Creating
Winning Trial Strategies and Graphics

G. Christopher Ritter

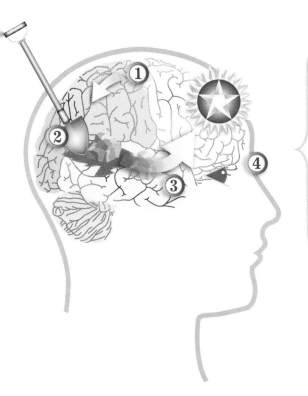

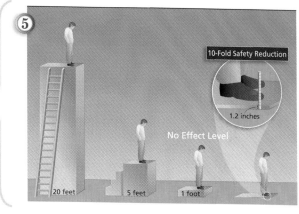

10-Fold Safety Reduction

1.2 inches

No Effect Level

20 feet   5 feet   1 foot

Defending Liberty
Pursuing Justice

American Bar Association
Tort Trial and Insurance Practice Section

Printed in the United States of America.

08 07 06 05 04   5 4 3 2 1

Library of Congress Cataloging-in-Publication Data

Ritter, G. Christopher.
  Creating winning trial strategies and graphics / by G. Christopher Ritter.
    p.   cm.
  Includes bibliographical references and index.
  ISBN 1-59031-330-5
    1. Trial practice—United States. 2. Trial practice—Graphic methods. I. Title.

KF8915.Z9R58 2004
347 .73975—dc22

                                        2004019037

To my wife, Jill Stevenson-Ritter
To our children, Andrew, Kelsey, and Erich Ritter
To my parents, Gene and Connie Ritter
Thank you!

Summary Contents

Contents

Table of Illustrations

Acknowledgments

When Zen monks gather to eat, they recite a meal chant that traditionally contains these words, "Innumerable labors have brought us this food, may we know how it comes to us." The same could clearly be said here—innumerable labors have brought you this book, may you know *some* of the people who brought it to you.

Nothing in this book would have been possible without the unconditional love and support of my immediate family. To my dearest friend and life partner, Jill Stevenson-Ritter, thank you for your unfailing support and for bearing more burdens than I will ever be able to fully recount. Your faith in me is exceeded only by my gratitude for that faith. To our children—Andrew, Kelsey, and Erich—your patience, encouragement, editorial comments, and wacky senses of humor sustained me more times than you can even imagine. For that, I will always be grateful. A special thanks to my parents, Dr. Gene and Connie Ritter. I conscripted my poor father to be this book's first editor. He must have read the manuscript a dozen times, each time without complaint. Dad, I still do not know when to use a semicolon, but I am certain that this book is substantially better because of your generous efforts. Mom, thanks for putting up with my many late night visits to drop off and retrieve edited text.

I am one of those lucky people who loves what he does for a living. In large part, my joy is due to three groups of people, each of which contributed enormously to this book. First, there are my friends, Andrew Spingler, Linda Spingler, Brian Ward, and Scott Hilton—who (not coincidentally) are fellow Members at The Focal Point LLC. Each unselfishly took on more than his or her fair share of work so that I could have more than my fair share of time to think and write. I know that there were days when you (and I) thought we would never get this book done. With your help, we did and, for that, I thank each of you.

The second group that makes my professional life so fulfilling includes all of my other friends and colleagues at The Focal Point, each of whom contributed in his or her own unique way. Some edited text or graphics; some debated points with me; some offered suggestions and examples; some offered kind words—all made a big difference. Specifically, my thanks go to my friends and colleagues: Yousif AbdelAziz, Marc Aure, Joel ben Izzy, Kelly Bloom, Lou Castro, Michelle Zeiter Diago, Dennis Duong, Nina Ellsworth, Erica Golding, Steve Haskins, Sadie Jernigan, Jason Lundy, Cheryl Masilang, Elena Mitschkowetz, Mary Patrick, Heather Perry, Laura Slate, Jerry Smith, Gordon Spingler, Shana Van Ort, and Jeremy Young.

Without diminishing the substantial contributions of any of the above listed people, I want to single out and to thank especially five of my colleagues at The Focal Point: Lillian Meldola, Guy Grogan, Andrew Spingler, Christina Gray, and Richard Cho. To the extent that you admire any of the graphics in this book (and there is a lot to admire), the credit goes to Lillian, whose artistic skills are legendary and clearly evident. I know two things with complete certainty—all of us at The Focal Point have benefited from her generosity and this book would be a poor shadow of itself without her contributions. Guy created the whimsical sketches and oversaw endless hours necessary to create the Visual Resource CD-ROM that accompanies this book. He did so like the master that he is. Andy, Christina, and Richard had the unenviable task of bringing necessary order to my often unstructured approach to life and work. They took my nebulous concepts for a book and moved them from the realms of possibility to probability to certainty. Trust me; this was no simple task.

The final group of people who consistently make my work so enjoyable and writing this book so much fun are The Focal Point's clients. I have the honor of getting to work every day with some of this country's best trial lawyers. Rarely a case goes by where I don't learn something new from one of these extraordinarily talented people. Since there have been more than a 1,000 cases, I cannot possibly thank everyone in the limited space allocated by the editors. The fact that I cannot do so does not in any way diminish the substantial contributions you have each made. Thank you all.

Last, but certainly not least, there are several people who have lent their considerable technical skills to the process of creating this book. Both the American Bar Association and I are fortunate to have the opportunity to work with Richard G. Paszkiet, Executive Editor. Rick, thank you for your foresight, guidance, editorial skills, and for making this book as colorful as it is. I would also like to thank Jill Nuppenau, Maureen Grey, Jeff Lachina, and John Rhead for their sharp eyes and minds in producing this book. Thanks to Robert E. Gordon, Esq., for his assistance in navigating through copyright issues. Lili Pratt King of Career Advocates in Walnut Creek, California, deserves special credit for help in scores of different directions. For their help with issues related to animations, I thank Stuart Gold of Shadow and Light Productions and Zac Rymland of Liquid Picture, both of which are in Berkeley, California. Finally, I want to thank Lynn Towne and Nicolas C. Vaca, Esq., who remain my friends after more than 20 years and who were the first people to suggest, "You should write a book."

About the Author

G. Christopher Ritter is a member of The Focal Point LLC., which has offices in Oakland, California, and Santa Fe, New Mexico. The Focal Point consults with trial lawyers throughout the country to find ways to make cases easier to understand and, as a result, more persuasive to juries. Chris is a former partner at a major San Francisco law firm, where he tried numerous cases in State and Federal Courts. For more than 12 years, he was also an adjunct faculty member at University of California—Hastings School of Law, where he taught Legal Writing, Evidence, and Trial Practice courses. Chris has over 20 years experience in litigation and graphic strategy. He has also regularly taught programs for such organizations as the National Institute of Trial Advocacy, California's Continuing Education of the Bar, and the Litigation Section of the State Bar of California. Chris was graduated from the University of Chicago Law School and is an active member of The State Bar of California. He, his wife Jill Stevenson-Ritter, and their three children Andrew, Kelsey, and Erich live in Alamo, California. He can be reached at gcr@thefocalpoint.com.

Chapter 1

Introduction

Give the Jury What It Wants

I grew up in southern Indiana, in a small town down at the bottom third of the state. Every Sunday, my brother David and I would get up early to watch one of our favorite television programs. Wedged between *The Farm Bureau Round Up*, which ended at 7:30 A.M., and the religious programming, which droned on from 8:00 A.M. until too long into the afternoon, Channel 4 would run *Earle Stahl—Hoosier Fisherman*.

In our corner of the world, Earle Stahl was a legend. Each week, he and his cameraman would round up a local celebrity—the high school basketball coach, the owner of our town's only Roy Rogers Restaurant franchise, or some other big shot—and they would go out fishing.

EARL STAHL - HOOSIER FISHERMAN: "If you wanna catch fish, you best give 'em what they want!"

Earle and his guests *always* caught fish. Big fish, too—catfish, large-mouth bass, even trout imported into the reservoir from the nearby Department of Forestry's hatcheries. Every Sunday, Earle would use his television program to show off what he and his guest had caught.

In all the years David and I watched him, Earle always ended his show the same way. There would be a close-up of Earle's fishing cap with the logo "Stahl's Cheese Bait—Fish Ask For It!" stitched above the brim. The camera would then pull back slowly until you could see that Earle was holding a large fish across his even larger belly. He would stare at the camera, grin, and each week offer up the same advice: "If you want to catch fish, you best give 'em what they want!"

1

If I had to distill the advice in this book down to a single sentence, I could not do any better than to paraphrase Earle—"If you want to catch jurors, you best give 'em what they want!"

What This Book Is About

For more than fifteen years, my colleagues at The Focal Point LLC and I have worked with many of this country's best trial lawyers to make their courtroom presentations more persuasive by making their cases easier for judges and juries to understand. We have worked on well over a thousand cases involving every conceivable topic and type of dispute, developing trial graphics that convey information in an organized, clear, and convincing manner.

Often our cases include carefully orchestrated mock trials with recorded jury deliberations. By observing these mock trials and through other aspects of our work, my colleagues and I have developed a unique perspective from which to answer the question, "What do jurors want?"

Although we produce thousands of trial graphics and other tools each year, we do something far more important than just make pretty pictures. We use the *process* of creating trial graphics as a way to encourage lawyers to step back, reevaluate what is important about their cases, and, based on what they find, simplify their entire courtroom presentation. Through this process, we help our clients develop the tools that judges and jurors need in order to understand, accept, remember, and use our clients' versions of the facts.

The point of this book is to provide you with a better understanding of what jurors want and suggest ways—mostly through the process of designing and using trial graphics—to give them exactly that.

The most successful trial lawyers are advocates who take the time (and I will warn you right now—it usually takes much longer than most lawyers think) to learn, really learn, what is important about their cases. Successful trial lawyers then use this knowledge to educate their jurors about (1) the key events leading up to the lawsuit; (2) the reasons why the jurors, who up until jury selection had no prior interest in any of these events, should suddenly care about what happens; and (3) the steps jurors can take during deliberations to persuade others to accept the lawyer's case.

Trial graphics are an important tool in this learning/teaching process. Graphics allow jurors to see what you are saying and why it is important *for them*. A picture is worth a thousand words; we all know that. Unfortunately, what many lawyers do not know is that *creating* the picture is worth much, much more. If the lawyer does it right, the process of creating trial graphics should yield far more than just pretty pictures. The process of transforming an idea into a trial graphic provides far-ranging benefits that begin accumulating long before the case goes to court; the benefits extend through opening statement and continue on, past closing argument, all the way to the end of the jury's deliberations.

The final *product* (i.e., the trial graphic itself) helps the lawyer teach the judge and jurors. The process that trial lawyers go through to create that product makes them better-educated teachers and, as a result, more effective advocates. This is true regardless of whether they "spontaneously" sketch trial graphics on newsprint or use the latest technology to project professionally prepared illustrations across the courtroom.

The process of illustrating key aspects of your case forces you to organize your presentation in a more logical, understandable, and persuasive manner. This book is about the process that you should go through to simplify each of your cases, so that you can more easily educate your jurors and convince them that they should not only accept but also actively endorse and effectively advance your version of the facts during deliberations.

This book provides trial lawyers with a process they can use to simplify their cases by filtering out what is distracting or unimportant. The process also helps lawyers clarify and develop essential themes and other tools that jurors need to evaluate, retain, and understand complex issues.

As you can see by flipping through the following pages, this book is full of trial graphics. These include examples that we have developed for use throughout the United States. While professionally prepared trial graphics are an integral part of this book, they are *not* what this book is really about. This book is about a *process*—a process that yields scores of benefits, only one of which includes trial graphics. This book is about a process that you should go through with every one of your cases, *regardless of whether you ultimately create a single trial graphic*. This book is about a process that maximizes your opportunities to persuade jurors and, in so doing, increase your chances of winning your trial.

All of the trial graphics displayed in this book began the same way. Each started with a story that the lawyer needed to tell, a handful of colored pens, and a blank sheet of paper. Don't be fooled by its apparent simplicity; a blank sheet of paper is a very powerful tool—powerful precisely because it has a limited amount of space upon which you cannot possibly put all of your facts. In order to get your case to "fit," you must eliminate excess, limit your "picture" to what really matters, and find the simplest way possible to display what's left to the jury.

Limitations can work to our advantage. As we will see throughout this book, restrictions often trick the brain into being more creative, not less.

The rules of Japanese haiku are exact and unbending. Each poem must be three lines long and consist of seventeen syllables. The first line must have five syllables, the second line seven, and the third line five. It is hard to imagine a more restrictive medium. Yet for centuries these limitations have actually encouraged writers to create an amazing body of poetry—works that capture an event in an instant or an emotion in its simplest form.

Likewise, you should use the artificial limitations imposed by the four corners of a sheet of paper to enhance rather than stifle your creativity. I often challenge our clients to reduce their entire story so that its essence fits on a single sheet of paper. Obviously, not every fact will fit. That is the point—not all of a story is worth fitting. What is important will fit; what is not, won't.

With apologies to The Rolling Stones…

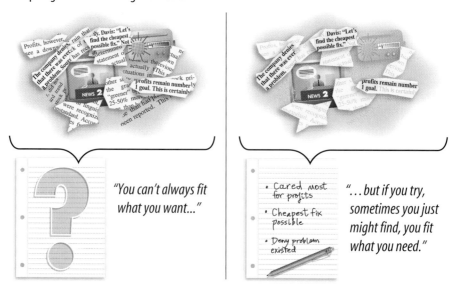

"You can't always fit what you want…"

- Cared most for profits
- Cheapest fix possible
- Deny problem existed

"…but if you try, sometimes you just might find, you fit what you need."

This book details this refining process and describes how it makes trial lawyers more persuasive by making their cases easier for judges and jurors to understand.

What Is in This Book

The balance of this book is divided into eight chapters.

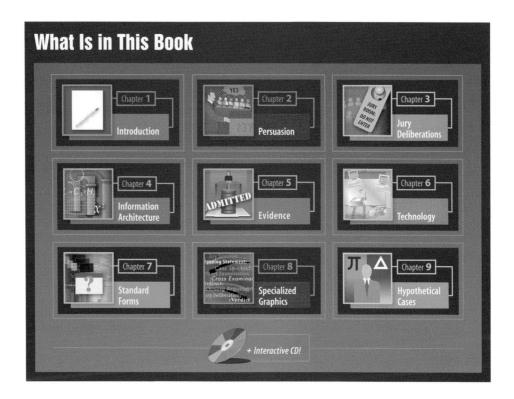

Chapter 2 deals with a trial lawyer's stock in trade—persuasion. No one can win every case. The great trial lawyer Edward Bennett Williams once observed that a third of the cases can never be won, a third can never be lost, and it is the battle over the remaining third that makes or breaks a trial lawyer's reputation.

There are at least five characteristics common to highly persuasive advocates. These are the trial lawyers who routinely win that remaining third of their cases— the cases that make reputations.

First, highly persuasive advocates spend their time at trial educating jurors. These advocates are teachers, not fighters; yet by taking the time to educate jurors, these lawyers usually are much more effective fighters than most of their more openly hostile counterparts.

Second, highly persuasive advocates are able to simultaneously see the trees *and* the forest. They develop an understanding from two different perspectives, which I call "under and over." That is, they develop an *under*standing of the *under*lying facts, while maintaining an *over*view of the *over*all case. These lawyers know the individual facts of the case and revel in this level of detail. At the same time, they never lose sight of what they want the final, overall picture to look like.

From these two perspectives, the trial lawyer knows, among other things, which of the facts are most important and which battles are really worth fighting in order to best convince the jurors.

Third, highly persuasive advocates take the time to make their cases simpler, not more complex. Over time, their trial estimates get shorter, not longer; their witness lists have fewer names, not more; the number of their exhibits decreases, not increases.

Fourth, from the very beginning of their cases, highly persuasive advocates make time to engage in a process I call mental mining in order to uncover stories, analogies, and other images that are universally understood by jurors. They then find ways to explain key and/or complicated points to the jury using these already familiar images.

Finally, highly persuasive trial lawyers combine the right mixture of the prior four skills to convince jurors to "give a damn." That is, these lawyers know how to transform the jurors from passive, neutral observers to partisans favoring one side over the other.

Chapter 2 focuses on each of these five characteristics/skills and suggests ways for you to develop them more effectively.

Chapter 3 describes what happens during jury deliberations. This chapter focuses on how jurors make their decisions and the tools you can provide them to increase your chances that they will decide the case in your favor.

Despite what exhausted trial lawyers may think, efforts at persuasion do not end when they sit down after closing. Arguments (often very forceful ones) continue on during deliberations between the lawyers' "surrogates," that is, the "Active Jurors" who favor one side over the other.

On any given issue, the participants in these fights can be classified as falling somewhere along a spectrum. (See Illustration 1-1.) At one end are the Active Jurors who strongly favor the plaintiff; at the other are the Active Jurors who strongly favor the defendant. The trial lawyers' battle, fought during deliberations by their Active Jurors, is for the middle (i.e., the "neutral" jurors who have not yet made a decision or who are not firmly committed to one side or the other).

The prevailing party usually is the one whose trial lawyer provides tools to its Active Jurors—tools that those jurors use to persuade fellow jurors to vote a particular way. These include tools that:

- Convey a single coherent storyline rather than a series of alternative arguments that are often contradictory.
- Address the issue of motive, even when motive (or its close relative, "state of mind") is not technically a prima facie element of the claim or defense.
- Allow jurors to use already familiar concepts as a way to understand complex issues that they encounter for the first time at trial.
- Appeal to values commonly shared, understood, and applied in the community from which the jurors are pooled.
- Provide ammunition with which "your" jurors can counter arguments raised by jurors who favor your opponent.

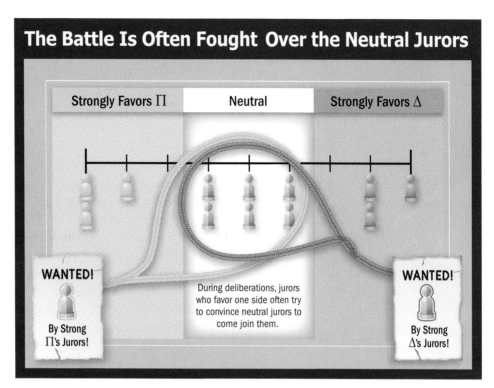

The Battle Is Often Fought Over the Neutral Jurors

Strongly Favors Π   Neutral   Strongly Favors Δ

WANTED!
By Strong
Π's Jurors!

During deliberations, jurors who favor one side often try to convince neutral jurors to come join them.

WANTED!
By Strong
Δ's Jurors!

ILLUSTRATION 1-1

Trial lawyers who take the time to provide tools such as these to the Active Jurors who favor their side have a substantial advantage during deliberations over the lawyers who do not.

Chapter 4 is "Information Architecture for Trial Lawyers." For several decades, a small (but fortunately expanding) group of professionals has devoted its considerable talents to finding and developing ways to convey complex information to a target audience in as simple a manner as possible. I hope that after you read Chapter 4, you will begin to appreciate how much we trial lawyers can learn from these information architects who have made "explaining how to explain" their careers.

Chapter 5 is the only chapter that deals with what is traditionally a legal issue. In this chapter, I briefly discuss the rules of evidence and the question of admissibility. Obviously, it is impossible for a book such as this to address the nuances of evidence law in all jurisdictions. Instead, Chapter 5 focuses on certain practical observations made over the years about how judges (consciously or otherwise) apply the rules of evidence to trial graphics, especially graphics that rely on state-of-the-art technology.[1]

---

1. Whenever I describe "state-of-the-art" technology in this book, I do so at some peril. By definition, what is state-of-the-art as I currently write this book will not be when you read what I have written. Whatever the state-of-the-art may be, I am confident that the basic principles outlined in this book will still apply.

Chapter 6 provides an overview of the technology available to display exhibits and other graphics at trial. As a general rule, there is an inverse relationship between a lawyer's age and his general knowledge of courtroom technology. Given this fact, Chapter 6 may be one that some younger "second chair" trial lawyers can afford to skip. On the other hand, many older "first chairs," particularly those who, like me, relied on typewriters in law school, should not do so![2]

Don't worry; the focus of Chapter 6 is not overly technical, nor does it have to be. Technology is just one of the factors that trial lawyers need to consider in designing graphics. It is very important to remember that the medium should never drive the message. Technology should never be the primary reason for creating or limiting the creation of a trial graphic. Instead, you should first identify the concept that you need to communicate. Next, design the best possible graphic that accomplishes this goal. Then, and only then, determine the optimum way to display your trial graphic to the jury. This process should never flow backward; i.e., you must resist the temptation to think, "Gee, I spent a lot of money on all of this whiz-bang, state-of-the-art equipment. How can I design a trial graphic to show off the equipment that will otherwise just be sitting here?"

Unfortunately, as technology gets less expensive and easier to use, many lawyers become so enamored with new equipment that they forget something very important. They forget that a poorly conceived or executed graphic does not get better merely because it is displayed using state-of-the-art technology. The only thing that happens by displaying a poorly conceived graphic using expensive high-tech equipment is that you end up with a more expensive poorly conceived graphic.

Chapter 7 is divided into sections dealing with the standard forms of trial graphics, including timelines, textpulls, tutorials, outlines, checklists, flowcharts, and other ways of illustrating your case. These are the types of trial graphics that you will likely use throughout your case. I include various examples, explanations of what does and does not work, a list of things to consider before using a particular type of graphic, and suggestions as to how and when you might want to do so.

In Chapter 8, I offer some observations concerning three parts of your jury trial that are especially well suited for graphics—the opening statement, expert witness testimony, and the closing argument.

In Chapter 9, I analyze a series of hypothetical cases and prepare several graphics for each of them.

This book includes a CD-ROM. Whenever you see this symbol next to an illustration in the text, a version of that graphic is also included on the accompanying Visual Resource CD-ROM. Many of these graphics are buildable; that is, you can use the CD-ROM to see how a trial lawyer might use the graphic during trial.

---

2. In my defense, it was an electric typewriter.

How to Use This Book

I designed this book so that you can read it two different ways: (1) the way I would like you to read it and (2) the way you are likely to read it—at least the first time.

As for the way that I would like you to read it, I hope you will read through it once and then repeatedly browse through this and other books related to trial graphics and information architecture long before you need any of this material for a particular case. One of the best ways to design trial graphics is to look at examples and let them knock around in your head until the situation arises when you need them. For those readers who have the time, I encourage you to look at the examples both in the book and on the accompanying Visual Resource CD-ROM. Read the book as a whole; then re-read those sections that most interest you. Repeat this process as time and interest permit. I firmly believe that when the time comes, this process of mental composting will provide a fertile environment in which you can design trial graphics for your specific case.

But as a recovering trial lawyer, I know that the way you are likely to read this book (at least the first time) is different from the way I just suggested. Chances are you are on the verge of trial. You need concrete results for a specific case; you need those results right away. In such an instance, I suggest that you read Chapters 2, 3, 4, 5, 6, 7, 8, and 9—*but in reverse order.*

Consider following these steps:

- Start by reviewing the hypothetical cases in Chapter 9 for inspiration and to see what you might want some of your trial graphics to look like.
- Then turn to Chapter 8 for suggestions related to key sections of your trial—places particularly well suited for special types of graphics.
- Next review Chapter 7 for ideas of what general types of graphics (text-pulls, timelines, tutorials, outlines, etc.) might be effective.
- You should then consult Chapter 6 to determine what technology you want to use to display these graphics in court and Chapter 5 to determine some of the evidentiary issues you may need to consider before doing so.
- Last, but definitely not least, review the basic concepts outlined in Chapters 4, 3, and 2. By ending your review this way, you will conclude with the most important concepts of persuasion fresh in your mind. Take these concepts, follow the process described in the other chapters, and get to work.

Following this procedure should take you a long way toward producing effective trial graphics. The process will yield far more than pretty pictures. The process will help you simplify your case by weeding out unimportant issues. It will also help you educate "your" jurors so that they can more easily accept your version of the facts and, during deliberations, encourage other jurors to do so as well.

If you read this book in a crisis mode, which at some point I know you will (in fact, you may be doing so right now), please come back when the crisis ends and re-read this book as I designed it to be read—in numerous sittings, looking at the graphics and thinking about the process that led to their creation. I promise that this kind of repeated meandering without a sense of urgency will most certainly make your future graphics and trial presentations even more effective.

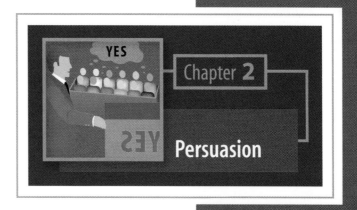

Chapter **2**

Persuasion

Make Mine the Truth!

Several years ago, a lawyer friend of mine decided to upgrade his firm's marketing material. One evening over dinner, he mentioned this to his children and asked them for their suggestions.

His younger son immediately announced, "You know what you need? You need a catchy slogan."

"A slogan? Like what?" asked my friend.

"I know," said his son excitedly, "Your slogan should be, 'Our trial lawyers make your version the TRUTH!'"[1]

Now, that's a catchy slogan! I doubt if you can find a better definition for "persuasion" or a more intuitive description of what we work so hard to achieve at trial. As trial lawyers, our tools are all tools of persuasion. Whenever we use one, the goal is to make our client's version "the truth."

Persuasion doesn't just happen. It takes time; it demands considerable focus and sustained effort. Persuasive trial lawyers often share five characteristics. First, they are strongly committed to helping the jurors—who, after all, are the finders of fact—understand the facts. Rather than squabbling in front of the jurors, persuasive lawyers spend their time educating the jurors as to what really matters.

A lawyer's desire to teach is not entirely rooted in altruism; the objective is usually far more practical and immediate—winning the case. Nevertheless, whatever it is that motivates these highly persuasive lawyers, two facts remain: (1) there is a genuine need to educate jurors, and (2) this educational process plays a crucial role in making a lawyer's version "the truth."

A casual observer might conclude that lawyers who spend their time teaching are not "fighters" and somehow cannot be "real" advocates. That is wrong. Trial lawyers who take the time to educate jurors are often far more persuasive and effective advocates than their more traditionally belligerent opposing counsel.

---

1. My thanks to Kristjan Vaca for the slogan and Nicolas C. Vaca, Esq., for telling me this story.

Second, highly persuasive trial lawyers can shift (often in ways that appear effortless) between two perspectives—one "under" and one "over." These advocates simultaneously develop an *under*standing of the *under*lying facts and an *over*view of their *over*all case. They revel in the details, all the while keeping their mind's eye focused on the broader, more comprehensive picture. With these two perspectives, these lawyers know which facts are important and which battles are worth fighting.

Third, highly persuasive trial lawyers make it their ongoing task to simplify their cases. With practice, the stories they tell become less rambling and more focused; their trials get shorter, not longer; the number of exhibits they use decreases, not increases; the number of witnesses needed to prove their case gets smaller, not larger.

Fourth, highly persuasive advocates spend considerable time engaged in a process I call mental mining (discussed later in this chapter). They start this process as soon as they first get the file. They continue on with it in their offices, during long drives, on walks, in the shower, and during other moments when they can profitably ponder two crucial questions: (1) "After cutting through all of the crap, what is this case *really* about?" and (2) "What is the simplest way for me to show the jury what this case is really about?"

By using this process, these lawyers find ways to take relevant stories, analogies, and other concepts with which the jurors are already familiar and use these educational tools to help jurors understand unfamiliar and often complicated evidence.

Finally, highly persuasive trial lawyers know how to combine each of the four previously discussed skills in just the right proportion and manner in order to get jurors to "give a damn"; that is, these lawyers know how to get members of the jury to shift from being passive, neutral observers to being advocates actively lobbying during jury deliberations for one side over the other.

This chapter examines these five characteristics and suggests how you can develop and incorporate them into the way you persuade jurors.

Yosemite Sam Never Taught Nothin' to Nobody

About two weeks after our older son, Andrew, started kindergarten, my wife, Jill, and I formally met with his teacher for the first time. After several minutes of pleasantries, the teacher suddenly turned to me and asked rather abruptly, "Mr. Ritter, what do you do for a living?"

"I am a trial lawyer," I replied.

"Oh, now that's interesting . . .," the teacher said with surprise. "Andrew has been bragging to all the children that you 'drive sick people to the hospital.'"

After I thought about this for a while, it dawned on me that a few weeks before, my brother-in-law had jokingly called me an "ambulance chaser." To a six-year-old, that could mean only one thing—his father drove sick people to the hospital. It was hard breaking the news to Andrew that I did not drive a fast car, let alone one with flashing red lights and a siren.

I tell this true story to convey a serious point. People, including six-year-olds, often have very strange perceptions of what trial lawyers do, misperceptions we trial lawyers ourselves often create, contribute to, and perpetuate. For example, we assure our younger colleagues that "trials are war and war is hell" as if these words of encouragement make it easier for them to stay up all night drafting those 442 interrogatories (with sub-parts) that we intend to propound on our opposing counsel three weeks before Christmas. We smile at bumper stickers that boast, "My lawyer can beat up your lawyer." We do nothing to discourage the perception that a successful trial lawyer is a mad dog, son-of-a-bitch mercenary. We do all this and still we are dismayed that the public generally does not respect us. We are annoyed by the lawyer jokes and shocked when one of our colleagues is injured by a disgruntled former client.

Litigation (pleading fights, discovery battles, and other things done before trial or outside the presence of the jury) may be war. Certainly many of these activities and their resulting disputes are often as senseless and wasteful as war.

But trials—trials should be different.

Do trials involve disputes? Of course! Do disputes cause emotions to run hot? Undoubtedly, and jurors expect them to. But is trial the time for jurors to perceive you as a blind partisan indiscriminately slashing and burning on your long march through Georgia? No! In fact, when jurors see that you are pursuing such a reckless course rather than helping them uncover the truth, there are likely to be three casualties—you, your client, and your case.

In most trials, jurors believe that there is a *right answer*. They want to uncover the facts; they want to find that elusive thing called "the truth"; and they want your help in doing so.

Jurors instinctively doubt that some "mean-as-a-snake trial lawyer" is capable of recognizing, let alone preserving, anything so delicate as the truth. As a juror once confided to me about a particularly partisan warrior in the courtroom, "He kind of reminded us [the jury] of Yosemite Sam. You know, that cartoon character that is always running around wild, swearing, and randomly shooting his pistols up into the air. Sometimes all his ranting and raving was fun to watch. But you know what? We never really trusted very much of what he said."

So Mr. or Ms. Trial Lawyer, let me ask you the caterpillar's famous question from *Alice's Adventures in Wonderland*—"Who are you?"

A standard answer is, "Trial lawyers are storytellers." This answer is far better than "Trial lawyers are low-down, egg-sucking cutthroats." But to say that a trial lawyer is a storyteller is too narrow a description, because it confuses *one* of a trial lawyer's techniques (storytelling) with a trial lawyer's role.

I do not intend that last statement to be perceived in any way as trivializing the art of storytelling. Storytelling is one of the most effective and powerful tools of persuasion. However, for purposes of this immediate discussion, it is important to understand that there is a difference between a role and a technique used while in that role.

So, I repeat—"Who are you?"

Successful trial lawyers are advocates who take the time and make the extra effort to do two things very well. They (1) learn the important facts of the case and (2) use this knowledge to educate jurors as to what really matters. In short, the most accomplished lawyers are also the most accomplished *teachers*.

The historian Arthur M. Schlesinger, Jr., observed that successful politics (and we know that every jury trial involves politics) required three steps: education, persuasion, and consensus building. Of these three, Schlesinger noted that education was the most important because neither persuasion nor consensus building can occur without it.

Your job is to teach the jurors what they need to know so that they are not only persuaded to vote for you but are also able to use what you have taught them to actively build the consensus in the jury room necessary to decide the case in your favor. Never underestimate the importance of educating your jury. You are responsible for teaching the jurors everything that they will ever learn about what happened at that intersection, in that boardroom, or down that dark alley.

Take the time to educate your jurors. If you do not do so, your opponent almost certainly will. If neither of you takes the time to educate the jurors, you will, in all but the simplest cases, end up with a horribly muddled and angry group of fact finders. In such instances, trial graphics, no matter how brilliantly conceived or beautifully executed, will *not* save you, your client, or your case.

If you need additional incentive to convince yourself to make the effort to educate your jury, consider this: Jurors respect teachers and will often reward the side that takes the time to educate them. Jurors perceive educational efforts not only as helpful (and remember, they are looking to you for help) but also as a sign of respect and proof positive that the side making the effort is unafraid of and is more likely offering the truth.

Occasionally, one of our lawyer clients will conclude that because I stress the need to educate the jury, I am suggesting that lawyers abandon their traditional role as an advocate. I could not disagree more. It is the job of all trial lawyers to advocate on behalf of their clients and to make an effort to see that their clients prevail. An important part of an advocate's job includes selecting the most effective tools to legitimately win the case. For the most successful advocates, these tools include those that educate the jury. The truth is that by teaching, these advocates are more effective and win a greater number of cases. Isn't this the best possible reason for you to be one of these advocates?

Play Like Monk and Coltrane

During the summer and fall of 1957, Thelonious Monk and John Coltrane played jazz together at New York City's Five Spot Café. Ira Gitler, the jazz critic, observed that during this time Coltrane underwent an important artistic transformation after Monk taught him to experiment with "sheets of sound." Specifically, Monk showed the tenor saxophon-ist how to play a single note while thinking "in groups of notes rather than one note at a time."

This is the same perspec-tive that trial lawyers need to apply to each case—attention to the immediate detail, while keeping a broader, overall per-spective in mind. Successful trial lawyers view their cases from the "under" and "over" vantage points. As stated above, they develop an *under*standing of the *under*lying facts, while maintaining an *over*-view of their *over*all case. These lawyers can simultaneously see both the trees *and* the forest.

These lawyers absorb detail and are fascinated—but never overwhelmed—by it. They instinctively separate that which is important from that which is not, until what remains is a comprehensive, overall picture that they seemed to have known was there all along. Successful trial lawyers use this picture to educate their jurors, motivating them to move past being neutral finders of fact to becoming active advocates for one party over the other.

UNDERSTAND THE UNDERLYING FACTS

There is a difference between *learning* the facts and *using* those facts effectively. Learning the facts involves memorization. It requires that the lawyer develop the ability to recall names and dates. This is the skill that allows you to not only quickly locate a key document but also to find a specific topic or phrase within that document.

The process of learning the facts (what I previously referred to as *understanding the underlying facts*) usually occurs on more or less a mechanical level. By referring to this process as "mechanical," I am not in any way trivializing its importance. It is crucial that you learn, really learn, the underlying facts in your case. Unless you do so, your ability to perform any of the other steps outlined in this chapter will be severely limited, if not impossible.

Acquiring all of this necessary raw data can be a daunting task—so much so that some lawyers think that once they learn the facts they can stop analyzing their case. You should not be so shortsighted.

If the only thing trial lawyers have to offer the jury is a list of facts, then the best that they can do is to provide a dry chronology. This is the functional equivalent of a train schedule that lists the stops between Chicago and Altoona. While a train schedule provides important information necessary to getting you where you want to go, very few jurors are likely to get excited by it. Certainly, no one is going to feel compelled to award punitive damages based merely on a dry recitation of the names of the Chicago suburbs southeast of Union Station. In short, if you are going to reach your destination, you need this schedule and you need *more*.

DEVELOP AND MAINTAIN AN OVERVIEW OF THE OVERALL CASE

The underlying facts are of only limited value unless you know how to use them. You can not fully use them until after you develop "perspective." This is what I referred to earlier as maintaining an *overview* of the *overall* case and thinking in "sheets of sound." Perspective requires that you determine which facts matter and then find ways to show the jury what these facts are, how these facts are connected, and why the jurors should care.

Perspective allows you to appreciate and use nuance, to understand the thematic glue that holds the facts together, and to perceive and articulate what really motivated the key players to do whatever it is that they did. If information is power, then the types of information you obtain by developing and maintaining perspective are among the most powerful.

THE MASTER CHRONOLOGY: A TOOL TO HELP YOU LEARN ABOUT YOUR CASE

So, how do you get to know your facts and, at the same time, develop perspective? You must first emulate a good truffle pig; put your head down and root nose-first through the layers of facts in the case file. The more of this process that you do yourself, the more you will benefit. Of course you may have to rely on others to

help sift through mountains of documents, transcripts, and facts. But, whenever possible, read the key deposition transcripts rather than the summaries; look at the actual documents rather than relying on secondary source material that "interprets" these documents for you. As a teacher once told me, "Read the books, not the book reports."

The single most helpful tool in rooting through the underlying facts of a case is the master chronology. I draw a distinction between a chronology and a timeline. Whenever I use the term *chronology,* I am referring to a collection of *written* information that lists and summarizes the key events, key documents, and other relevant information in chronological order. While the information in a timeline often comes from a chronology, a timeline is more graphically based with entries usually placed at scaled intervals along a time bar. (Chronologies and timelines are discussed in greater detail in Chapter 7.)

In creating a master chronology, you should pull together every available bit of information without prematurely judging its value (e.g., this fact is good, this one bad, this is helpful, this is not) or segregating the information by category or theme. The master chronology should include both undisputed and disputed facts, with the disputed facts being marked accordingly.

Other than these extremely broad requirements, there is no set or universal format for a master chronology. You should feel entirely free to tailor this important tool to meet your individual needs and the unique ways that you learn, process, and use information. In fact, unless you take the time to personalize your master chronology, this learning tool will prove to be of little benefit.

Illustration 2-1 is an example of the format that I use when I create a master chronology. In this particular instance, the master chronology focuses on a hypothetical set of facts involving an insured's efforts to tender a third-party claim to his insurance company. Before we discuss the contents of the master chronology in any more detail, please take a minute to review Illustration 2-1. As with any master chronology, after such a review, you should have a good understanding of the facts and documents in this hypothetical case.

There are no rules as to what goes into a master chronology. Most master chronologies (1) list events, (2) describe key documents, (3) cross-reference events to documents, (4) pull key quotations from documents, and (5) serve as a repository for possible graphics. (See Illustration 2-2.)

Creating a master chronology takes time, both initially and on an ongoing basis. You must first spend time consolidating, digesting, and summarizing your material. Then you must make an ongoing commitment to update your master chronology as you develop new facts. If you skimp at either step, the value of your master chronology will rapidly drop.

Master Chronology

1/4 Automobile accident – 3rd and Clay
"Vehicle 1 (Young) ran red light hit Vehicle 2 (Jernigan). Minor damage to Vehicle 2; driver has neck injury." *[Doc. 5– Police Report]*

1/6 Initial contact with Big Insurance Company, Inc.
Young calls insurance agent. Claims Rep. Haskins faxes "Initial Report Form" to Young.

1/7 Young returns faxes "Initial Claims Report Form" to Big Insurance Company, Inc. *[Doc. 1– Completed form and fax transmittal]*

2/10 Jernigan faxes first letter to Young
"I hope you are well. My neck really hurts, but all I want is to get my car fixed. Please have your insurance company call me. It's been 5 weeks. I have estimate for $500, which is all I want." *[Doc. 2– Ltr 2/10 Jernigan to Young]*

　　Note: First letter seems very friendly compared with later ones after Young cannot get insurer to settle.

　　Young forwards Jernigan 2/10 letter to Big Insurance Company, Inc. "Please take care of this while she [Jernigan] is still reasonable." *[Doc 3– Ltr 2/10 Young to Haskins]*

3/15 Jernigan calls Young to see if "can't we just resolve this"
"I said – 'I haven't heard from you. I just want my car fixed. I am starting to get upset.' He said, 'I would love to help, but my insurance company won't call me back.'" *[Jernigan Depo. 19:1-7]*

　　Young calls Haskins and reports Jernigan's phone call. Leaves message: "I told him [Haskins] what she said and for the 20th time I asked him to please call me." *[Young Depo. 3:4–5]*

4/20 Young pays his monthly insurance premium to Big Insurance Company, Inc.
　　Note: Get copies of canceled checks to show Young kept his side of bargain with insurance company.

A *Master Chronology* is a basic learning tool for trial lawyers

5/21 Big Insurance Co. replies with form letter to Young
"We'll get to you as soon as possible. Have a nice day." *[Doc 6– Ltr 5/21 Haskins to Young]*

5/25 Jernigan faxes Young
"I am really upset. If your insurer doesn't get a hold me by 5:00 today I am going to be forced to sue you for lot more than $500. Please let's settle this and get this mess behind us." *[Doc 8– Ltr 5/25 Jernigan to Young]*

　　Young faxes letter to Haskins
"Please! Help me resolve this. I still haven't heard from you." *[Doc 4– Ltr 5/25 Young to Haskins]*

5/30 Big Insurance Co. sends second form letter to Young
"Thank you for your recent inquiry. We will be in touch. Have a nice day." *[Doc 7– Ltr 5/30 Haskins to Young]*

6/3 Jernigan calls Young
"I am tired of waiting for your insurance company. Resolve this by June 4 or this is going to my attorney." *[Tape from Mr. Young's answering machine]*
　　Note: What do we have to do to get audio tape admitted?

　　Young calls Haskins
Leaves message updating Haskins on what is happening.

6/12 Attorney Shana Van Ort files/serves complaint
Alleges Jernigan suffered property and bodily injury 5 times greater than Mr. Young's policy limits.

6/20 Haskins sends third form letter to Young
"Can't find your Initial Claims Report. We need to start this process all over again. Please send/re-send notice of claim. We look forward to serving you." *[Doc 10– Ltr 6/20 Haskins to Young]*

　　✳ *possible exhibit* →

ILLUSTRATION 2-1. Master Chronology: An Example

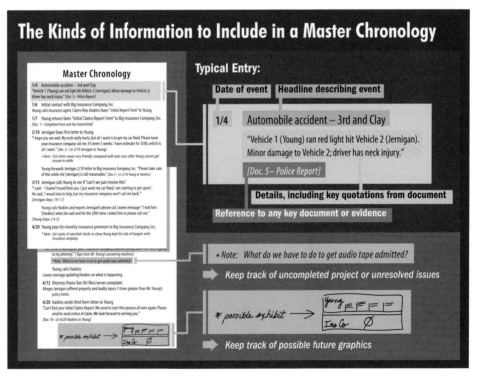

ILLUSTRATION 2-2

Are such efforts worth your while? Yes! You should make your master chronology as detailed as your client can afford to hire you to make it. Such efforts will ultimately prove worth your while for at least three reasons. First, chronological order is the Western brain's default mechanism for organizing material. When we want to know "what happened," we naturally begin to organize and learn facts in terms of what happened first, next, and last. Second, putting the material in this order helps us to see the patterns and connections upon which perspective is ultimately based. Finally, as we shall see in Chapter 7, the master chronology provides an additional bonus—it is the source document from which you can draw information to create a variety of other important tools and graphics, ones that you yourself can learn from and then use to teach the jury about what happened in your case.

"'Tis a Gift to Be Simple. . . ."

Our life is frittered away by detail . . .
Simplify, Simplify.
> —Henry David Thoreau

This is great advice—and not just because he's Thoreau.

We know that a trial lawyer must constantly refine his mastery of the facts and use this mastery to simplify every case. We know that unless we simplify our case, the jury will likely get lost along the way and the verdict (if there even is one) will become a matter of chance based on factors over which we have little or no control. We know all of this; knowledge is not the problem. The problem is finding a way to do what we already know needs to be done, that is, finding ways to "simplify, simplify" when we can't spend the next few months by a quiet, maple-tree-lined pond contemplating an upcoming trial.

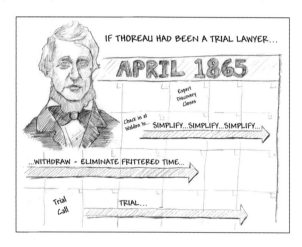

PRELIMINARY CONSIDERATIONS

Before we discuss ways to simplify your case, we need to examine three important and related concepts. First, we need to review how each juror's ability to understand evidence is affected by the competing mental functions of comprehension and boredom. Second, we need to examine how information fits on what I call the Complexity Scale. This scale ranks information based on how difficult it is for the jury to understand. Finally, we need to combine what we have learned in both of these areas to determine the best way to simplify different types of cases.[2]

Competition Between Comprehension and Boredom

Over time, each juror's ability to understand any topic is a function of two competing mental forces—comprehension and boredom.

There is generally a positive, or direct, correlation between time and comprehension. The more time you spend educating your jurors about a particular subject, the greater their comprehension of that topic will normally be. The resulting line expressing this relationship is the Comprehension Curve. (See Illustration 2-3.)

Given this fact, wouldn't it stand to reason that you should spend as much time as possible teaching the jurors about each and every topic? The answer is no, because excessive time carries a cost hidden within it—boredom.

I measure boredom in units of "juror interest." In contrast to comprehension, there is generally an inverse, or negative, correlation between time and juror interest. As a general rule, the more time you spend on a single subject, the less interested most jurors are likely to become and, as a result, the less new evidence jurors can willingly absorb. The inverse relationship between time and jurors' interest creates what I call the Interest Curve. (See Illustration 2-4.)

The Comprehension Curve

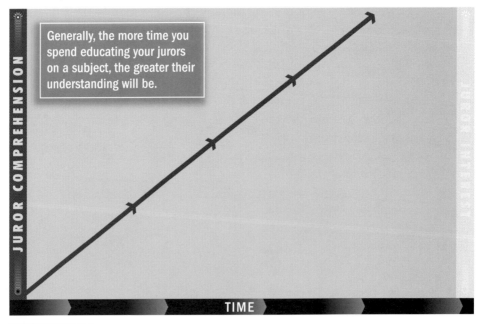

Generally, the more time you spend educating your jurors on a subject, the greater their understanding will be.

ILLUSTRATION 2-3

---

2. What follows is not an empirical study; in fact, I am not sure that such a study would even be possible. Instead, the following sections illustrate key observations that I have made over the past few years.

The Interest Curve

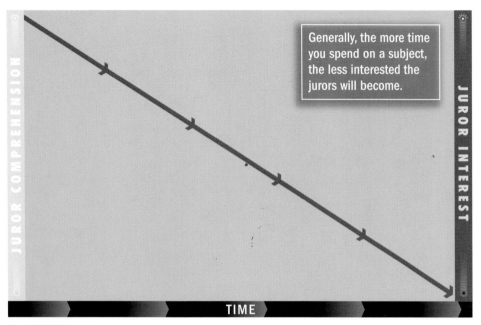

> Generally, the more time you spend on a subject, the less interested the jurors will become.

JUROR COMPREHENSION

JUROR INTEREST

TIME

ILLUSTRATION 2-4

When combined, a graph of these two mental functions (comprehension and boredom) spread over time looks like Illustration 2-5. The point at which the rising Comprehension Curve intersects the declining Interest Curve is what my colleague Guy Grogan calls the Sweet Spot. The Sweet Spot is the place where jurors are most receptive and capable of understanding the testimony that you are presenting to them.

While I am not able to quantitatively measure the Sweet Spot's exact location, I can qualitatively describe it. This is the place where you have invested, but not overinvested, your time and educational resources. It is the place where you have spent enough time so that the jurors understand the issues, but you have not spent so much time that the jurors have become bored with what you are teaching them.

The challenge for trial lawyers, as it is for all educators, is to push this learning process right up to the Sweet Spot, but not to stop either before or after it. If you stop too early, you have sold the jurors short. (See Illustration 2-6.) They are still interested and have additional capacity to learn, yet you have squandered the opportunity; additional time educating the jury on that particular topic would have yielded a positive return for your effort. Without losing their attention, you could have provided more information to your jurors—information that jurors would hopefully have used to convince others to vote in your favor.

If you carry on too long, you will push past the Sweet Spot and begin to go down along the falling Interest Curve. (See Illustration 2-7.) Here the horse has been repeatedly beaten and is already dead. Any additional gains are *not* worth the increased time that you are putting into the process. Any small gain you may make in jury comprehension is more than offset by a greater loss directly attributable to jury boredom; your efforts are providing a negative return.

The Comprehension and Interest Curves

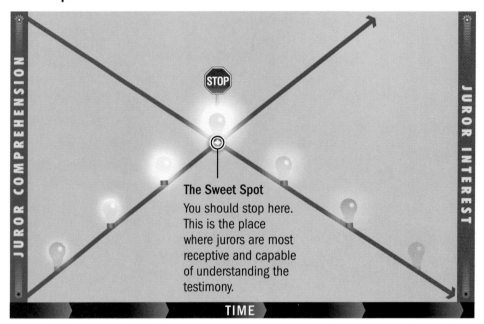

ILLUSTRATION 2-5

Don't Stop Too Early

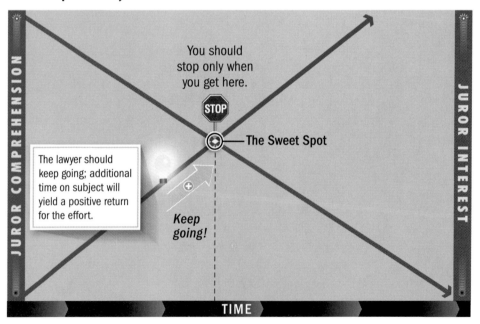

ILLUSTRATION 2-6

Don't Go On for Too Long

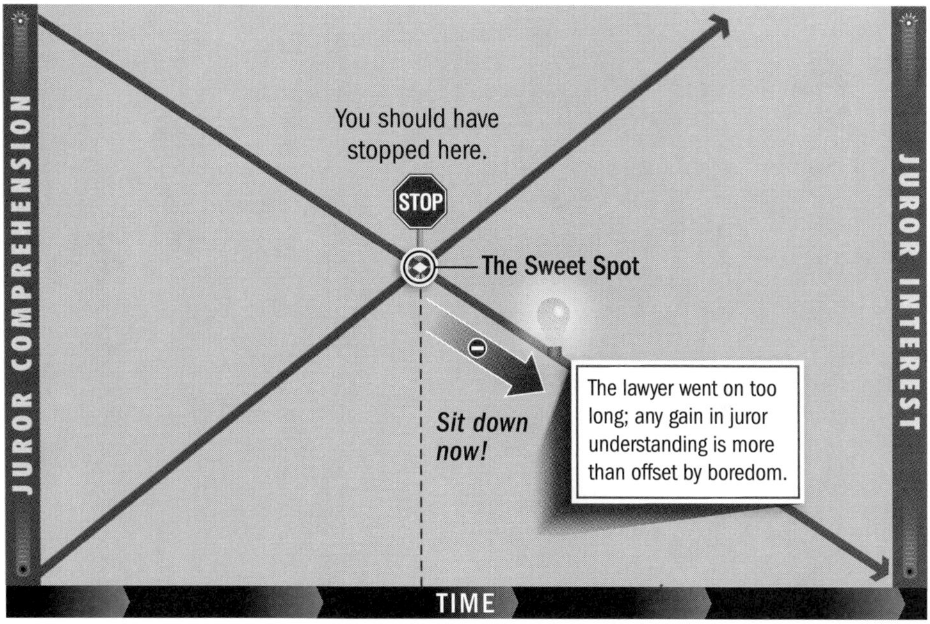

JUROR COMPREHENSION

JUROR INTEREST

You should have stopped here.

STOP

The Sweet Spot

Sit down now!

The lawyer went on too long; any gain in juror understanding is more than offset by boredom.

TIME

ILLUSTRATION 2-7

The Complexity Scale

The Complexity Scale divides evidence into three levels based on how difficult the information is for the jurors to understand. (See Illustration 2-8a.) From the bottom of the scale and moving upward, these levels are: (1) "Bottom Level—Information *Everybody* Can Understand," (2) "Middle Level—Information Only *Some* People Can Understand," and (3) "Top Level—Information Nobody I Know *Can* Understand or *Wants* to Understand." When I say "nobody I know," I am referring to the average nonexpert—your typical neighbor, friend, parent of your kid's friend, the kind of person who is likely to be on your jury.

When a witness begins to testify, the information is bottom-level "basic stuff"—basic facts, basic arguments, basic examples, basic metaphors, analogies— things everyone can understand. (See Illustration 2-8b.) As the testimony or argument continues, the information generally moves up the Complexity Scale and it gets harder and harder for some of the jurors to understand. Eventually, the information becomes sufficiently complicated that it crosses into the middle level of the scale; that is, it becomes "testimony only *some* people can understand." (See Illustration 2-8c.) As the testimony or arguments continue, the inevitable happens—the information becomes so complex that it crosses into the top level. Information is in this level when it is material that "nobody I know *can* understand or *wants* to understand." (See Illustration 2-8d.)

The Complexity Scale

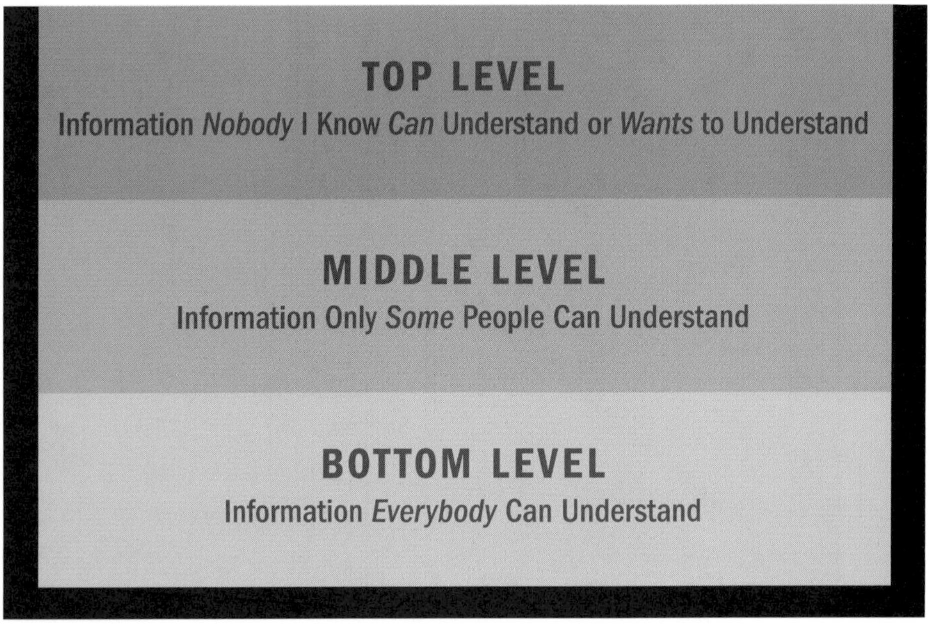

TOP LEVEL
Information *Nobody* I Know *Can* Understand or *Wants* to Understand

MIDDLE LEVEL
Information Only *Some* People Can Understand

BOTTOM LEVEL
Information *Everybody* Can Understand

ILLUSTRATION 2-8a

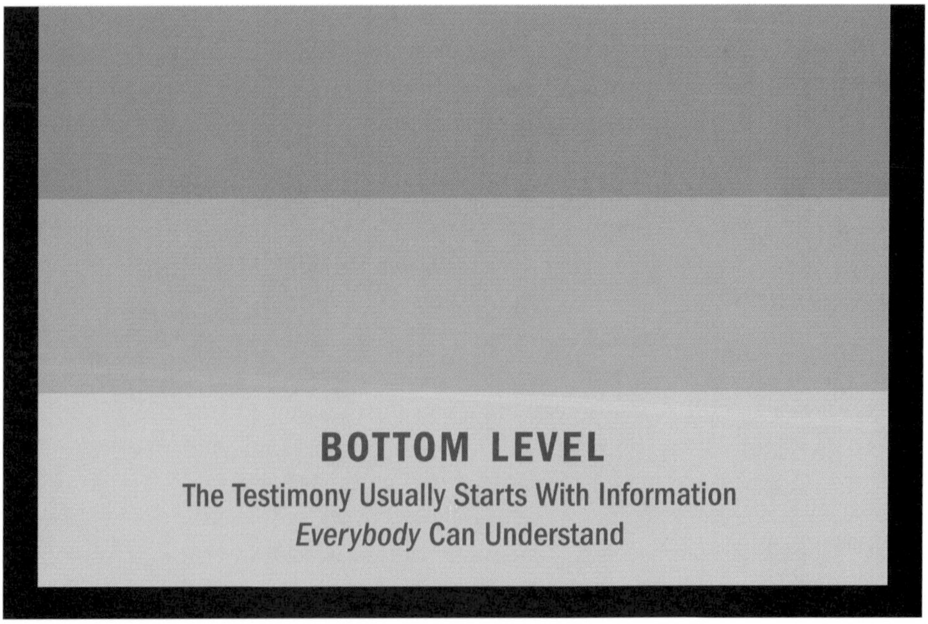

BOTTOM LEVEL
The Testimony Usually Starts With Information
Everybody Can Understand

ILLUSTRATION 2-8b

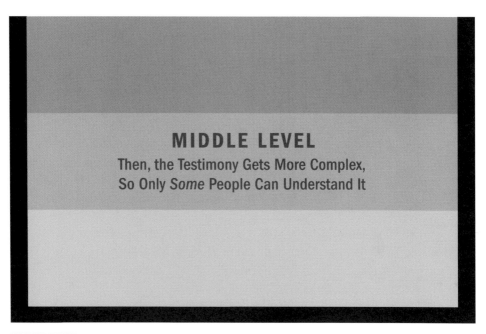

ILLUSTRATION 2-8c

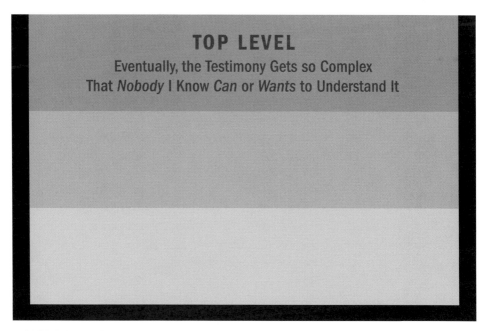

ILLUSTRATION 2-8d

It is important to note the *or* in "can understand or wants to understand." Material works its way into the top level of the Complexity Scale in one of two ways. First, the information can be such that "no one I know *can* understand" because it is too complicated. This is complex information that no average person can possibly fully appreciate given the limitations of trial. For example, at some point an expert may rely on an arcane formula or calculation that took years to learn and apply. While the law may require that you introduce such evidence in your case, no one really believes that a typical juror is able to understand this material.

The second way information qualifies for the top level of the Complexity Scale is for it to be of a nature that "no one I know *wants* to understand." At the back of an accountant's report are typically a dozen or more schedules, each of which establishes an element necessary for the accountant's final conclusion. Accountants carefully present this material in a way such that, if it is not always easy to follow, it is sufficiently logical that you could probably figure it out if you really wanted to. But who really wants to review this stuff? No one on the jury does! That is why it qualifies for the top level of the Complexity Scale.

As soon as you cross from the bottom to the middle level of the Complexity Scale, you begin losing some of your jurors. And unless you have an expert (or an extremely intelligent person) on your jury, no one in the jury box is likely to understand or want to understand evidence in the top level. Consequently, more often than not, the jury will make its decision based on evidence in the bottom and middle levels.

"So," you might ask, "why would anyone want to present evidence to the jurors if there is little chance that any of them will actually understand it? Why would you ever bother offering evidence from the top level to the jury?" This is a trick question. You see, even though it is a jury trial, the jury is not your only audience. There are at least two other spectators that you need to keep in mind: the trial judge and the justices on the Court of Appeals.

Whether the jury comprehends, uses, or even appreciates evidence in the top level is really not the point. The target audience of this testimony is usually not the jury; it is the court. Even if the jurors never understand it, the court still requires such evidence in virtually every case. If you fail to offer the "necessary stuff," you may subject yourself to a nonsuit or motion for directed verdict from the trial court. Additionally, unless you introduce foundation-necessary evidence from the top level of the Complexity Scale, the trial court may bar you from presenting other highly persuasive and understandable evidence from the lower two levels.

Likewise, if you skip presenting evidence from the top level because it is "bo-o-o-o-ring," the Court of Appeals may decide that you failed to make the required prima facie showing and reverse any victory you were able to convince the jurors to award you.

Let me offer an example. Assume that an accountant is on the stand. She starts by describing basic information—what it is that an accountant does, basic principles of accounting, etc. Here you are in the bottom level of the Complexity Scale; *everyone* (all the jurors and the judge) understands this information.

After a few minutes, your witness begins to describe contribution margins, explaining that they represent "the difference between sales and variable costs." By now, you have probably crossed into the middle level. The court understands the evidence. Some of the jurors understand; others do not. Hopefully, those who do will favor your side of the case.

Eventually, your accountant begins discussing the steps and procedures she followed to calculate the contribution margin at issue. She writes out the exact formulas she used. She describes her supporting documents and other arcane—but necessary—evidence. At this point very few jurors, if any, understand what has just taken place; you are in the top level. But remember, the target audience at this point is not the jury; it is the trial court and the Court of Appeals. They are the audience that will require you to meet certain necessary prima facie or foundational requirements. Whether the jury understands this relatively small bit of complex evidence is of only secondary importance. So, you swallow hard and introduce all of the accountant's workpapers with all of the calculations and bottom-line numbers on them. Your jury is probably temporarily asleep, but the legal integrity of your case is preserved.

Let me end this section with an important clarification. When some lawyers (and expert witnesses) hear my philosophy on this subject, they conclude that material in the top level of the Comprehension Curve cannot possibly be simplified. This is not the case. I believe that given enough time, all complex information can be substantially simplified. But given that time is not infinite, the point of this section is really threefold. First, concentrate a considerable percentage of your efforts on the two lower levels of the Comprehension Curve; this is where most jurors get the information necessary to make their decisions. Second, make sure that you provide the jurors with the right proportions of material from these two levels so as to keep them interested and focused on your case as long as possible. Finally, with all this effort, don't forget that you still need to add enough information (which can sometimes be very complicated) from the top level to meet your burden of proof and other legal requirements.

How the Competing Factors of Understanding and Boredom Interact Within the Complexity Scale

While it is impossible to quantitatively graph an example of "perfect" trial testimony, it is possible to illustrate its salient features by applying the principles just discussed (i.e., how comprehension and boredom interact and the concept of the "Complexity Scale"). I envision that a graph of perfect testimony might look like that shown in Illustration 2-9.

As you can see in Illustration 2-9, we have superimposed the upward-sloping Comprehension Curve (representing increasing comprehension over time) and the downward-sloping Interest Curve (representing declining interest over time) onto a base graph reflecting the three levels of a Complexity Scale.

Perhaps the most important feature of this illustration is the location of the Sweet Spot. The Comprehension Curve and the Interest Curve intersect near the

Perfect Trial Testimony

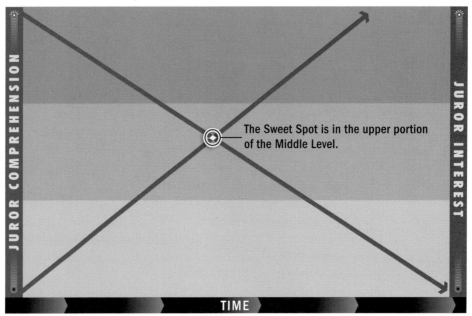

ILLUSTRATION 2-9

transition between the middle and top levels of the Complexity Scale. This is the perfect place for the Sweet Spot because it means that the lawyer and the witness have kept some of the jurors interested in the testimony well into the middle level. True, some of the jurors will not understand the information in this level, but those who do have not only learned the information, they have done so without getting so bored as to have been turned off by your teaching process.

If you do it right, those jurors who are not bored and who continue to absorb the testimony will explain the evidence to the rest of the jurors during deliberations. If you really do it right, the jurors who are doing the explaining will be "your" jurors and will do so in a way that favors your case.

SIMPLIFYING YOUR TESTIMONY

I have found four methods that help with the simplification process. These four methods—Simplification by Subtraction, Simplification by Addition, Simplification by Division, and Simplification by Multiplication—correspond to each of the basic mathematical functions, as shown in Illustration 2-10.

Simplification by Subtraction

Overview. Unfortunately, not all testimony goes as smoothly as displayed in Illustration 2-9. For example, in some cases, if we could plot the testimony, the Comprehension Curve would move upward far too slowly and result in a graph that looks something like that in Illustration 2-11a.

Simplification by	When You Need It	Solution
⊖ Subtraction	• Too much material • Repetition	• Reduce data to include only the most essential elements
⊕ Addition	• Basic information is excluded • Context is missing	• Focus on teaching concepts and facts • Use tutorials
÷ Division	• Jurors overwhelmed with data in short period • Material is too complex	• Break down complex data • Eliminate what you don't need
✕ Multiplication	• The "whole" is too big and incomprehensible • "Parts" are manageable by jurors	• Start with a discrete part • Move to the whole

ILLUSTRATION 2-10. Four Methods for Simplifying Testimony

There is too much unnecessary preliminary material or repetition in the testimony represented by this Comprehension Curve. The "wind up" is too long, as illustrated by the fact that the slope of the Comprehension Curve rises too gently. The curve does not cross into the middle level until far too late in the testimony. What this means is that, even though the material may not be overly complex, the jurors will eventually get bored, causing the Interest Curve to drop precipitously. As a result, the Sweet Spot in Illustration 2-11a is far too low; it is still in the bottom level of the Complexity Scale.

Because of the unnecessarily long wind-up, even the brightest jurors will have mentally "checked out" by the time you get to the topics in the middle level. Even though some of the jurors are capable of understanding more complex issues, many of them will be so bored that they will not be willing to do so. You have effectively lost the attention of the brighter members of your jury *before* getting to the material for which you most likely need them—material in the middle level of the Complexity Scale.

Now that we have identified the problem, how do we simplify the testimony so as to eliminate, or at least reduce, this problem? We use Simplification by Subtraction, the process of removing excessive and unnecessary clutter. (See Illustration 2-11b.) This can be visualized as shortening the Comprehension Curve and thereby increasing its slope to more closely approximate that of "ideal testimony." (See Illustration 2-11c.)

By cutting out the excess, you make the Comprehension Curve look more like the one we drew to illustrate perfect testimony. With less extraneous material, the Interest Curve also flattens out and does not drop as precipitously. The net result is that the Sweet Spot is raised higher up, closer to its ideal location in the middle level of the Complexity Scale. (See Illustration 2-11d.)

Too Much Preliminary Material

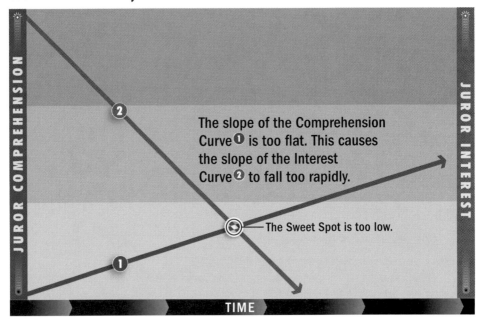

The slope of the Comprehension Curve ❶ is too flat. This causes the slope of the Interest Curve ❷ to fall too rapidly.

The Sweet Spot is too low.

ILLUSTRATION 2-11a

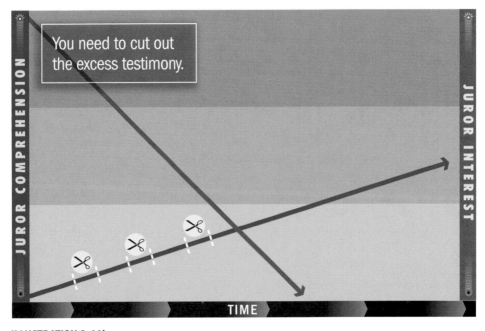

You need to cut out the excess testimony.

ILLUSTRATION 2-11b

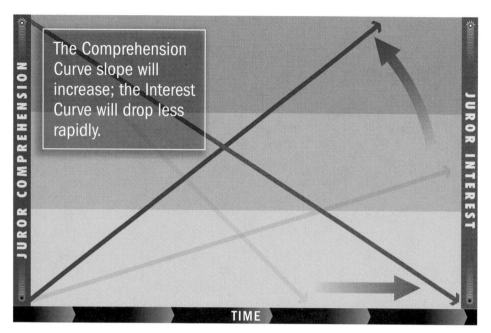

ILLUSTRATION 2-11c

ILLUSTRATION 2-11d

How to Use Simplification by Subtraction. How hard can it be to eliminate excessive ideas, testimony, or arguments? The answer is, "Harder than you may think." Coming up with new ideas is usually easier than getting rid of old ones. Unfortunately, eliminating material, even the long-held ideas that you have grown to love, is exactly what you must do.

Like all things, ideas have a natural life. The majority are short-lived; they surface during the mental mining process (discussed below), inspire other ideas, and then quickly fade away. Some ideas will survive to middle age, but most will eventually lead to dead ends, dry up, and disappear. In the end, only a handful of the remaining ideas will make it all the way to "trial prep." I call these hardy ideas, and the information and arguments that have coalesced around each of them, Survivors.

Often, I become so enamored with a Survivor that it is almost impossible for me to let it go, even after it has fully served its purpose. Maybe it is a form of inertia or the fact that I have lived with the idea for so long. Unfortunately, letting go is exactly what I need to do with some Survivors.

When the time comes, take a deep breath and start the often painful process of pruning away as many unneeded Survivors as possible. Do so, no matter how old these Survivors may be. Longevity, in and of itself, means nothing if the Survivor does not strengthen the central theme of your case.

Why all this chopping and hacking away of excess material? Because anything that does not help you hurts by obscuring the jurors' view of what really matters.

The jury will miss important facts that are buried in muck. Your chances of persuading the jury increase when you take the time to reduce the dispute down to its essence and pursue only those issues that really matter. This means having the confidence to let go of certain claims, ideas, and approaches (even potentially winning ones) in order to maximize your overall chances of convincing the jury to find in your client's favor.

How do you determine what to eliminate? Well, the very first thing you have to do is to reformulate the last question. You should *not* ask yourself, "How do you determine what to eliminate?"—instead, the proper question is, "How do you determine what to keep?" The difference between the two questions is significant. The first presumes that material remains unless it needs to be eliminated. The second presumes that material is eliminated *unless* you find a reason for it to remain.

The best way to start this winnowing process is to consult your jury instructions, which list the minimum of what you need to prove in order to establish your claim or defense. Once you have this information, determine how to make your prima facie case with as few witnesses and exhibits as reasonably possible. Then (and only then) add those additional facts back in that help capture or keep the jurors' interest, help the jury understand your case, or provide you with the material that you will eventually need for your closing argument.

Some of the "stuff" that you should throw out will be obvious. My grandfather, who was the most honest automobile mechanic I ever met, used to say, "You can't sell what you don't buy." Follow his advice and eliminate anything that does not pass the "Smell Test"—eliminate anything that smells fishy. If you have a prob-

Do not ask: "What to Eliminate?"... | Ask: "What to Keep?"

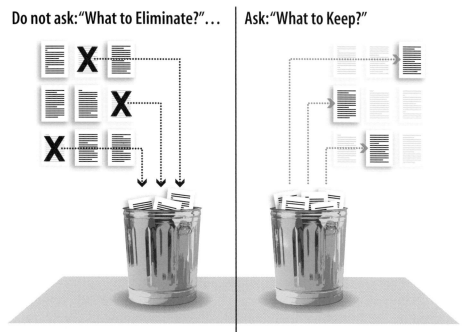

Presumption: Data *in* unless taken out | Presumption: Data *out* unless it needs to be in

lem applying the Smell Test, consider what I call the Sigh Test. An argument fails the Sigh Test if you find yourself (either actually or emotionally) taking a deep breath before you start to make the argument and then letting out a sigh when you finish it.

Abraham Lincoln once advised: "In law, it is good policy to never plead what you need not, lest you obligate yourself to prove what you cannot." Throw out your weak positions, no matter how clever. Throw out theories or causes of action that impose too great a burden of proof on you.

Another place to cut back is in the details. In some cases, details are necessary; in others, they are not. This often depends on who is in the audience. If your jury consists of only brain surgeons (I know, what are the chances of that—but this is a hypothetical), make sure you let them know that the injury is to the parieto-occipital sulcus. If you have a more typical jury, eliminate this detail and just tell them that the injury is "over here at the back of the brain." The first hypothetical jury wants that level of detail; the second will not likely understand it.

Simplification by Addition

Overview. We all have relatives or friends like this: the ones you used to know well, but now the only time you hear from them is at the end of the year when they send you (and probably scores of others) a photocopied Holiday letter, detailing all that has happened to them over the past year. The fact that you have not seen or spoken to these people for years does not matter; the letters just keep on coming—holiday season after holiday season.

The person sending you the letter always assumes that you know more about what is going on in his life than you really do know or care to know. To make matters worse, the sender usually refers to people mentioned in the letter only by their first names—"Steve and Heather visited us again this year." Any context a last name might provide is completely lost. Who the heck are Steve and Heather?

In this instance, the problem is not having *too much* information; it is having *too little*. In trials, the analogous situation happens all the time, often with expert witnesses. Expert witnesses are notorious for forgetting what it is like to need the most basic information in order to understand a particularly arcane topic. In such instances, the Comprehension Curve rises too rapidly and the Interest Curve falls even more rapidly. (See Illustration 2-12a.) This reflects the fact that the testimony either started at too high a level or got too complex too fast. Without context, the jurors have little understanding; with little understanding comes even less interest. The result: not only is the Sweet Spot too low, it also occurs too early in the testimony.

The way to resolve this problem is to add additional background information, to use what I previously referred to as "Simplification by Addition." (See Illustration 2-12b.) By doing so, you increase the length of the Comprehension Curve and thereby decrease its slope. The effect is also to make the downward slope of the Interest Curve less steep. (See Illustration 2-12c.) As a result the Sweet Spot moves upward, closer to its ideal position in the Middle Level of the Complexity Scale. (See Illustration 2-12d.)

How to Use Simplification by Addition. We are so preconditioned to believe that simplification involves *eliminating* material that some people have trouble believing that it is possible to simplify a case by expanding it. Adding information to simplify a topic may at first glance seem counterintuitive. How does this process work?

As I discuss below in greater detail, learning cannot take place in a void. Students, including jurors, cannot begin to learn until they first find and latch onto something they already understand. Think about how hard it would be to learn something entirely new beginning with a topic about which you had absolutely no knowledge. It would be like one of those nightmares everybody has where you are somehow enrolled in an advanced calculus class; on the first day the teacher decides to start with "just a quick refresher of some of last semester's easier topics" and you have no idea what she is talking about.

Simplification by Addition allows you to add enough information to your presentation so that the jurors begin their analysis in comfortable and familiar surroundings. This familiarity will occasionally serve as a seed from which understanding begins to germinate.

Whatever you do, never lose sight of your goal, which is to find ways to help jurors understand your case. You increase your chances of accomplishing this objective if you make the case as simple as possible. If simplicity comes from cutting back, do it. If you determine it is easier for the jurors to understand your case by adding material, do not be afraid to do so.

Not Enough Preliminary Material

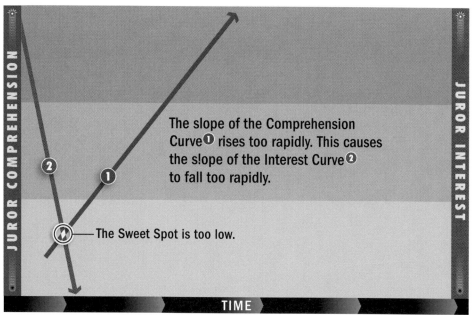

The slope of the Comprehension Curve❶ rises too rapidly. This causes the slope of the Interest Curve❷ to fall too rapidly.

The Sweet Spot is too low.

ILLUSTRATION 2-12a

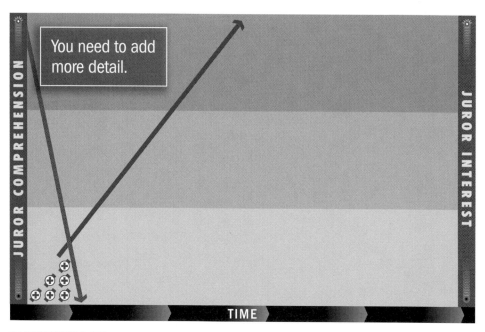

You need to add more detail.

ILLUSTRATION 2-12b

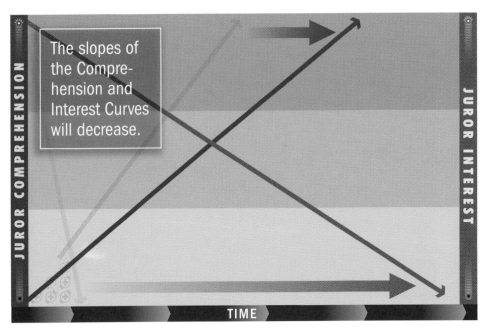

ILLUSTRATION 2-12c

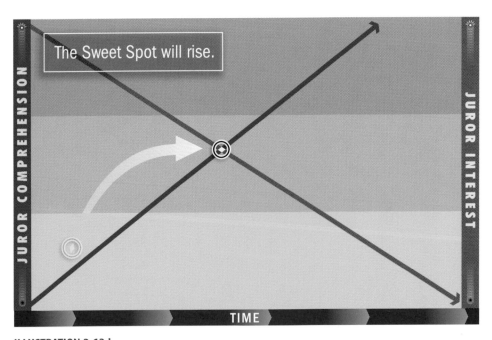

ILLUSTRATION 2-12d

In virtually every trial, there are concepts that require additional teaching, ones that the jury will not understand unless you take extra time to explain. In such instances, it is important to use tutorials so that you can simplify your case.

Tutorials do not need to be fancy. In fact, they do not even necessarily require graphics. What they do require are two things. First, tutorials require that you take the time to identify what issues you need to clarify. Second, tutorials require that you find simple and memorable ways to explain these concepts to the jury.

Some of your tutorials may be as simple as taking a little extra time to explain an important concept or term of art. Others may involve nothing more than a simple glossary to explain key terms. Still others will require a level of greater preparation. (Tutorials are discussed in Chapter 7.)

Simplification by Division

Occasionally, there will be what I can best describe as a "knot" in the testimony. This occurs when a witness, usually without much warning, unleashes a barrage of difficult information over a relatively short period of time. If it were possible to graph this testimony, the result would closely resemble a snake that has just eaten too large a meal. (See Illustration 2-13a.)

A "Knot" in the Testimony

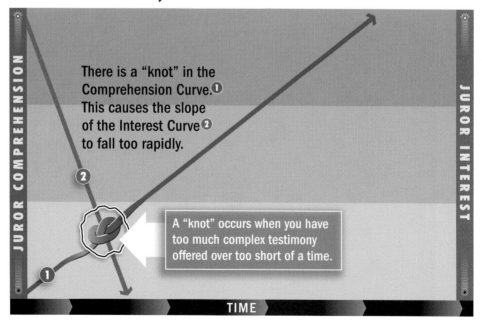

There is a "knot" in the Comprehension Curve.❶ This causes the slope of the Interest Curve❷ to fall too rapidly.

A "knot" occurs when you have too much complex testimony offered over too short of a time.

JUROR COMPREHENSION

JUROR INTEREST

TIME

ILLUSTRATION 2-13a

This mass of information often confuses and discourages the jurors. As a result, boredom quickly sets in and there is a rapid decline in juror interest. In such instance, the Sweet Spot often occurs at too low a level and results in premature juror boredom and a loss of juror comprehension.

Here, you need to rely on Simplification by Division, which involves three steps. First, divide the single mass of material into smaller units. This requires merely that you break down the complex issue into sub-issues and, if necessary, further break down the sub-issues into sub-sub-issues. (See Illustration 2-13b.) The easiest way to do this is to rely on the basic outlining techniques that you have used since your early student days.

Next, eliminate any excess. This second step requires that you apply the techniques that you learned from Simplification by Subtraction. (See Illustration 2-13c.)

Finally, spread these remaining smaller units of information out over time. You accomplish this final step by having your witness take a few minutes to testify about each of the key remaining sub-units. With your jury understanding the issue, the slope of the Interest Curve decreases and the Sweet Spot moves upward to the middle level of the Complexity Scale. (See Illustrations 2-13d and 2-13e.) Dividing a subject into discrete understandable bits may mean that you spend more time in front of the jury, but it also often eliminates the subject's complexity. Remember that eliminating complexity is the goal. If keeping the witness on the stand longer accomplishes this goal, then it is worth doing.

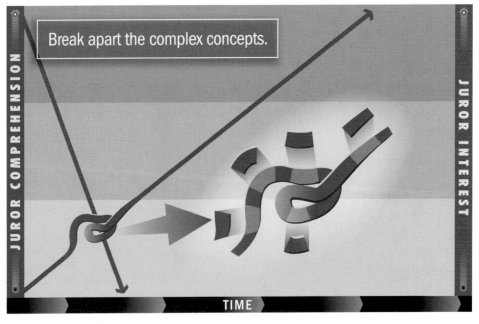

ILLUSTRATION 2-13b

ILLUSTRATION 2-13c

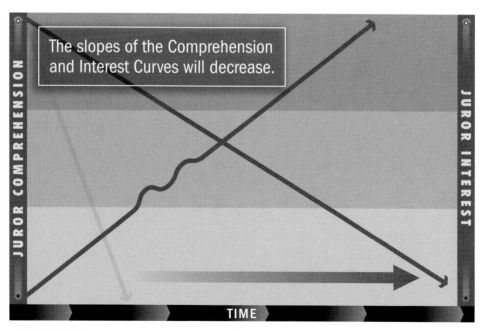

ILLUSTRATION 2-13d

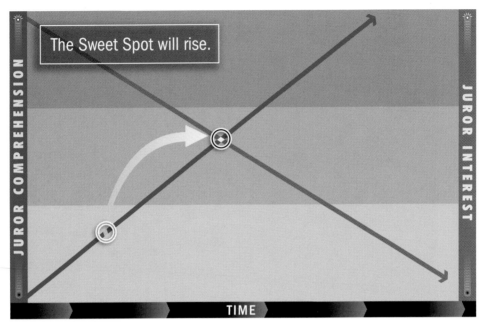

The Sweet Spot will rise.

JUROR COMPREHENSION

JUROR INTEREST

TIME

ILLUSTRATION 2-13e

Simplification by Multiplication

Simplification by Multiplication is the process of helping jurors feel comfortable moving from a discrete understandable part to a larger, otherwise virtually incomprehensible whole. It is the process of helping a jury feel comfortable with a single tree and then using what that jury just learned to help them understand and appreciate the entire forest.

By way of an example, I worked on a case where 3,000 plaintiffs sought $90 million for unpaid overtime work done over a four-year period. Ninety million dollars is a lot of money—so much so that during mock jury trials, the jurors often had trouble awarding such a large amount to the plaintiffs, even when there were 3,000 of them.

Initially, we attempted to persuade the mock jurors using Simplification by Division. We started with $90 million, divided that amount by the number of class members, and then divided the resulting number by four years to show that the average amount per year per plaintiff was $7,500. We thought this would work because, while $7,500 per year was still significant, it was not an unreasonable amount to award each plaintiff. Even with this detailed explanation and 3,000 plaintiffs, the mock jurors still had problems awarding $90 million.

Eventually, it occurred to me that we were doing this backward. Instead of starting with the whole and scaling down to the individual, we needed to start with the individual and scale up to the entire class. This scaling-up process is Simplification by Multiplication.

In this case, we started the process with an individual, the name plaintiff. She told the jury that she routinely worked sixty to seventy hours a week for only forty hours of pay. She testified that she even had to work without pay on the Saturday morning of her wedding day. We repeated this process with a handful of other plaintiffs, each of whom had an equally compelling story. By the time these representative witnesses were done testifying, the jury had no problem understanding why each of them was individually entitled on the average to $7,500 per year in overtime salary. (See Illustration 2-14a.)

Once the jurors were comfortable with the individual figure, we invited them to calculate the total damages using the individual data. Specifically, we asked them to multiply this individual amount by the number of class members (3,000) and the number of years (four years). The result was, of course, $90 million, which is the amount that the jury eventually awarded to the class. (See Illustration 2-14b.)

⊗ Simplification by Multiplication

Step 1: Help Jurors Feel Comfortable with an Understandable "Part"

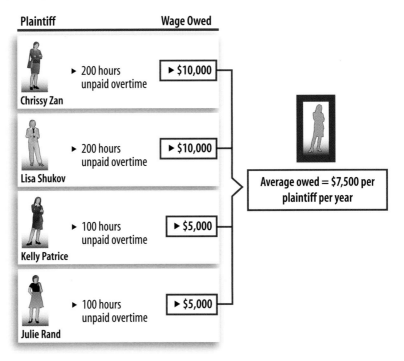

Plaintiff		Wage Owed
Chrissy Zan	▸ 200 hours unpaid overtime	▸ $10,000
Lisa Shukov	▸ 200 hours unpaid overtime	▸ $10,000
Kelly Patrice	▸ 100 hours unpaid overtime	▸ $5,000
Julie Rand	▸ 100 hours unpaid overtime	▸ $5,000

Average owed = $7,500 per plaintiff per year

ILLUSTRATION 2-14a

Step 2: Move the Jurors from the "Part" to the "Whole"

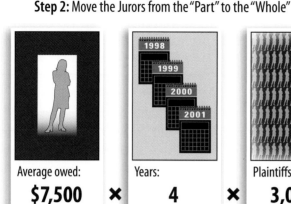

Average owed:		Years:		Plaintiffs:	
$7,500	**×**	**4**	**×**	**3,000**	**= $90 Million**

ILLUSTRATION 2-14b

Make Time to Mentally Mine

WHAT MENTAL MINING IS AND WHY IT IS IMPORTANT

Mental mining is the conscious effort to dislodge, bring forth, and examine the subconscious understanding that you have developed about a topic—in this instance, your case. Unless you make a conscious effort to bring forth this unconscious understanding, it will generally remain hidden and be of little use to you.

When you are learning the basics about your case, two things are happening simultaneously. (See Illustration 2-15.) First (and most obviously), you are consciously memorizing such vital information as names, dates, places, etc. Second (and less obviously—at least until you start actively mentally mining), your subconscious is finding ways to deal with all of the new facts with which you are inundating it. The subconscious often accomplishes this by (1) arranging the facts into a story and (2) more or less simultaneously comparing this newly created story to various other guideposts or bits of information with which it is already familiar.

To rephrase my original definition above, mental mining is the conscious effort to bring forth the underlying stories and the related guideposts that your subconscious has developed to help your conscious mind make sense of the otherwise overwhelming facts in your case. Once you uncover these stories and guideposts, your conscious mind can refine and develop them as ways to help you explain and the jury understand what happened. (See Illustration 2-16.)

Let me illustrate by describing what happens in a typical mental mining session. The vast majority of these efforts follow the same pattern. I often start off by asking my client, usually a lawyer preparing for trial, to tell me the story of his case. Many lawyers begin merely listing facts or pointing to a document or two. At this point, I stop my client and politely but firmly ask him to start over, but this time to tell me the *story.* For many lawyers, this is an awkward moment. Some

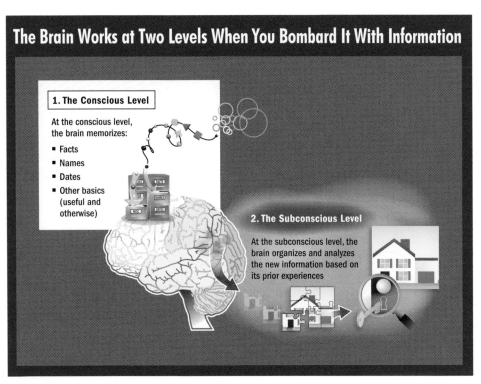

ILLUSTRATION 2-15

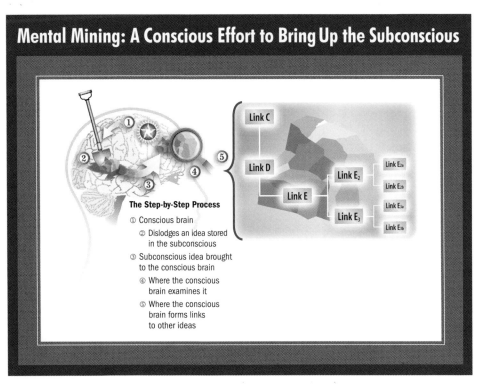

ILLUSTRATION 2-16

think that listing facts is telling a story. But with gentle prodding, the client begins to do more than list facts; he begins to tell a story.

Initially, the story is not always understandable. Often the client has to go back, fill in blanks, and restart the process. But eventually a coherent story emerges. Actually, what emerges is almost always more than just a story. (See Illustration 2-17.) Usually, what comes out of this process includes:

- A better-articulated understanding of what is really in dispute—this is often your "case theme" (discussed in Chapter 3).
- A better understanding of what really inspires the key player—this is the key element of "motive" (discussed in Chapter 3).
- One or more basic links between the lawyers' particular and unique case and various analogies, expressions, and metaphors commonly understood by potential jurors—these are your key ("educational tools") (discussed in Chapter 3).
- A list of areas in the story that are unclear and need more work in order to be better understood by the lawyer and, eventually, the jury—these are your "problem spots," places where no mental pictures arise in the listener's mind.

It is always amazing to see what emerges from this process, what connections exist buried deep within your brain—old Monty Python skits, songs, commercials, punch lines from jokes, and more. As we will see, all of this is potential buried treasure.

Let me offer you three real-world examples of such buried treasures.

First Example of Buried Mental Mining Treasure

I had a case involving a stockbroker who made 3,000 unauthorized trades that took over 350 of his clients, all of whom were retirees, out of the stock market just before the Dow Jones Industrial Average went from 7,000 to 11,000. The net result was that his clients lost over $11 million dollars.

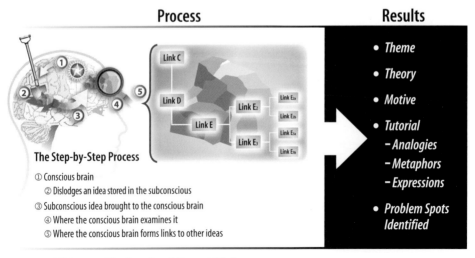

ILLUSTRATION 2-17. The Results of Mental Mining

This was the single largest series of unauthorized trades in the history of the defendant brokerage company. The brokerage company, which discovered the unauthorized trades within days of their having been made, could have easily reversed the trades at a relatively low cost to itself and restored all of the clients back to where they had been. The brokerage company not only failed to do this but also began to escape liability by hiding the illegal trades from the clients by limiting the amount and types of information that the broker provided to them.

One of the defense experts claimed that limiting the information that the investors received about the illegal trade was not so bad; after all—this expert claimed—one role that a broker plays, especially for older and less sophisticated investors, "is to act as an 'information filter' making sure that the customer does not get overwhelmed by all of the confusing information that is out there."

When I thought about the phrase "information filter," I started thinking about what the difference was between a filter and a censor and, for some strange reason, I was reminded of a toy my kids used to have. The toy had blocks of different shapes. You would store the blocks in a hollow sphere. On the outside of the sphere there were holes of different shapes. The object was to slide the differently shaped blocks into the corresponding holes. For example, the square block would go through the square hole, but it would not go through the round hole.

My memory of this toy led to the following graphics for closing argument.

▼ ▼ ▼

Defendant Adam Sorensen[3] says he wasn't a censor; he only acted as a filter. What's the difference? Let's see what the dictionary says.

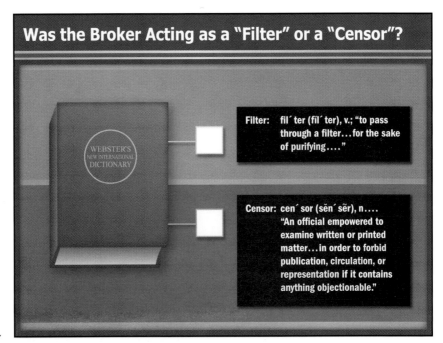

Was the Broker Acting as a "Filter" or a "Censor"?

Filter: fil´ ter (fil´ ter), v.; "to pass through a filter... for the sake of purifying...."

Censor: cen´ sor (sĕn´ sẽr), n.... "An official empowered to examine written or printed matter... in order to forbid publication, circulation, or representation if it contains anything objectionable."

---

3. The real names have been changed in this and other examples.

So, which was he? Was Adam Sorensen a filter or a censor? Mr. Sorensen says all that he did was act as an information filter. All he did was filter out extraneous information—information that the investors really did not need. They just would have gotten confused if he hadn't done so.

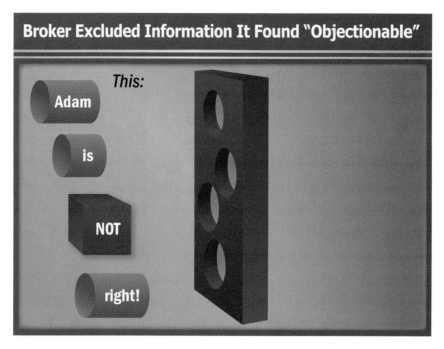

That's **not** what happened. The evidence shows that what Mr. Sorensen did was to exclude anything that he found objectionable. In this instance, what was objectionable to Mr. Sorensen was the truth!

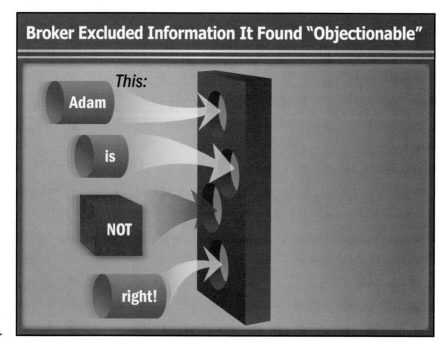

If the information helped Adam Sorensen, that information passed through and made it to the investors.

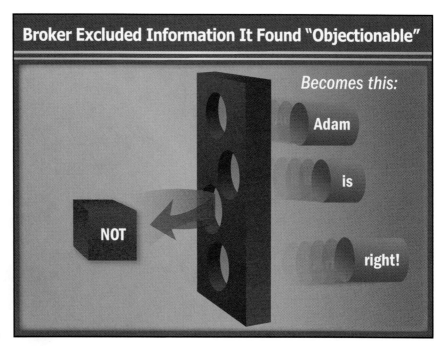

If Adam Sorensen decided that he was hurt by the information, well, that material just never made it through—the investors never got those facts. Defendant changed the truth—"Adam is not right!" He changed it into "Adam is right!"

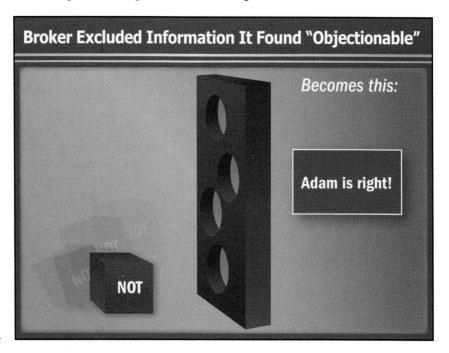

Adam Sorensen found the truth to be objectionable, so he excluded the truth. That is a censor, a censor of the truth, a censor who wants to help only himself.

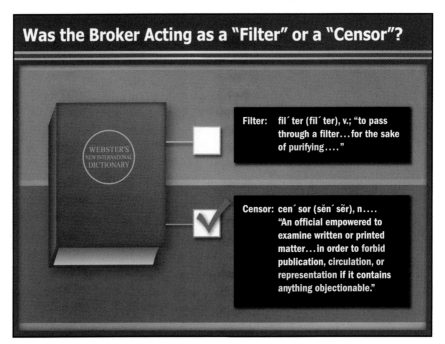

Second Example of Buried Mental Mining Treasure

I was once involved in a case where the defendant company, which was not my client, had repeatedly tried to suppress evidence of its own wrongdoing. At first, this was relatively easy to do. Eventually, as an increasing amount of evidence began to accumulate, it got progressively more difficult for the defendant to hide what it had done and it began taking increasingly extreme steps to hide the information. Finally, the evidence became so overwhelming that, despite every possible effort, the defendant could no longer conceal what it did and all hell broke loose.

Our client, a class of plaintiffs, wanted to illustrate this point. As I heard this story, I immediately began to think about one of my favorite *I Love Lucy* programs, the one in which Lucy and Ethel are working along a conveyor belt at a chocolate factory. Their job is to package the candy as it comes down the line. At first, the work is easy; as the pieces come down the line, Lucy and Ethel carefully put them in boxes. Then the pace of the assembly line begins to get faster and faster. At first, Lucy and Ethel are able to handle the challenge. But as the speed increases, so does their desperation as they try to figure out how to stop the candy from getting past them. They begin stuffing the candy in boxes, in their mouths, in their clothes, anywhere they can. The result is complete bedlam.

This mental mining effort worked. I had not seen *I Love Lucy* in years, but I could clearly visualize this particular episode and the analogy fit perfectly. Even more amazingly, when I informally tested the analogy on various people ranging from ten to seventy-five years old, they all knew exactly which episode I was referring to and immediately understood the point.

Third Example of Buried Mental Mining Treasure

I was asked to work with a class of police officers. They were employed by a county that maintained two separate law enforcement agencies. One was the county sheriff's department, which consisted of mostly white officers; the other was the county police department, which consisted mostly of black and Hispanic officers who did comparable work but were paid only 60 percent of what the sheriffs were paid.

For more than a decade, the county police officers presented evidence of this discrimination to the county and for equally as long, the county ignored the evidence. The evidence kept mounting up and the county kept ignoring it. In fact, the county admitted that it had thrown away at least two independent reports criticizing its history of discriminatory action.

As I heard this story, I was reminded of the legendary (and I am afraid now all too forgotten) comic genius Buster Keaton and his elephant Bimbo. In 1964, Mr. Keaton was photographed with an elephant for a U.S. Steel advertisement. The photograph shows Mr. Keaton seated on a stool. He is wearing his trademark hat; he has raised his hand over his eyes to emphasize he is intently staring off far in the distance and is completely unaware (or pretending to be unaware) of what is happening around him. Immediately behind him is Bimbo, a fully grown Indian elephant. Bimbo is standing patiently. Her trunk is wrapped around one of Mr. Keaton's arms. The tip of her trunk probes one of Mr. Keaton's vest pockets. Bimbo is as close and as obvious as an elephant can possibly be and yet Mr. Keaton does not see—or does not want to see—the truth. When I was a kid and first saw the picture I could just hear Mr. Keaton saying, "Elephant? I don't see no elephant!" (See Illustration 2-18.)

ILLUSTRATION 2-18. "Elephant? I Don't See No Elephant!"

Our clients eventually used this image in their closing argument. They spoke about how the evidence of discrimination had been accumulating for years and had been ignored. They concluded that except for the tragic fact that several hundred hard-working law enforcement officers had been injured for more than a decade, the lengths to which the county went so that it could ignore the evidence might even be funny, almost like the picture of Buster Keaton pretending to ignore the elephant. But no matter how hard Buster Keaton tried to ignore the truth, it was still there. Likewise, no matter how much the county tried to ignore discrimination, it was real and still very much there.

In the Red Corner, the Waltons; in the Blue Corner, the Stevenson-Ritters

So, how do you engage in mental mining?

Let me start with an observation that may help answer this question. It is my belief that, when it comes to eating dinner, there are two entirely different types of families. On the one hand, you have the "traditional" family, perhaps best exemplified by the Waltons—you know, that family they named the television show after. In this family, three generations of Waltons would sit peacefully at the dining table. On the other hand, there is my immediate family, the Stevenson-Ritters. If I had to describe our dinners, I would say that they are one big free-for-all.

At the Waltons' dining room table, food was passed quietly all in the same direction. There was only one discussion going on at any one time. If someone had a comment to offer, he patiently waited his turn. If, with all of this waiting, the unspoken idea died or was forgotten, it was no big deal to the Waltons—at least the quiet order at dinner had been maintained. A stenographer would find transcribing such an event a piece of cake, a walk in the park, no big deal.

At the Stevenson-Ritter table, constrained (but only slightly constrained) chaos prevails during dinner. There are at least three conversations going on at the same time and you are nothing if you can't simultaneously participate in all of them. If you have what you feel is a comment, you offer it without hesitation. If you have a better idea, there is no reason to wait your turn—get it out there. Throughout all of this there is usually at least one running joke that surfaces, disappears, and surfaces again later on. In short, none of the Waltons would survive long at the Stevenson-Ritters' table. Good night, John-Boy!

When you are in the process of mental mining, you will find that you are far more productive if you model your session on dinner at the Stevenson-Ritters rather than at the Waltons.

The best mental mining sessions are those where no one holds back; where no idea is too silly to be raised; where multiple ideas are being simultaneously tossed out for consideration. Participants should be encouraged to take risks. If they have comments, they make them even if it means talking with their mouths full. Delay will kill your best ideas; embarrassment will smother them. The lesson you were forced to learn as a kid about walking quietly in straight lines does not apply in mental mining.

You Say Tomato, I Say… *PAR*-ty!

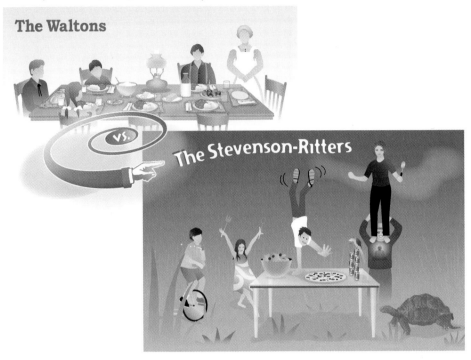

Many people perceive the mental mining process as being entirely spontaneous, loud, and rambunctious. Perhaps this is because that is the way most people perceive trial lawyers and the way that many of us perceive ourselves. There is, however, a very important part of the process that substantially benefits from careful pre-planning and structure; that is the preparation leading up to the mental mining session itself. Before you go into a no-holds-barred mental mining session (like the kind described above), provide some background information to your Critical Listeners (this is a group that we will describe in further detail in the next section). You want to provide them with enough information to start the mental composting process, but not so much information that their thinking becomes fixed.

Rather than distributing material that is unbiased or entirely neutral, I find it more helpful to hand out adversarial material that promotes your position (a settlement conference filing, a summary judgment motion, a trial brief, etc.). At least initially, you want the participants thinking like advocates *for your position*. Later you can ask these same Critical Listeners to do mental mining once more while pretending to be your opposing counsel, but not at first.

Providing material to your Critical Listeners before the mental mining session serves two very valuable functions, depending on the personality type of the participant. Some of your Critical Listeners will review the material very quickly and then not consciously think much more about it again until just before the mental mining session begins. That is fine. For these people, even a brief preview will get the idea-composting process unconsciously going, the results of which will rapidly surface during the mental mining session itself.

Other Critical Listeners will likely take your material, go somewhere by themselves, review it repeatedly, and consciously think about how to best provide you with the material that you requested. At the mental mining session, these people will come prepared with ideas and likely present them to you in a very organized and coherent manner. These carefully reasoned ideas are likely to be every bit as helpful as those that are conceived during the session itself.

You Need a Critical Listener

Mental mining works best when at least two people participate: (1) the lawyer, who is very familiar with the case, and (2) a Critical Listener, who is not. (See Illustration 2-19.)

A Critical Listener is crucial. This person must be someone who is able to do at least four things at the same time. (See Illustration 2-20.) First, the Critical Listener must be able to listen, really listen, to the lawyer's story. This is not passive or polite listening. It is critical listening, paying close attention to what the lawyer is saying directly and what he is saying indirectly by way of inference. This is a special skill that I would liken to that of a good therapist.

Second, while carefully listening, the Critical Listener must be willing (without any hesitation) to interrupt the lawyer. When something does not make sense or when the lawyer's description leaves the listener with no mental picture, the Critical Listener must feel free to say so immediately. When there is a question, the Critical Listener must not be afraid to ask it. This requires that the Critical Listener feel free, without fearing any adverse consequences, to repeatedly look the lawyer in the eye and say, "I have no idea what the heck you were just trying to say. Go back and explain that again."

Third, the Critical Listener needs to be able to record any images, analogies, or other descriptions that the lawyer spontaneously offers while telling his story. To me, this is actually one of the most interesting aspects of the mental mining process. There is rarely a session where the lawyer during the middle of telling his story doesn't say something like: "What happened here reminds me of a story my grandfather told me . . . ," or "This case is an example of . . . ," or "This case just goes to prove the adage. . . ." These comments are verbal pictures. The Critical Listener must, first, be able to write all of them down regardless of whether they seem to be helpful or not and, second, follow up with probing questions, such as "What do you mean by that?" or "Tell me the story that your grandfather told you." This is crucial.

Finally, the Critical Listener needs to record any verbal pictures that come to mind while listening to the lawyer's story.

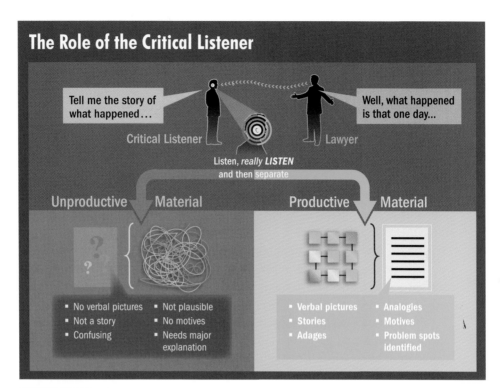

ILLUSTRATION 2-19

Characteristics of a Successful Critical Listener

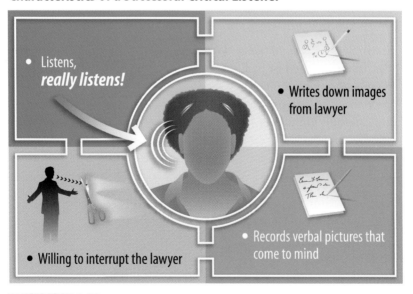

ILLUSTRATION 2-20

Follow Auntie Rita's Lead

When you engage in mental mining, you want to come up with as many different ideas as possible. You want to gather ideas without prejudging them and only later separate the good from the bad. I liken this process to the way Auntie Rita used to go shopping. Obviously, this requires some explanation.

For several years, my family and I lived in Honolulu across the street from a woman who everyone in the neighborhood called Auntie Rita. In Hawaii, calling someone who is not related to you "Auntie" or "Uncle" is a way of expressing affection and respect for them. Auntie Rita was almost pure Hawaiian. She was a large woman with powerful arms and legs. Yet when she moved, it was with considerable grace. She loved everyone and I do not know of anyone who did not feel the same toward her.

Auntie Rita loved to go shopping for clothes, but only when things were on sale at large discount stores. Auntie Rita would go and buy things not only for herself but also for anyone else she felt could fit into and would look nice in a particularly good bargain.

Auntie Rita's technique for getting the best bargain was simple and highly effective. She would go to the table with the sale items on it—let's say shirts. She would grab huge armfuls of the shirts without even worrying about whether they were the right size or color. She would then go to another part of the store where the other shoppers would not disturb her and leisurely examine what she had indiscriminately grabbed, sorting them into two piles: items that were worth keeping and rejects to take back to the sale table. Auntie Rita would then return to the sale table and repeat the whole process until she had everything she needed or could afford to buy.

Be like Auntie Rita when you engage in mental mining:

- Assemble all kinds of ideas without prejudging them. Do not screen the ideas as being good or bad, helpful or not helpful. Be truly nondiscriminating in gathering your ideas.
- Once the first sweep is made, sift through the material slowly, deliberately, and carefully. Only then start the process of determining what to keep and what to send back. Err on the side of trying out ideas at least once.
- Go through this process repeatedly. (See Illustration 2-21.) Every time you do, start fresh. Maintain what Zen students call "beginner's mind."[4]

Be fearless in your suggestions and do not in any way inhibit your colleagues from feeling that they can be equally fearless in offering suggestions to you. Before

---

4. "In the beginner's mind there are many possibilities, but in the expert's mind there are few." Shunryu Suzuki-Roshi.

he starts many of his mental mining sessions, my colleague, Andrew Spingler, advises new participants that mental mining is similar to that old television show *The Gong Show*. No idea is too crazy to be at least tried and no one can shoot down an idea until the person offering it has had adequate time to make his case for the idea—no matter how bizarre it may be. Don't forget, a brilliant concept is often the grandchild of a silly idea.

Active mental mining is like a soufflé. It takes time and suffers greatly if rushed or unnecessarily subjected to loud, unrelated noise. The mental mining process is a meander, not a straight-out sprint. Therefore, start the process as early as possible. Active mental mining works best when you are uninterrupted and not distracted by the hundred or so other things that somehow make themselves seem equally important. When you are in this process, go somewhere you will not be disturbed. Turn off the phone, the pager, or whatever means by which the outside world disturbs you. Focus on one thing—how to make your case make sense.

The Mental Mining Process

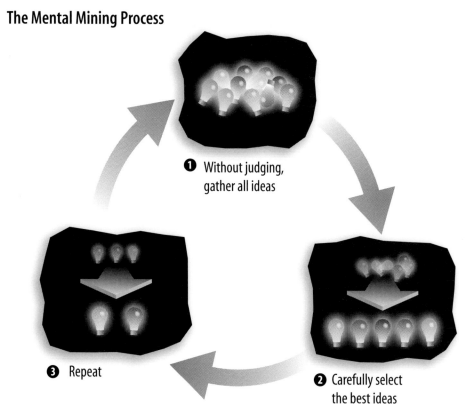

❶ Without judging, gather all ideas

❷ Carefully select the best ideas

❸ Repeat

ILLUSTRATION 2-21

LET PASSIVE MENTAL MINING OCCUR AND BE READY FOR IT WHEN IT DOES

There is another form of mental mining—passive mental mining. This is the mental mining that occurs when you are doing other things. Remember that I defined active mental mining as the conscious effort to bring forth and examine your subconscious thoughts. Occasionally, this process will appear to happen spontaneously. Who hasn't stumbled on a new idea while taking a shower, driving along in the car, walking to an appointment, etc.? Active mental mining brings ideas up from the subconscious to the more freely accessible conscious. Sometimes, these arguments do not break entirely free during the active mental mining session and can be claimed only when they break through at some wholly unanticipated moment.

Duke Ellington once described the process like this:

After you've absorbed the day and you get all settled down, you're quiet and you're already to go to sleep. You turn out the light and you put your head on the pillow and you get your sleeping stance together and there's an idea you've been looking for all day long and you get up and put the light on, get the paper, jot it down, and usually before you go to sleep, you got the next part of it.

You cannot force these moments, but you can be ready for them. Keep a pen and pad of paper next to your bed or in your pocket. And, for goodness sake, when these ideas come, write them down, trust them, and refine them.

Thomas Edison is reported to have once observed that everyone had great ideas while taking a bath. According to Edison, the only difference between him and everyone else was that when he got out of the bath with a great idea, he did something about it. You should, too.

Get Jurors to "Give A Damn" Based on the Facts

If you think about it, we impose a great deal on jurors. We take twelve normal people, all of whom have their own problems, and we complicate their lives by making them take on and resolve a problem for two or more parties that the jurors have never met.

Voir dire virtually guarantees that the jurors are blank slates. They do not know the parties; they know nothing about the dispute; to the extent that the dispute involves any specialized knowledge, the jurors generally have none of it.

The jurors are supposed to be disinterested; they are not supposed to be uninterested as well. Highly skilled trial lawyers know that they must take all necessary steps to prevent tedium. These lawyers know how to get jurors to "give a damn." They know how to get members of the jury to care enough about the case to shift from being passive, neutral observers to being advocates actively lobbying for one side over the other during jury deliberations.

These lawyers inspire this partisan response from the jurors by combining each of the four skills discussed in this chapter—educating the jurors, focusing on both "under" and "over" perspectives, simplifying cases, and engaging in mental mining—in just the right proportion and then using these skills to present *the facts* to the jurors.

I often talk with lawyers who stress how important it is to persuade jurors using emotion. These lawyers suggest that what sells to the jurors are not mundane facts, but the sizzle of an emotional appeal. I suppose that there is some truth to this. But, in my experience, these lawyers rely too much on the notion of emotion. Of course you want jurors to be emotional, but they must be emotional as a *result* of something. That something is usually the facts.

The jurors will decide your case on facts. They are, after all, the finders of fact. They want the facts. It is your job to teach them the facts. I can hear you saying, "Wait! If all that you need is the facts, why did I just read this entire chapter? Why the heck do I need all of the techniques described here?"

You need these techniques because a closed mind and/or an uninterested mind will not absorb facts. Without the facts, there is nothing to be emotional about. The techniques described in this chapter are designed to help keep the jury interested—to help keep their minds open. They are intended to help you find ways to keep the jury awake. They are designed to help you make your version the *truth*.

How Jurors Deliberate and How to Help Them Do So in Your Favor

Jurors often get two raw deals and a bum rap.

Compensation is the first and most obvious raw deal. Jury duty can be a financial disaster. Jurors in my home county are paid an amount that places their wages somewhere between that of Albanian and Nepalese day laborers. To add insult to injury, these jurors do not actually receive any cold hard cash until thirty days after their conscription ends. In the meantime, while they are performing their civic duty, jurors must pay for their own parking and buy their own lunches at a mediocre restaurant next to the courthouse.

If they are actually chosen to serve, jurors get their second raw deal—considerable disrespect from the lawyers throughout the trial.

Wait, how can that be? We appreciate our jurors, don't we? After all, at the beginning and end of every trial both sides traditionally thank their jurors by reminding them (with these or other similarly meaningless words) "that jury service is an honored privilege/duty extending back to 1215 A.D. and the days of the Magna Carta."

Yet between these automatic expressions of thanks, many of us blindly subject our jurors to considerable disrespect. We think nothing of:

- Wasting jurors' time in a myriad of ways.
- Forcing jurors to sit through badly edited and poorly structured trials.
- Forcing jurors to experience the emotional discomfort of making crucial decisions with inadequate information.
- Failing to provide jurors with the necessary tools to understand key testimony
- Boring the jurors beyond the point of numbness.

These two raw deals—inadequate compensation and lawyer disrespect—make the jury's "bum rap" all that more unfair. Lawyers (usually those who have lost) too often blame the jury for their own shortcomings at trial. Trial counsel routinely claim that "lay" jurors are incapable of deciding complex issues. Such criticism is usually then followed by horror stories about how "the jury just never got it" or how the jury was more interested in what a witness wore than the substance of her testimony.

Saying that "the jurors never got it" or that "the jurors were more interested in clothing than testimony" is often far more damning of the lawyer's abilities than the jurors'. Will every juror fully understand every case? Of course not; but you better have tried hard, really hard, to make your case simpler and more interesting before you make comments such as these.

Ultimately, lawyers' complaints about the jury system are meaningless for at least three reasons. First, for every story of disgust (told by the losing attorney), there is inevitably a contradicting story of praise (advanced by the winning side).

Second, the complaining lawyer's assessment at the end of trial rarely corresponds to her assessment at the beginning. A juror who a lawyer labels "incompetent" at the time of a verdict is often the very same juror who the lawyer deemed "perfect" immediately after voir dire. Such are the clarifying effects of an adverse judgment.

Finally, as much as we complain about its imperfections, we will never eliminate the jury system. Secretly, we know that we need it more than it needs us. To

this extent, our relationship with the jury system reminds me of the old joke Woody Allen used to tell about the man who goes to a psychiatrist seeking help for his crazy brother. The man says, "Doc, my brother is completely nuts; he runs around all day believing that he is a chicken." The doctor (usually with a German accent) replies, "Vell, vy don't you bring him in?" And the man answers, "I would, but we need the eggs."

As Mr. Allen so accurately understands, sometimes, no matter how crazy and frustrating something may be, we can't just get rid of it because we have gotten far too used to having the eggs.

Jurors take their jobs very seriously. They may complain about jury duty, yet most jurors believe that they have a personal stake in ensuring that the system works. As such, jurors generally apply the law as well as they can to the facts, as they best understand them.

Jurors believe that there is a "right" answer. The jury believes "the truth is out there!" They want to find it. Imagine how discouraging it would be to sit through a six-week trial, missing work, paying for your own parking, buying your own crummy lunches, and then, when it is all over, concluding that you came up with the wrong answer.

Often the only thing jurors find at all rewarding about jury service is feeling that they did the right thing. As a juror once told me, "After the hassles of listening to the case, all the while knowing that my regular work was piling up at the office, the only consolation was knowing that we [the jurors] came to the right conclusion."

Another juror told me, "I felt like that optimistic kid in the joke who keeps digging through the horse manure convinced that there just has to be a pony in there somewhere. I kept justifying all the time I spent on the jury by thinking that if we could find a way to dig through all this crap [at trial] we would find the truth buried in there somewhere."

Jurors believe that if you give them the right tools, they can and will find the right answer. Without feeling that you are unduly wasting their time, jurors want you to give them as much meaningful information as possible. They want to understand what is going on in the courtroom. This understanding not only helps them find the right answer, it makes the whole process considerably more interesting. Remember, it is the interested mind that most readily absorbs what you are trying to teach it.

Jurors are often willing to fight very hard to make sure that the "right side" wins. Active Jurors (we will define who they are in a bit) are your surrogates during deliberations; they continue your battle in the jury room. These jurors will often push hard to see that the "right side" (i.e., the side they favor) wins.

This chapter focuses on what happens during jury deliberations and how, through the processes of mental mining and designing graphics, you can increase the chances that jurors will reach the decision that you want.

A Jury of Our Peers?

A jury is a diverse group, whose members often appear as if they share very little in common with one another and even less in common with the witnesses, parties, lawyers, and judge involved in the case. With the possible exception of an emergency room at a large metropolitan hospital or the bleacher section at a professional baseball game, I cannot imagine any other location or event attracting and holding the attention of such an apparently diverse group of individuals.

A colleague of mine once observed that the members of her jury shared nothing except the "same area code and an inability to come up with an excuse to get struck for cause." Another colleague noted, after surveying her jury, that the only time that she had seen a more diverse group was in the cantina scene in the original *Star Wars* movie.

How is it possible that this group of twelve apparently dissimilar people, who sit together in the jury box and who will collectively decide the case, can do so as a jury of the parties' peers? What can this jury possibly have in common with the experts and the other witnesses who are going to testify?

The answer is, "A lot."

As a collective body, jurors have much more in common with the parties, the witnesses, and the lawyers than we give them credit for. In fact, it is exactly this common connection that makes the jury's collective decision-making process possible. It is this common connection that allows trial lawyers to communicate with and, hopefully, convince jurors. It is this common connection that allows one group of jurors to persuade another during deliberations.

When I say that jurors and other participants share much in common, I use the term to highlight the fact that the trial participants (parties, lawyers, witnesses, judge, and jury) share a collective wisdom that each has inherited merely by being part of the same culture. (See Illustration 3-1.) In other words, regardless of who ends up on your jury, you do not have to start at ground zero in order to educate

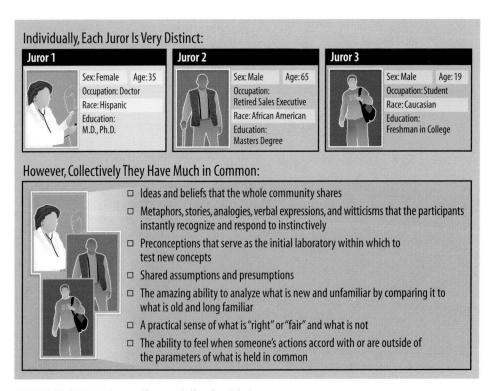

ILLUSTRATION 3-1. Jurors Share a Collective Wisdom

and persuade them. Your jurors come to the courtroom with certain "pre-wiring," with certain collective wisdom "pre-installed," such as:

- Ideas and beliefs that the whole community shares.
- Metaphors, stories, analogies, verbal expressions, and witticisms that the participants instantly recognize and respond to instinctively.
- Preconceptions that serve as the initial laboratory within which to test new concepts.
- Shared assumptions and presumptions.
- The amazing ability to analyze what is new and unfamiliar by comparing it to what is old and long familiar.
- A practical sense of what is "right" or "fair" and what is not.
- The ability to feel when someone's actions accord with or are outside of the parameters of what most members of society hold in common.

The closest single word that I know to describe this common wisdom is *prajna*. (Let me pause right here to acknowledge to my Buddhist friends that what follows is a very twisted interpretation of a complex theological concept. I thank them in advance for their indulgence.) Prajna is a term that comes from northern India and Nepal. The word is sometimes translated as "intuitive wisdom," "heart wisdom," or "wisdom beyond wisdom." For purposes of this discussion, I contort the definition to mean the instinct or wisdom derived from real world experience that most of us simultaneously feel in our gut and understand in our brain.

While not an exact match, the closest Western concept that I know to prajna may be the theory of the collective unconscious. (Let me pause again right here to acknowledge to my Jungian friends that what follows is a very twisted interpretation of a complex psychological concept. I thank them in advance for their indulgence.) According to psychoanalysis pioneer Carl Jung, a part of every person's psyche includes a form of inherited instinct—information that crosses generations and societies and is shared by all human beings. The collective unconscious includes images, patterns, and motifs that all humans understand, simply because they are human.

If, as Jungians believe, individuals from different societies on different continents at different times share and can instinctively understand certain common symbols and images, then consider how much stronger the bond or connection must be among twelve jurors who live within a thirty-mile radius of the courthouse and have been sitting together for six weeks at trial listening to the same evidence.

Prajna and the collective unconscious often manifest themselves when jurors use the following three-step reasoning process: (1) "I do not *know* about [*some complex issue*], (2) but I do *feel* [*some commonly shared principle*], (3) which is why I *believe* [*name of one of the parties*] should win." For example: "I don't *know* very much about inverse multiplexing, but I do *feel* that it is not right to take things that do not belong to you, which is why I *believe* the plaintiff should win."

In order to avoid possible later confusion, let me quickly point out that when I talk about appealing to jurors' feelings, I am *not* suggesting that you play to passion or base emotion. "Feeling" that a conclusion is right and coming to a conclusion based on passion can be overlapping processes, but they are *not* the same thing. In this context, when I say that jurors share certain common feelings, I am referring more to "intuitive wisdom," "instinctive wisdom," "heart wisdom," or "gut intelligence."

Whatever you want to call it, that which the jurors have in common is the framework upon which every single case, no matter how complex it factually may be, is ultimately resolved. By combining this intuitive wisdom with basic learning tools, jurors analyze, deal with, debate, and ultimately decide questions that they have never before encountered. The jurors will supply the prajna and/or collective unconscious; you need to arm your jurors with some of the tools described below so that they can advocate your position during deliberations, thereby increasing your chances of winning the case.

What Goes On in the Jury Room?

TYPES OF JURORS

Immediately after closing arguments, each juror can be plotted along two continua. These continua are important because ours is an adversarial system that requires a predetermined number of jurors, usually a supermajority, to agree on a verdict. More often than not, this requires that the jurors form one or more coalitions in the jury room—a process that can be as chaotic, boisterous, and adversarial as anything that occurs between counsel—a process that, if you are going to win, your jurors must control.

The first continuum measures how strongly a particular juror favors one party over the other. (See Illustration 3-2.) At one end of this continuum are those jurors who strongly favor the plaintiff and at the other end are those who strongly favor the defendant. In between these extremes are jurors who are neutral or whose support for one side or the other is not particularly strong. During jury deliberations, most of the battles take place over the middle of the continuum as jurors at the extremes try to persuade the neutral jurors to join them on one side of the spectrum or the other.

While each juror may ultimately have an equal vote, not all jurors have equal influence during deliberations. The second continuum measures potential influence by determining how strongly a particular juror is willing to push in order to see that the party she favors prevails. (See Illustration 3-3.)

As you can see from the illustration of the second continuum, I believe that most jurors fall into one of two categories—those whom I call "I Just Am" Jurors and others I refer to as Active Jurors.

I gave the "I Just Am" Jurors their name because this is the answer they usually give when another juror asks them to justify why they are voting a certain way. As in:

Juror 1: "Why are you voting for plaintiff?"
Juror 2: "I don't know. I just am!"

First Continuum:
Measures How Strongly Each Juror Favors One Party Over the Other

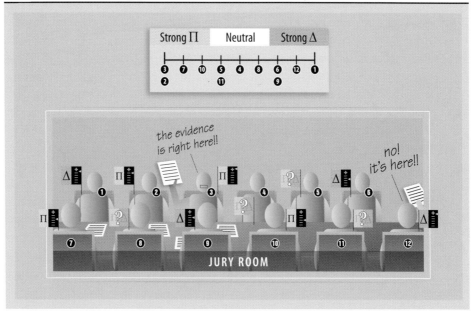

ILLUSTRATION 3-2

Second Continuum:
Measures How Strongly Each Juror Is Willing to Push for Her Side

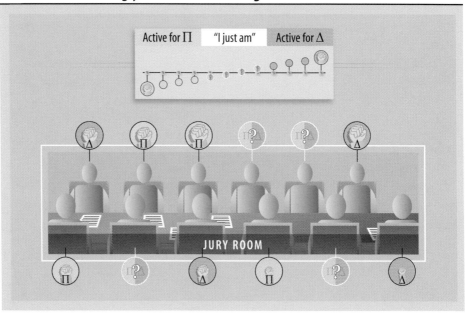

ILLUSTRATION 3-3

"I Just Am" Jurors are not your long-term friends. They tend to be of little benefit to whichever side they initially favor. Jurors who cannot articulate meaningful reasons why they are voting for one side over another have very little influence over any one else in the jury room and easily change their minds when confronted by opposing arguments.

You want as many Active Jurors as possible to be on your side. These jurors not only have listened to the evidence and decided in their own minds which side is "right" and why, but also are willing to advocate (often strongly) on behalf of that side during deliberations. Your side is their side; your arguments in closing are their arguments during deliberations; your victory is ultimately their victory. (See Illustration 3-4.)

Needless to say, the stronger and more complete the ties, the more likely the juror is to advocate your position and the less likely that juror is to switch sides when confronted by arguments from your opponent or her jurors. Active Jurors are able to articulate why they are voting a particular way and are willing to try to convince other jurors to do so as well.

These jurors are bound with both halves of their brains. An Active Juror's ability to say, "Here are the *reasons* for my decision . . ." binds herself with the intellect of the brain's left hemisphere. An Active Juror's ability to say, "I *feel* this is the correct decision . . ." binds herself with the emotion of the right hemisphere.

Having made this neurological observation, I must confess that I have no idea whether there is a genuine physiological connection, but I suspect there is. However, even if there is *not,* I always keep this concept in mind to remind myself of

Differences Between "I Just Am" Jurors and "Active" Jurors

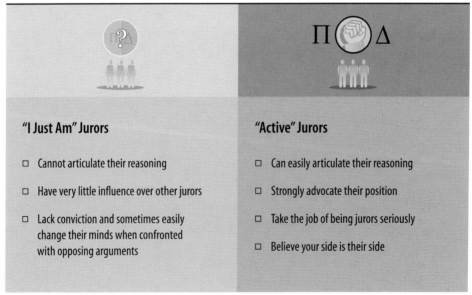

"I Just Am" Jurors	"Active" Jurors
☐ Cannot articulate their reasoning	☐ Can easily articulate their reasoning
☐ Have very little influence over other jurors	☐ Strongly advocate their position
☐ Lack conviction and sometimes easily change their minds when confronted with opposing arguments	☐ Take the job of being jurors seriously
	☐ Believe your side is their side

ILLUSTRATION 3-4

two things: (1) the best jurors are those who not only feel you are right but also can explain why, and (2) your best arguments need to satisfy both the jurors' feelings *and* intellect.

ACTIVE JURORS OFTEN PLAY TWO IMPORTANT ROLES

Between the time you make your opening statement and the clerk reads the verdict, most Active Jurors will play two different roles. They begin the trial as "searchers for the truth." Later, once you have convinced Active Jurors that you have what they are looking for (i.e., the truth), they become "advocates of the truth," which is what they perceive your story to be (or at least they perceive it is closer to the truth than your opposing counsel's).

Many lawyers do not appreciate the fact that each of the Active Juror's roles (searcher versus advocate) is considerably different from the other and, as such, Active Jurors rely on different skills and need different tools at different times in the trial. If you are smart, you will make every effort to provide these tools to your Active Jurors well in advance of when they need them. (See Illustration 3-5.)

How Active Jurors Search for the Truth

As a searcher for the truth, an Active Juror's first task is to find some way to cope with the mass of information that you present at trial. In all but the simplest cases, this material is new and potentially complex.

Life Cycle of an Active Juror

Phase of Case	Summons for Jury Duty	Voir Dire	Trial	Deliberation	Verdict
Juror's Role	Uninterested member of general community		Searcher for the truth	Advocate of the truth	
Juror's Needs	An excuse to get out of jury duty		Learning tools to make sense of the case	Tools to argue on behalf of the "Right Side"	A good stiff drink!

ILLUSTRATION 3-5

Once selected to serve on a jury, jurors find themselves in a position like that of first-year law school students, only worse. Like first-years, the jurors are often bombarded with too much information, much of which initially makes no sense whatsoever to them. Unlike first-year students, the jurors cannot skip class or sit all the way in the back row of the classroom staring at the ground, mumbling "pass" whenever asked a question to which they do not know the answer. There is no way for the jurors to sidestep not only that they have to come up with an answer but also that society has formally charged them with the added responsibility of coming up with the right answer.

Does this mean that jurors must understand every single fact in order to rule in your favor? No, of course not. Chances are that jurors will never understand all of the nuances of your case. You cannot expect them to do so. It took you months, if not years, to master the facts and, if you are like most trial lawyers, you continue to be surprised by new facts right through trial. Even if by some miracle you were allowed to keep everybody in the courtroom long enough to teach them all that there is to know about your case, the jurors would still not know everything because they would have become brain-dead weeks before you finished the process of "educating" them.

The fact is that jurors neither want nor need to understand every single nuance of your case. Jurors want enough information to make the right decision, to do so with a clear conscience, and then move on. Unlike many parties embroiled for years in litigation, jurors do not need to be admonished to "get a life"; they already have full and complete ones, which they have been forced to suspend in order to make time to resolve your case.

So, how do jurors learn? How much information do they need? How can you help them? To answer these questions, we must first spend a few moments discussing what a juror's brain does when it is bombarded by *too* much information all at once. Then we will examine how a juror's brain deals with this situation and begins to grasp new and complex facts.

The Brain in Retreat. The brain can grasp and process only a certain amount of new information at any one time. Whenever it is confronted with more information than it can easily handle, the brain begins to retreat. The more incomprehensible the material, the deeper the retreat.

I envision this retreat as progressing in three phases, each successive phase a bit deeper than the one before it. In a Phase I Retreat, the brain perceives the information as a whole. But before it can analyze anything, the brain triggers what I call the Yikes! Alarm. This is the name of the physical reaction typified by a sudden inhalation of breath and the thought "Yikes, there is way too much information here." Or, "Yikes, I don't know about this." (See Illustration 3-6.)

As soon as this happens, the brain begins a process of worrying about whether it is capable of understanding the information on the graphic. This internal mental struggle goes on for a few moments, during which time the brain is forced to makes one of two decisions—it either begins to comprehend what is there (i.e.,

The *Yikes!* Alarm

FIND THE MAXIMUM & THE MINIMUM VALUE FOR THE CONTINUOUS FUNCTION $f(x,y)=\sqrt{|xy|}$ $-3e^{-x^2-y^2}-x-y$ IN THE COMPACT REGION $\{(x,y): x^{2/3}+y^{2/3}\leq ...\}$

Retreat Phase I

The brain
- Worries
- Tries to figure it out

OR

Figures out a little part

Retreat Phase II

The brain
- Retreats further
- Thinks maybe eventually it will "get it"

OR

Gets some of it

Retreat Phase III

The brain
- Shuts down
- Begins wandering...

ILLUSTRATION 3-6

stops retreating) or it moves on to a Phase II Retreat. The best you can hope for in a Phase II Retreat is that the brain will understand a small percentage of the trial graphic.

Sometimes the brain cannot even do that. In such an instance, the brain goes into a Phase III Retreat, ignores the graphic entirely, and very happily wonders about where its owner might be able to get a good lunch or some other topic wholly unrelated to the case. Whichever phase the juror's brain gets to, once the Yikes! Alarm is triggered you and your graphic lose. Even if the brain can eventually grasp everything, it has wasted precious time worrying and struggling to determine what it should do and, as we will discuss later, these first few seconds are often crucial if you are going to capture a juror's attention.

How the Brain Copes. Learning something new always involves a certain sense of insecurity as the student (in this case, the juror) tries to relate to something that is unfamiliar. In such situations, jurors, like all human beings, have developed what I have observed to be a two-stage coping process to help them understand that which would otherwise not be understandable.

In the first stage the jurors find ways to overcome this insecurity so that they can start the learning/understanding process. They do so by connecting some of the unfamiliar facts, which they are hearing for the first time at trial, to familiar facts, concepts, or emotions with which they have comfortably dealt for years. Once they are able to do so, jurors progress to the second stage of learning. In this second stage, the jurors develop their understanding incrementally, by way of a series of baby steps that lead outward to and through unfamiliar information. So that the concept is not missed, let me stress that the second phase progresses best when you serve the information in logically sized and ordered pieces. We will discuss this again in Chapter 4 when we deal with pacing devices.

There are a number of ways to visualize this two-stage learning process. I sometimes describe it as "building a mosaic," where the plaster mastic connects the familiar facts to those which are new. Others describe these two steps using the analogy of garden latticework, where plants (the new facts) are strapped to and eventually grow onto an already existing framework (the familiar facts, concepts, or emotions). Still others liken the process to the way that pearls are cultured, where layers of new material are deposited onto and eventually become indistinguishable from the original "seed" planted in the oyster.

I use the three descriptions in the previous paragraph because I want to highlight one of the most common tools that jurors use so they can begin to understand new facts in your case. Jurors rely on and use analogies—simple analogies. Needless to say, if you want to teach and persuade the jury, you should rely on them as well. (Analogies are discussed further later in this chapter.)

How Active Jurors Advocate the Truth

Closing arguments do not end when both attorneys sit down at counsel table. The venue merely shifts; the participants become more numerous and the formal rules virtually disappear. No, this is not an advertisement for World Wrestling Federation; it describes what goes on in the jury room as various jurors embrace or reject your client's position and advocate that other jurors do the same.

One way I judge the effectiveness of a mock closing argument is to see how much of it continues on in the jury room during the deliberations. Your closing argument is successful when one (and hopefully more) of the Active Jurors picks up where you left off and *continues* to argue your position. This occurs because at least one Active Juror has made the shift from being a searcher for the truth to an advocate of the truth. As advocates, Active Jurors work to convince other jurors (jurors that are neutral or support the other side) to vote with them. Obviously, the side whose Active Jurors are most successful usually prevails.

Arm Your Active Jurors

One of your goals throughout trial is to provide your Active Jurors with ammunition they can use to convince their less committed colleagues (and hopefully a few of the Active Jurors on your opponent's side) that your version is the truth. Experienced trial lawyers take special care to see that their Active Jurors are fully armed before deliberations. You need to provision your allies on the jury with some basic tools—tools that they can use to explain the reasons why they are voting for you, to persuade others to do so as well, and to counter arguments raised by the other side's Active Jurors.

Some jurors, most particularly active ones, will do more than merely articulate reasons why they are voting for you. You want to give these Active Jurors the tools to continue making your closing argument in the jury room while you are pacing the floor in the courthouse coffeeshop waiting for a verdict.

These tools are very important. In fact, it is precisely because they are so important that you should spend considerable time, starting long before trial, identifying and refining exactly which ones you want to provide to those people you care most about—Active Jurors willing to argue on your behalf during deliberations.

WHAT THESE TOOLS MUST HAVE IN COMMON

Before we discuss these tools individually, let's spend a few minutes examining the one thing that each must have in order to be effective: They all must be *user-friendly*. (See Illustration 3-7.) If your Active Jurors cannot use the tool, then you have wasted your time and, more importantly, theirs.

You can make tools user-friendly if you are careful to do four things. First, be succinct and use only everyday, real-world language. I am not advocating that you dumb down your presentation. Instead, remember that learning something new is easier for the jurors if you keep your concepts as simple as possible. You get the luxury of having months to understand the important parts of your case; the jury does not.

Second, make sure that each tool relates to something with which the jurors are already familiar. Jurors can relate to and understand something new only if they can compare it to something with which they are already familiar. You need to be able to relate important facts to the jurors by comparing the new facts to things that the jurors already understand.

ILLUSTRATION 3-7. Make Your Trial Tools User-Friendly

Third, be certain that your concept is memorable. Ideally you will provide the jurors with tools that they will remember long after you finally sit down. Hopefully, through careful preparation for trial, you will find some fact about your case that the jurors will not only remember but also repeat at cocktail parties for years to come.

Finally, you want to find tools that have what I call the buzz factor. Tools with the buzz factor are difficult to define, but you will instantly recognize them. Such tools create a palpable buzz in the jury box when you first use them. Andy Spingler insists that he can spot this result by looking for what he calls the lean-to effect. That is, he knows that he has accomplished his goal when the jury members sit straight up and "lean to" the front of the jury box in response to an argument or trial graphic.

Another way Andy Spingler knows that he has created a buzz is when he sees the jurors chuckle after a lawyer makes a key point. I am not suggesting a belly laugh—although sometimes you get this from jurors. Instead, it is more like the laugh we all make when we suddenly understand something and there is a release of emotional tension, a "thank goodness I get it" kind of laugh.

You do not want all of your trial tools to have this buzz. If they do, the buzz will become a constant distracting hum; trial tools that deserve a lean-to will be indistinguishable from those that do not.

OK, how about an example of a tool that meets all of these criteria?

You represent a company that runs a nuclear power plant. People living near the plant have filed an action to stop its operation. They allege that, even without an accident, just the normal operation of the plant will expose nearby residents to an additional millirem of radiation per year.

Radiation is scary. Nevertheless, your experts have convinced you that any increase in radiation will be minimal and will have no real adverse health impacts. Now, it is your job to convince the jury.

One effective way to do so would be to show the jurors that they, like most other people, routinely *and voluntarily* expose themselves to an additional millirem of radiation with no adverse effect. So, how do you not only do this but also do so with user-friendly data that (1) explains the concept succinctly in everyday language; (2) allows the jurors to answer the question, "Compared to what?"; (3) is memorable; and (4) hopefully, creates some buzz with the jury?

With some trepidation, you interview your radiation expert and ask her to tell you what it means to be exposed to one millirem of radiation. "No problem," she replies, "It's easy. I will just tell the jury that a millirem is one thousandth of the dosage of an ionizing radiation that will cause the same biological effect as one roentgen of X-ray or gamma-ray dosage."

At this point, your trepidation should turn to fear. You should be afraid, very afraid, *not* about the radiation, but about your own expert witness. Your expert's proposed explanation tells your jurors nothing—absolutely nothing. Actually, it tells them worse than nothing. It tells them that you don't care enough to take the time to teach them or to give them information that they can understand and use.

So, you keep probing with your expert. You put on a "beginner's mind" and start asking questions, listening carefully to the answers, and continuing to ask questions and listen to the answers. "Is a millirem a lot or a little? . . . Even without the power plant, how long would it take for an individual to be exposed to an additional millirem of radiation? . . . How would such radiation exposure likely occur? . . . Would *you* be afraid of getting exposed to an additional millirem of radiation a year?"

Your expert starts giving you useful information. She tells you that we are surrounded by virtually limitless sources of natural, low-level, radiation coming from the sun, rocks, etc. In fact, in a given year, an average person is exposed to 360 millirems of "background radiation" from these natural sources. This radiation is so common that the Nuclear Regulatory Commission deems a single dose exposure of ten millirems or less to be insignificant and not a threat to anyone's health.

These facts are better. With them, you know that 1 millirem is 1/360th of what we get naturally each year. It is an amount approximately equal to what an average person gets in a single day of normal activities. You also know that it is one tenth of what the United States government deems to be an acceptable one-time dose. With this information you can create a graphic like the one in Illustration 3-8a.

This graphic is OK, but it is definitely not great. This graphic is better than mentioning roentgens of X-ray and gamma ray dosages—*but it does not really create a buzz*. And if there is any fact that requires a buzz to win over a skeptical jury, this is one.

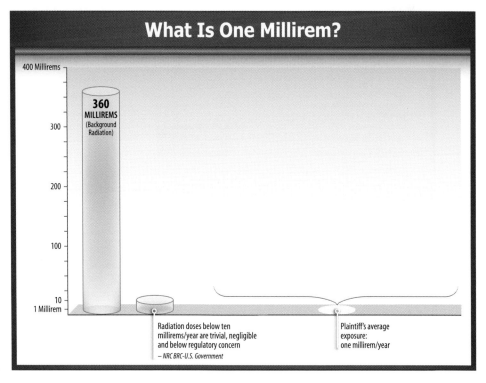

ILLUSTRATION 3-8a. An OK Graphic

You push your expert witness for more concrete examples of when people will, during their ordinary lives, voluntarily expose themselves to an additional millirem of radiation. You ask her about the last time she remembers doing so. Bingo! It turns out that your expert exposed herself to an additional millirem of radiation just last week when she was a passenger in a commercial airplane flying from Sacramento to Denver. She goes on to explain that passengers on planes are exposed to an additional millirem of radiation on such trips because, since there is less atmospheric protection at 30,000 feet, there is more exposure to cosmic radiation. The facts are starting to buzz. So, you illustrate this point and add it to your trial graphic. (See Illustration 3-8b.)

Your expert is now on a roll. She tells you that when people go skiing in the mountains for a weekend, they expose themselves to an additional millirem of radiation because the thinner atmosphere at the higher elevation blocks less of the sun's rays. Since your hypothetical jurors all live in northern California, you know that they will easily relate to this fact. Many of them spend much of the winter either going or wanting to go up to the higher elevations of Lake Tahoe to ski for

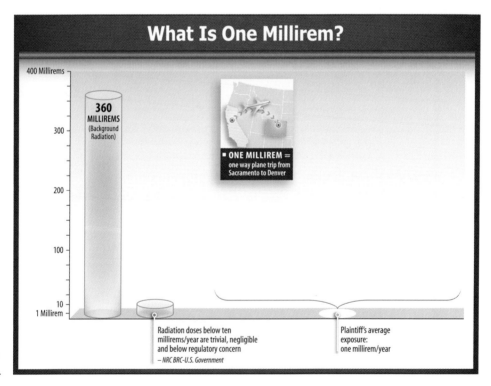

ILLUSTRATION 3-8b. The Beginnings of a Much Better Graphic

ONE MILLIREM =
one weekend skiing
at Lake Tahoe

the weekend. In fact, they are so eager to do so that they often spend hours in bumper-to-bumper traffic just to get the opportunity to escape to nature and expose themselves to that additional millirem of radiation on the slopes—commentary that you file away to be used later in closing argument. So you illustrate this point and add it to your graphic.

Your expert is now enjoying coming up with examples as much as you appreciate receiving them. She tells you that smoking one cigarette in your lifetime exposes you to an additional millirem of radiation and that if you live in a stone house for six days rather than in a wooden one, you get an additional millirem of radiation. You illustrate these points and add them to your trial graphic.

ONE MILLIREM =
smoking one cigarette
in a lifetime

By now, you know that this graphic will help the jury understand what a millirem is. But something is missing—the final zinger fact, the one that the jury will remember and tell others long after the trial is over. You keep pushing your expert and you eventually discover the fact that will not only cause the jury to lean forward, but also will cause most of them to laugh and confirm that you have made your point.

Here it is.

It turns out that many foods give off a low dose of radiation. For example, bananas contain potassium, which has various radioactive isotopes. Banana eaters actually emit very low levels of these radioactive isotopes.

ONE MILLIREM =
six days in brick vs.
wood building

If you sleep next to a banana eater for six months, you will have exposed yourself to—you got it—an additional millirem of radiation. As you eventually will point out to your jury, there is a far greater chance that a snoring companion will force you to sleep on a couch than that an irradiated one will. You illustrate this final point and add it to your graphic, which is now complete. (See Illustration 3-9.)

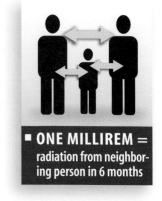

ONE MILLIREM =
radiation from neighboring person in 6 months

Now you know that your jury will understand and not be bored by explanations of biological exposure to roentgens of X-rays. Your jury will appreciate the fact that you took the time to explain a key concept to them in an understandable manner. Your Active Jurors will remember and use this fact as ammunition throughout jury deliberations.

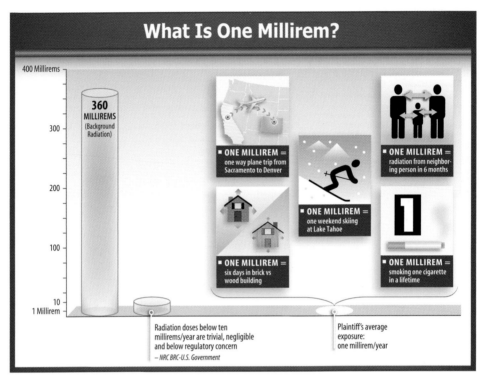

ILLUSTRATION 3-9. This Graphic Creates a Buzz and Answers Its Title's Question

TOOLS TO PROVIDE TO YOUR ACTIVE JURORS

The tools that you should make available to your Active Jurors include:

- A single coherent story line.
- Case themes that add credibility to your explanation of what is really going on.
- Analogies or other familiar concepts, which, as discussed above, help introduce new ideas to the jurors.
- "Plans of attack" that allow your Active Jurors to organize, understand, and use the facts you provided to them in the most effective way possible to persuade others.
- Tools that provide jurors with the ability to "see" things that are not otherwise visible in court.
- Tools that allow jurors to easily compare and contrast testimony and other evidence.
- Tools that allow the jurors to answer the crucial question, "Compared to what?"
- Tools that enhance the jurors' abilities to understand how events relate chronologically.
- Glossaries or other ways for the jurors to quickly define and use key terms in ways that you want them to.
- Tools that allow your jurors to better understand and make your key argument on your behalf during deliberations.

Many of these tools lend themselves to being presented through trial graphics. All of these tools naturally flow from and become apparent *if you see trial graphics not only as an end product but also as a process.*

Active Jurors Need a Single Coherent Storyline

Jurors often need a single, coherent story. To have a *single* storyline, you need to avoid arguing in the alternative. To have a *coherent* story, you need to have one with a plot that makes sense, is internally consistent, explains motive, and incorporates all of the relevant undisputed facts, regardless of whether these facts are "good" or "bad."

Avoid Arguing in the Alternative. After three years of law school and whatever time you have spent practicing law, arguing in the alternative has probably become something that you accept as routine. But, that was not always the case. Think about the first time that you heard such an argument and see whether you can remember your initial reaction to it.

The first time I was conscious of hearing anyone argue in the alternative was in criminal law class during my first year in law school. The professor introduced the technique by hypothetically defending a man whose goat ate all of his neighbor's cabbages. In his defense, the imaginary goat owner argued:

- "I do not own a goat!"
- "If I own a goat, you did not own any cabbages."
- "If I own a goat and you owned cabbages, it was not my goat that ate your cabbages."
- "If I own a goat and you owned cabbages and it was my goat that ate your cabbages, my goat was legally justified in doing so."
- "If I own a goat and you owned cabbages and it was my goat that ate your cabbages, and if my goat was not legally justified in eating your cabbages, then there is no liability because my goat was legally insane at the time."

When I first told this story to my wife (who is not a lawyer), she had the same reaction I had when I first heard it. "The only one who's insane is the person who believes that someone would actually buy that story. If I heard a lawyer make that argument, I would not trust anything else she said."

My wife is right! Alternative arguments provide a perfect illustration of the proverbial slippery slope. With the first part of the argument, the lawyer is on relatively solid ground. With the addition of each new alternative argument, the lawyer begins a rapid slide downward.

Jurors see alternative arguments as confusing and disingenuous. It is *not* hard to imagine them at the conclusion of a criminal trial saying to themselves, "Wait, there is no way that the defendant was framed for murder, but at the same time acted in self-defense. So, she must be guilty!"

Whenever possible, give the jurors a single story. But how do you avoid arguing in the alternative? Sometimes it is not a problem; there is one logical explanation

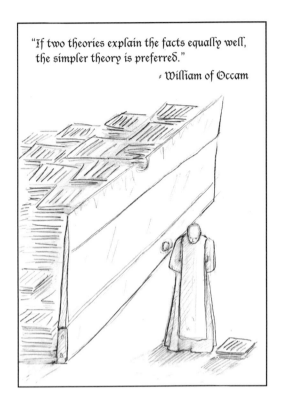

"If two theories explain the facts equally well, the simpler theory is preferred."

, William of Occam

and that (and that alone) is what you argue. But what do you do when there seem to be multiple possible arguments?

Generally, I suggest two things. First, apply the theory of Occam's Razor. This theory, which was developed hundreds of years ago by a radical Franciscan monk named William of Occam, provides that if two theories explain the facts equally well, then the simpler theory is to be preferred. In other words, the simple explanation is the more plausible and more likely to be the correct one. The simpler explanation is also the one that jurors are most likely to understand. So, between two equally competing arguments, generally trust the one that is less complex.

Second, if, after eliminating as many alternatives as possible, you are still left with more than one possible argument, take a step back and see if there is a way to unify the alternative arguments. Ask yourself, "Are these two [or more] arguments completely separate or, as is often the case, are they merely subparts of a larger overarching argument?" If they are, use that overarching argument to make your point.

This is not to say that there is no place for arguing in the alternative. Such an approach may work very well when arguing before a judge. But two things are different here than when you face a jury. First, the judge has been to law school and, while there, undoubtedly studied under the equivalent of my criminal law professor. The judge is familiar with this argumentative technique and the reasons we lawyers use it.

Second, the alternative arguments raised before the judge are usually *legal* alternatives rather than *factual* ones. You do not lose much credibility with your judge (who, as already noted, understands and is comfortable with the technique) when, for example, you argue the alternative theories of statutes of frauds and lack of consideration, both of which are primarily legal (not factual) issues.

Now that you have a single storyline, you need to make sure that it makes sense; you need a story that is coherent. Coherent stories have at least three things in common: a carefully chosen plot, a strong beginning and ending, and a way to deal with *all* undisputed facts.

Choose Your Plot Carefully. A proficient storyteller carefully considers and chooses his story's plot. When I use the word "plot," I mean not just what happens but, more importantly, the *order* in which the storyteller reveals what happens to the listener.

Most stories are told chronologically. Chronological stories are often the easiest to assemble, memorize, tell, and understand; however, chronological stories are not always the most interesting.

In fact, strict chronological order can bore the hell out of you, particularly when it is coupled with too much detail. For example, when my younger son, Erich, was in kindergarten, his teacher gave him the assignment of keeping a journal for a week. Since Erich could not yet write, this process consisted of his dictating a description of his day to me, which I would faithfully write out word for word. Since he was a stickler for accuracy, Erich's story would go something like this: "First I got to school. Then I took off my coat. Next I hung my coat up in the closet. Then Mrs. Cooper told us to sit down. Then I sat down. Next she told us . . . ." You get the picture. As cute as some of these overly detailed chronological stories might have started off being, they get to be overwhelming awfully fast. And I say this as an adoring parent—imagine the effect of such stories on the jurors, who may not even like you that much.

Because of this, some of the most interesting and gripping stories are not told in strict chronological order. For example, Quentin Tarantino did not tell the story in *Pulp Fiction* in a chronological order. In fact, I still do not know exactly what that order was; yet, when I saw the movie, people in the audience were generally riveted to their seats, partly because of the order in which Mr. Tarantino chose to reveal what happened. Likewise, William Styron's novel *Sophie's Choice* plays fast and loose with chronological order; yet I am not sure that there was any better way to present this haunting story.

As a general rule, the more complex a case is, the *less* of an opportunity there is for the lawyer to tell the story in pure chronological order. In order to make complex cases understandable, lawyers often need to interrupt the chronological flow of the story to explain key concepts to the jury. (See Illustration 3-10.) Without these diversions, most jurors could not remain interested in, let alone understand, the story's plot. The challenge to the trial lawyer is twofold: (1) keeping the juror's attention during these necessary and sometimes difficult side trips and (2) determining where in the story these diversions need to be placed.

Evan S. Connell, in his book *Son of the Morning Star,* provides a wonderful example of how this is possible. Mr. Connell's book traces the events leading up to the defeat of General George Armstrong Custer at the Little Big Horn. Because the subject is essentially historical, the overall structure of the book must be chronological. But, as is the case of any story told in strict chronological order, the listener/reader/juror can easily miss supporting details that are important and interesting.

So, instead of telling the story in a strictly chronological order, Mr. Connell digresses whenever he feels that the reader needs additional background or when he has material that is likely to increase the reader's interest. For example, Mr. Connell starts a chapter by writing about the horse that Custer was riding when the battle started. Instead of moving to the next moment of the battle, the author writes about how horses were generally supplied to the cavalry and how the government often paid too much for its military supplies. This additional information

Simple vs. More Complex Plot

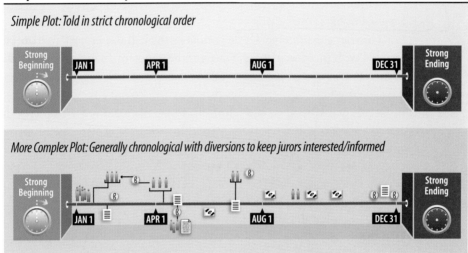

Simple Plot: Told in strict chronological order

Strong Beginning | JAN 1 | APR 1 | AUG 1 | DEC 31 | **Strong Ending**

More Complex Plot: Generally chronological with diversions to keep jurors interested/informed

Strong Beginning | JAN 1 | APR 1 | AUG 1 | DEC 31 | **Strong Ending**

ILLUSTRATION 3-10

not only keeps the reader's attention, but it also explains facts that the reader will eventually need to understand why certain events happened the way they did.

Good storytellers like Mr. Connell allow these digressions to punctuate the strict order of "first event, second event, third event." They understand that occasionally branches of the story need to diverge from the main trunk. So, the story Mr. Connell tells may go something like this: "first event, second event, the story of the cavalry man who got drunk and unwittingly married a transvestite tavern owner, third event," and so forth. (If that does not convince you to at least look at Mr. Connell's book, nothing will.) Here, diversions do not distract; they inform and ultimately increase the listener's interest in and commitment to the main story line. Learn to tell your stories this way and you too will keep your jury not only interested but also well informed as to why your side should win.

When you consider the plot for your next case, what format should you use? The answer is that there is no automatic answer. The important point is that you have options. Take the time and make the conscious decision of how you can best use them. If chronological order works best, great! If there is a better way, take that path!

Have a Strong Beginning and Ending. Coherent stories have a strong beginning and a strong ending.

I know, you are thinking, "That's self-evident." We all know the concept of primacy and recency. Right?

Well, if we do, why do so many stories told in the courtroom seem to take forever to get off the ground and/or leave the jury wondering at the end, "What the heck was that all about?"

A Strong Beginning. A journalist is taught to write the first paragraph of a newspaper article so that it tells readers all they need to know about the story. There is good reason for this—the first paragraph is all that most readers read of a story. Many readers do not have the time to read the continuation on page A-8. Others will turn to page A-8 *if and only if* the reporter first captures their interest with the first paragraph of the story.

Jurors are the same way. Don't waste your time at the beginning of your opening statement introducing yourself; remember, you were already introduced at least once in voir dire. Do not waste your time telling the jury about the history of the common law; this is not a jurisprudence class.

Instead, start with a strong introduction that frames the major issues of the dispute. At the beginning explain why you are there, establish your case themes, and summarize your story. This is a tall order and it may technically take more than your first paragraph. But you have a limited amount of time to connect with the jury. Do not waste it.

A Strong Ending. There are certain phrases that magically reinvigorate a jury. You say "in conclusion" and it is like an alarm clock suddenly going off. You say, "so now that we are at the end of the case, let's talk about what you need to do" and most of the jurors, including those who have been sitting in a catatonic state for the past hour, suddenly sit straight up and start listening again.

Why? Because we have been conditioned to believe that the end of any event is important and something to which we better pay attention. In a story, it is the end when the truth is revealed, the villain unmasked, the punch line delivered. Take advantage of this conditioning. Use the end of your argument wisely to make key points with the jury.

Stories that end with a whimper are like the clock that strikes thirteen times; not only is the last chime wrong, but it puts all that preceded it into question. The end of your story should always come quickly and it should be strong.

Explain Motive. Perhaps the most often overlooked detail in a story is motive. Technically, most civil cases do not require that you establish the party's motive or state of mind. Since it is not required, many lawyers ignore it. This strategy is wrong! Jurors do not ignore motive; in fact, it is often a crucial part of their analysis. You run a considerable risk by not providing such information to them.

I have observed numerous mock juries stop deliberating when one juror spontaneously asks the question that they all have been wondering—"So, come on, why do you think the defendant really did what she did?" Even jurors who have said nothing concerning the significant issues in dispute will jump in with their pet theory of what really motivated the parties' actions. Conspiracies come out of the shadows; speculation about unrequited (and requited) love surfaces.

In such situations, I have watched trial lawyers sit perplexed, watching televised mock deliberations and wondering out loud: "Where did the jury ever get that idea? There is no support for that fact; the jury is making this sound like a soap opera."

What happened? What caused the jurors to come up with their own explanation of the facts? The answer is that none of the lawyers took the time to explain "why"; no one explained motive. As such, the jurors will often spend considerable time debating the reasons for some party's actions. While these discussions can often be very psychologically revealing given that mock jurors often project their own personal characteristics on to the parties, these discussions distract the jurors away from what you really want them to do—decide the case in your favor.

So why is motive so important? I suspect that the reason goes back to our earlier discussion of how jurors deal with and learn about complex new topics. In order to start learning and forming an opinion, the jurors need to start with something with which they are familiar and readily understand. Once they have this seed, jurors can go on and begin to form opinions and conclusions about unfamiliar issues.

Motive is something that every single juror can relate to. It is one of those things that can be the seed upon which jurors begin to build their understanding of a case. Not every juror can understand the complexity of securities trading, but they each know what it is to be greedy; they each know what it is like to be hurt by a greedy person; they each know that there are certain base emotions that drive their fellow humans. These motives form a powerful familiar basis for beginning any complex analysis of unique facts.

How do you illustrate motive? Often you can't. Not because such motive does not exist—it does in every lawsuit—but because many courts frown on your doing it too directly in your opening statement or case in chief.

So what do you do? Sometimes, the best thing to do is to find ways to illustrate key facts that you will later use during closing to argue motive. Let me show you two examples.

The first comes from an insurance bad-faith case in which the insurance company allegedly destroyed key documents from its files that would have established that it had to provide billions of dollars in coverage for tens of thousands of asbestos bodily injury claims.

There was no doubt that the insurer had ordered the documents destroyed; in fact, there were two key memoranda from upper management ordering various employees to "purge your files." However, the insurance company argued that these memoranda were merely part of a proper "document retention program" and had nothing to do with its increasing asbestos liability.

Illustration 3-11 is a timeline that was created to help the jurors understand when the order to destroy documents occurred in relationship to other key activities in the asbestos litigation field. As you can see, it was not hard based on these facts for the policyholder to argue that the document destruction was *not* routine. Instead, the destruction was motivated by the insurance company's desire to avoid extensive liability for which it knew it was responsible. The order to destroy the documents came shortly after plaintiffs' counsel announced that they would actively pursue a claim against the insured and after the cost of litigation began to skyrocket.

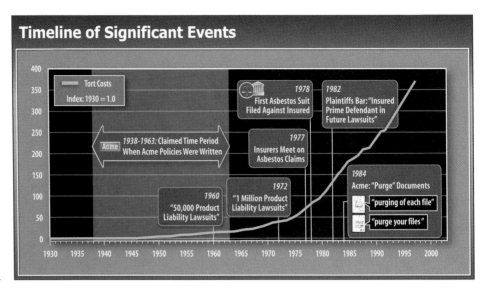

ILLUSTRATION 3-11. This Timeline Helps Establish Motive

The second example of using graphics to help establish motive comes from a criminal case. In closing argument, defense counsel wanted to argue that, in bringing the case, the prosecutor was not motivated by justice. Instead, the prosecutor was motivated by an overwhelming desire to selectively punish a politically unpopular individual. Counsel used the graphic shown in Illustration 3-12 to bolster her argument.

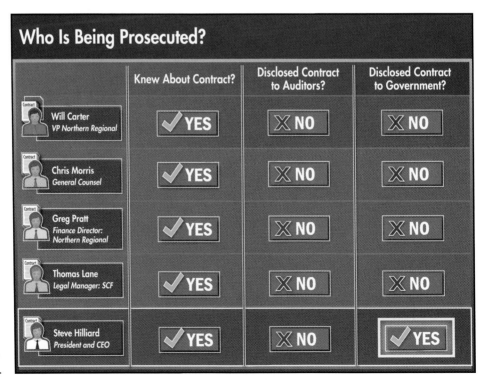

ILLUSTRATION 3-12. Using Graphics to Establish Motive

Deal With All Undisputed Facts. Abraham Lincoln's most famous trial (which Henry Fonda made even more famous in the movie *Young Mr. Lincoln*) was a criminal case in which Lincoln successfully defended a man wrongly accused of murder. The fatal blow occurred late at night. The prosecution's only witness claimed that he saw the killing. When pressed by Lincoln on cross-examination, the witness claimed that he could clearly see who committed the murder because the moon was so bright that night. Lincoln then destroyed the prosecution's witness by pulling out a copy of *The Farmer's Almanac* (which Lincoln—or at least Henry Fonda—always conveniently carried in his hip pocket) to show that the moon had long set by the time of the murder.

Almost miraculously, the actual trial transcript of Lincoln's cross-examination in this case (*People of the State of Illinois v. Armstrong,* Cass County, Ill., 1858) was preserved and makes for fascinating reading.

Q: Did you actually see the fight?
A: Yes.

Q: And you stood very near to them?
A: No, it was one hundred and fifty feet or more.

Q: In the open field?
A: No, in the timber.

Q: What kind of timber?
A: Beech timber.

Q: Leaves on it are rather thick in August?
A: It looks like it.

Q: What time did all this occur?
A: Eleven o'clock at night.

Q: Did you have a candle there?
A: No, what would I want a candle for?

Q: How could you see from a distance of one hundred and fifty feet or more, without a candle, at eleven o'clock at night?
A: The moon was shining real bright.

Q: Full moon?
A: Yes, a full moon.

The record reflects that Lincoln referred to a blue-covered almanac, offered it into evidence, and the court received the almanac as evidence without objection. The cross-examination resumed.

Q: Does not the almanac say that on August 29 the moon was barely past the first quarter instead of being full?
A: (No answer.)

Q: Does not the almanac also say that the moon had disappeared by eleven o'clock?
A: (No answer.)

> **Q:** Is it not a fact that it was too dark to see anything from fifty feet, let alone one hundred and fifty feet?
>
> **A:** (No answer.)

The transcript concludes by noting that the jury acquitted Armstrong.

Traditionally, when lawyers and historians review this transcript they always focus on what Lincoln did right. Alternatively, I suggest that we can learn more by looking at *what the prosecutor did wrong.* Specifically, the prosecutor *failed to identify and incorporate all undisputed facts into the story* he presented to the jury.

Was the fact that the moon had set prior to the murder an undisputed fact? Yes, in fact so much so that the extraordinary evidence teacher Irving Younger often used the Lincoln example to illustrate the concept of judicial notice. Professor Younger would point out that the fact of when the moon set was so undisputed that the judge could take judicial notice of this fact and, even if there was no evidence on the point, instruct the jurors that they must accept this fact as true.

In every case there are facts that cannot be disputed. Some of them will help you. Some will hurt you. None of them can be ignored if you are going to construct a coherent story for the jury.

No matter how brilliantly crafted, a story that fails to incorporate or explain all of the undisputed facts is doomed to fail, particularly in an adversarial system such as ours, where your opponent is paid to find and make the most of flaws in your case.

Identify the undisputed issues and deal with *all* of them, not just the ones that you like.

Active Jurors Need Case Themes

The author Willa Cather observed that, while the specific subject matter may differ from story to story, all literature is based on one of a half dozen or so recurring themes. Many years ago, while working in a legal-aid clinic, I made a similar observation as I interviewed a half-dozen or so potential clients each night. When listening to these potential clients tell their stories, I was always surprised how often I could "see it coming" long before the clients got anywhere close to finishing their stories. Human nature being what it is, I could predict not only *how* the story would end; I would know who did what, how they did it, and what the result was, but also, even more important, nine times out of ten I knew *why* people had acted the way they had.

In making these observations, I am not minimizing the very real problems that my clients at the legal aid clinic faced. Nor am I suggesting that the process of writing fine literature is formulaic—if there were a simple formula, there would be fewer lawyers and many more successful writers. Instead, I see Ms. Cather's comment and my observations from the legal aid clinic as having two very important implications to our work as trial lawyers.

First, let's start with the obvious—lawsuits are stories of conflict. While the specifics (generally, the *who, what, where,* and *when*) of each case may be unique, the underlying themes (generally, but not always, the *why*) are recurring and, as such, almost always strike jurors as being familiar. What I am suggesting is that the only reason most literature and almost all trials make sense is that the reader/lawyer/ juror shares an intuitive understanding of human nature and can often predict how it will manifest itself in certain situations. This knowledge is what makes it possible for jurors to begin to understand a series of events that they themselves did not actually experience. It is this same knowledge that allows fiction readers to relate to a world that may never have actually existed.

The second observation is that familiar themes can and often do serve as the means by which jurors begin to analyze unfamiliar facts. To borrow from my earlier analogies, the themes form the seed at the middle of the pearl, the latticework in the garden, or the mastic backing the mosaic of your story.

Case themes by themselves usually have no independent legal significance. The theme is rarely part of your technical prima facie case. Rather, case themes often add moral support to your story. Case themes are often rooted in people's understandings of fundamental decency and the way things should work or the way they would like to be treated by others.

Themes can also arise from various preconceptions or prejudices broadly held by society. I recognize how politically incorrect it is to make such an observation, but it is nonetheless true. Fortunately, the basest examples of reliance on these prejudices (stereotypes based on race, gender, sexual preference, religion, etc.) have been officially banned from the courtroom. Rightly or wrongly, other prejudices remain and can serve as a basis for a theme—for example, government bureaucrats bumble about and fail to do things in the most effective manner; insurance companies are predisposed to unfairly deny claims; and corporations care more about the bottom line than people.

Here are some examples of these types of themes:

- Plaintiff violated defendant's trust.
- Plaintiff did not play by the rules.
- Defendant is trying to take something that is not his.
- Acme Co. is pursing profits at the expense of people's health.
- Defendant was warned; but since he disregarded that warning, he deserved what he got.
- Sometimes things happen that are not the fault of anyone.
- Plaintiff wants to have his cake and eat it, too.
- What is sauce for the goose is sauce for the gander.

Themes serve another purpose as well. Rightly or wrongly, themes sometimes provide jurors with an escape route to avoid critical or analytical thought; jurors will sometimes use themes as a shortcut around hard work. Jurors usually pay close attention to the evidence and try to understand it. At the same time, jurors are human; when they reach areas that they cannot understand, jurors look for things that appear familiar and, thus, easier to deal with. Simple and familiar themes serve as a way for the jurors to begin to understand your complex case. In short, jurors look for and need guideposts to help them to begin to analyze the case. Oftentimes, your case theme gives them these aids.

Active Jurors Need Analogies

Analogies are powerful tools.

I use the word "analogy" as a shorthand reference to rhetorical tools that increase understanding by tying two apparently disparate concepts together. These rhetorical devices include:

- *Analogy*—the inference that if two or more things agree with one another in some respects they will probably agree in others; resemblance in some particulars between things otherwise unlike.
- *Archetype*—an inherited idea or mode of thought that is derived from the experience of the human race and is present in the unconscious of the individual.
- *Metaphor*—a figure of speech in which a word or phrase literally denoting one kind of object or idea is used in place of another to suggest a likeness or analogy between them.
- *Simile*—a figure of speech comparing two unlike things that is often introduced by *like* or *as*.

Analogies allow you to turn common zippers into replicating strands of DNA. Analogies help the auto mechanic on your jury to more easily understand a complex machine because you explain how these parts are similar to those on your 1984 Volvo. Analogies permit you to use the parking lot next to the courtroom, which is divided into lettered rows, which in turn are then divided into uniquely numbered slots, to explain how computer memory is divided on a disk drive. Analogies allow you to introduce the concept of mitigating damages to jurors who have never been parties to a commercial contract by saying "a stitch in time saves nine"—a phrase with which jurors have been familiar since childhood. Analogies guarantee that your jurors will understand what you mean when you refer to your client as "David" in a battle against "Goliath."

Rhetoricians sometimes point out to me that analogies are a weak form of argument. Those who study rhetoric and persuasion argue that when something is *like* something else, the two items, by definition, are not the same and, as such, if you push the analogy long enough, differences will appear and the analogy will eventually breakdown.

While true, the problem with this argument is that the rhetoricians are staring through a magnifying glass at the wrong end of the analogy. Analogies provide effective *introductions*. Their strength comes at the *beginning* of the story or when you first introduce a new concept. Analogies allow jurors to obtain an orienting view of a subject through the use of their peripheral vision rather than being forced to stare at all of the potentially overwhelming details or hard-to-accept truth straight on.

Having said this, I will be the first to remind you that whether jurors actually accept your analogy ultimately depends on whether you are able to successfully make the next step of supplementing this analogy with real and sufficient supporting facts.

While there are no limits to the analogies that the creative mind can develop, for purposes of a trial, analogies most often serve three purposes: (1) to introduce key terms or concepts, (2) to explain the relevance of key numbers, and (3) to illustrate overall case themes. We will look at examples of each type of analogies at various points in this book and the accompanying Visual Resource CD-ROM, both of which contain numerous analogies in a variety of trial graphics. For the purpose of our immediate discussion, let's focus for a moment on three examples.

The first explains a basic legal concept. When is a contract a contract? More specifically, if certain terms of a contract are missing or have not been fully agreed to by the parties, is there still a legally binding agreement between them?

At the risk of greatly oversimplifying the law, in certain jurisdictions the answer to this question often turns on whether the missing terms are "significant." If the missing terms are relatively insignificant, then the law will "fill them in" and enforce the agreement. However, if the missing terms are significant, the law will not fill them in and the contract is deemed void by the court. A missing term is significant if its inclusion/exclusion will substantially alter the terms of the contract.

How do you illustrate this point? How do you show the difference between significant and insignificant terms? One way would be to merely quote the case law; another way is to use the analogy of a puzzle, as in Illustration 3-13, to show how filling a gap can sometimes change the picture 180 degrees.

The second analogy deals with a problem common in toxic tort cases. Most scientists acknowledge that for all chemicals there is a concentration below which the chemical poses no harm to humans. This concentration is called the "no-effect level." Regulatory agencies sometimes set their safety standards (the amount below which exposure to the chemical is permitted in the workplace, etc.) at one-tenth of the no-effect level.

Plaintiffs usually dispute these assumptions and assert that if the chemical poses *any* kind of risk to humans at *any* level (including a high concentration), then the chemical should *always* be considered dangerous at *all* concentrations, no matter how small.

To demonstrate the logical defect with defendant's argument that if something causes harm at one level it causes harm at all levels, we created the following graphic. Instead of using a harmful chemical to illustrate the point, we used an analogy based on gravity. As you can see in Illustration 3-14, the first portion shows a man standing on twenty-foot-high platform. At this level, gravity is likely to be dangerous in that if the man were to fall from this platform he would undoubtedly be hurt, perhaps even seriously. At five feet, gravity is still dangerous such that if the man were to fall from the second platform, he might still be hurt, but less so than if he were on a platform at twenty feet. At some point, gravity stops being a threat. If the man fell off a one-foot platform, there would be very little chance of injury. For gravity, this height could be considered the no-effect

ILLUSTRATION 3-13. Using an Analogy to Illustrate a Legal Concept

The lawyer who used this graphic started off by pointing out that if the missing piece were part of the sky or grass, the court could fill in this part of the puzzle without affecting the overall effect of the picture. The lawyer continued by arguing that this was not the case in this particular dispute. Here, the judge was being asked to fill in the missing central piece of the contract, which would clearly alter the entire agreement.

level. Likewise, if he fell off a platform that was 1.2 inches tall (i.e., one-tenth of the no-effect level, a ratio that is often used to set the safety standards), there would be no chance of injury whatsoever. In short, just because gravity is harmful at one level (e.g., at twenty feet) does not mean that it is harmful at all levels (e.g., at one foot or at 1.2 inches).

The final example of an analogy is one that could be used by plaintiff to thematically counter defendant's affirmative defense.[1] In this instance, let's assume that the affirmative defense consists of a series of elements, *all* of which must be satisfied in order for the defense to be effective. In other words, if defendant fails to prove any one element, the defense crumbles.

By way of an analogy, you might highlight the difference between a brick wall and a Roman arch. (See Illustration 3-15.) With a brick wall, if you do not have all the pieces, the wall will still remain standing. Not so with a Roman arch; if one piece—any piece—is missing, then the entire structure will collapse. You could then

---

1. As you will see, this same analogy could be used by a defendant to argue that a plaintiff's claim should be dismissed for failing to establish all necessary elements.

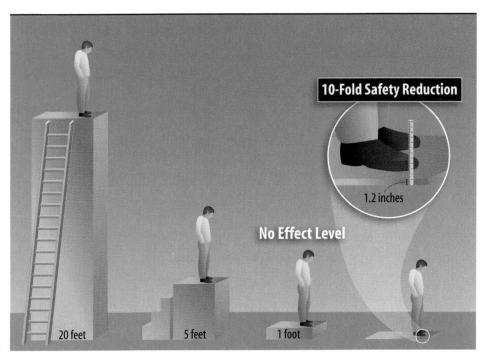

ILLUSTRATION 3-14. **Using an Analogy to Expose Logical Defects**

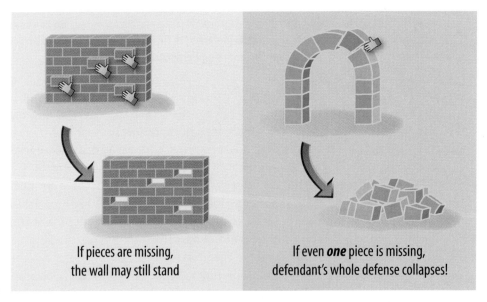

ILLUSTRATION 3-15. **Using an Analogy to Explain Necessary Elements**

argue that the same is true with defendant's affirmative defense and follow this up by pointing out the missing element(s) responsible for the affirmative defense's entire collapse.

Active Jurors Need Help Getting Organized

I know many lawyers who will write and re-write their opening statements and closing arguments dozens of times. Often these advocates want to get everything in just the right order. They believe (probably correctly) that the outcome of an argument will differ depending on the order in which it is made. Consequently, these lawyers will make considerable effort to set up the arguments in a way that most effectively funnels the jurors in the direction that the lawyer wants them to go.

I make this point because many of these same lawyers will forget or fail to see the need to provide similar tangible organizational tools to their jurors in deliberations. These lawyers will whip the jurors up into a frenzy during closing argument and send them off completely jazzed into jury deliberations. Then what happens? The jurors go into deliberations fully committed to doing the right thing. They sit down, pens out, ready to pounce on the verdict form. They read the verdict form. And do you know what happens? Nothing! These inspired, well-meaning jurors often run smack dab into a brick wall. The jurors look at each other. They begin to feel less and less enthusiastic and more and more self-conscious. Eventually someone asks the question that is on all of their minds: "OK, what are we supposed to do now?"

Don't let this happen. Jurors need help getting organized. They need and appreciate help in getting information about how to systematically analyze the facts of the case, how to make sense of the law, how to complete the verdict form, etc.

When one side provides a coherent plan and the other does not, the side that does has a distinct advantage. For one thing, jurors who favor the side that provides the guidelines are usually out of the blocks faster during jury deliberations and are more likely to dominate the early (and important) discussions about the trial. These jurors can do so because they do not need to spend time at the outset trying to figure out how to go about analyzing the facts. They can jump right into discussing the matter based on a process of analysis that experienced counsel has already provided to them.

How do you provide this organization? There are a variety of ways, many of which are discussed throughout this book. For purposes of this immediate section, I would like to show you an organizational tool that we designed for the prosecution to use in a highly publicized and tragic criminal case. We designed it so that jurors would have a systematic way to analyze what was probably the key issue in this dispute.

In this case, the defendants owned two very vicious and large dogs that they kept in their small San Francisco apartment. Based on more than thirty earlier violent incidents, the defendants were well aware of how vicious their dogs were capable of being, but did very little to restrain the animals. Neighbors, veterinarians, even complete strangers had warned the defendants that the dogs were likely to kill someone someday. Unfortunately, that's exactly what happened.

One of the defendants took the dogs out for a walk without putting any kind of muzzle on them. On the way out of the apartment, the dogs encountered a neighbor in the apartment hallway. Without warning, one of the two dogs attacked and killed the neighbor. The district attorney decided to prosecute both owners, one for second-degree murder. In order to do so, it was crucial that he convince the jurors that the defendant who had been walking the dog at the time of the fatal attack had acted with implied malice.

We suspected that jurors would have a problem with the concept of implied malice. While people understood malice, they had genuine problems understanding how malice could be implied. Mock jurors repeatedly asked: "Isn't malice always intentional and always against someone you know and don't like? How can malice be implied and how can it occur against someone that the defendant did not have any specific desire to harm?"

Here is the series of graphics and approximately what was said by the prosecutor to help jurors organize their thinking on this matter.

Whether defendant is guilty of second-degree murder will turn on your determination of whether she acted with implied malice. That is one of the crucial questions you face: Is there implied malice?

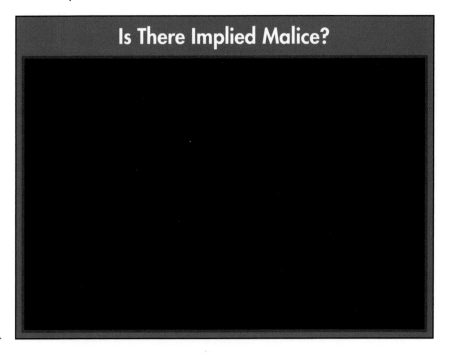

The judge is going to instruct you that there is implied malice if you find four things: (1) an intentionally dangerous act, (2) defendant realized the risk, (3) defendant acted with a total disregard of the danger, and (4) as a result there was a human death.

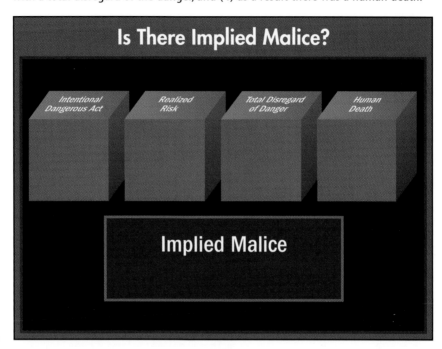

Let's look at each element and see if each one existed at the moment that the dogs killed Mary Clarkson. Was there an intentional dangerous act? Yes! Defendant walked both dogs without a muzzle.

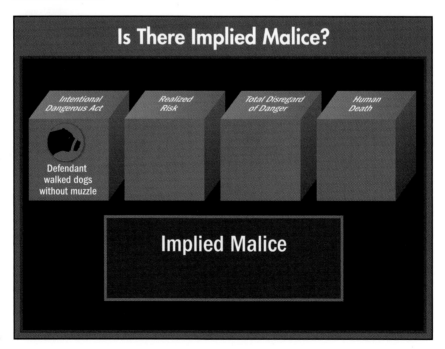

Should defendant have realized the risk? Yes! As we showed you in trial, there were over thirty prior incidents in which the dogs attacked or attempted to attack other animals and people. Defendant's veterinarian, neighbors, even strangers warned them that the dogs would likely kill someone someday. Defendant saw the warning signs; she realized the risk.

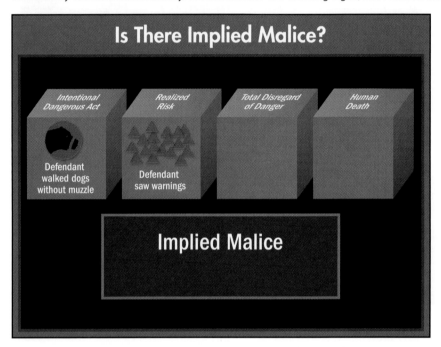

Did Defendant totally disregard the risk? Yes, clearly; despite the warning, she took the dogs, these huge and vicious dogs, for a walk without any protection for the people that they would encounter.

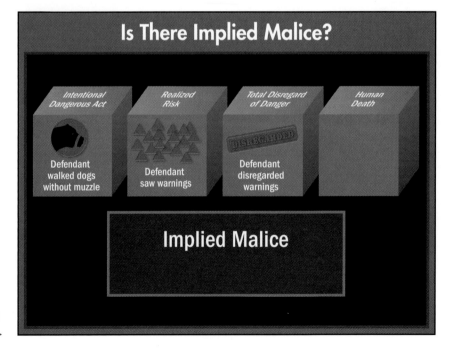

Finally, was there a human death? Tragically, yes. Mary Clarkson's death. The defendant and her dogs killed Mary Clarkson in the shared hallway of their apartment building.

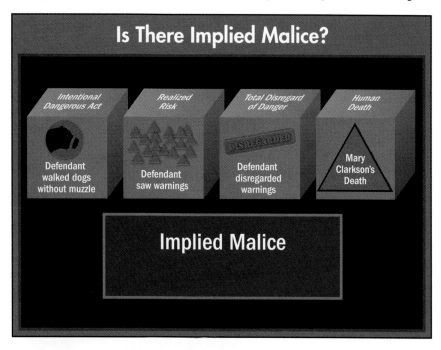

We have proven to you each and every element to establish implied malice and, as such, you must convict the defendant of second-degree murder.

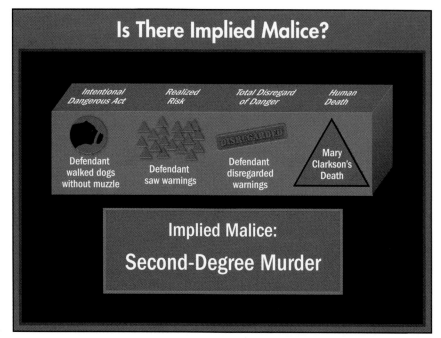

Active Jurors Need Tools to Help Them "See" Things Not Otherwise Visible in Court

I have a problem with the adage "Seeing is believing." It is not that I doubt that the saying is true—it is. My problem is that I think that some trial lawyers take these words too literally. These attorneys would translate the expression as "Stimulation of your optical nerves is believing." Instead, I would translate the adage as "Perceiving/ Understanding (through whatever sense and by any means possible) is believing."

Jurors, especially curious Active Jurors, want to "see" things in court. When they do, you have an increased chance that these jurors will be persuaded to become "your" jurors and, in turn, they will be better able to persuade undecided jurors to do the same.

Some things are easy to see in court—a contract, a pistol, a cancelled check. Other things are not. It is on this latter category of items that I want to focus our discussion in this section of the book.

Intangible Concepts. Certain things cannot be seen because they do not exist in any physically visible form. I am not exclusively talking about quarks or some other particles from theoretical physics, although they certainly fit in this sub-category. I am also including in this category certain concepts or principles. For example, there is nothing inherently silly in a juror saying, "Show me a fiduciary duty. What does it look like? Is it big or small? What color is it?"

If these things do not physically exist, how do you show them to the jury? The short answer is to remind you what many trial lawyers forget: This is one of the things that analogies, tutorials, and trial graphics can do, and can do very effectively.

Here is an example.

In patent law, coming up with a good idea is not enough. You cannot get a patent for merely having thought about something, sketched possible ideas, or coming up with models that do not work. In order to successfully patent an invention, the inventor must do more, including "enable" the idea.

"So," a juror might ask, "what does enablement look like? How will we know it if we see it?"

One way to answer that question is to provide a long explanation involving definitions. This is *not* likely to hold the juror's attention.

Another way (and I suggest a more effective way) would be to give the jurors an illustrated example of enablement and help them understand why the concept makes sense and is important. Your expert witness might start off by explaining that having an idea is not the same thing as "enabling" an idea. Lots of people have ideas that they either never pursue or are never able to get to work. The United States Patent and Trademark Office is not going to let these people get patents on these technological dead-ends. In order to patent something, inventors must do more. They must successfully enable the idea, that is, make the idea actually work.

Your expert can then offer an example known by every schoolchild. She can talk about how people tried for centuries to figure out how to fly. In the late 1400s, even the genius Leonardo da Vinci spent considerable time sketching possible ways to create a flying machine—all to no avail. In fact, at the end of his notebook on the subject, the Great Leonardo is reputed to have admitted, with respect to these efforts, "I have wasted my time."

More recently, thousands of people tried all kinds of crazy designs; in fact, a good number of these people died trying to make a flying machine—again to no avail. Undoubtedly, many of the jurors have seen historical filmed footage of people trying to get all kinds of inventions off the ground; all to no avail and often with disastrous results.

None of these "inventors," including Leonardo, could have received a patent on their work because none of them had successfully enabled the idea.

All of this changed on December 17, 1903, when brothers Orville and Wilbur Wright were the first to build and successfully fly the first airplane. Unlike everyone before them, these two Ohio bicycle makers successfully enabled the idea by making a machine that actually flew—it was for only a few seconds, but it flew. As a result, the United States Patent Office granted the Wright brothers a patent to protect their years of hard work. (See Illustration 3-16.)

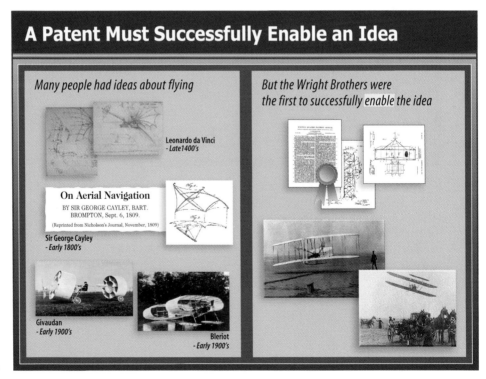

ILLUSTRATION 3-16. Explaining Intangible Concepts

Too Small, Too Big, Too Fast, or Too Slow. The second category of items cannot be seen in court because they involve extremes. Some of these items are too small or too big to ordinarily be seen in court. Others involve events that occur too quickly or too slowly to become part of ordinary, real-time testimony.

For example, how do you help a jury see one part in a billion? Here is a trial graphic and what the lawyer could have said to the jury to help make this point.

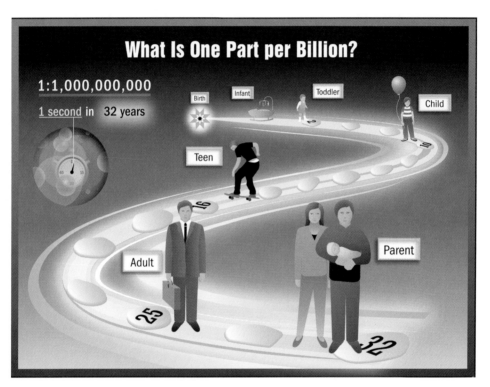

Dr. Van Ort told you about how she measures things in "parts per billion"—parts per *billion*, with a "b." I don't know about you, but I have a hard time visualize what exactly that means— one part in a billion parts. Dr. Van Ort explained this when she told you that one second.— [lawyer claps at one-second interval] Mississippi One—is one billionth of thirty-two years. In other words, if you take the second that a child is born, that child is going to be thirty-two years old before a billion seconds elapse.

Another example—we once had to help a jury in Los Angeles visualize how many people lived in American Samoa. Obviously, our client could not bring everyone into the courtroom and just listing the number 46,733 would not be overly helpful. What we did was to compare the number of American Samoans to something that the jury could readily relate to—the Los Angeles Coliseum. (See Illustration 3-17.)

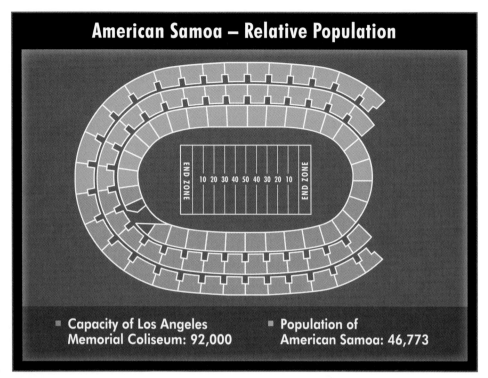

ILLUSTRATION 3-17

Active Jurors Need Tools to Help Them Compare and Contrast Evidence

Because of the way that trials are structured, evidence often goes in in a rather disjointed manner. Since evidence is usually broken down and presented by party and witness rather than by topic, evidence on one subject can arise on one day and then not be supported or contradicted until days or even weeks later.

Active Jurors often appreciate and rely on tools that make it easy for them to compare and contrast the evidence that has accumulated over the course of the trial. Jurors use these graphics as scorecards to determine whether the evidence supports or contradicts your key arguments and to judge witness credibility, based on whether the evidence squares with that witness's testimony.

Let's look at three examples. The first was designed to bolster a key argument in a products liability case. This defendant manufactured glass for large commercial greenhouses. Certain flowers grow best in specific wavelengths of light. To be successful, a grower must very carefully maintain the glass used in the greenhouse. If a grower fails to clean the glass every six months, accumulated dirt can affect the amount and wavelength of light that passes though into the greenhouse. Such changes can have a devastating affect on the grower's yield.

Under cross-examination, the plaintiff in our example testified at the beginning of the trial that she had cleaned the glass only once in the ten years that she owned her greenhouses. At the time, this fact was merely one of scores of other facts, many of which had no independent importance to the jurors. Several weeks later, one of the defendant's experts testified that the standard industry practice was to clean the glass once every six months.

Obviously, there is considerable contrast between what these two witnesses told the jury—plaintiff: "I only washed the glass once in ten years" versus defendant's expert: "The industry standard is to wash the glass once every six months." Unfortunately, the impact of this disparity was lessened because there were several weeks and a dozen witnesses between the two pieces of testimony.

Here is the graphic the lawyer used and approximately what she said in closing argument to help sharpen the contrast in this testimony.

▼▼▼

Two days ago, Dr. Brian Ward testified. As I am sure you all remember, Dr. Ward is a professor of botany and, for the past twenty years or so, has been one of the primary advisors for the AAFG—the American Association of Flower Growers. I am also sure that you remember that the AAFG is the trade group that Plaintiff, Laura Slate, belongs to and whose guidelines she says she relies on in operating her business. Dr. Ward testified that the standard in the industry requires that Ms. Slate clean these windows once every six months. So, according to these standards, Plaintiff should have cleaned the glass on her greenhouses twenty different times—twice a year for ten years. Here is what Ms. Slate should have done:

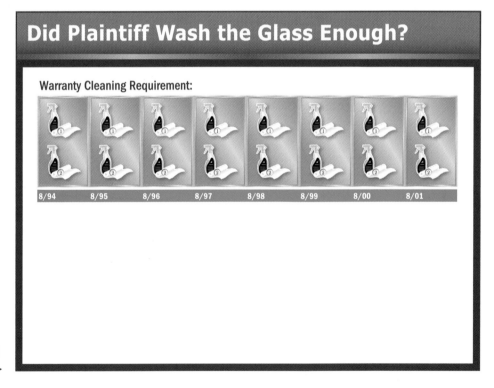

Here is what Ms. Slate actually did:

The second example of a tool that helps jurors compare and contrast evidence, as shown on the following two pages, was used against a plaintiff who was involved in an automobile accident in which she claimed she suffered considerable injury. On four different occasions, plaintiff filed answers to interrogatories claiming that prior to the accident she had "never been to a chiropractor and had no pain before."

▼▼▼

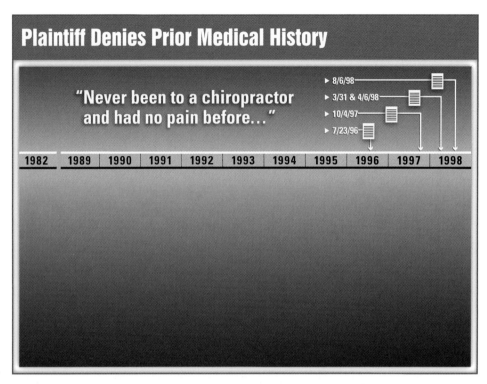

Discovery did not support plaintiff's claim of no prior injury or medical treatment.

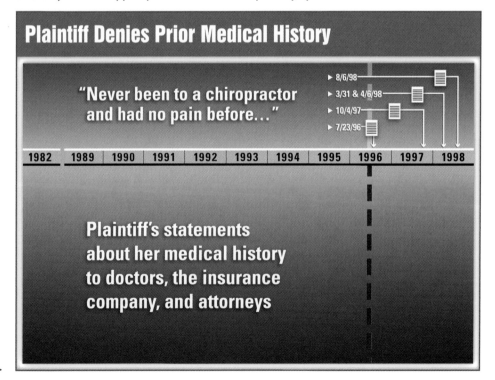

It turned out that plaintiff had in fact seen at least one chiropractor and three physicians prior to the accident in question.

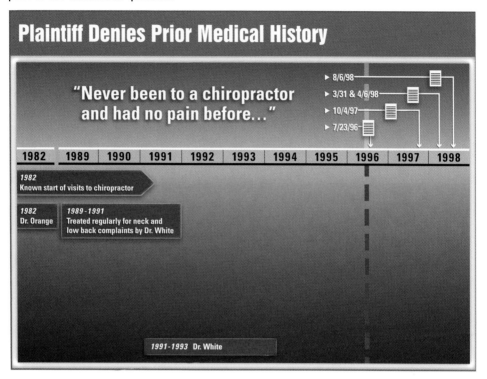

The plaintiff also had numerous pre-existing complaints, including pain in her shoulder, neck, back, and arms.

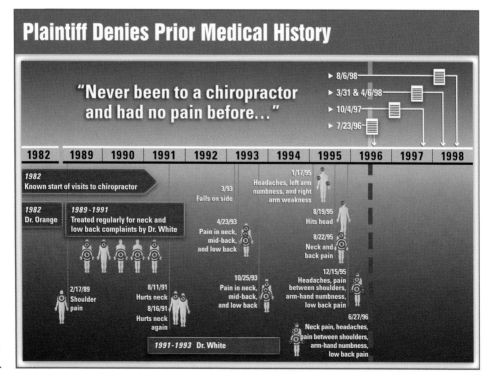

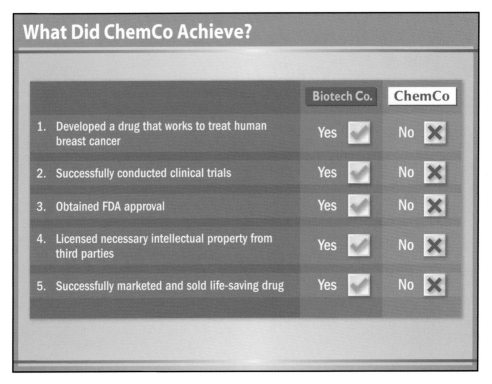

	Biotech Co.	ChemCo
What Did ChemCo Achieve?		
1. Developed a drug that works to treat human breast cancer	Yes ✓	No ✗
2. Successfully conducted clinical trials	Yes ✓	No ✗
3. Obtained FDA approval	Yes ✓	No ✗
4. Licensed necessary intellectual property from third parties	Yes ✓	No ✗
5. Successfully marketed and sold life-saving drug	Yes ✓	No ✗

ILLUSTRATION 3-18. Comparing Testimony With a Checklist

The final example of a graphic that trial lawyers can use to compare and contrast testimony is a simple checklist. (See Illustration 3-18.) For more information concerning this type of graphic, see Chapter 7.

Active Jurors Need to Be Able to Answer the Question "Compared to What?"

I used to have a colleague who, as a "joke," developed stock answers to stock questions. For example, whenever an unsuspecting young associate approached him with "I have a question," my colleague would immediately reply, "I have an answer; it's thirty-seven."

Whenever I heard his automatic response, I always thought that, whether my colleague intended it or not, his comment illustrated a crucial point: Data without context is meaningless.

The acknowledged dean of information architecture, Edward R. Tufte of Yale, emphasizes the same point when he stresses that all good graphics must answer the same basic question—"Compared to what?" Much of Chapter 4 will focus on the importance of providing jurors with sufficient tools to be able to answer this question.

For now, let's just focus on two of the most common ways to help Active Jurors make such a comparison and then use this information during deliberations. The first method, which is probably the easiest, is to juxtapose two accurately scaled illustrations—one of an object with which the jurors are familiar and the second of the object you are showing or telling the jurors about for the first time.

For example, several miles southwest of where I live is an air force base. From the highway that runs along one side of it you can clearly see an enormous building that prior to World War II was used as a hangar for zeppelins, some of the largest vehicles ever constructed. The U.S.S. Macon, which used to be stored at this hangar, was 785 feet long and 133 feet wide. Those are large numbers, but it was not until I saw a simple picture that showed that the Macon was three times larger than a Boeing 747 that I truly understood how big. (See Illustration 3-19.)

This type of graphic is not limited to comparing size. For example, Illustration 3-20 compares numbers of items. It puts into context how difficult it is to create a marketable prescription drug—specifically, how only one in 2.5 million tested compounds eventually becomes a marketable drug.

The second common way to help jurors compare objects is to offer them an analogy. We had a case where we needed to illustrate technology that could find defects as small as one micron on eight-inch silicon wafers. Merely saying that a micron is "really, really, really small" does not answer the key question of "Compared to what?" Showing the jury the analogy in Illustration 3-21 does.

Active Jurors Need Tools to Help Them Understand How Events Relate Chronologically

After mock trials, I will sometimes review the notes that jurors leave behind after their deliberations. These notes very often contain information that the jurors gleaned from timelines or other tools that helped jurors understand how events related chronologically.

This is not really surprising—chronological order is the Western mind's default method of organizing. For most people, organizing events chronologically is the first step in learning and understanding what happened. It is as if the mind needs to walk through the calendar as a way of helping things make sense by seeing what happened first, second, third, etc. In Chapter 7 we will explore the types of trial graphics that help you display this information.

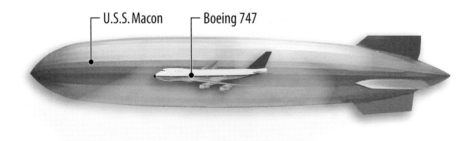

ILLUSTRATION 3-19. **Measuring Against a Known Object**

This simple but powerful graphic makes its point because it juxtaposes a known object— a Boeing 747 (which most people already consider to be large)—against an unknown object that is three times larger.

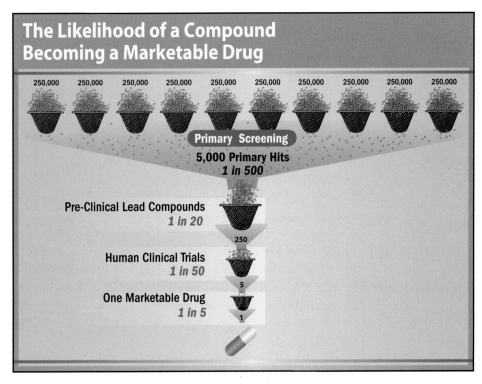

ILLUSTRATION 3-20. Picturing the Numbers

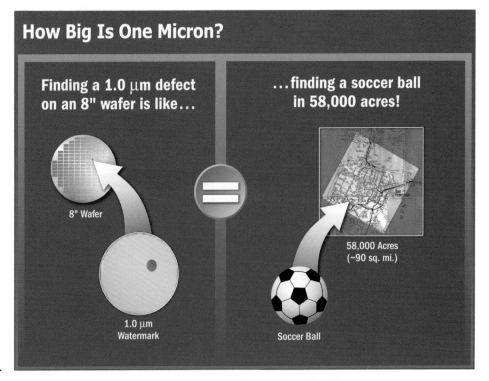

ILLUSTRATION 3-21. Answering the Question, "Compared to What?"

Arranging facts in chronological order has another benefit—often it is the only way for you to show patterns to Active Jurors. Let me show you two examples. Helping a jury to see a pattern was crucial in defending against a criminal case that the federal government brought against an executive accused of fraudulently and intentionally completing claim forms in a raisin crop insurance program. Honest—the federal government insures raisin crops against destruction by rain and hail. Fortunately for the government, virtually all of this country's raisins are grown in the Central Valley of California, which is an area generally known for hot and dry weather. There are relatively few claims for weather-related crop destruction and, as such, the program is extremely profitable for the government. In fact, the government counts on the profits from raisin crop insurance to offset less profitable programs such as wheat crop insurance, where some claims need to be paid almost every year.

In order to make sure that the raisin crop insurance program remains profitable, the government always changes the rules and regulations after each bad year. The fact that claims do not happen very often and the fact that the government changes the rules and regulation after each bad year virtually guarantees three things: (1) claims agents do not complete the required claims forms very often; (2) when they do, the forms and the rules governing those forms are new and being used by the claims agent for the first time; and (3) if the forms are inaccurate or not completed correctly, it is often because of ignorance and not criminal intent. The graphic that we used to illustrate these facts is shown in Illustration 3-22. This last point was the basis of our client's defense, that if he paid too much, it was an honest mistake, not part of a criminal scheme.

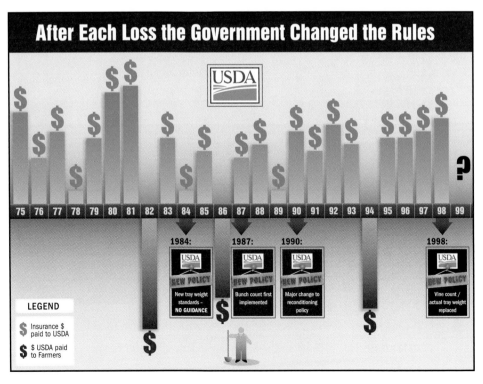

ILLUSTRATION 3-22. A Chronology Establishes the Pattern

The second case was one where a city was attempting to prevent one of its residents from legally using her home to care for six Alzheimer's patients by using the city building and police departments to harass her. A simple timeline helped establish what we believed to be the city's tag-team tactic—first send in the building department, and when it had done all it could do, send in the police. The graphic that established this pattern is shown in Illustration 3-23.

Active Jurors Need Tools to Quickly Define and Use Key Terms to Favor Your Version of the Facts

A trial graphic that defines key terms fairly, but in a way that favors your position, is an extremely powerful tool, one that is surprisingly often overlooked by trial lawyers. I once watched a trial in which none of the lawyers bothered to explain what they meant by the phrase "insurance underwriting." None of the jurors was brave enough to raise a hand or to send a note to the judge to ask counsel to explain what the phrase meant. This is an example of a missed opportunity. Consider the advantage that one side would have had if it had taken the time to educate the jury and provide them with a definition that was fair, but more favorable to that side's position. To the extent that the jury is using definitions, why shouldn't they be yours?

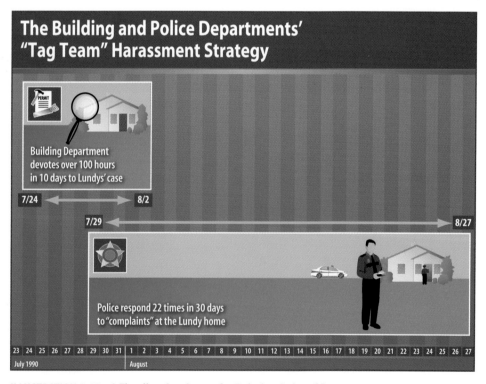

ILLUSTRATION 3-23. A Timeline Can Stress the Relative Order of Events

Here is an example of what I call an "annotated definition." It examines the difference between "identical" and "equivalent." To the casual user the two terms may easily pass for one another in everyday conversation. To a patent lawyer, the terms are significantly different. It is a violation of the patent laws to develop and improperly sell a product that is equivalent to a patented product. The product does not have to be identical to violate the patent, merely equivalent.

Because the terms are sufficiently close in meaning, defense counsel (usually the party who allegedly infringed on the patent) will often suggest that the jurors must find the infringing product to be *identical* to the patented one in order to find that the defendant violated the law. Plaintiff's counsel will argue that the product must be merely equivalent (not identical) to violate the patent laws.

How do you show that these words mean different things? One way is to use language, to use the dictionary, to use words. Here is an example:

"Equivalent" and "Identical" Are Not the Same

According to Webster's *New Collegiate Dictionary*:

"Equivalent – equal in force, amount or value; equal in area or volume but not admitting of superposition; corresponding or virtually identical esp. in effect or function."

vs.

"Identical – being the same, having such close resemblance as to be essentially the same."

This is an OK graphic, but it is not great. One of the problems with this graphic is that it uses the problem to resolve the problem. That is, it uses words to try to clarify a problem created by words. A more effective way would be to use pictures to illustrate an analogy. The following trial graphic takes an ordinary object—a key, something that you can pull out of your own pocket—to make the point that identical and equivalent are not the same.

This trial graphic successfully uses an analogy to illustrate the difference and does so much more effectively than if you had relied merely on written or spoken words. Specifically, you have two keys. The jury can quickly see that they are not identical. But, for the part of the key that matters, the end that goes into the key-hole, both will do the same thing. Both will open the same lock. They are equivalent; however, they are not identical.

Active Jurors Need Tools to Help Them Understand and Make Your Argument During Deliberations

As noted earlier, Active Jurors often play two roles during trial: they start out as searchers of the truth and eventually become advocates of the truth. As advocates of the truth, these Active Jurors are your surrogates in the jury room; your arguments during closing become their arguments in deliberations. As I previously pointed out, one of the criteria that I apply to determine if a mock closing has been effective is to observe whether one or more jurors pick up right where the lawyer left off and continue to make the argument on behalf of one party or the other. The chances of this happening increase when you provide jurors with tools that help them better understand and articulate your key points or arguments.

Here are two examples of such tools.

In the first instance, we represented a manufacturer of a private airplane that crashed, killing the pilot and one passenger. The families of the victims sued the manufacturer alleging that the airplane was defective.

The defendant denied that there was anything wrong with the airplane. Instead, the defendant believed that pilot error had caused the crash. Specifically, the pilot, who was in his 70s, decided to fly at night and to attempt a landing at a small unstaffed air strip rather than waiting to fly the next morning into a larger, better equipped airport.

To help make this argument clear to the jurors, the defendant's lawyer prepared two graphics. The first used a picture of the crashed airplane as its baseboard. Onto it the lawyer placed a series of images illustrating the mistakes that the pilot made. For example, these images highlighted that the pilot had set his altimeter incorrectly, he decided to land at night on an air strip with no air traffic control, he chose a short runway with a number of obstacles, and he tried to land knowing that there was considerable fog at the airstrip.

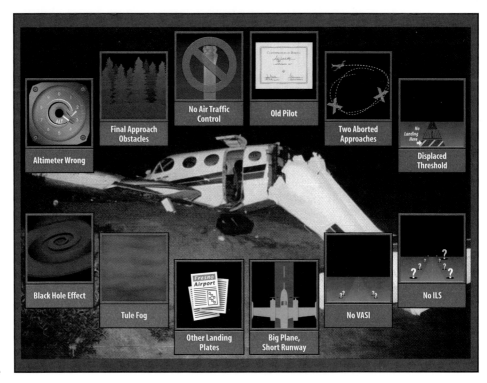

The second graphic had a photograph of the alternative airport that the pilot could have flown to the next morning. On this baseboard, the trial lawyer added a series of images clearly demonstrating why this would have been the far smarter and safer decision, including the facts that the airport had a longer runway, it had air traffic control, and there were no final approach obstacles.

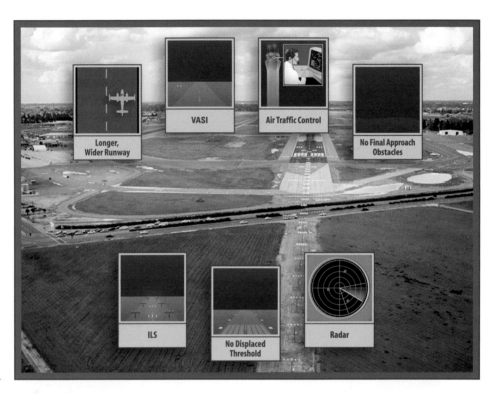

Taken together, these graphics illustrate defendant's closing argument. During deliberations, the Active Jurors used the information on these graphics to argue successfully for a defense verdict.

The second example of how to illustrate your argument comes from a case in which a major biopharmaceutical company had developed a drug that substantially improved the condition of women suffering from severe breast cancer. The company had spent years, hundreds of millions of dollars, and untold other resources developing the drug. After all of this work, another company, which had been at best a peripheral player, attempted to claim a substantial portion of the credit for and income from the drug. Illustration 3-24 is an argumentative graphic that shows the ridiculousness of the second company's claim by contrasting how much each company contributed to the development of the drug.

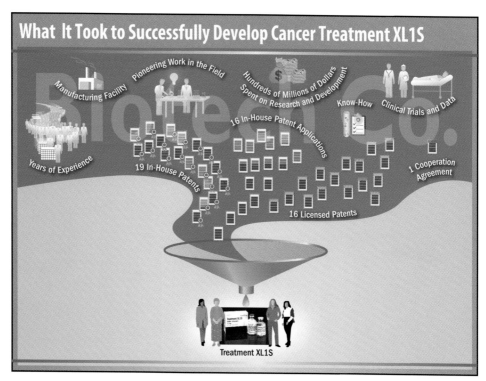

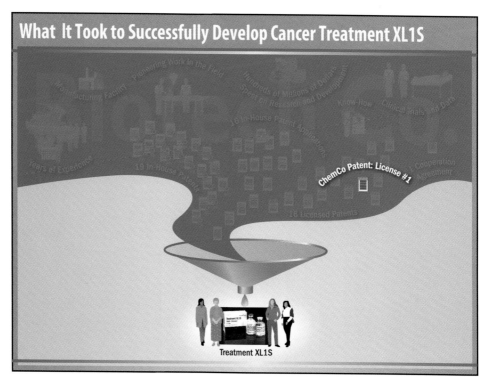

ILLUSTRATION 3-24. Contrasting How Much Each Party Contributed

Conclusion

It is said that the processes of making sausages and crafting legislation should not be watched by the faint-hearted. The same is true for jury deliberations. Trial lawyers who observe mock juries deliberate are often humbled as they watch jurors raise obvious questions that counsel never considered, speculate about relationships counsel never saw, and catch things counsel thought they had successfully buried. Perhaps most importantly, counsel realize that, as with any bum rap, our complaints about jurors are unfair and that jurors often deserve better than we are giving them. Use some of the tools in this chapter to do so.

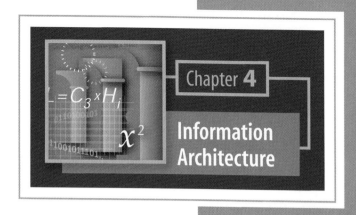

Chapter 4

Information Architecture

Information Architecture for Trial Lawyers

Information architects are professionals who specialize in conveying complex information to a target audience in a *simple and honest* manner. Until recently, few of these specialists have been trial lawyers. Instead, most have focused their skills on such diverse projects as designing textbooks, illustrating news and scientific publications, writing instructional programs for high-tech products, creating Web sites, organizing museum exhibits, or integrating interactive databases that link texts, images, and sounds.

"What," you may ask, "do these projects have in common with each other and, more importantly, what characteristics do they share with a jury trial?" It is no coincidence—they all focus on finding *simple and honest* ways to educate a select audience about usually complex topics.

The information that you must present at your next jury trial came to you by the crateload without instructions, organizing principles, or sorting tools. You need to separate what matters from what does not, find and identify patterns, organize this data, and develop ways to present it coherently to a group of average citizens who know nothing about you, your client, or the events that bring you into court. While this would prove to be an overwhelming task for most people, for information architects such an opportunity combines all of the excitement of Christmas morning and New Year's Eve.

Trial lawyers have much to learn about *explaining how to explain*. That is what this chapter is about.

The Twin Functions of Information Architects

INFORMATION ARCHITECTS LOWER BARRIERS TO LEARNING

My family and I once unexpectedly had to have repair work done on the lower level of our home; water had seeped into one of the rooms. In order to protect the workmen from our four sometimes obnoxious and always curious cats, we erected a temporary barrier at the top of the stairs leading to the area where the repair work was being done. "Barrier" is actually too strong a word for what we created; while it kept the cats out, the temporary gate did virtually nothing to prevent human trips up or down the stairs. It took at most three additional seconds to open the temporary gate, pass through, and then close it against a potential feline attack.

One of our downstairs rooms contains a good-sized television and several comfortable chairs. For years, this was the place where anyone who wanted to watch television for more than just a few minutes would go. Another room downstairs is the laundry room; everyone in my family is under strict orders to deposit their dirty clothes there at the end of each day.

None of the repair work affected the television room or anyone's ability to watch television there. Likewise, none of the repair work affected the laundry room or anyone's ability to take clothes downstairs. Yet a curious thing happened.

As soon as we installed our minimal barrier, virtually no one made the extra effort (remember, it was only three extra seconds) to go downstairs to watch television or to take clothes down to the baskets in the laundry room. Instead, my wife, three children, and I clustered around a much smaller television in our considerably less comfortable kitchen, and piles of dirty clothes accumulated upstairs.

There was absolutely no proportional relationship between the three-second barrier and the dramatic change in my family's television viewing and laundry habits. Yet this shift was real and the cause was the flimsiest of barriers. While I half expected this change with respect to burdensome tasks, like taking dirty clothes

"Not worth it"

Oftentimes it takes only a small obstacle to cause a person to simply give up doing something.

downstairs to the laundry basket, I was genuinely surprised at how little it took for people to forgo more pleasant activities, for example, watching their favorite shows on a nice television while sitting in a comfortable chair.

Seeing this result helped me realize how disruptive barriers (even relatively minor ones) can be. Oftentimes it takes only a small obstacle to cause a person to simply give up doing something. This observation has real-world applications far wider than just watching television or washing clothes. Imagine for a moment what effect barriers to learning (even small barriers like the functional equivalent of a three-second delay in going up or down steps) can have on jurors whose entire time in the courtroom must seem to them more like dealing with dirty clothes than watching a comedy show on television.

The first thing that information architects must do in order to be successful is to lower and whenever possible break down barriers to learning. Information architects are constantly vigilant, looking far enough ahead to identify such barriers and then eliminate or navigate around as many of them as possible. Throughout this chapter you will notice a variety of methods to accomplish these crucial tasks.

INFORMATION ARCHITECTS HELP THOSE WITH INFORMATION ENGAGE THOSE WHO NEED IT

Optimal learning (or anything approaching it) requires engagement—engagement between the person offering the information and the person receiving/processing it. Engagement can be direct; that is, it can be straight from the teacher's mouth to the student's ears/brain/heart. Other times engagement is indirect; the information ends up in the same place but it gets there through a device (e.g., a story or a graphic). (See Illustration 4-1.) The chances of engagement occurring increase as the number of barriers to understanding decrease.

Engagement requires interest and understanding. It often takes place in sudden bursts. As much as we want jurors to be fully engaged all of the time, if this happened, their brains would explode. Consequently, we need to maximize the times that engagement occurs and carefully select the message that we transmit when it does.

Information architecture is all about reducing barriers and increasing engagement. The discipline finds ways to increase the chances of there being a connection between the lawyer and the jurors. Some of these methods are prohibitive—"Whenever possible, thou shall not. . . ." Others are prescriptive—"Whenever possible, thou shall. . . ." None is absolute; all require flexibility.

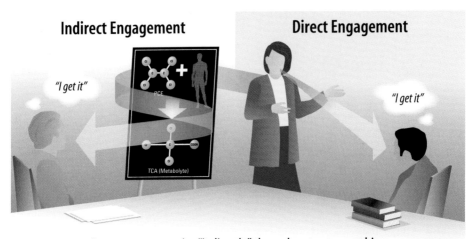

Engagement can arise "indirectly" through a story or graphic or "directly" from the teacher straight to the student.

ILLUSTRATION 4-1

If, as I suggest in Chapter 2, our job as trial lawyers is to teach the jury about what really matters, then we can learn much from information architects, their projects, and the basic principles they employ. At the same time, as trial lawyers we face a challenge; we must carefully select what we borrow from other information architects. We must never forget that we operate in a strange arena. The courtroom is an artificial world governed by centuries-old rules of evidence and procedure—a venue different from the places where most information architects have developed their basic principles.

Much of what information architects have learned is directly applicable and useful at trial; some is not. Trial lawyers need to learn not only the basics of information architecture but also how then to select those techniques that show promise and tailor them to serve our clients in the unique confines of the courtroom.

Don't Forget That Trials Are Odd Creatures

It is pretty near impossible for something to have been around for eight hundred years and not have acquired a few quirks. The jury trial is no exception. For reasons that sometimes make complete sense and other times do not, our adversarial system has developed certain idiosyncrasies, including those we call the rules of evidence and procedure. In certain instances, these idiosyncrasies saddle a trial lawyer with disadvantages that do not affect information architects in other fields. In other instances, these idiosyncrasies provide the lawyer with certain offsetting advantages. As you prepare for trial, you must keep both these advantages and disadvantages squarely in mind and adapt your techniques accordingly.

TRIAL LAWYERS HAVE ONE BIG DISADVANTAGE

Trial lawyers face one big disadvantage not universally shared by other information architects. To better understand it, let's take a look at what many consider to be one of the greatest informational graphics ever[1] and consider why this amazing graphic might *not* do well in front of your next municipal court jury.

In 1812, Napoleon and over 422,000 of his men began marching to Moscow. Three months later, when Napoleon reached his destination, he had only 122,000 men. While some of the original force had been sent on auxiliary missions, the vast majority of the 300,000 missing men were either dead or had deserted.

Shortly after arriving in Moscow, Napoleon and his remaining troops retreated back across Russia. The retreat was even more disastrous than the march to Moscow. The winter of 1812–1813 was unusually brutal. At no time during the entire two and a half months of Napoleon's retreat did the temperature ever get above zero degrees Celsius. In fact, for much of the time the temperature hovered in the range of twenty to thirty degrees Celsius *below zero*. Every time the temperature dropped and every time Napoleon's troops retreated across a major river (where they were often forced to fight battles), they suffered devastating losses. By the time Napoleon reached the relative safety of Lithuania, he had only 10,000 of his original 422,000 soldiers—approximately 2.5 percent of the troops with which he started.

In 1861, a French engineer named Charles Joseph Minard wanted to display the history of these losses graphically. He hoped his creation would be a powerful way of protesting against the wastes of war. Illustration 4-2a shows what Minard produced. By the way, if you do not immediately see how amazing this graphic is, don't worry. With enough pondering you will—and, as we will discover, the fact that pondering is required is exactly why this great graphic would *not* work well in a typical jury trial.

You should notice certain features of Minard's graphic. For example, two bands run across the entire exhibit. The first, the lighter-colored one, traces the advancing movement of Napoleon's troops to Moscow. (See Illustration 4-2b, Point 1.) The second band, the darker-colored one, traces his retreat. (See Illustration 4-2b, Point 2.) The width of each band reflects the number of Napoleon's troops at any given point in the campaign; notice how the rapid narrowing of the bands reflects his dwindling troop strength. As evidence of this, compare the width of the band at the beginning of the campaign, when there were 422,000 soldiers, to the end, when only 10,000 remained. (See Illustration 4-2b, Point 3.)

Minard's graphic allows you to trace the route that Napoleon and his men traveled to Moscow and back. Their path is indicated by the various cities named

---

1. Edward R. Tufte, professor emeritus at Yale and expert on informational design, noted that Minard's work "may well be the best statistical graphic ever drawn." Tufte, *The Visual Display of Quantitative Information* (Cheshire, Connecticut: Graphic Press, 1983), 40.

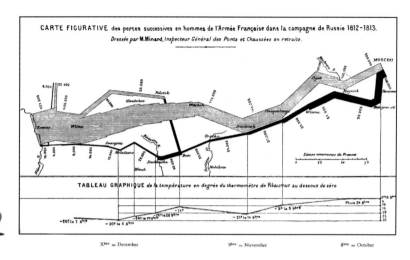

ILLUSTRATION 4-2a. A Great Graphic, but Not for Trial

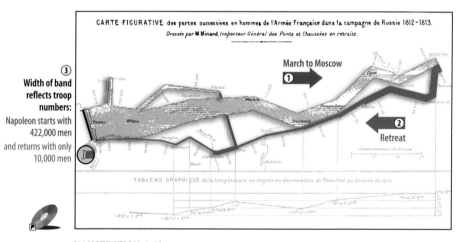

ILLUSTRATION 4-2b

inside or next to each of the main bands. (See Illustration 4-2c, Point 4.) Additionally, Minard included various rivers and other geographic obstacles that the French encountered during their retreat. (See Illustration 4-2c, Point 5.)

From this graphic you can also analyze auxiliary troop movements in considerable detail. You can determine when the auxiliary troops separated from the main force, where this separation occurred, how many men were in the auxiliary troops, where the auxiliary troops went, what kinds of casualties they experienced, when the auxiliary troops rejoined the main force, and where the unification took place. For example, one such movement, which occurred shortly after Napoleon left Poland, sent 22,000 men north. Only 6,000 of these soldiers survived and eventually were able to rejoin Napoleon's main force. (See Illustration 4-2d, Points 6 and 7.)

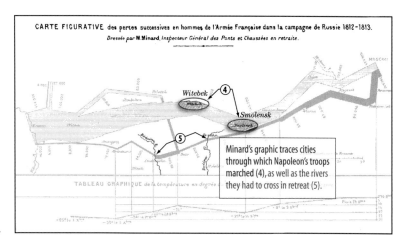

ILLUSTRATION 4-2c

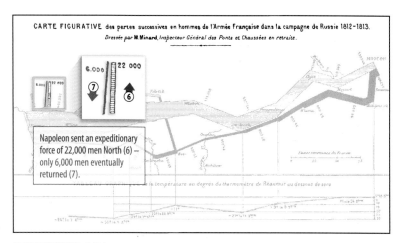

ILLUSTRATION 4-2d

Each time the retreating dark band intersects a river, you can see the number of men who died there either attempting to cross or at the battles that often took place at such locations. For example, Napoleon lost 22,000 of his 50,000 remaining men when his troops crossed the Brezina River. (See Illustration 4-2e, Point 8.) Many of the men who died at the Brezina were part of an auxiliary force that had just recently rejoined Napoleon's main troops. (See Illustration 4-2e, Points 9 and 10.)

As mentioned above, during the retreat, the winter temperatures remained below zero degrees Celsius for more than two months. This fact is reflected in a simple line graph at the bottom of the graphic that plots the temperature from the time that the retreat started on October 8, 1812, until it ended on December 7, 1812. For the viewer's convenience, Minard provides various lines showing where

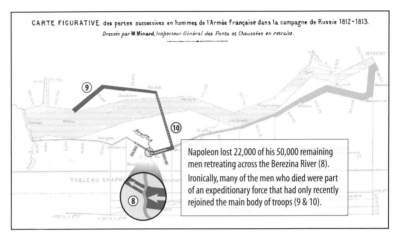

ILLUSTRATION 4-2e

the troops were with each major temperature drop. (See Illustration 4-2f, Point 11.) Not surprisingly, a large number of troops died at each of these points, a fact that is also directly observable in the narrowing width of the darker retreating band. (See Illustration 4-2f, Point 12.)

The more I ponder Minard's work, the more I appreciate that it is a work of genius. It is a marvel of planning and execution. One graphic with at least seven variables—trust me, not easy.

Unfortunately, this graphic also helps illustrate the primary *disadvantage* that lawyers have at trial—a disadvantage not always experienced by informational architects in other fields. Many of the best examples of information graphics are designed to be pondered. That is, an information architect often designs graphics with the expectation that viewers will have an opportunity to examine them intensely, uninterrupted, in silence, for as long as the viewers wish.

Jurors do not always get the time necessary to ponder a trial graphic. This is so for two reasons. First, even though the jurors are supposed to be the ones learning the facts of the case, the pace at which information is presented at a trial is usually set by people other than the jurors. Many trial judges, either on their own or with minimal urging by opposing counsel, will push a lawyer to present the evidence and "move on, Counsel," regardless of whether the jurors have fully learned what it is they are being taught.

Second, many trial graphics do not physically go into the jury room during deliberations. Some do; these are the graphics that are marked and actually admitted into evidence. Many do not; these are the graphics that lawyers offer for illustrative purposes, the ones that help reinforce a point at the time it is made. (We will discuss this point in detail later in Chapter 5.) Unfortunately, it is this latter category of graphics, the ones that do *not* get to go into the jury room, that would most often benefit from being pondered by the jury.

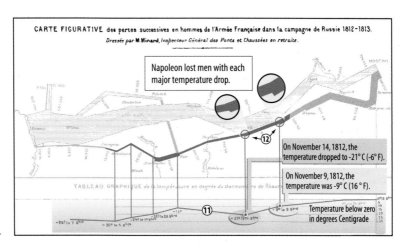

ILLUSTRATION 4-2f

Why does this matter? It matters because we need to be aware of this limitation and, as we shall see in subsequent sections of this chapter, figure out ways to design around it.

TRIAL LAWYERS HAVE TWO ADVANTAGES

The news is not all bad! Fortunately for us, the idiosyncrasies that created the disadvantage (i.e., the rules of evidence and procedure) also provide trial lawyers with certain offsetting benefits. Trial lawyers have two advantages not always available to information architects in other fields. First, we not only can, but usually are required to, "introduce"[2] our graphics to the jury. As a result, our trial graphics rarely hit the jury cold. Instead, we often have the advantage of supplementing or explaining our graphics with witness testimony or lawyer statements or arguments.

Of course, the best graphics generally are those that make their point with minimal additional explanation. These graphics provide more information visually than could otherwise be conveyed by a similar number of spoken or written words. Nevertheless, with all of the pressures we face at trial, it is comforting to know that this first advantage exists; if you need to explain your graphic, there are usually sufficient opportunities to do so. Make use of this advantage when necessary, but do not get lazy and rely on it too heavily.

Since trials are segmented, they are often intentionally repetitious. This is the trial lawyer's second advantage and we must make good use of it. I want to caution you that when I talk about repetition, I am *not* suggesting excessive repetition.

2. I use this term both as formally defined by the Federal Rules of Evidence and in a more generic sense.

There is a major difference between repetition that educates the brain and repetition that dulls the mind.

In order to fully understand any graphic, jurors need to appreciate it from three different perspectives. They need to grasp the graphic's *format* (i.e., how the information in the graphic is organized), the graphic's *content* (i.e., what type of information is in the graphic and what that information means), and the graphic's *context* (i.e., how and where the information in a single graphic fits in with the overall case).

Occasionally, the jury grasps all three perspectives at once. Bingo! Slap to the side of the head! Kensho! Instant understanding! However, more often these three perspectives arise separately at different points in the trial.

The rules of evidence and procedure broadly divide a trial into three phases— the parties' opening statements, their cases-in-chief, and their closing arguments. Fortunately for us, each phase is particularly well suited for developing one or more of these perspectives. For example, during opening statement you can speak directly to the jurors about the *format* and *content* of certain graphics that the jurors are going to see again later in the trial. During witness testimony (usually direct, but sometimes cross), you can show the jurors the graphic a second time and use witness testimony to help them focus on the graphic's *content*. Finally, in closing argument, you can provide the jurors with *context* by stressing how the graphic relates to other facts or arguments. After these repeated exposures, the jurors should have no problem understanding and remembering your key graphics.

Time and Space Are Limited Commodities

When I was in high school, one of my classmates, Daryl Honeycutt, believed that he had discovered a way to ace our biology final without studying. Our teacher announced that he would permit each student to bring a three-by-five-inch index card to the examination with as much information on it as that student could fit. Instead of studying, Daryl spent hours copying whole sections of the textbook verbatim onto the card. He did so in handwriting that would even impress those carnival vendors who claim to be able to write your name on a grain of rice. After the exam I asked Daryl how he had done. "Bad!" he replied, "I did not have enough time to find much of the stuff on the card and when I did it was too small for me to read."

While I didn't know it at the time, Daryl Honeycutt had stumbled upon one of the most important facts about all informational graphics—*the most limited (and therefore precious) elements for any trial graphic are time and space.*

Time is a precious commodity because it is restricted in two ways. First, the judge will give you only so much time before warning you, "That's been more than adequately covered, Counsel." Time is further limited because jurors will spend only so much of it before they begin to rapidly lose interest, get bored, and stop listening to you.

Space is precious because trial graphics have concrete boundaries beyond which you cannot go. Additionally, you can put only a limited amount of information within those boundaries and still have your exhibit be legible and make sense.

Daryl Honeycutt discovers that the most precious elements of any graphic are time and space.

It is the information architect's job—and yours—to deal with the limitations of time and space. You must (1) *turn* these limitations to your advantage, (2) *allocate* these scarce resources effectively, and (3) whenever possible, *overcome* these limitations.

TURN THE LIMITATIONS OF TIME AND SPACE TO YOUR ADVANTAGE

We tend to think of limitations as always hampering creative expression. This conclusion is wrong; in fact, often the opposite is the case. Limitations actually force us to be *more* creative, not less. We need to turn the limitations of time and space to our advantage by finding ways to use these restrictions to encourage (not stifle) creativity.

Let me give you an example. I am a fan of haiku. The rules establishing this form of Japanese poetry are exact, unbending, and extremely restrictive. Each poem must contain seventeen syllables—no more and no less. Those seventeen syllables must be arranged in three lines. The first line must have five syllables, the second line seven, and the third line five syllables.[3] At first glance, you might ask yourself, "How can anyone be creative within these tight restrictions? Impossible!" Yet for

---

3. With apologies to Basho and the other great haiku masters:

> On newsprint paper
> Ideas find safe harbor
> Few survive the trial.

centuries these extreme limitations have encouraged writers to create an amazing body of poetry—works that capture an event in an instant or an emotion in its simplest form.

Limitations, even simple limitations such as the four corners of a sheet of paper or the boundaries of a trial graphic, actually force you to be more creative, not less. The restrictions (which are often psychological) created by the limited usable area of a trial graphic force you to eliminate what does not matter and to concentrate on what does. In order to get your case to "fit," you must simplify. You must eliminate excess, limit your "picture" to what really matters, and find the best possible way to display what's left to the jury.

For this reason, as strange as it may sound, a pencil and blank sheet of paper are two of the most powerful tools in your office for purposes of encouraging (some would say forcing) brevity and creativity. Just as nature abhors a vacuum, lawyers abhor blank sheets of paper. The paper's blankness virtually demands that the trial lawyer do something to fill it with the details of his case. At the same time, the sheet's four corners limit this process. He can put only so much information on the sheet before it becomes so full as to be useless—which is what Daryl Honeycutt taught me.

There is an inherent tension between the desire to provide more information and the need to limit how much you actually provide. From this tension comes creativity; take advantage of it.

ALLOCATE TIME AND SPACE EFFECTIVELY

As with any scarce resource, you need to allocate time and space carefully. I have found three rules to be particularly helpful in this regard. To better understand these three rules and the principles behind them, let's look at how they apply to three different examples.

The First Rule of Time and Space

Not all information is of equal value. Never be afraid to pass up the *good* in favor of the *great*.

As mentioned in Chapter 3, I once worked on a case involving extensive abuse of power by a city against one of its citizens. My client represented a woman whom I will call Ms. Lundy. Ms. Lundy wanted to use her own home, which was in an upscale community, as a residential facility for up to six Alzheimer's patients, including her own father who was dying of complications related to this devastating disease. Her plan was entirely legal and she should have been able to open the home.

When Ms. Lundy's neighbors found out about the possibility of the group care home, they launched a personal and political attack against her, the likes of which I have never before seen. Unfortunately for Ms. Lundy, two of the politicians (and I use this word in its worst possible sense) on the city council had openly set their

The First Rule of Time and Space:
Not all information is of equal value. Never be
afraid to pass up the *good* in favor of the *great*.

| OK | Better than OK | Good | Very Good | Great! |

sights on higher political office and opportunistically seized upon this dispute as a way to advance their own careers.

The politicians persuaded the city's building department (in a writing that they foolishly never thought could be discovered) to go through Ms. Lundy's home with a fine-tooth comb and cite her for hundreds of code violations, violations that as a practical matter exist in almost every house. The building department also agreed to criminally prosecute Ms. Lundy for these technical violations—the first such prosecution in at least thirty years. As if this were not bad enough, the building department agreed to this strategy of "cite and prosecute" *before* any inspectors ever set foot in Ms. Lundy's home.

The city's harassment did not stop there. The councilmembers held neighborhood meetings in which they instructed neighbors in how to spy on Ms. Lundy and report her activities to the police. The police were constantly investigating supposed illegal activity and issuing tickets to anyone who might be visiting Ms. Lundy; one such ticket was for parking nineteen inches from the curb (the police officer had actually measured) instead of the statutory maximum of eighteen inches.

The city, relying on the pretext of needing to protect potential residents of Ms. Lundy's home, spent more than $100,000 on private investigators and accountants who pored over Ms. Lundy's personal life and financial records looking for possible evidence with which to challenge her application for a state license to open the home. Newspaper articles began to appear daily condemning the project and Ms. Lundy personally. Unknown individuals began vandalizing Ms. Lundy's home, and when her son called and complained to the police, the police threatened to arrest him for disturbing the peace.

The lowest blow came when the city located one of Ms. Lundy's sons who lived out of state and had been institutionalized for several years for severe emotional problems. The city paid to bring the son to testify in an administrative hearing that his mother was unfit. The city then ordered an expedited transcript of his testimony, distributed it widely, and, of course, never bothered to tell any of the recipients of the material about the young man's history of emotional problems. There were scores of other examples of harassment and abuse of official power.

The lawyer with whom I worked on this case became a close friend of Ms. Lundy. He empathized with her and genuinely shared the pain that she experienced as a result of each of these horrible acts. The lawyer asked me to review and make suggestions about his opening statement. The draft he sent me was over two hundred pages long and I estimate would have taken at least four hours to deliver. The draft listed a hundred or so examples of governmental abuse in detail; my lawyer client could not let go of any of them. In some ways I understand why he did this. Each of the examples was relevant; none was trivial; each had caused Ms. Lundy considerable pain. It was almost as if my client believed that if he did not highlight every single instance of governmental abuse, Ms. Lundy would have suffered in vain with respect to those unmentioned events.

No matter how much I tried, I could not get my client to let go of some of the less important facts. The result was a draft opening statement that bored prospective jurors by overwhelming them with too much detail. In desperation, I consulted with my colleague Joel ben Izzy. Joel listened to my dilemma and provided me with the advice that eventually helped my client let go of much of his excess material and create a very powerful opening statement and case. Joel's advice was, "Never be afraid to pass up the *good* in favor of the *great*." This advice has saved me (and my clients) on countless occasions and is the essence of my First Rule of Time and Space.

I have never worked on a case with too few facts. Prioritize your facts; choose those that are important and tell a compelling story; eliminate everything else. You have neither the time nor the space to squander on things that are not "great."

The Second Rule of Time and Space

Allocate time and space in direct relationship to the information's importance. The more important the information, the more time and space you should allocate to it.

To better understand the Second Rule, let's start by examining a trial graphic that violates it. We will take that graphic apart, noting the various violations, and then use that same underlying information to reconstruct a new and better trial graphic consistent with the Second Rule.

Illustration 4-3 consists of two pages from a deposition transcript. What we are really interested in is the party admission, "I don't think that they defrauded us . . . ." (page 181, line 23, through page 182, line 8). You do not know anything about the case from which this document came, but I suspect that this admission is sufficiently significant that you can probably guess how I want to use it at trial. I want not only to show this sentence to the jurors but also to have the phrase jump out at them and then have it become one of crucial themes of my client's fraud defense. Unfortunately, the quotation is well buried in the transcript and, to make matters worse, it is buried on not just on one page, but two.

So, how do we best accomplish these goals?

The first option would be simply to enlarge the two pages of transcript to a size that the jury could read at a distance, put the blown-up pages on an easel or two, and use a yellow highlighter to emphasize the phrase "I don't think that they defrauded us. . . ." When I started practicing law, this approach was consid-

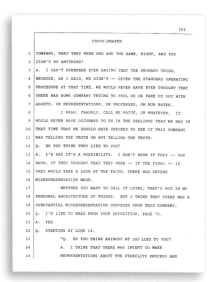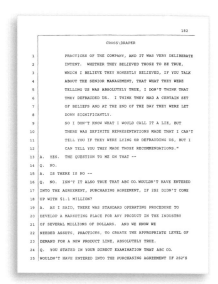

ILLUSTRATION 4-3. Poor Use of Time and Space

ered the sign of an innovative trial lawyer. After all, back then most lawyers were merely reading the transcript to the jury or going through the added hassle of repeatedly turning off and on all of the courtroom lights so that they could display an 8½ × 11 inch acetate copy using an antiquated overhead projector.

While this technique may at one point have been de rigueur, merely enlarging two pages of deposition transcript is not a very effective way to isolate and display crucial information to the jury.

For the purpose of educating the jury, the format of the deposition pages squanders time and space. Such a waste should not be surprising. The court reporter who prepared the original material intended it to be in a booklet format read word for word by lawyers holding it a few inches from their noses. It was not the court reporter's job to lay out the transcript in a format that identifies what is important and then can be easily read and understood by a jury sitting fifteen feet away. That is *your* job.

Illustration 4-3 violates the Rules of Time and Space in a variety of ways. Most specifically, it neither attempts to differentiate between what is important and unimportant nor allocates the graphic's limited space to what really matters. For example, look at the size of the print itself. The numbers at the left of each line are as big as the crucial words "I don't think that they defrauded us. . . ."

Even with the highlighting, the key admission is still buried. You can find the admission, but that is just it, you have to *find* the admission; it definitely does not jump out at you. Additionally, the admission is surrounded by surplusage that you probably do not want the jury to read—not because there is anything wrong with the material, but because it takes valuable time and distracts the reader from what is really important.

In addition to violating the Second Rule of Time and Space, there are other related problems with Illustration 4-3. For example, there is nothing to "authenticate" or let the jury know the information came from a real document, not just the lawyer's imagination.[4] Likewise, there is no way for jurors who might on their own look at the graphic two weeks later to quickly remind themselves of the point that you made when using this graphic. Finally, such an exhibit is not easy to read. The black text on a white background is legible only at close range, definitely not from fifteen feet away. In short, merely blowing up the original document does nothing to eliminate any of these problems. You need to find a better way to show this crucial information to the jury.

We have redone this trial graphic so that it is consistent with the Second Rule of Time and Space and so that it eliminates the problems described above. (See Illustration 4-4.)

Consistent with the Second Rule of Time and Space, we have made sure that the important portion of the deposition transcript dominates the exhibit, instead of being buried in it. The easiest way to see this is to focus on three aspects of the graphic: its overall design format, the varying type sizes within that format, and the added highlighting.

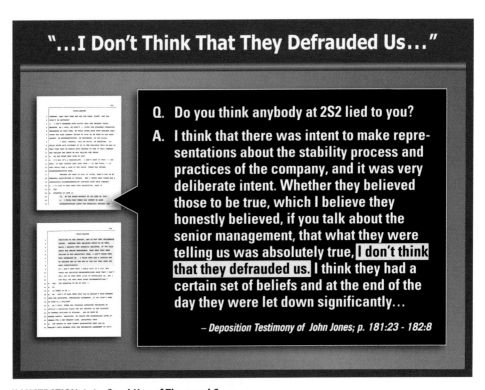

ILLUSTRATION 4-4. Good Use of Time and Space

---

4. As discussed later in the text, "trial graphic authentication" is different from "evidentiary authentication." The former provides context to the jurors so that they see that the document is real and ties back to an actual document that you will provide to them unedited as an exhibit. "Evidentiary authentication" refers to the requirement in the rules of evidence that an exhibit "is what it purports to be."

As shown in Illustration 4-5a, the graphic is divided into four sections: a title bar (Point 1), a scan of the deposition transcript itself (Point 2), and a textpull containing the key admission (Point 3) followed by the deposition citation (Point 4).

Within this format, as shown in Illustration 4-5b, there are four different "fonts" or type sizes. The largest type size is used for the title; the textpull type is slightly smaller; the deposition citation is smaller still; and the copied deposition transcript pages are in the smallest type of all.

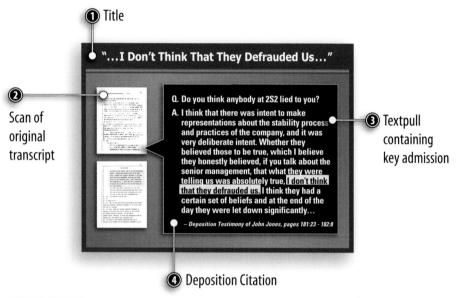

ILLUSTRATION 4-5a

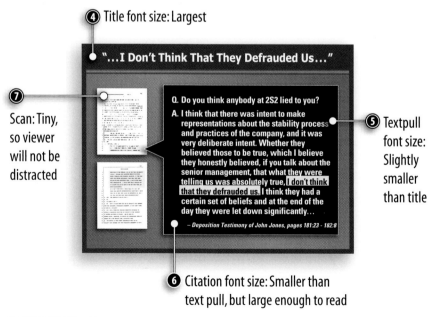

ILLUSTRATION 4-5b

Consistent with the Second Rule of Time and Space, you can usually determine how important certain information is by observing how much space is allocated to that material and what size type (remember that print size is really just another way to allocate space) is used within that space. For example, the crucial deposition question and answer takes up well over 50 percent of the trial graphic's available space and uses a relatively large type size. In "real space" (the actual space devoted to the information in the real document) this crucial question and answer takes up less than 20 percent of the original document and is in the same font (size and style of type) used throughout the entire deposition transcript, as shown in Illustration 4-3. The allocation of space and type size in Illustration 4-4 shows that the information in the textpull is the most important information in the trial graphic.

Continuing on with this analysis, note that after the textpull itself, the title is the next most prominent aspect of the graphic. While the title space is physically smaller than the area assigned to the document scan, the title space more than makes up for this difference by using the largest type in the graphic and being at the very top of the graphic, a place many people look first. This technique allows the title, which I consider to be the second most important part of the trial graphic, to dominate over the scanned text but not overwhelm the textpull itself.

There is a tie for the least prominent aspects of the graphic; a tie between the scanned document itself and the deposition citation. The information conveyed by the scan and the actual citation are important enough to be part of the graphic, but not so important as to dominate its limited space. If you think about it, this is entirely appropriate because the scan and the citation both serve the same purpose—to "authenticate" where the specific admission comes from. The deposition transcript pages themselves are large enough to assure the viewer that the information comes from a real document, but not so large as to allow the viewer to be distracted by reading the extraneous text in the scan. The citation is at the end of the quotation. We placed it here both to assure the viewer that the testimony is authentic and to make it easy for the lawyer to quickly provide the deposition citation to the court, witness, or opposing counsel.

At the outset of this section, I mentioned that Illustration 4-3 had other problems as well; for example, there was no quick way for jurors on their own to remind themselves later what the graphic was about, and it was difficult to read the dark text on a light background. We have eliminated these problems as well in Illustration 4-4. Specifically, we have added a title to the new exhibit to help the jurors understand why the graphic is important and help them remember this fact later in the trial. (Titles are further discussed later in this chapter.) In order to improve the graphic's readability we have reversed the color of the type and background in the two most important portions of the text.

The original deposition transcript, like this book, consists of a light background on which is placed dark text. There is a reason for this. Items that are designed to be read up close usually have dark print on a light (generally white) background. This format makes it easier for people to read books, newspapers, and deposition transcripts. This combination of light background and dark ink does not work as well when the reader is at a distance from the text. In this instance, it is far easier to read the text if it is reversed (i.e., light-colored text, usually white, surrounded by a dark-colored background, usually black). Reversed type has an additional advantage; since we do not see it all that often, this kind of printing is dramatic and immediately attracts the reader's attention. For these reasons, we chose to reverse the majority of the important text in Illustration 4-4.

The Third Rule of Time and Space

When important information requires it, never be afraid to use as much time and space as you need to make your point.

Some lawyers, after initially encountering the First and Second Rules, conclude that good trial graphics must *always* minimize time and space. This is *incorrect*. While you should never waste either resource, certain trial graphics effectively use the commodities of time and space themselves to argue or make a key point quite effectively. Consequently, the Third Rule of Time and Space recognizes that when information is important enough to really require it, you should never be afraid to use as much time and space as you need to make your point.

Let's look at an example.

One of the occupational hazards of doing what I do is that I often find myself wondering how I would display interesting information even when I am not looking at it for purposes of a case.[5] I once read about a dispute between the South Tahoe Public Utility District—or as it is also known, STPUD (honest, I did not make that up)—and various gasoline producers. The dispute centered on what concentration of methyl tertiary-butyl ether (MTBE) in drinking water adversely affected human health.

The material that I read (which was admittedly biased in favor of the gasoline producers) argued that the standards applied by STPUD were extreme and unduly restrictive. The author noted that the U.S. Environmental Protection Agency had concluded that the chemical posed no health risks to humans in concentrations of less than 40 parts per billion (ppb). The California Department of Health Services found that concentrations below 13 ppb posed no potential health dangers and concluded that concentrations below 3 ppb could not be reliably detected by any then known technology.

Consequently, the article argued, STPUD's proposed limit of 0.2 ppb (1/200th of the federal limits, 1/65th of the state limits, and 1/15th of what the scientists could even detect) bore no relationship to any established scientific data. The author then concluded by offering this ineffective table summarizing these disparities. (See Illustration 4-6.)

---

5. You do not need to remind me how sad this is; my family does so constantly.

Agency	Poses Health Risk At:	Not Measureable Below:
US EPA	40 ppb	3 ppb
CA DHS	13 ppb	3 ppb
STPUD	.2 ppb	3 ppb

ILLUSTRATION 4-6. This Table Is Unexciting

In my mind, this was definitely *not* the way to make an impact with this information. Instead, I would have invoked the Third Rule of Time and Space, allocated time and space to a point that mattered, and created a graphic that looked something like the one in Illustration 4-7.

Notice the dimensions of this trial graphic, specifically that the mockup calls for the final version to be nine and one half feet wide with considerable empty space between STPUD's standards and that of the other agencies. Does this graphic use a lot of space? Yes, absolutely so. Does it waste that space? No, it does not. The point of this graphic is to *show* how far apart the parties are or, if you were the spokesperson for the gas companies, how extreme STPUD's position is compared to that of the state and federal agencies. The use of large amounts of space highlights these differences and *shows* (shows, not tells) the extent of the disparity without having to use words. This is an instance in which a considerable amount of space is intentionally used to make a point; the space itself has become an important element of the argument.

OVERCOME THE RESTRICTIONS OF TIME AND SPACE

Information architects have accomplished something more often associated with theoretical physics or science fiction novels than with the courtroom. They have found ways to overcome the limitations of time and space.

The techniques information architects use do not involve traveling backward at the speed of light or anything so exciting. Instead, information architects overcome these limitations by using what they have learned about how the brain processes information. This knowledge allows them to "expand time" by increasing how long jurors will spend focusing on trial graphics and to "overcome the limitations of space" by compressing more relevant information into the four corners of a graphic and still have it make sense.

One of the simplest ways for a trial lawyer to overcome the limitations of time and space is to use pacing devices. These are simple tools; in fact, many lawyers instinctively rely on them without even realizing it. Pacing devices allow a lawyer to repeatedly reuse the same baseboard, adding a little bit more information to it each time, until in the end, the trial lawyer has created a powerful and relatively complex graphic without triggering the jurors' Yikes! Alarm (defined in Chapter 3).

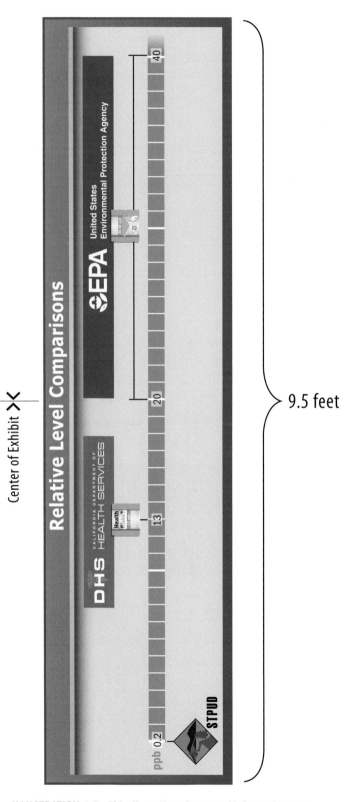

ILLUSTRATION 4-7. This Chart Uses Space to Make an Impact

Before we review pacing devices in detail, we must first understand how and why such tools work. Specifically, we need to appreciate the *interplay* of four important principles that I call (1) Selectavision, (2) the Answer Board Phenomenon, (3) the Billboard Principle, and (4) the Informational Honeymoon.

The Principles Underlying Pacing Devices

Selectavision. Three strange things happen when you reuse the same baseboard to present graphical information bit by bit to jurors. When you offer jurors the *first* bit of information, their brains focus on it. Then, when you add a *second* piece of information, the first piece of information becomes transparent in the jurors' minds, allowing them to focus on and study the second bit of information to the exclusion of everything else. This procedure (i.e., the process of information "appearing" when first offered and "disappearing" when new material appears) continues on until you have constructed your entire graphic. *Finally,* once your graphic is complete (i.e., you have added all of the parts), the viewer's brain, as if by magic, widens its perspective; all of the pieces that had previously disappeared reappear, and the viewer is able to see the information all at once in its entirety. I call this process Selectavision.

I realize that this process may sound confusing, so let's look at an example.

▼▼▼

We add our first bit of information to our baseboard. Here is what the graphic actually looks like:

We add our second bit of information. Here is what the graphic actually looks like:

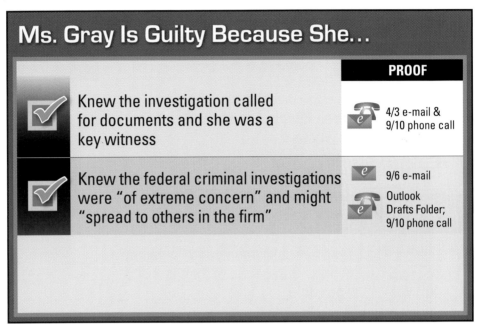

Now, here is what Selectavision allows the brain to "see" and focus on:

We add our final bit of information. Here is what the graphic actually looks like:

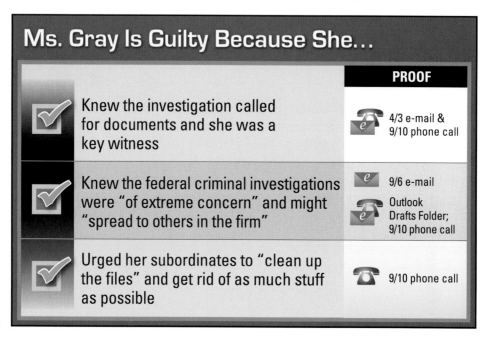

Here is what Selectavision allows the brain to sees and focus on first:

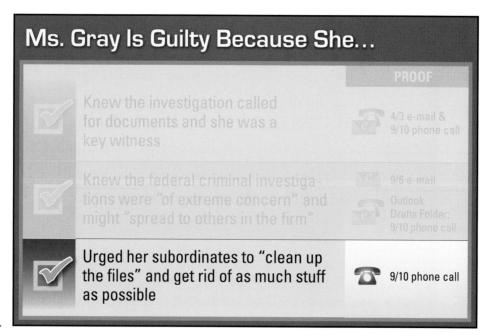

Once the brain understands the final addition to the graphic (this may take a second or less), the brain automatically turns off Selectavision, widens its perspective, and, for the first time, focuses on the graphic as a whole and connects all of the pieces. Here is what it sees.

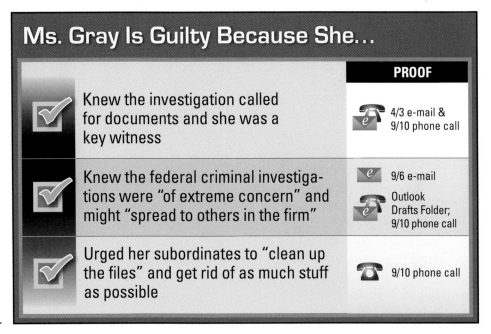

When my brother David was in college he was notorious for eating at very inexpensive (this was a polite way of saying "not very good") restaurants. Once when I asked him if he wanted to go someplace nicer (this was a polite way of saying "more expensive"), he responded, "Why should we? No matter how much it costs, the food all ends up in the same place."

Admittedly, since there is some logic in David's response, I suspect that more than a few readers viewing the previous graphics are wondering, "If the end result is the same, then why bother with all the extra steps?" The main reason is that jurors are likely to be overwhelmed if they see all of the information at once. Offering the same information step by step—breaking the whole into smaller, related bits—leads (some say "tricks") the brain into using Selectavision so that it can focus on a bit of information, get used to it, and understand that bit before having to do so again with the second bit, third bit, etc.

The Answer Board Phenomenon. Television game shows use two techniques that we should keep in mind when we design and use trial graphics. I collectively call these techniques the Answer Board Phenomenon. The first technique, a form of conditioning, is the "answer board" used to help keep the viewers focused on the game. The game show host uses the board as a central location from which to reveal answers to the show's questions one by one.

The viewers are quickly conditioned to rely on the board; after all, it is the only place they can go to get the answers. The more the viewers are conditioned to rely on the board, the more comfortable they become with its format and hopefully the more they trust the board and the information on it.

The same thing happens when you encourage jurors to repeatedly rely on a particular trial graphic. Jurors are less threatened and consequently are more open to learning when you bring them back to something with which they are already familiar, including a graphic that they have seen and relied on before. We explored one aspect of this when we discussed the process of encouraging jurors to compare concepts they encounter for the first time at trial with older, more familiar ones.

As we will see, pacing devices take advantage of this familiarity. The trial lawyer introduces a graphic to the jurors, gets them familiar with it, and over a period of time repeatedly brings the jurors back to this same graphic, adding something new each time. Because the graphic is something with which the jurors are already familiar, it takes less time and mental energy for the jurors to use the graphic a second, third, and fourth time, thereby hopefully increasing their comfort with the graphic and its contents.

The second technique you should consider taking away from television game shows is the rate at which their hosts reveal the answers on the answer boards. I do not know of any game that gives out all of the answers at once. Instead, the hosts reveal the information at a measured pace, with at least some period passing between the times that the answer board is used. A similar process occurs when we use pacing devices. You establish and condition the jury to accept the following dance steps: Show the jurors a graphic; get them interested in it; make your point; go away for awhile; come back to the graphic again; get the jury interested again; make your second point; go away for awhile; come back again; and repeat as often as necessary. I will show you how this works later in this chapter.

The Billboard Principle. People who design outdoor advertising adhere to something they call the Billboard Principle, which provides that a typical driver will spend no more than six seconds looking at a sign. During this short period, the driver must be able to visually latch on to the billboard, focus on it, comprehend the message, and avoid crashing. Because of this limitation, billboard designers have learned the importance of making a billboard "pop"; that is, the message must be carefully chosen and it must be clearly presented so that the viewer can get the point quickly and with minimal effort.

We need to keep this principle in mind when designing trial graphics. While I am not convinced that we are limited to six seconds (in other words, I think jurors are a slightly more captive audience and are willing, or forced, to give us a little more time than most drivers), the essence of the billboard principle is equally applicable in court. Trial graphics need to pop!

The Informational Honeymoon. Rufus Choate, the nineteenth-century lawyer and orator, once claimed, "The lawyer's vacation is the space between the question put to a witness and his answer." Personally, I think this is a bit extreme. I prefer my

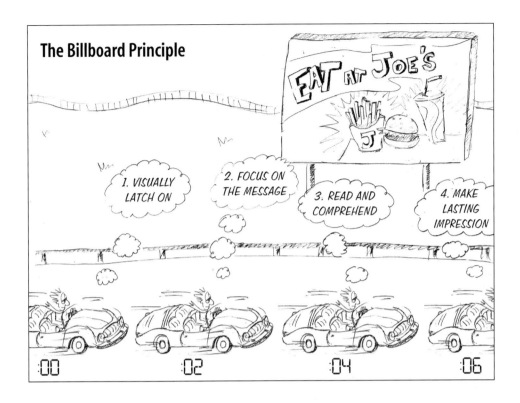

vacation to be the slightly longer space (actually it is more of a pause) immediately following each time that you display a trial graphic to the jury. I call this interval the Informational Honeymoon.

Human curiosity is such that jurors will generally give each trial graphic a brief "honeymoon" for a few moments after you show it to them. That is, whenever you present a new graphic, most jurors, even those who are otherwise uninterested in what is going on around them, will sit up and take notice. Some jurors will pay attention for a good long time. For others, this honeymoon may be short-lived. But, regardless of your jury's makeup, I can virtually guarantee that everyone in the jury box (unless they are asleep and then you have bigger problems) will initially pay attention and examine your graphic for some period of time.

Informational Honeymoons are not necessarily one-time affairs. If you do it right, you can get the jury to give you a series of such honeymoons, even with a single graphic. Each time that you bring the jurors back to a graphic by adding a new fact to it, you wake them up and get additional honeymoon time. It does not matter whether you are showing them a different graphic or merely adding something new to an already familiar one.

The phenomenon of multiple or sequential Informational Honeymoons from one graphic is extremely important and can provide a considerable advantage. Assume for a moment that the jury's interest is piqued each time you add something to a graphic (i.e., there is an Informational Honeymoon) and that each time this interest lasts for at least six seconds (the Billboard Principle). Further assume that at five different points in the trial you add new bits of information to the same baseboard. The jury will now give you a total of thirty seconds of attention, that is, six seconds on five different occasions. While it might not initially sound like it, thirty seconds of concentration is likely to have a significant impact on the jurors' ability to review and remember your graphic.

How Pacing Devices Work

Pacing devices rely on a combination of Selectavision, the Answer Board Phenomenon, the Billboard Principle, and the Informational Honeymoon. Pacing devices allow a trial lawyer to use the same basic graphic repeatedly, each time adding a little bit more information to it until he has created a powerful graphic with which the jurors have enjoyed a series of Informational Honeymoons.

Allan Odell intuitively understood the power of pacing devices. In 1925, he used this simple teaching technique to create one of the most influential advertising campaigns in American history. Odell's family owned a small company that manufactured a "brushless shaving cream" called Burma-Shave. Sales were minimal. Odell used $200 of his family's money to buy lumber from which he made hundreds of small red signs. The signs were identical in size and shape; each was a basic T or cross shape. The only difference was that Odell wrote different short phrases in white paint on each sign.

Odell then posted four to seven of these signs at hundred-yard intervals along the side of country roads. Collectively, these signs would contain an advertising jingle, with one line of the multipart rhyme on each of the signs. The final sign in the series was always the name of the sponsoring product, Burma-Shave. By today's standards, these jingles seem almost embarrassingly hokey. Some advertised Burma-Shave directly, for example:

Ben Met Anna
[One hundred yard gap]
Made a Hit
[One hundred yard gap]
Neglected Beard
[One hundred yard gap]
Ben & Anna Split
[One hundred yard gap]
Burma-Shave

and

My Job Is
Keeping Faces Clean
And Nobody Knows
The Stubble
I've Seen
Burma-Shave

Others contained some of the first public service announcements designed to encourage safe driving, for example:

A Man Who Drives

When He Is Drunk

Should Haul His Coffin

In His Trunk

Burma-Shave

Because each advertising jingle was different and was presented in a segmented form, the viewer had to look for and read each of the signs to understand the full message. People would actively seek out these advertisements. When they found the beginning of a new slogan, the drivers and passengers would often compete to see who could first guess the final line of the rhyme. The technique was so effective that Burma-Shave soon became the second largest company of its kind in the United States and the signs began appearing throughout the entire country. Over the next forty years Burma-Shave produced several hundred such slogans, which it placed to great success on tens of thousands of signs.

The Burma-Shave advertisements were an early form of pacing devices. Each series of signs relied on Selectavision, the Answer Board Phenomenon, the Billboard Principle, and serial Informational Honeymoons.

Specifically, Burma-Shave started with an identical baseboard, that is, the same size, shape, and color wooden sign upon which each of the answers was revealed; the readers are already familiar with it and are not required to expend as much mental energy as they would if the graphic were entirely new each time (the Answer Board Phenomenon). Burma-Shave used reversed text, white lettering on a red background. Burma-Shave added information to that board bit by bit as opposed to all at once (the Answer Board Phenomenon). Each time it added a bit of information, it got its readers to focus on that new information to the exclusion of everything else (Selectavision). Burma-Shave designed each added bit of information to pop, that is, quickly grab (the Billboard Principle) and hold (the Informational Honeymoon) the readers' attention. Because Burma-Shave used multiple boards, it got not just one Informational Honeymoon but anywhere from four to seven such opportunities, thereby multiplying the amount of time the viewers spent focusing on the signs.

Let's see how you might use the same principles at trial. The plaintiff in this example is married to a worker at a nuclear power plant. The plaintiff suffers from a form of cancer for which the only known cause is exposure to radiation and alleges that the radiation that caused her illness came from the plant. Specifically, she claims that her husband brought home one or more "radioactive fleas" (microscopic particles of radioactive material) and that she was exposed to this radiation while washing his clothes.

During discovery defendant determined that plaintiff, who was forty-three, had smoked two packs of cigarettes a day for twenty years. Among other by-products, cigarette smoke contains low but harmful levels of polonium, a radioactive isotope.

By smoking forty cigarettes a day for twenty years, plaintiff exposed herself to 38,000 millirems of radiation.

Defendant's expert also determined that the plaintiff had been exposed to several other sources of radiation in far greater amounts than could ever have come from the power plant. For example, an average person living forty-three years is exposed to 15,480 millirems of naturally occurring terrestrial radiation (i.e., radiation from the sun, rocks, and other sources). Additionally, the expert calculated that plaintiff had been exposed to 2,325 millirems of radiation from medical sources (medical X-rays, dental X-rays, etc.).

The expert's study reveals two other relevant and important exposure levels. First, based on daily inspections, plaintiff's husband had been exposed to a total of 387 millirems of radiation during all of his years working at the power plant, yet he shows no signs of cancer. Finally, the largest theoretical dosage of alleged off-site radiation to which plaintiff could have been exposed from a radioactive flea was *two* millirems.

What we want the jury to focus on is the huge disparity between 38,000 millirems of radiation caused by cigarette smoking and two millirems of radiation, the maximum theoretical dosage that could have come from the "fleas"—specifically, the 19,000-to-1 ratio of cigarette radiation to "flea" radiation. Secondarily, we want the jury to be aware of the other sources of radiation and how much greater these amounts are than the exposure allegedly coming from the power plant.

So, how do you show this information and keep it interesting to the jury? One possible way is to have the expert orally testify concerning these numbers and offer *no* graphics to assist the jury. The impact of such crucial information on the jury is likely to be limited.

A second alternative is to have that same expert witness orally testify and offer support for his numbers using a "show it all at once" chart like that in Illustration 4-8.

Millirem Dose	Exposure
38,000	20 years of smoking 2 packs of cigarettes a day
15,480	43 years of natural background radiation
2,325	43 years of medical radiation
387	Husband's exposure
2	Theoretical dose from ingesting largest off-site radiation source

ILLUSTRATION 4-8.
A "Show It All at Once" Chart

This technique is likely to be more effective than merely offering oral expert testimony. But, as we will see, there is a major problem with Illustration 4-8—it will produce only limited jury interest and it will not hold that interest for more than just a few seconds. Here is what is likely to happen.

Your action: You put up Illustration 4-8 with everything exposed at once.

The jury's reaction: They sit up and pay attention—this is the Informational Honeymoon.

Your action: You start talking about the first entry.

The jury's reaction: They spend the Informational Honeymoon looking at first entry, but they do not stop. They move on, reading the second, third, fourth, and fifth entries while you are still talking about the first entry.

Your action: You start talking about the second entry.

The jury's reaction: They have considerably less interest. They have already looked at the second entry and have only limited interest in what you have to say. Some of the jurors are zoning out; some have glazed eyes. They have already read all of the entries; why should they listen to what you have to say? It is old news. Other jurors whose Yikes! Alarm was triggered when you first showed them the graphic are already thinking about what they will have for lunch.

Your action: You see the glazed eyes of the jurors and realize that you have five more sections to talk about and the jury is zoning out. You swallow hard and wish you had not shown them the entire exhibit all at once.

Let's do it again, but this time we will use a series of pacing devices. The following hypothetical testimony takes place after your expert, Dr. AbdelAziz, has been qualified as an expert in all relevant areas.

Q. Dr. AbdelAziz, how old was Ms. Morris when she was diagnosed with cancer?

A. She was forty-three years old.

Q. Did you do any studies comparing the types and amounts of radiation that Ms. Morris was likely to have been exposed to during those forty-three years?

A. Yes, based on my various studies and the scientifically accepted work of others, I determined the types of radiation that Ms. Morris was likely to have been exposed to during those forty-three years and calculated the exposure that she would have likely received from each type of exposure.

Q. What did you find?

A. Well, I determined that she was likely to have been exposed to at least five different sources of radiation.

Q. What was the first source?

A. We know that plaintiff was a heavy smoker. She smoked an average of two packs of cigarettes each day for twenty years. When tobacco burns, it creates various radioactive isotopes that the smoker inhales directly into her lungs. Over the years, these radioactive isotopes can account for a substantial amount of radioactive exposure. I calculated that as a result of her smoking Ms. Morris exposed herself to 38,000 millirems of radiation.

As I said, I examined five types of exposure, the first one being cigarette smoking. To help the jury make some sense of this and to put these numbers into perspective, I have prepared this chart.

Defendant's attorney puts up the baseboard for the buildable chart that is about to follow.

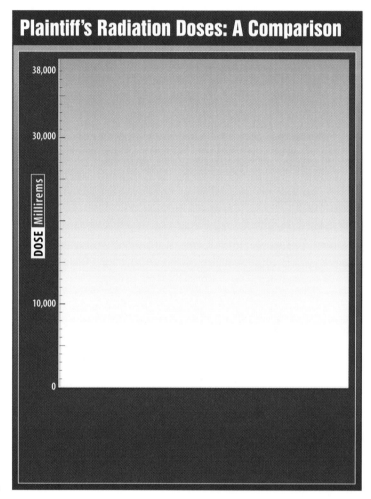

Ms. Morris exposed herself to 38,000 millirems of radiation by smoking two packs of cigarettes a day for twenty years. I recognize that it may be difficult to keep these numbers in perspective, so I have prepared a chart that shows the relative amounts of radioactive exposure from each of these sources. Here is the first entry on this chart. It sets 38,000 millirems as the height of the Empire State Building in New York.

The expert adds the first pacing device to the chart.

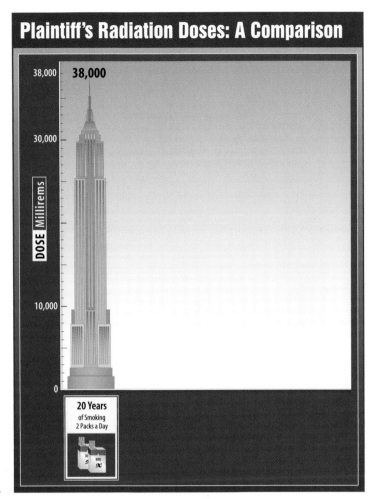

Note that you could immediately continue on with this examination or you can come back to it later. With pacing devices it is not important. You have got the baseboard and the first addition to the baseboard in front of the jurors—to whom this is now familiar ground.

Q. What was the second type of radiation that you examined?

A. It is what we call terrestrial radiation, or natural background radiation. This is the naturally occurring radiation that we are all exposed to just living on earth. Minor amounts of radiation come from natural sources like the sun, rocks, even some foods like bananas. The average person who lives forty-three years, as the plaintiff has, has been exposed to 15,480 millirems of terrestrial radiation. So going back to the chart, if 38,000 millirems of radiation from the plaintiff's smoking is equivalent to the entire Empire State Building, then the amount of radiation that she has been exposed to from terrestrial sources would be the same as about halfway up the building. It would look like this.

Expert puts up the second pacing device panel.

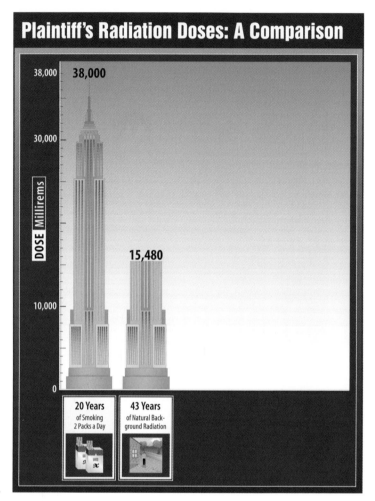

Note that again you can decide how long to wait for the next addition to the graphic. The baseboard has been established, you have set the pattern of putting material on it, and, in so doing, you are encouraging the jury to come back to an already familiar graphic.

Q. What was the third type of exposure that you examined?

A. That was medical radiation. Every time that we are X-rayed by a doctor or a dentist, we are exposed to a certain level of radiation. Based on Ms. Morris's medical records, I calculated that she was exposed to approximately 2,325 millirems of radiation. So, going back to the chart, this amount of radiation for this source would be equivalent to less than one tenth of the Empire State Building.

Expert puts up the third pacing device panel.

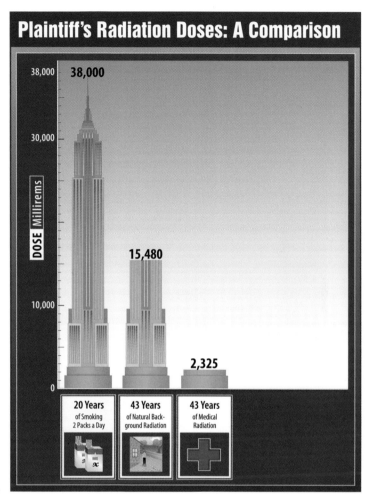

Q. By the way, does Mr. Morris, the plaintiff's husband, suffer from cancer?

A. He does not.

Q. What was the fourth type of radiation that you examined?

A. I checked the records of plaintiff's husband, Phillip, and found that based on daily measurements, he was exposed to a total of 387 millirems. That is about one one-hundredth of the amount that plaintiff exposed herself to by smoking. So using the same chart, when we graph this amount, we see that this would be equivalent to a small part of the foundation of the entire Empire State Building.

Expert puts up the fourth pacing device panel.

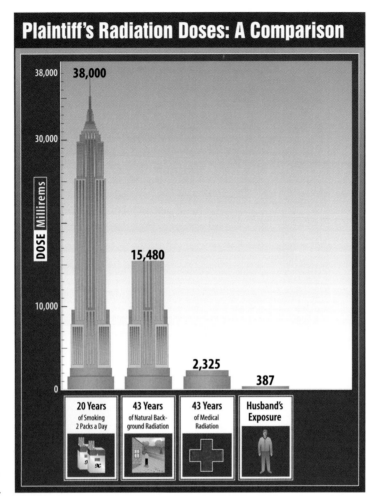

Q. What was the final type of exposure and how does it compare?

A. The final measurement was the maximum theoretical amount of radiation to which plaintiff could have been exposed if there was a leak. Now, bear in mind that I am not saying there was a leak. I am merely asking, "What if there were?" The answer is that if there were a leak, the maximum total exposure to plaintiff would have been 2 millirems. As this graph shows, plaintiff exposed herself to 19,000 times more radiation by smoking. Comparing the amount of exposure she had from twenty years of smoking to a possible amount of radiation from the plant is like comparing the Empire State Building to less than an inch.

Expert puts up the final pacing device.

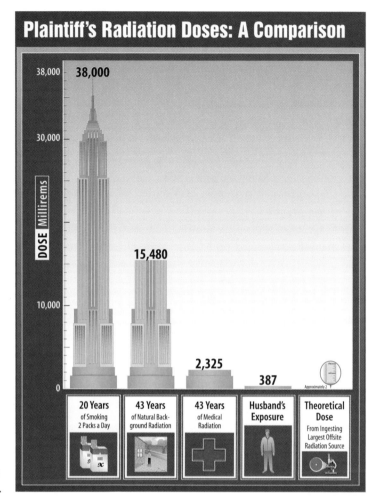

Let's examine what happened. The lawyer and the expert built the graphic bit by bit on a familiar background or baseboard. The graphic and the lawyer's comments encourage the jurors to come back to the same baseboard to refresh their interest in new information as well as in material presented earlier. The jurors have seen the baseboard before; familiarity has bred further familiarity; each time they view the board it is easier for them to comprehend the information placed there. Additionally, the graphic relates complex information with which most jurors have not had prior contact to real-world objects with which the jurors are familiar. This is a powerful trial graphic presented in a highly effective manner using simple pacing devices.

Whenever Possible, Use Symbols

I have observed an interesting incongruity. While we readily accept the notion that a picture is worth a thousand words, trial lawyers are nonetheless occasionally reluctant to put pictures in our graphics. More specifically, they too often fail to make good use of symbols.

Using symbols has at least four advantages. First, as powerful as words may be, they have their own limitations. Symbols are shorthand, powerful shorthand. Because symbols define a concept visually, a juror understands them immediately without excessive spoken or written words. Symbols can convey nuance that would otherwise require too many words to explain.

Second, symbols often invoke a wide range of conscious and subconscious associations that could not be expressed effectively in any other manner. When jurors encounter a symbol they do not see *just* a picture; instead, they incorporate all kinds of common experiences and understandings about the symbol into their analysis of the graphic.

Third, symbols are an economic way to communicate. They are economic because they allow you to put a lot more information into a limited space. For example, assume that you want to place a series of telephone calls on a timeline. Instead of repeatedly using the words "Telephone Call," which takes up considerable space, you could convey the same information using a universally understood symbol. (See Illustration 4-9.)

Finally, when you display the same symbol repeatedly, the cluster of symbols takes advantage of what is called the theory of small multiples, which we will discuss in greater detail after we look at this example.

I previously described in Chapter 3 a tragic criminal case that we worked on involving the killing of a young woman by two enormous and vicious dogs. The San Francisco district attorney prosecuted the owners of the dogs for second-degree murder. In an attempt to exonerate themselves, the defendants claimed that prior

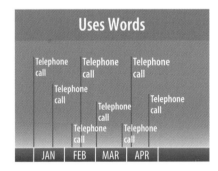
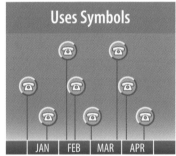

ILLUSTRATION 4-9. Symbols Are Economical

to the killing, their dogs had never before been violent. This was simply untrue. An investigation found dozens of violent incidents involving the dogs prior to the alleged second-degree murder.

To assist the prosecutor, we designed a buildable timeline for him to use throughout the trial. In this specific graphic, we began with the death of the victim, which we symbolized with a red triangle on a timeline. We deliberately chose this symbol since a triangle is often used to indicate caution or warning. (See Illustration 4-10.)

After describing the sad circumstance surrounding the killing represented by the red triangle symbol, the prosecutor then noted, "The defendants claim that this was the first time the dogs had been violent. The evidence will show that this is not true." The prosecutor then began describing each incident in *reverse order*. (See Illustration 4-11a.) He talked about an attack by one of the dogs a few days before the murder; then a similar attack a few weeks before that; then another two weeks before, etc. Eventually, he revealed and described thirty separate incidents, each represented by a red triangle with a number in it. (See Illustration 4-11b.)

This graphic derives much of its power from the use of a symbol—the red triangle. It takes advantage of each of the four benefits described above. Specifically, after first being introduced by the prosecutor, the symbol of the red triangle

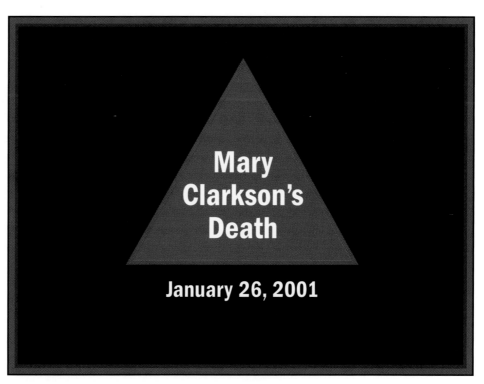

ILLUSTRATION 4-10. A Red Triangle Symbolizes Danger

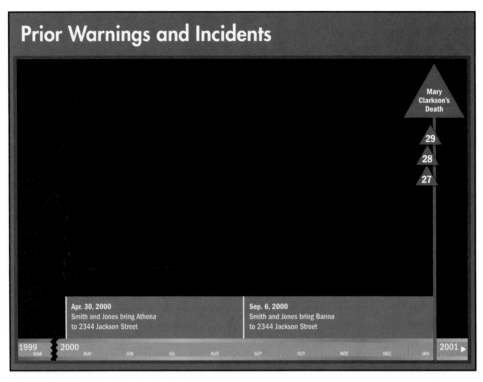

ILLUSTRATION 4-11a. The Symbol as Shorthand

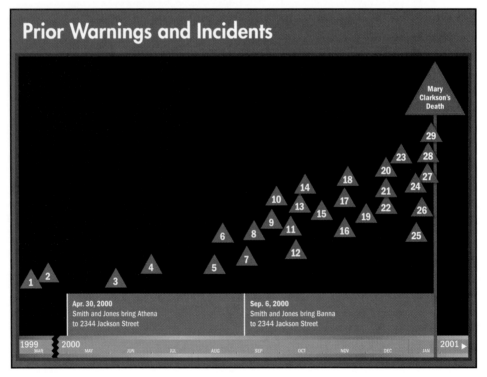

ILLUSTRATION 4-11b

becomes powerful shorthand—a symbol that conveys a concept simply and eloquently without using an excessive number of additional words. Not coincidently, we chose to introduce the symbol to the jurors in connection with the most severe of the incidents—the death of the victim. The severity of this incident became a part of the symbol's shorthand and was carried over in the jurors' minds each time they viewed the symbol.

Second, the symbol of the red triangle invokes a wide range of conscious and subconscious associations that could not be expressed effectively in any other manner. As noted above, most jurors (either consciously or not) are aware that the triangle has come to be associated with danger or warning. For example, the red triangular yield sign warns that a driver needs to be careful merging into a lane where there are likely to be faster-moving cars. This inherent understanding is reinforced by the prosecutor's brief explanation of what the symbol specifically means in this case.

Third, the red triangle symbol conveys this information economically. Like the symbol for the telephone in Illustration 4-9, we do not need an elaborate statement that takes up considerable room on the timeline; the symbol alone suffices.

Finally, the use of a cluster of red triangles takes advantage of the theory of small multiples, which, now that we have an example, I can describe.

The theory of small multiples provides that a collection or cluster of symbols can provide more information than the sum of the collection's individual parts. Said differently, symbols allow you to provide information on both an individual, or micro, level as well as with an overall, or macro, perspective.

Individually, each of the red triangles in Illustration 4-11a represents a distinct and separate event that occurred at a particular place, at a particular time, etc. The graphic can be used as a starting point to analyze each of these individual events in considerable detail.

Collectively, a large number of these symbols (particularly if the jury sees this collection all at once, as in Illustration 4-11b) alerts the jury not only to the individual events but also to something more. Exactly what that extra message is will vary from case to case depending upon the point you are attempting to make with the particular symbol. In the instance of the red triangles, the collection spoke profoundly to the fact that the defendants were not only lying but also that no reasonable person could have concluded anything other than that the dogs were dangerous.

Let's look at another example. I previously described a case in Chapter 3 where a city harassed a woman who wanted to legally use her home as a extended-care facility for people suffering from Alzheimer's disease. Over a period of five and a half weeks, the family was harassed over 250 times. Each of the icons in Illustration 4-12 represents an individual incident. Collectively, through the theory of small multiples, the graphic conveys an almost unimaginable level of harassment.

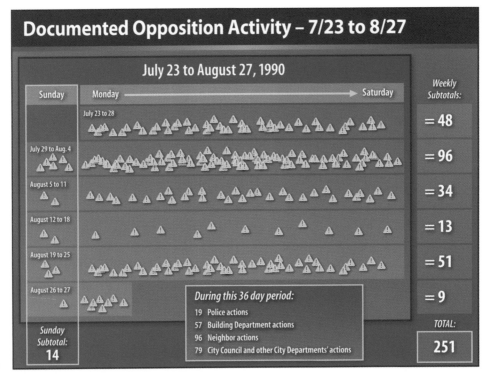

ILLUSTRATION 4-12. The Power of Small Multiples

Help Keep Jurors From Getting Lost

It is no fun getting lost; in fact, some of my most miserable memories involve driving around and around trying to figure out where I was. When they get lost, I know of two groups who just cannot ask for directions. The first are men, who stereotypically can't bring themselves to do so. The second are jurors, who are generally never given such an opportunity by the court. Because of this limitation, it is important for trial lawyers to provide jurors with tools to help keep them from getting lost.

In Chapter 7 we will examine various types of graphics that help keep jurors oriented, including timelines, checklists, and other organizing tools. In this chapter, I focus on two techniques that you can use with virtually any type of graphic to help provide directions to jurors—Titles and Icons.

TITLES HELP REMIND JURORS WHERE THEY ARE IN THE CASE

Many of the examples in this book and on the accompanying Visual Resource CD-ROM have titles. There is a reason for this. One of the easiest ways to pull even more meaning out of an exhibit is to give it a title. Titles provide important clues to jurors. The title bar (i.e., the space at the top of the exhibit) is often the first and last place that many jurors will concentrate their efforts.

Titles enhance a trial graphic in at least three ways. First, a carefully chosen title tells the viewer exactly why a particular graphic is important. Second, the title conveys this information quickly and in a way that helps the exhibit pop. Finally, titles provide reading material to bored jurors when their interest is wandering. When they get bored, many jurors will scan the courtroom for something to catch their attention, something of interest that they can read even if it is for only a few seconds. If you are the kind of lawyer who prints your key graphics on boards and then "just happens" to leave these graphics out in plain view leaning up against the podium or counsel table during trial, the jurors will often focus their waning attention on the titles of these materials even when what is then being discussed in court has nothing to do with that particular graphic.

Lawyers usually commit two mistakes with respect to titles. First, lawyers tend to ignore them. They either forget to put titles on their own exhibits, which is a missed opportunity to advocate a position, or they fail to read and think about the titles on their opposing counsel's exhibits, which provides the other side with an unopposed opportunity to advocate a position. Don't make this mistake; pay attention to titles, both on your exhibits and on your opponent's exhibits.

The second mistake that lawyers make is that they put unhelpful titles on their exhibits. Here is an example. Assume that you have a case where water is permeating through the wall of a building, causing severe damage to the structure. During discovery, you found a "hot doc" in which one of the engineers responsible for designing the building warned the general contractor that leaking might someday be a problem.

Illustration 4-13a is an exhibit designed to highlight the engineer's conclusions, which obviously helps your case. For this example, we deliberately have not included a title.

Now it is up to you to pick an appropriate title. Let's look at three options. The most obvious is to simply use the name of the case as the graphic title: "Cho vs. Lonnie & Son Construction." This is not a good choice, because using the name of the case is not helpful. The jury has been sitting in the box for two weeks earning $5.00 per day, paying twice that amount for lunch and parking. They know the name of the case. You know the name of the case. The judge knows the name of the case. You do not need to waste precious space highlighting the name of the case. Weeks later, if any jurors come back and look at this graphic on their own, the title will not tell them why this document is important. In short, this title is a complete waste because it focuses on something about which none of your jurors need or want to be reminded.

Another option is to put the trial exhibit number and a brief description of the document in the title, such as "Trial Exhibit 4: Engineering Report." This is better than using the case name, but it is far from great. At least this second title option will help *you* identify what the exhibit is. But the title really does not do much more than that. Would you ever consider just giving your exhibit list to the jury and then telling them to figure out what the case was about based upon your neutral description of the potential exhibits? Of course not. So why waste important space with this type of title?

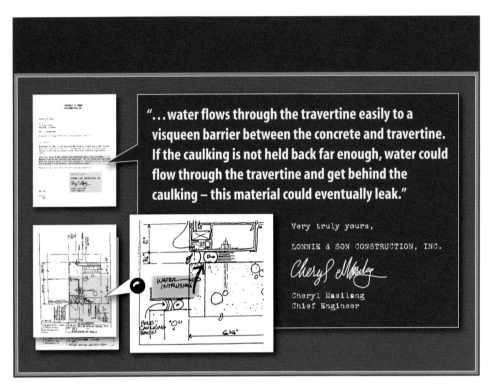

ILLUSTRATION 4-13a. This Exhibit Needs a Title

A third title option is to use a direct quotation from the document itself: "'This Material Could Eventually Leak . . .' Cheryl Masilang, Chief Engineer." Of the three options, this is the best. It makes the significance of the exhibit very clear. Even weeks after you use this exhibit, it will remind the jurors exactly why the exhibit was important, the point you made with it, and why it is so important for them to remember this exhibit during deliberations. Illustration 4-13b shows the graphic again, but this time with our third option as the title.

Our clients will commonly ask us: "Don't you get in trouble with titles that are too argumentative?" This is a legitimate question, and the answer is "Yes." At the same time, there are certain tips that can maximize the effectiveness of your titles and minimize the possibility that the court will find the titles improperly argumentative.

Title tip one: Do not unduly censor yourself. Argument is permitted in only one place in a trial—closing. Some lawyers assume that because something is "effective" it must be argumentative. Unfortunately, this happens sufficiently often that some lawyers get gun shy. That is, they subconsciously assume that effectiveness may draw an objection. So they self-censor—or at least they pull too far back. Don't do this. Or at least, don't do this without first thinking very carefully.

Title tip two: Whenever possible, take the title from the document itself. Let's take the title "This Material Could Eventually Leak . . ." in Illustration 4-13b and the title "I Don't Think That They Defrauded Us. . . ." in Illustration 4-4. For the

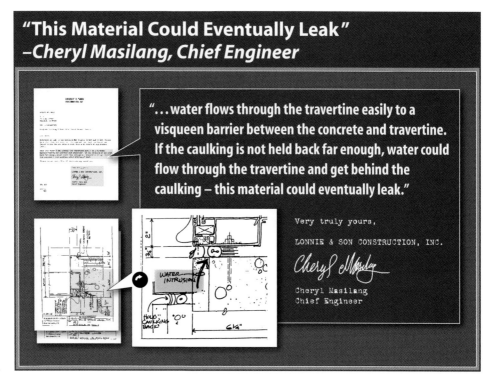

ILLUSTRATION 4-13b. The Same Exhibit With an Effective Title

reasons noted above, these are extremely effective titles. I would strongly argue (and in fact have argued) that titles like these are not argumentative. In both instances, the title merely quotes something that is in an otherwise admissible document. If the document is admissible (which it needs to be or you are wasting your money having an artist graphically highlight it), then there is no legitimate reason to prohibit the use of the title such as this. While I obviously do not know the law in every jurisdiction, there is logic to this argument and it has been very successful in cases on which we have worked.

Title tip three: Titles posed in the form of a relevant question generally are not found to be objectionable. Take a look at the graphic in Illustration 4-14.

The title of this trial graphic is in the form of a question. On the surface the question is a neutral one. The question deals with an issue that is relevant to the case and helps orient the jury. Once jurors develop an answer, they are instinctively reminded of it every time they see the question.

Title tip four: Even if the title is argumentative, don't worry too much. The problem can be fixed relatively easily, or you can hold the graphic back and use it later in closing argument.

What do you do if the court says that your graphic is too argumentative for opening or for your case-in-chief? The simplest thing is to offer to cover up the title. This can be done very easily by (1) merely covering the title with a strip of opaque paper; (2) having the person who printed the board prepare a blank strip

ILLUSTRATION 4-14. Is the Title of This Graphic Argumentative? I Don't Think So.

that you can add over the original title, or (3) having the person who printed the poster prepare a strip with an alternative, nonargumentative title on it. These solutions work well if the exhibit is used in opening or during witness testimony. They have the added advantage that you can often take these strips off during closing argument with a flourish, thereby further reinforcing your key point.

ICONS HELP CONNECT TWO OR MORE GRAPHICS TOGETHER

Several years ago, a clothing manufacturer came up with a brilliant idea of how to help young children learn how to get dressed by themselves in clothes that actually matched. The manufacturer stitched small versions of various animals on the clothing. The child understood that so long as he wore a pair of pants and a shirt with the same animal icon embossed on it, the outfit would match. So, for example, the child would look very natty if he chose to wear a pair of pants with a lion icon on it and a shirt with that same icon. There was no such assurance if he matched a zebra-embossed shirt with a panda-embossed pair of pants.

By now, you should have noticed that many of the graphics in this book include small illustrations, usually in the upper left corner. These illustrations, which are called icons, serve more than just an aesthetic purpose; they are intended to be used (consciously or otherwise) by the jurors to help connect different graphics and different portions of your overall case.

ILLUSTRATION 4-15. Using Icons to Link Graphics

Recall Illustration 4-11b, the timeline using a series of red triangles in the case involving the killing of a young woman by a pair of vicious dogs. On the timeline, each triangle was numbered to represent a specific incident. We created a series of other graphics that linked each numbered icon to a more detailed analysis of what happened. (See Illustration 4-15.)

Avoid Chartjunk

Information architect Edward Tufte is a purist. He correctly insists that every line, every illustration, every element of a graphic must serve a particular purpose. Anything in the graphic that does not serve a specific purpose detracts from the graphic and should be considered what Tufte calls chartjunk.

If there is such a thing as malpractice for an information architect, it is chartjunk. Unfortunately, there is an increasing amount of it in the courtroom. Much of this is due to two factors. First, trial lawyers do not take adequate time to go through the process of creating and refining their trial graphics. Second, inexpensive computer programs, clip-art libraries, and printers that can produce hundreds of different colors permit lawyers to create some truly bad trial graphics. Chartjunk can lead to a statement such as this: "Mr. Witness, please explain the significance in Graph 437 of this chartreuse bar next to the peppermint circles, just below this drawing of the scales of justice." May such words never pass your lips.

Illustration 4-16a shows one of the best examples of chartjunk and, hence, one of the worst trial graphics that I have come across. *We did not create this graphic.* The party that did ended up losing over $110 million dollars to our client in this case. Did the graphic alone cause the defendant to lose this case? Of course not! But the graphic is evidence of a condition that very well may have caused the loss. The graphic is evidence that the lawyer and witness did not take the time or did not care to help make the material understandable to the jury. A teacher who cared about his students would not use such a graphic. Why should a trial lawyer?

Let's talk about the things that are wrong with this graphic from an information architecture perspective. Actually, there are a lot of things that are wrong, but let's focus on six such elements.

First, note the title. (See Illustration 4-16b.) Actually, I am not sure how much of what is in the title bar is intended to be the title. To the extent that the title is the name of the case, "SmithMade v. SignCo," this is a useless title and a waste of key informational real estate. To the extent that the title is supposed to be all of the material in the title bar, none of this information is understandable. Additionally, even if the lawyer tells the jury what this information means, it is not likely to be the kind of material that the jury will remember weeks later.

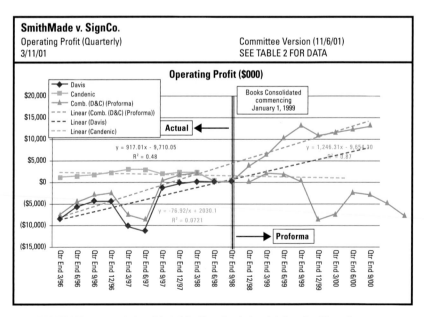

IILLUSTRATION 4-16a. A Graphic With Chartjunk (and Other Problems)

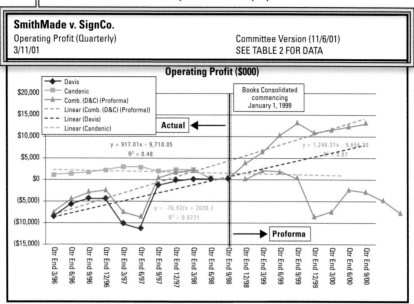

ILLUSTRATION 4-16b

Second, part of the title bar in this graphic instructs the viewer to "See Table 2 for Data." (See Illustration 4-16c). There is no explanation as to what Table 2 is or why the data is important. In fact, during the entire trial in which this graphic was used, no one ever discussed or offered any evidence about anything called "Table 2."

Third, the graphic uses a key (See Illustration 4-16d.). While there is nothing per se wrong about a key, you should try to avoid using them when possible. When you need to use a key, it should be intuitive and user-friendly. In this graphic, there is no intuitive connection between "Davis" and a red line with a diamond or between "Candenic" and a green line with a square. The best keys are ones that somehow connect the symbol used in the key with the information being displayed in the trial graphic. This connection reduces the number of times that viewers have to divert their attention from the data to the key.

Fourth, imagine seeing this material appear all at once. (See Illustration 4-16e.) It is virtually impossible for such a graphic not to trigger each and every juror's Yikes! Alarm. There is no way for anyone to look at this material and not immediately feel the dread of being overwhelmed. At a minimum this dread will delay and more likely completely prevent the jurors from learning anything from this graphic.

Fifth, there are various statistical formulas interspersed in this graphic. (See Illustration 4-16f.) What does "$y = 917.01x - 9,710.05$" mean? For most jurors, the answer is, "Nothing!" The formula unnecessarily takes up space. Additionally, if the multicolor lines does not trigger the jury's Yikes! Alarm, I guarantee "$y = 917.01x - 9,710.05$" will!

Where is Table 2? Flipping back and forth between Table 2 and this graph is a waste of time.

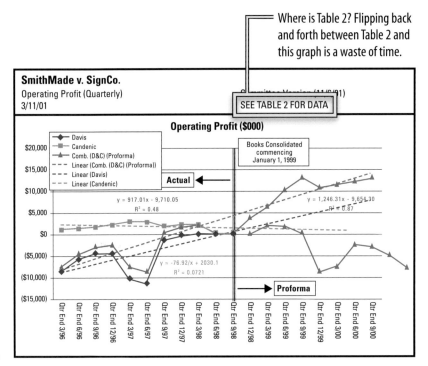

SEE TABLE 2 FOR DATA

ILLUSTRATION 4-16c

This key is not very user friendly. The symbols are difficult to read and there is no connection between the symbols and what they represent.

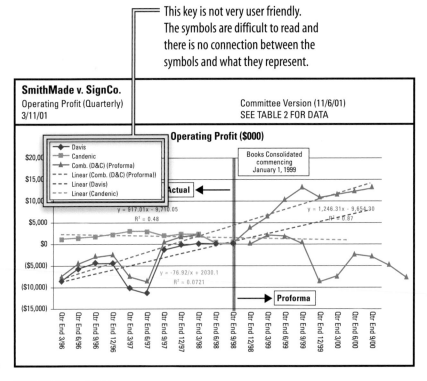

ILLUSTRATION 4-16d

Close your eyes for 5 seconds and then reopen them while looking at this chart…
You have just recreated the process of seeing this entire graphic at one time.
The effect is an overwhelming trigger of the "Yikes Alarm."

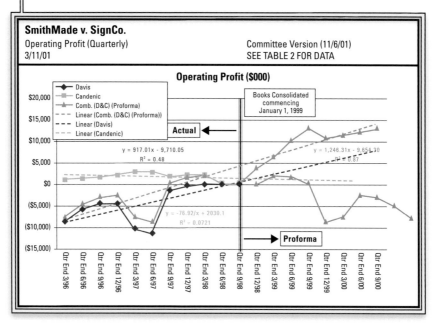

ILLUSTRATION 4-16e

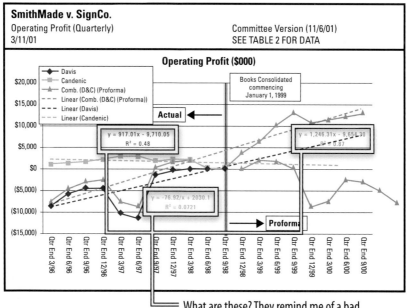

What are these? They remind me of a bad
dream where you are in front of an entire
math class and asked to solve a problem
you cannot even begin to understand.

ILLUSTRATION 4-16f

Finally, there is nothing intuitive or familiar about this graphic. There is nothing in the graphic that allows jurors to answer the question "Compared to what?" There is nothing that connects the data in the graphic to anything that jurors understand or have otherwise experienced in the real world.

Convey Material Honestly

If a picture is worth a thousand words, then the last thing you want to do is to get caught using a thousand untrue or false ones. As I noted at the outset of this chapter, successful informational architects must make sure that they convey information to their target audience in a simple *and* honest manner. Be warned: Honesty without simplicity wastes the jurors' time because they will not understand the material. Simplicity without honesty will more likely than not eventually bite you in your backside. If not fatal, such bites will take a long, long time to heal—longer than you may have at trial.

There is no excuse for using misleading or distorted material. I don't care how beautiful the graphic may be or how elegantly simple it makes your point. You are better off to have not used anything than to have been caught using something that is not honest.

In case honesty itself is not its own reward, there is another practical reason for your graphics to be honest. Andrew Spingler calls this the halo effect. The party that the jurors perceive as being fair is seen as wearing a metaphorical angel's halo. This halo and the benefits that come from it continue on throughout the entire trial, providing the lawyer with an intangible but powerful advantage.

Chapter **5**

Evidence

Evidence Rules for Trial Graphics and Other Persuasion Tools

What follows is *not* your traditional review of evidence law. Someone far smarter than I has already taught you the basics or, at a minimum, where to go to find answers to most of your evidentiary questions.

This chapter deals with certain practical issues that affect a trial lawyer's ability to use graphics and other persuasion tools at trial. Reading it will undoubtedly cause many evidence professors to shudder since it does not contain a single case or statutory citation and because it oversimplifies (some might even argue that it ignores) a massive body of important case law. This is all true. But it is true for two good reasons. First, such an analysis is clearly beyond the scope of this book. Second, and more important, this chapter focuses on principles that are *not* formally codified but nonetheless have a very real effect on what you can and cannot do in court. As such, you need to be aware of them as much as you need to know the section numbers of key provisions of your jurisdiction's official evidence code.

Categories of Persuasion Tools

Let's start with some basic definitions.

Trial lawyers often refer to anything that they show, say, argue, or otherwise use in court as "evidence." This is too broad a definition. Instead, I refer to this hodgepodge of material as "persuasion tools" and specifically save the word "evidence" to describe a far narrower subset of these tools.

Persuasion tools can be divided into two broad categories: (1) those tools that are *not* formally admitted into evidence and (2) those that are. (See Illustration 5-1.)

The first category (i.e., those that are *not* formally admitted into evidence) contains teaching tools that lawyers most often describe as "being offered for illustrative purposes only." Lawyers use these tools to help judges and jurors understand live testimony, other evidence, and arguments. Illustrative tools (which can include graphics, models, etc.) are *not* themselves facts and, therefore, not admitted into evidence. They are more like study guides for the facts.

ILLUSTRATION 5-1

The second category contains the facts, which get this designation because the court has formally admitted each of them into evidence. While substantive evidence can be used as a teaching tool, it is also something far more—it is an actual manifestation (rather than a mere illustration) of the "truth."

Obviously there will be conflicting versions of the truth, and it is up to the jurors to consider which ones they will ultimately accept. But that is exactly the point. The jurors consider these persuasion tools as evidence when they retire to deliberate. Technically, jurors do not have the same opportunity with material offered for illustrative purposes only.

Evidence itself can be divided into oral evidence and tangible evidence. This book does not examine the art of introducing oral evidence. There are three types of tangible evidence: real evidence, documentary evidence, and demonstrative evidence. (See Illustration 5-2.)

Real evidence is, as its very name states, the real thing. It is the actual gun used in the holdup, the very tire that was improperly manufactured and blew out while moving at a high speed, etc.

Documentary evidence includes letters, contracts, and other written or printed materials. A very strong case can be made that documentary evidence is really just a special form of real evidence (e.g., the "real" contract signed by parties). Nevertheless, I treat documentary evidence as its own subcategory because of certain distinct rules (the best-evidence rule, hearsay, etc.) that commonly apply to documents but often do not apply to other items we traditionally consider real evidence.

Demonstrative evidence is *admissible* material used to illustrate a witness's testimony or make other evidence more comprehensible to jurors. It can include diagrams, models, drawings, charts, and graphs.

If demonstrative evidence sounds a lot like material offered for illustrative purposes, that is because there is often considerable overlap and, with only one exception, no bright-line test to distinguish between the two. The distinguishing characteristic is somewhat obvious—demonstrative evidence is formally admitted by the court into evidence and illustrative tools are not.

I realize that the distinction that I have drawn between demonstrative evidence and illustrative tools appears to be outcome driven. It is, and it is in the real world as well.

I was counsel in a large case where the judge ordered all lawyers to appear in her courtroom once a month for over a year to provide her with case status reports. These appearances always seemed to be late in the afternoon and usually involved a lot of sitting around waiting.

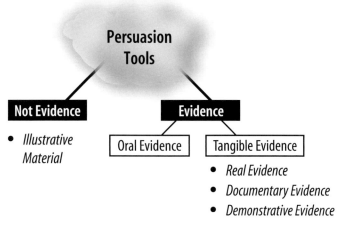

ILLUSTRATION 5-2

Because I was there so regularly and usually had time to kill, I soon became familiar with the general comings and goings in the courtroom. One thing that I specifically noticed was a collection of enlarged graphics mounted on plastic-foam boards in the very back, behind where the spectators would usually sit. The clerk had neatly stacked these boards on end and leaned them against a filing cabinet—very similar to the way you see street vendors display posters for sale.

I recognized that the boards dealt with topics that had been tried in that courtroom over the preceding months. Every few weeks, the collection would change, with new boards appearing and others disappearing.

One afternoon, while we were waiting for the judge, I asked the clerk, "What are all those boards back there?"

"Oh, those," replied the clerk, "those are what I call the 'bone pile.' It is where all the things that you lawyers say are 'being offered for illustrative purposes only' seem to end up after a trial."

The clerk explained that as far as she could see, trial graphics and other similar material that lawyers used in court ended up in one of two places. Some would go with the jurors into the jury room where jurors used them during deliberations. Other material, that which the lawyers usually told the judge were being offered "for illustrative purposes only," never left the courtroom itself and stayed there until they were disposed of.

The clerk went on to explain that when a case was over, she would collect the materials that were admitted into evidence from the room where the jury deliberated and assemble them as part of the official trial record. As for the illustrative material (those items that never left the courtroom), people on the winning side were usually too excited to collect their graphics as they ran off to celebrate. People on the losing side left these graphics behind because they never wanted to see them again. Consequently, after trial, material used "for illustrative purposes only" went into the bone pile at the back of the courtroom and stayed there until the clerk took some of the pieces home for her kids to use in elementary school art or science fair projects.

When I heard this, I realized that the clerk had found a wonderful way to differentiate between the two main types of persuasion tools. As the clerk correctly observed, illustrative tools usually go to the bone pile. Persuasion tools offered as substantive evidence usually end their days more gloriously than their "for illustrative purposes only" cousins. Jurors take this evidence into deliberations with them. After the verdict, the clerk collects all of this evidence and preserves it as part of the official trial record. If the case is appealed from the trial court, this record, including the persuasion tools admitted as substantive evidence, goes to the court of appeal. (See Illustration 5-3.)

Having noted this difference, let me quickly point out that as a practical matter, this distinction may be meaningless when it comes to persuading juries. To say that illustrative material is not evidence is like saying that opening statements and closing arguments are not evidence. While that is true, well-designed illustrative material, like well-delivered opening statements and closing arguments, stick with the jurors and have an impact on them during deliberations.

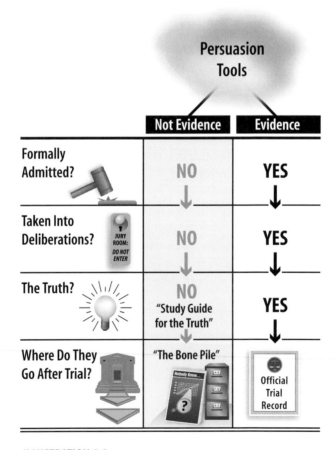

ILLUSTRATION 5-3

In fact, in my mind, persuasion tools offered for illustrative purposes only are often far more powerful and persuasive than actual admitted evidence. That is because there are fewer restrictions on what counsel can put into illustrative material; consequently, an imaginative lawyer can be creative in designing and using these tools at trial.

Yes, it is true that illustrative material does not physically retire with the jury into formal deliberations. But the memory of such well-designed illustrative material has an impact on the way jurors think about the case. For this reason, I often smile to myself when counsel says to the court, "This is *merely* being offered for illustrative purposes." There should be nothing "merely" about your illustrative material—this material should create a lasting impact.

This book focuses on (1) material offered for illustrative purposes and (2) demonstrative evidence. There is a reason for this. These are the only persuasion tools that counsel is expressly permitted to "create" for trial. By definition, trial lawyers do not create real or documentary evidence for trial. These items were originally created for purposes separate from what goes on in court. For example, the company that manufactured the tire that exploded on the freeway created that object for use as a car tire, not a jury exhibit. The people who drafted and signed the contract did so to facilitate a deal, not to illustrate at trial how that commercial transaction was supposed to work.

By contrast, lawyers routinely create demonstrative evidence and illustrative tools for trial. In fact, but for the trial, such material would never likely exist. The ability to effectively design and use this material separates trial lawyers who are creative from those who are not. This material makes the difference between a jury understanding a point and not.

Standards of Usability: The Purpose Continuum

Judges apply different standards of usability depending on the purpose for which you offer the persuasion tool. To illustrate this, let's create what we will call the purpose continuum.

As you move up the purpose continuum, the court and trial lawyer increasingly value the persuasion tool for its "truth." The material goes from being *argument about the truth* (illustrative graphics used to make an argument in closing), to *illustrations of the truth* (illustrative graphics the lawyer plans on using with her witnesses during their testimony or in her opening as a "road map" to such testimony), to finally being *actual manifestations of the truth* (substantive evidence the trial lawyer plans on offering and having admitted into the official record). (See Illustration 5-4.)

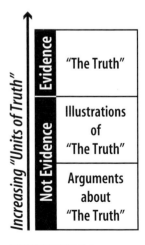

ILLUSTRATION 5-4.
The Purpose Continuum

Not surprisingly, just as the perceived value of the persuasion tool increases (as measured in some hypothetical "units of truth"), so do the number of preconditions that you must meet before the judge will allow you to use the material in court.

At a minimum, *every* persuasion tool regardless of where it falls on the purpose continuum must meet three requirements in order for it to be used for *any* purpose at trial. First, the persuasion tool cannot violate any substantive rules of evidence. Second, the persuasion tool must contain relevant information. Third, the court must find the persuasion tool to be sufficiently fair and accurate. Persuasion tools that lawyers offer as substantive evidence (i.e., material at the top of the purpose continuum) must also meet a fourth criteria. In order to be admissible, such material must meet certain basic evidentiary foundational requirements. (See Illustration 5-5.)

Let's examine these requirements in greater detail.

PERSUASION TOOLS MUST NOT VIOLATE
ANY SUBSTANTIVE RULE OF EVIDENCE

Regardless of how you plan on using it, a persuasion tool cannot violate any of the substantive rules of evidence. This is a pretty obvious limitation. Blowing up and highlighting a document that contains inadmissible hearsay does not make the material any more admissible than if it were left alone in its original form. Likewise, no matter how beautiful you make your tutorial graphics, if your jurisdiction prohibits using existence of insurance for purposes of establishing liability (or any other relatively clear rule of evidence), your efforts will not make such information admissible. This is common sense—enough said about this first evidentiary screen, which is equally applicable to all persuasion tools, regardless of where they falls on the purpose continuum. (See Illustration 5-5.)

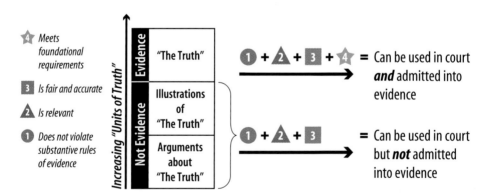

ILLUSTRATION 5-5. Can Your Persuasion Tool Be Used in Court? Is It Admissible Into Evidence?

PERSUASION TOOLS MUST BE RELEVANT

The second evidentiary requirement is relevance. (See Illustration 5-5.) Simply put, the content of your persuasion tool must bear some logical relationship to the case. Many lay people rightfully fail to see how this is much of a requirement. After all, if your trial material does not have a logical connection to the case, why would you even bother creating it?

From a legal standpoint, something is relevant if it has a tendency ("no matter how small," my evidence professor would stress) to make an issue that matters in the case (i.e., a material issue) more or less likely.

I have a friend who used to spend his summers working as an archery instructor in a camp for preteen boys. Nerves of steel, that guy. According to him, the archery range was one of the most popular places at the camp. It was also one of the most dangerous. Since most of the boys thought that being male was the only necessary prerequisite for archery, none of them would wait very long to listen to instructions. Because of the campers' short attention span, my friend said that he stressed two (and only two) rules.

First rule: In order to prevent bodily injury, he would tell his campers, "You have been assigned a target, always aim at it! That is the only target that matters. Do not aim at anything that is not a target and do not aim at a target that is not yours!"

Second rule: In order to prevent ego injury (a fate far worse for most preteen boys than bodily injury), my friend would tell the campers, "It does not matter if you hit the bull's eye; hitting your target *anywhere* is good enough!"

These two rules are applicable to the two most important concepts of relevance. First, "you have been assigned a target"—the issues that matter are those necessary to establish the prima facie elements of your case. These are the "material" issues; always aim at them. Do not aim at anything that does not matter (i.e., at immaterial issues). Second, do not worry about hitting the bull's eye. Your persuasion tool is relevant so long as it hits *any* part of your target.

Based on this, the court should assess relevance by applying a binary standard: Something either is relevant or it is not. One would think that if the contents of a document are found to be relevant, they should be relevant for *all* purposes anywhere along the purpose continuum. As a practical matter—not a legal matter, but as an observed practical matter—this is not always the case.

The farther up you go on the purpose continuum, the more concerned judges are likely to be and the more likely they are to sustain relevancy objections. In other words, what might pass the relevance test if it were being used only as an illustrative tool may not pass if the content is being introduced as substantive evidence.

PERSUASION TOOLS MUST BE GENERALLY FAIR AND ACCURATE

The third evidentiary screen applicable to all exhibits regardless of where they fall along the purpose continuum is that of accuracy. (See Illustration 5-5.) The trial graphic must be fair and accurate. Another way of making this point is to say that a court has the right (I would argue, has the duty) to exclude the use of any graphic that is confusing, misleading, or just plain inaccurate.

Does this mean that every single persuasion tool must be completely accurate in order for you to use it? I guess that depends on the answer to two questions: (1) What do you mean by "completely accurate?" and (2) For what purpose do you intend to use the exhibit?

If by "completely accurate" you mean that the facts have to be universally accepted before they can be used, then the answer is "No." In virtually every case, the most important "facts" are always contested. The only facts that are uncontested are those to which the parties have stipulated or those which the court must take judicial notice.

Merely because something is disputed does not mean that the exhibit should be excluded. So, for example, your opposing counsel may not like and may strongly disagree with the content of your graphic. But that does not automatically give her the right to prevent you from using it. Similarly, an illustrative exhibit used in argument that sets forth the facts as you see them should not be excluded merely because your opponent sees the facts differently.

The purpose to which you put your persuasion tool will affect the degree to which the court will require that a persuasion tool be "accurate." The court will generally require a greater degree of fairness and accuracy as you move up the purpose continuum. The threshold will be lower for persuasion tools offered for illustrative purposes in closing argument and higher when the lawyer offers the item as substantive evidence.

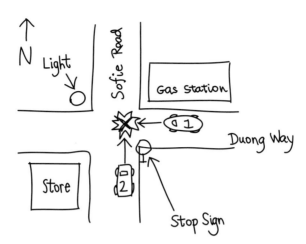

ILLUSTRATION 5-6. Rough, but Probably Permissible

If you want to show the jurors something for illustrative purposes only, courts rarely require that your material be exactly to scale or completely accurate. It is very likely that a court would permit jurors to see a sketch as basic as Illustration 5-6 to help illustrate the relative location or important features of a particular intersection.

Likewise, minor inaccuracies in proffered substantive evidence will generally not render such material inadmissible. It is not always possible, nor is it always necessary, for things to be 100 percent accurate in order for them to be of value to a jury. "Being of value to the jury" is often a key judicial consideration in determining whether to allow a trial lawyer to use a particular persuasion tool at trial.

The court usually concludes that claims of minor inaccuracies by your opposing counsel go to the *weight* of the proffered evidence, not its admissibility. If proffered evidence meets a certain threshold (the exact parameters of which only your particular court can determine), then the court is likely to admit the evidence and allow a party to use it subject to a limiting instruction and/or cross-examination by opposing counsel. This allows the jurors to decide for themselves how much they want to rely on a particular piece of evidence. Such a philosophy reflects the court's recognition that nothing is perfect and demonstrates judicial trust of the jurors' common sense.

TO BE ADMISSIBLE AS EVIDENCE, PERSUASION TOOLS MUST ALSO MEET FOUNDATIONAL REQUIREMENTS

As you keep moving up the purpose continuum, you eventually enter the region reserved for substantive evidence. In order to use such material, the court will generally require that your persuasion tool pass through a fourth screen; that is, it must meet certain basic foundational requirements. (See Illustration 5-5.)

The court imposes this fourth screen in order to increase the chances that such material is reliable. For example, let's assume that you have prepared a chart that summarizes considerable data. You want the court to admit this chart as substantive evidence. Before the court will do so, it will initially require that your chart pass the first three screens; that is, the chart (1) does not violate any substantive evidentiary law, (2) is relevant, and (3) is generally fair and accurate. Provided that you can pass through the first three screens, the court will then insist that you satisfy a fourth; that is, your chart must meet certain foundational requirements, which for this particular piece of potential evidence include the following:

- The exhibit fairly and accurately conveys the data that you purport it conveys.
- The exhibit is based on underlying data that is too voluminous to be conveniently examined in court.
- The data upon which you base your chart is otherwise independently admissible.
- You have reasonably offered to make the underlying material available for opposing counsel to examine prior to your use of the exhibit.

The exact foundational requirements will vary depending upon the specific piece of evidence that you are seeking to introduce into the record. How do you know exactly what these foundational requirements are? Here is where you need to go to the law library. The requirements are generally codified in each jurisdiction's rules of evidence. As I noted at the outset, a detailed listing and analysis of these foundational requirements is beyond the scope of this book.

Usability and Display Methods: The Technology Continuum

A judge's willingness to let you use a particular persuasion tool is sometimes affected by a variable seldom discussed in any evidence text—the method by which you display your material in court.

In order to discuss this point, let us start by creating the "technology continuum." As shown in Illustration 5-7, this continuum roughly ranks the various methods of displaying persuasion tools in increasing relative order of sophistication or technology. At the bottom are "spontaneously" produced graphics (such as drawings on newsprint paper or on blackboards); moving up, there are prepared exhibit boards; up a bit more are exhibits displayed electronically; higher still are models and two-dimensional animations; finally, at the top are three-dimensional animations or whatever else is state of the art at the time you read this chapter. (Each of these technologies is discussed in greater detail in Chapter 6.)

While I do not know of any formal rule to this effect, I have observed that the farther up the technology continuum (i.e., the more sophisticated your display methods become) the more carefully the judge will examine your persuasion tool, the more strictly she will apply the rules of evidence, and the more willing she will be to grant objections against your being able to use the material.

The Technology Continuum

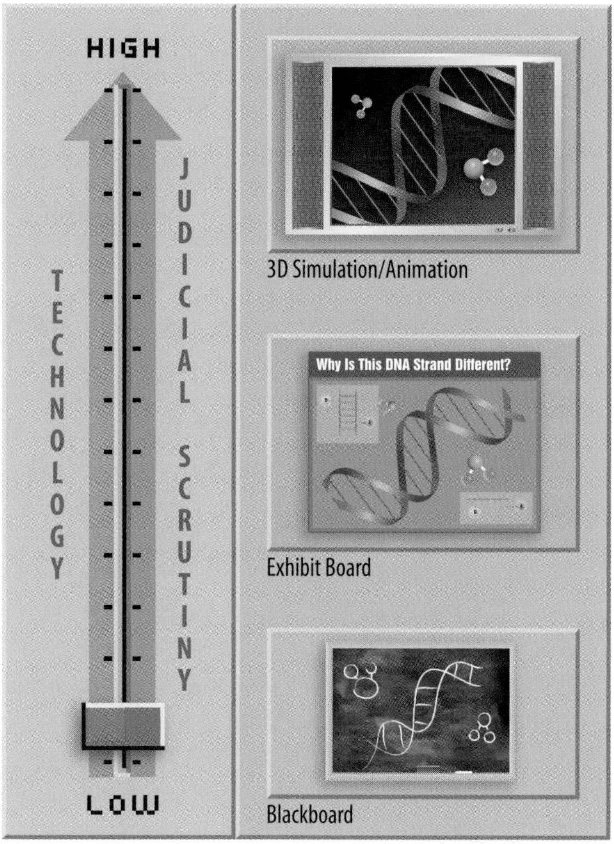

ILLUSTRATION 5-7 The level of judicial scrutiny increases as you go up the technology continuum.

I suspect that the level of judicial scrutiny increases as you go up the technology continuum because judges intuitively understand that as technology becomes more sophisticated, the greater the chances are that you can influence the jury with "smoke and mirrors" rather than substance and, as such, the greater the opportunity for possible attorney/witness mischief.

My suspicions were confirmed during a dinner that I had with a judge whom I very much respect. During that meal, the conversation turned to various blockbuster movies and the special effects that are used in them.

I mentioned that one of the technologies that Hollywood was using was something called motion capture ("mo-cap," if you want to sound like you are in the know). With motion capture the movie director can put an actor in a special suit on which there are scores of sensors. These sensors allow a computer to record exact movement of the actor and generate raw data from which other computers can generate amazingly accurate, lifelike animations.

After discussing the technology, I began waxing poetically (or at least I initially thought so) about how motion capture might be used to illustrate witness testimony and how much I was looking forward to being able to use it in court either as substantive evidence or for illustrative purposes. My dinner companion thought for a few moments, considered my hypothetical plans, and rightfully tempered my unabashed enthusiasm by making two important observations.

The judge's first observation confirmed that technology at the top of the technology continuum is likely to result in increased judicial scrutiny. As the judge pointed out:

> Cutting-edge technology puts a lot of pressure on the side offering it, the side opposing it, *and* the judge ruling on whether such material is usable in court. This pressure does not mean that there is anything wrong with the technology. In fact, if anything, the opposite is the case; the pressure comes from the fact that the technology is so powerful. If you are going to use the technology to create substantive evidence, I am going to feel pressure to make sure that your exhibit is admissible and I will feel a certain need to make absolutely sure that you dot every i and cross every t in your laying the foundation to show me that it is.

The second point that the judge made was about using cutting-edge technology to display material for "illustrative purposes only." He noted:

> Ironically, I think that using such technology for illustrative purposes potentially puts you in an even more difficult spot than using it as evidence. I probably would not feel comfortable saying, "OK, folks, what you are about to see is extremely realistic and looks an awful lot like how the events took place, but it is not evidence, it is merely an illustration." The technology you are describing [motion capture] is going to create material so visually powerful and realistic that I am afraid that no matter what kind of limiting instruction I give, the jurors are *not* going to see the graphic as being "merely illustrative." Every single one of them is going to disregard my instructions and assume that what you are showing them is evidence— that what they are seeing is the way it must have happened. Given this fact, I would be tempted to exercise my discretion and tell you that if you only want to illustrate a point that is fine, but you should probably use one of a dozen less powerful and potentially less prejudicial ways to do so. That way, you can still get your point across to the jury, but I will feel a whole lot more comfortable with the way you are doing it.

Let me clarify that the judge was not condemning a trial lawyer's use of such technology. He understood that increasingly sophisticated technology has it benefits and, as he had in the past, he would continue to welcome such technology in his courtroom. Instead, what the judge was doing was confirming an observation that I have made about using display methods from the top of the technology continuum.

As I previously noted, using such high technology will likely result in increased scrutiny by the court. Make sure that any benefit that you get from using sophisticated technology to present such persuasion tools is worth this extra hassle. Said differently, are you getting a sufficiently large persuasive impact for the procedural hassle? If the answer is "Yes"—and it very often is—then keep going with your plan. If the answer is "No," consider whether there is an equally effective way to present this type of illustrative material using a less complicated technology, thereby avoiding the evidentiary hassles associated with this increased scrutiny.

By way of an example of this last point, we were retained by a defendant in a high-profile criminal case where there was strong evidence showing that it was not physically or anatomically possible for the assault to have occurred in the way alleged by the victim. One of the methods we initially considered using to prove this fact was motion capture technology, similar to what I described earlier.

In the abstract, motion capture technology would have been perfect for the purpose we intended to use it. In the abstract, it all sounded good, but there was one problem. No case is ever actually tried in the abstract. This case was being tried in a real courtroom with real rules of evidence and real well-established burdens of proof.

The first mistake that I made in considering using this elaborate technology was acting like my client had to *prove* something—the fact was, he did not. In a criminal case, the prosecutor has to prove everything and has to do so "beyond a reasonable doubt." The defendant does not need to prove anything. All defense counsel must do is to create a reasonable doubt.[1] And, that is exactly the strategy our client, the defense counsel, wanted to adopt. He wanted to put the prosecutor to her proof; he wanted the prosecutor to be the one who had to struggle with the uphill battle of getting evidence admitted and used in court.

Consequently, our client wisely declined to try to present evidence using equipment from the uppermost end of the technology continuum. Why? Because he realized that any party offering such material as substantive evidence was voluntarily taking on a substantial evidentiary burden and that burden might not be worth it, particularly for the defendant. To be able to use the technology, our client would have to be ready to call one and possibly two expert witnesses to describe how the technology worked, its high degree of accuracy, what was done in this case, etc.

Taking on this additional evidentiary burden was completely antithetical to our client's overall strategy. So, our client made two very wise decisions. First, instead of using motion capture, he used a much lower form of technology (a blackboard and chalk) to roughly sketch out what he was claiming. Second, he did not offer the

---

1. For those readers who are criminal defense counsel, I know this is a lot harder than I am making it sound. I ask your patience and that you bear with me for just a moment longer.

persuasion tool as evidence; instead, he presented the material in closing argument as an illustration of the already established and admitted evidence. In short, he got all of the persuasive impact without the major procedural or evidentiary hassle.

Two Powerful Incentives for Judges to Allow Persuasion Tools

When it comes to persuasion tools, there are two things you should keep in mind, both of which usually work to your benefit. First, courts of appeal have generally concluded that the trial judge is in the best position to make the call on questions of using or admitting such material. Consequently, higher courts will not overturn a trial court's decision unless the trial judge is found to have substantially abused her discretion. It is my experience that when trial judges have such latitude, they often exercise it by letting the side offering these persuasion tools use them, particularly if the material is generally fair and accurate.

The second thing that you should keep in mind is what judges want. They want the jury to understand the evidence and to understand it as quickly and efficiently as reasonably possible. Properly prepared persuasion tools increase the likelihood of accomplishing these goals. As such, judges are likely to approve the use of such material—again, particularly if your tools are generally fair and accurate.

Does this mean that everything you create is going to be able to be used in court? Of course not. But it does mean that there is a high probability that you will be able to use your persuasion tools—particularly if they meet the general criteria discussed in this chapter.

Chapter **6**

Technology

What Is in This Chapter

I remember the first time that I went up against opposing counsel who used high-end technology to display his graphics. It was part of a two-day settlement conference. Plaintiff's lawyer arrived at the mediator's office a day early just to set up the equipment he needed to electronically project any document or videotaped deposition from the case onto a large screen. I had no idea what I was facing until the next morning when I arrived at the conference. I tell you, it was impressive, especially now that I know how much this high-end technology cost back then.

All I had was a flipchart with newsprint paper and three different colored pens. When I first saw all of the other side's technology, I knew what it was like to be part of the final battle scene in Episode VI of *Star Wars*. You know the fight between Darth Vader's best-equipped stormtroopers armed with super high-tech weapons and the Ewoks—those short, roundish, hairy creatures (which is how I looked) from the Stone Age (which is where I felt like I was from). I learned a lot during that mediation about how to display trial graphics, including the fact that more expensive technology is not always better—a fact we will review later in greater detail.

Courtroom technology scares some trial lawyers. Often these fears arise from two misperceptions. The first is that courtroom technology is something new and entirely unfamiliar, something with which most trial lawyers—particularly those like me who never consistently used a computer until after law school—have had little or no prior experience. This misperception is based on the mistaken belief that the only courtroom technologies that are effective and worth using are those that rely on sophisticated equipment developed in just the past few years.

Courtroom technology includes not only this type of equipment but also simple and powerful tools such as blackboards, newsprint paper, and blow-ups—tried and true technology used for generations. (See Illustration 6-1.) When trial lawyers realize this, they often respond like the character in one of Moliere's plays who, upon learning the definition of "prose," exclaims with relief, "For more than forty years I've been speaking in prose without even knowing it."

This is trial technology…

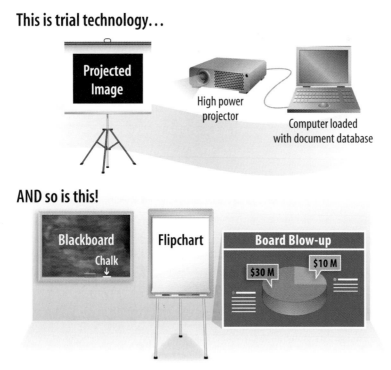

AND so is this!

ILLUSTRATION 6-1. **The Two Trial Technology Kingdoms**

The second misperception is that trial lawyers must acquire extensive technical expertise before they can use high-end technology effectively. *Acquiring technical expertise* and *using technology* are not the same things—a fact that I discovered several years ago when I decided to purchase a fax machine. I went to a large discount store and found two models that looked virtually identical, except that one cost $80 more than the other. When I finally tracked down a salesman, I asked him what the difference was between the machines. He paused for a second, started patting the more expensive model, and said with great confidence, "This baby's got more technology." With that, the salesman turned around, walked away, and went to help someone in the carpet department at the back of the store.

My point in telling this story is to assure readers who have limited technical expertise that they do not need to acquire a whole lot more of it before using (or for that matter selling) technology. This is good news for trial lawyers, all of whom stand to benefit substantially from using courtroom technology, yet very few of whom have the time, inclination, or interest in acquiring a detailed understanding of how these tools (especially those I refer to as "high-end") work.

So, if you do not need extensive technical expertise prior to using courtroom technology effectively, what do you need?

In my mind, you need three things. (See Illustration 6-2.) First, you need to understand technology's limitations. Simply put, there are certain things that technology does very well and others that it should never touch; there are things that it

Technology in the Courtroom

What you **don't** necessarily need to know:	What you **do** need to know:
	☑ Technology's general limitations
	☑ The relevant advantages of each technology type
	☑ How to factor this information into your mental mining process

ILLUSTRATION 6-2

should do and, more importantly, things it should not. You need to fully appreciate these differences.

Second, you need to develop a general understanding of what types of technologies are available. You should know not only each technology's advantages and disadvantages but also when it is best to use one type as opposed to another.

Finally, you need to know how to factor this general information about technology into your overall mental mining process and thereby improve your entire case preparation.

This chapter examines each of these three areas. But don't worry—just as a detailed analysis of every jurisdiction's evidence law is beyond the scope of Chapter 5, a detailed analysis of all forms of technology and how they work is equally beyond the scope of this chapter. Consistent with my belief that you do not need a whole lot of technical knowledge to use technology effectively (in fact, people who know me might say that I am living proof of this), I have deliberately kept the content of this chapter relatively simple.

My overall objective is twofold. The first is to provide you with just enough information so that you can choose the right technology, whether it is a blackboard or a 3-D animation. The second is to help make sure that you never feel like a short, roundish, hairy creature from the Stone Age.

Technology's Limitations

THE MEDIUM IS NOT THE MESSAGE

Despite what Marshall McLuhan once proclaimed, the medium is not the message; likewise, the message is not the medium. You must never make the mistake of confusing one for the other, at least not in the courtroom.

The message is a "what"; it is what you show the jury; it is the content, the substance. It is what you hope the jurors will take away from your case and use during their deliberations. For trial graphics, the message consists of two elements: (1) the content that you want the jurors to remember and (2) the design (including the layout and format) that best conveys the content to the jury. The themes and variations resulting from combining content and design to create the message in a trial graphic are infinite; examples of just a few are in this book and the accompanying Visual Resource CD-ROM.

This chapter focuses primarily on the medium—the technology—that you carefully select to present your message. For purposes of this discussion, I consider "medium" and "technology" to be synonymous. The medium is a "how"; that is, it is a delivery system through which you channel your message; it is a tangible thing (e.g., a blackboard or an animation). If the message is what you hope the jurors will take away, then the medium is often what you hope they will not even notice. Said differently, you are in trouble if the jury remembers that you used a magnetic board but does not recall the message you displayed using that technology.

In order to illustrate the relative importance of the medium and the message, let me tell you a story, one that will periodically resurface throughout this chapter.

A guy decides to buy a custom-made suit, so he goes to a tailor and tells the tailor in great detail exactly what he wants. Without even looking, the tailor reaches over to a rack of fifty identical suits, grabs one and announces, "Here is your custom suit!"

"Wait a minute," says the customer. "Don't you even have to measure me?"

"No," says the tailor, "just put on the suit."

The man does what he is told and, as you would expect, the suit looks terrible. The coat's right sleeve is too long, the left too short, and the pants are way too big in the backside. "This suit looks horrible!" says the man.

"There is nothing wrong with the suit!" insists the tailor. "Let me show you. Twist your leg to the left; move your back upward; move your bottom downward; stretch both arms outward; now pull the right arm back a bit."

The customer does exactly as the tailor tells him, stretching and distorting his body in all different directions just to fit into the suit. Sure enough, when he is done, the customer looks in the mirror and the suit looks great. So, he buys it and walks (or rather hobbles) out of the shop wearing his new suit.

A few yards down the street he passes two women. The first woman says, "Oh that poor, poor man. He must have been in a horrible accident. His legs were twisted to the left, his back was pushed upward; his bottom was forced downward; both arms were stretched outward."

Unless you are careful, you can end up like this uncomfortable man in this ill-fitting suit.

"Yes," said the second woman. "But what a nice suit!"

Many lawyers will laugh at this story without appreciating that, unless they are careful, there is a substantial chance that they will end up becoming that uncomfortable man in that ill-fitting suit. In order to prevent this, you must never let technology dominate your case; instead, you should confine it to a *secondary* role. Technology must never be the primary reason for creating or limiting the creation of a trial graphic. Do *not* begin by picking a particular method to display your trial graphic and then twist and distort the message to fit within your pre-chosen technology.

Sequentially, you should always follow the same three-step, one-directional process. You must first determine content by identifying the concept that you wish to communicate. Next, you need to choose the design that best communicates this content to the jury. Only then, when these first two steps are complete, should you finally think about what technology to use to display your trial graphic. (See Illustration 6-3.)

Never let this process flow backward. You must resist the temptation to start off by thinking, "Gee, I spent a lot of money on all of this whiz-bang, state-of-the-art technology. How can I design a trial graphic to show off that technology?" Unfortunately, as technology gets less expensive and easier to use, this is exactly where many lawyers begin their analysis. Those who do inevitably forget something very important—that a poorly conceived or executed graphic does not get any better merely because it is displayed using state-of-the-art technology. The only thing that happens is that you end up with a more expensive poorly conceived graphic. Do your best to avoid this common mistake.

COURTROOM TECHNOLOGY CANNOT THINK FOR YOU

Several years ago, my wife and I lived across the street from a family that would gather every Christmas Eve to make hundreds of tamales, which they distributed the next day to friends. In case you have never seen the process, making tamales is

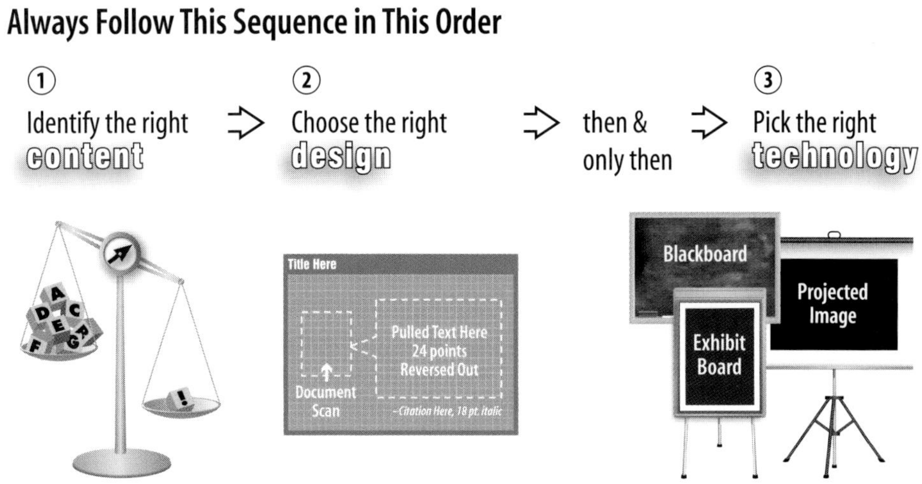

Always Follow This Sequence in This Order

① Identify the right **content** ⇒ ② Choose the right **design** ⇒ then & only then ⇒ ③ Pick the right **technology**

ILLUSTRATION 6-3

very labor-intensive, so much so that when you receive a dozen, you know that the giver truly values your friendship.

One Christmas Eve, after watching how hard everyone worked to make these gifts, I glibly commented that it was too bad there wasn't some kind of a machine that could do all the work for them. My comment evoked an immediate rebuke from one of our friends who politely, but very firmly, reminded me, "Chris, some things are far too important to be left to machines."

This same wisdom applies to the message that you need to convey at trial. No mater how sophisticated it becomes, technology's role in developing content and design will always be limited. There is good reason for this. You create your message using your brain in an organized and deliberate manner based on the unique particularities of your specific case. Technology requires no such specificity; the people who designed the computer program or built the screen that you use at trial did not ever know nor did they ever care one whit about you, your client, your judge, or your case.

Have I made technology sound impersonal? The fact is, it is impersonal! But so what? This should never be a problem so long as you always remember that *your choice of medium should never drive your message.* In case I was too subtle in the last sentence, let me repeat what I said—*your choice of medium should never drive your message.*

Edward Tufte published an article excoriating Microsoft and its PowerPoint software, specifically accusing those who use the program's AutoContent Wizard feature of replacing "serious analysis with chart-junk, over-produced layouts, cheerleader logotypes and branding, and corny clip art." According to Tufte, the result of using such a program is a homogenized generic end product that he disparagingly calls "PowerPointPhluff."[1]

For those who are unfamiliar with AutoContent Wizard, it is a "three-in-one program" that Microsoft seems to suggest is capable of (1) developing the right content for your message, (2) creating the best design for that message, and (3) displaying what it has created for you. (See Illustration 6-4.) All the user is supposed to have to do is select a template from among those prepared by Microsoft, answer a handful of questions, plug information into the resulting generic outline, and shazaam . . . you end up with just the right message, design, and display technology.

If this sounds too good to be true, that is because it is. AutoContent Wizard fails to live up to its own hype specifically because it fails to remember (or perhaps never understood) that the *medium should never drive the message.* Instead of following this fundamental rule, AutoContent Wizard's operating principle is that the medium trumps the message.

Microsoft's misplaced perspective means that the final product will be mediocre at best. AutoContent Wizard has six fundamental flaws. First, while AutoContent

---

1. Edward R. Tufte, *The Cognitive Style of PowerPoint* (Cheshire, Connecticut: Graphic Press, 2003), 4.

ILLUSTRATION 6-4. Launching AutoContent Wizard

Wizard takes the user through the creative process, it does so *backward*. As I mentioned earlier, creating and displaying just the right message for your judge or jurors requires three steps, *which must proceed in the following order:* (1) determine the content, (2) settle on the most persuasive design for that content, and (3) then (and only then) select the right technology or medium to display what you have created to the jury.

AutoContent Wizard takes the user through this process, but in reverse order. Instead of *waiting until the end,* the very first decision that AutoContent Wizard automatically makes for you is how your message will be displayed; that is, on PowerPoint, with all of its advantages and disadvantages. (See Illustration 6-5.)

Instead of waiting until after you have determined what the content of your message should be, AutoContent Wizard limits the format of your design to one option (bullet points in a horizontal template with considerable unused space) and it does so prior to even considering content (i.e., what is to be put inside that template).

Instead of starting with a critical assessment of what the message should be (which is the single most important decision in this process), AutoContent Wizard makes this the final step almost an afterthought—a decision made by a machine for you after the medium and design are already fixed.

"So what?" you may ask, "If you go through the process, what difference does it make if you do it backward, waiting to consider content until the very end?" The answer is, "A lot." Did I ever tell you the story about this guy who goes to this tailor to buy a custom made suit and the tailor randomly grabs a pre-made suit off a rack for the guy . . . ? Enough said on this point.

The second fundamental flaw with AutoContent Wizard is that it *discourages* (some might even argue *eliminates*) independent thought. Come on, this should not surprise anyone; I mean, just the name—"AutoContent Wizard"—doesn't that scare you a little bit? It should. But in case that is not enough, take a look at Illustration 6-6, which shows the outline that Microsoft suggests you follow in creating

The Right Way vs. the PowerPoint Way

- **The Right Way**

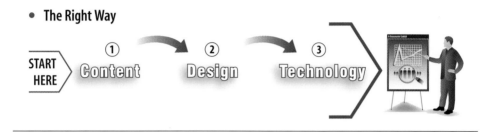

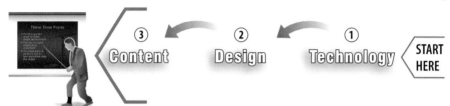

- **The PowerPoint Way**

ILLUSTRATION 6-5

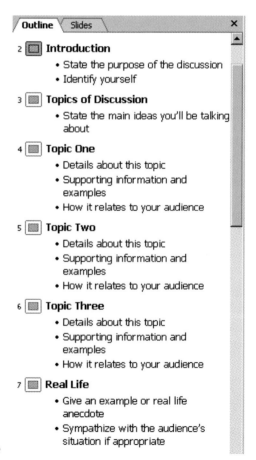

**ILLUSTRATION 6-6.
AutoContent Wizard's
One-Size-Fits-All Outline**

your graphics and structuring your presentation. This outline does nothing more than encourage you to adopt a "fill in the blanks" approach to persuasion.

Spending extensive time mentally mining your case is an essential element to any successful trial. It is something far too important to be left to a machine. Common sense should tell you that there is absolutely no way to get technology to do this analysis for you. Two kinds of lawyers ignore all this and make the mistake of relying on such technology to think for them. These are lawyers who undervalue the process of developing the message and lawyers who overvalue technology; don't be either one of them.

AutoContent Wizard's third fundamental flaw is that several of its features are just plain bad. For example, take a look at Illustration 6-7a, which shows one of the prepared templates that Microsoft includes as part of its program.

By now, some of problems with this design should be obvious to you. For example, look at the colors and the texture of the background design. Ask yourself: "Why? What purpose do these design features serve?" Personally, I see none. The color choices are unattractive and, more important, they are highly unlikely to have any connection to any important element of your case. From a purely practical matter, such a background and texture make it difficult for the viewer to read any of the written text and are more likely to distract rather than attract attention to your message.

Observe how Microsoft has allocated space in this template. (See Illustration 6-7b.) As I have previously pointed out, space is one of the two most important resources in any graphic (time being the other)—allocate it carefully. When you leave space blank, that space should serve a specific beneficial purpose; otherwise it is just a waste. Microsoft has built considerable blank space into each of its templates. I can see no valid purpose for it having done so. Instead of furthering a specific objective, all that the blank space does is decrease the amount of the template available for use, thereby making an already scarce resource even scarcer.

The fourth fundamental flaw that AutoContent Wizard has is that it automatically displays your text using bullet points. Just as Henry Ford told potential customers of the Model T that they could choose any color car as so long as it was black, AutoContent Wizard allows you to choose any display format, so long as it uses bullet points. There is nothing inherently wrong with bullet points; however, in this particular instance there is a problem because you have no other choice.

AutoContent Wizard's fifth fundamental flaw results from a combination of limited space and the forced use of bullet points. As Tufte points out, the average PowerPoint slide contains forty words, which an average viewer reads in five seconds. You generally will have more than five seconds' worth of discussion on any particular topic; after all, you are a lawyer.

By using these templates and the bullet point format, you end up with one of two results, neither of which is particularly desirable. You can leave the same forty words fixed on the screen while you take far longer than five seconds to explain your point, thereby potentially boring the jurors by making them stare at the same unchanging graphic. Alternatively, you can change PowerPoint slides every five or six seconds throughout the entirety of your presentation and end up giving your

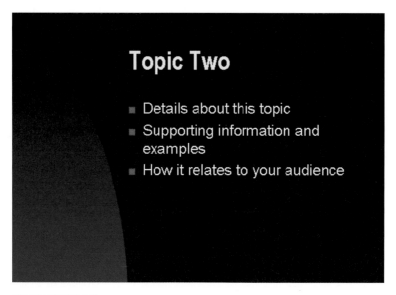

ILLUSTRATION 6-7a

Unless space serves a purpose it wastes a (1) valuable resource. This is a waste of space.

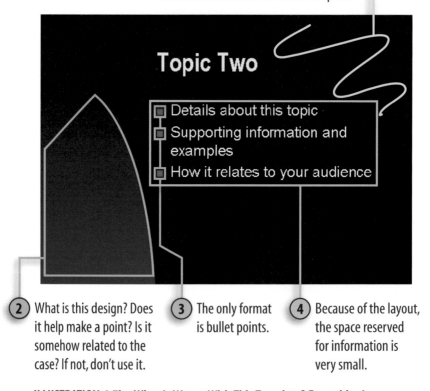

(2) What is this design? Does it help make a point? Is it somehow related to the case? If not, don't use it.

(3) The only format is bullet points.

(4) Because of the layout, the space reserved for information is very small.

ILLUSTRATION 6-7b. **What Is Wrong With This Template? Everything!**

jurors "visual whiplash" as they shift their gaze every few seconds from the lawyer to the slide, back to the lawyer, to the next slide, back to the lawyer, to the next slide, etc.

The fact that AutoContent Wizard's templates have extensive useless space and rely on a bullet point format creates an environment that encourages intellectual laziness in the person using the system. This is what I see as AutoContent Wizard's sixth major flaw. If all you have is a very small amount of space (remember an average of forty words per slide) and the only way to communicate your message is through bullet points, the natural tendency of most users is to jot down half-baked thoughts rather than spending the necessary time developing full-fledged arguments and evidence. These half-baked thoughts more often end up being personal notes or reminders for the speaker's own benefit rather than instructive material for the viewers. If all you want is to make notes for yourself, use note cards that only you see. Do not then take these personal notes and blow them up for your entire audience to share by way of PowerPoint.

Does all of this mean that PowerPoint has no redeeming features? My answer may surprise you. I think that PowerPoint and other programs like it can be effective—but this effectiveness occurs *if and only if* you (1) draw a clear line between the message and the medium, (2) throw out AutoContent Wizard, (3) recognize PowerPoint for what it really is—a way to display graphics, not create them, and (4) use a different and more thoughtful means to develop and craft your message.

Overview: Ways to Display Your Trial Graphics

In 1981, when I took the California bar exam, the proctors who administered the test divided applicants into two groups—those who handwrote their answers and those who used electric typewriters. An instructor in my bar review course loved to tell the story of how one year the electricity went out during the examination. According to him, the candidates who were using electric typewriters sat quietly at first waiting for the electricity to come back on. Moments passed to minutes and still there was no electricity. A wave of panic began to hit the typists; time was running out and they still had examination questions to answer. My instructor went on to explain how amazed the test proctors were that the typists had become so dependent on electricity and so focused on using it that, until one of the proctors made the suggestion, none of the applicants took out a pen to continue by handwriting their exam answers.

I use this story to introduce the first major division in trial technology taxonomy and to highlight the important fact that each species of technology comes with certain limitations.

Trial Technology Taxonomy

If the botanist Carl Linnaeus were to classify trial technology, the first division he would likely note is that these tools can be divided into two kingdoms—those that do not have electrical plugs and those that do. (See Illustration 6-8.)

There are three phyla within the Nonelectrical Kingdom. The first phylum is composed of graphics that are created through "spontaneous generation" at trial. These are the ones that lawyers or witnesses draw themselves during trial on a blackboard or on newsprint paper attached to a flipchart. The second includes prepared blow-ups, which I generally refer to as exhibit boards because they are attached to some form of firm backing, usually made of hard foam. The final phylum includes models—three-dimensional versions of either real objects or abstract concepts.

There are five phyla within the Electrical Kingdom. The first includes systems that electronically project an image of a document onto a screen. All that these tools do is project; they do not store images of the objects they are projecting in any kind of internal memory, such as a hard drive. These types of tools include simple systems like overhead projectors and slide projectors, both of which display documents and other graphics printed on acetate. This phylum also includes slightly more sophisticated machines such as an Elmo digital projector, which can project opaque sheets of paper, portions of books, and other small three-dimensional objects onto a screen without first transferring the image to acetate. These types of tools display the image of the item as is; that is, the user cannot manipulate any of this material by electronically adding layers, highlighting, or blowing up sections of the material being displayed.

The second phylum in the Electrical Kingdom includes tools that not only project enlarged still images but also store those images digitally on a computer hard drive. I call these tools integrated presentation systems. These tools usually require a computer, a projector or monitor, and software such as Trial Director,

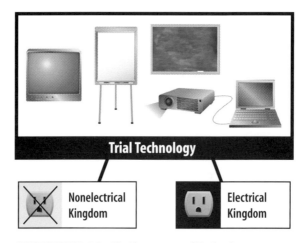

ILLUSTRATION 6-8. The Taxonomy of Technology

Sanction, and yes, even PowerPoint. These tools allow you to manipulate the original image by adding or subtracting layers and by enlarging and highlighting portions of the projected documents in real time during the trial.

The third phylum includes moving filmed images, such as videotaped deposition testimony, films of site visits, scientific experiments, etc.

The fourth phylum is simulations and animations. This phylum includes two-dimensional and three-dimensional versions of this technology.

The final phylum is the Flash program by MacroMedia, which is so powerful as to warrant its own phylum.

MORE TECHNOLOGY IS NOT NECESSARILY BETTER TECHNOLOGY

Before we go into detail about the specific forms of technology, I need to confront a common misconception: that the more high-tech your trial technology, the better and more persuasive it will be. I am not sure where this myth came from, except perhaps from our general societal belief that bigger, faster, and more expensive is always better. At least in the area of trial technology, following this myth is a mistake and does considerable damage to the way lawyers prepare for trial.

This belief dissuades two types of lawyers from following the creative process outlined in this book—those with unlimited budgets who think that they can avoid the process of mental mining by merely buying another expensive piece of technology, and those with very limited budgets who believe that just because they cannot afford to use expensive trial tools, there is no use going through the process. Both are mistaken. In no way does the amount of money you can or cannot spend affect your need to think—really think long and hard about your case. For the most part, this essential thinking process requires less than a dollar of technology—specifically, a pencil, an eraser, and a few sheets of paper. It is the best investment in technology that you will ever make.

No one should ever think that high-tech trial graphics or techniques are automatically better than their simpler relatives. Using the latest gizmo to display your trial graphic will not automatically make it better. In fact, as discussed below, there are numerous occasions when using anything other than an old-fashioned blackboard (which some would suggest is the epitome of low technology) will likely diminish rather than enhance the effect you are attempting to create. Remember that the medium you choose should never drive the message. If simpler technology works better for you, and it often will, use it and use it proudly!

When I am deciding what type of technology to use, I consider four broad variables. (See Illustration 6-9.) The first is what I call case-specific requirements, which include such considerations as the number of documents needed at trial, the number of exhibits, the case budget, courtroom limitations, and the judge's preferences/limitations. For the most part, these considerations are relatively straightforward. For example, is the courtroom big enough so that the lawyer can use boards that can take up space, particularly if there are a lot of them? Does the courtroom already have a screen on which you can project images? If not, is there room for

---

Considerations for Choosing the Right Technology

(1) Case-specific requirements

(2) Impression you want to make with the jury

(3) Number of graphics you are using

(4) Your preferences

ILLUSTRATION 6-9

one? Does the judge let the lawyers move around the courtroom or are they confined to the podium? How close can the lawyer get to the jury? Is this close enough for the jury to be able to read an exhibit board? This is all very important information that you need whether or not you decide to use graphics. Fortunately, if you do not know the particular judge or courtroom, this information is usually easily available from other trial lawyers, court clerks, and short visits to the courtroom itself.

The second consideration is the impression you want to make with the jury. For example, as we shall see later in this chapter, certain graphics are much more effective when the jury perceives that the lawyer or witness spontaneously creates them right there at trial. These graphics carry a certain sense of immediacy that does not exist in a highly coordinated prepared package assembled well in advance of anyone ever appearing in court. Walking up to the blackboard in front of the jury and drawing a simple sketch or writing down key words to emphasize a particular point helps further this perception of spontaneity—regardless of whether the lawyer or witness actually thought up the graphic on the spot or thought of and practiced drawing it weeks in advance. Showing a three-dimensional animation and claiming that you just "whipped it up during the lunch break" does not quite create the same desired effect.

Likewise, with respect to creating an impression with the jury, there are certain graphics that are so important that you want to squeeze every last bit of benefit from them. These are the graphics that "you just want to hug" and in so doing have all of their benefit magically transfer to you. Electronically projecting these documents on a screen twenty feet away from where you are standing does not create the same impression on the jury as displaying exactly the same material on an exhibit board that you place right next to you during your presentation.

The third criterion to consider in determining what medium to use is how many of the graphics need to be displayed at any one time. Certain graphics naturally complement and supplement each other, particularly if they are shown simultaneously. So, for example, I often recommend that a lawyer show a timeline to the jury while simultaneously displaying a particular document that was generated on one of the dates on the timeline. This technique allows the lawyer to go to the timeline, point out a particular date, show where that date is in relationship to other days, and then show the jury a copy of a letter or other document written on that day. The lawyer can repeat this process several times, comparing different letters sent at different times and pointing out the various events surrounding each letter by referring to the timeline. This requires that the lawyer use two graphics simultaneously—a timeline and a copy of one or more of the actual documents (usually with the key language pulled from or highlighted in the text). One way to simultaneously display this material is to have the timeline on an exhibit board next to the lawyer's podium while the lawyer electronically projects a copy of the key documents onto a screen. There is nothing particularly complex about this; the only requirement is that the technique be considered sufficiently in advance of the trial in order to make sure that the two technologies work well together.

The final consideration is the your personal preference and your unique way of trying a case.

My wife and I periodically engage in an important philosophical debate, which usually takes place after a very good dinner. It goes something like this: You have to give up one kind of food for the rest of your life. Would you give up chocolate or pasta?

If you ask me a similar question about methods of displaying my trial graphic— if I could use only one type of technology, electric or nonelectric, to display my trial graphics for the rest of my legal career—there is no doubt in my mind what the answer would be.

When I use trial graphics, my personal preference (obviously, I can't always do this but it is my first preference) is to surround myself with hard copy versions of the key graphics (i.e., technology not requiring electricity). I am personally most comfortable when I can put the graphics up on an easel next to me, physically tap on certain parts of an exhibit board to drive home a point with the jury, and hug the boards if appropriate. I like pausing to put the board up on an easel and using this pause to redirect and revive the jury's attention or to make a point more dramatically. Likewise, I also want to be able to sketch out simple graphics and write down key phrases on blackboards or on newsprint paper in front of the jury.

Other trial lawyers could not care less about being able to do any of these things. For them, given their styles, electronically displayed graphics are far more preferable. As noted earlier, this is purely a question of personal preference and style. The point is, when considering technology, you need to keep these personal preferences in mind and modify your media choices accordingly.

By the way, I would choose to keep pasta over chocolate any day; my wife thinks I am nuts.

Display Methods From the Nonelectrical Kingdom

BLACKBOARDS AND FLIPCHARTS

Let's start with the Rodney Dangerfields of trial technology. Blackboards and flipcharts don't get any respect and, like Mr. Dangerfield, they deserve a whole lot better.

When I say "blackboard," I am referring to any kind of erasable board. This includes writing with chalk on an actual black or green board as well as using erasable markers on a white board. When I use the term "flipchart," I am referring to a pad of newsprint paper. This paper is usually attached at one end, thereby allowing you to either tear individual sheets off the pad or flip between various pages that remain attached together.

Many trial lawyers have never completely appreciated nor fully utilized blackboards and flipcharts. Years ago, when a large number of our colleagues seemed to feel that they did not need to use *any* trial graphics, blackboards and flipcharts (which were about as high-tech as you could get back then) sat idle. Now that trial graphics are more commonly used, many of these same lawyers consider the blackboard and a flipchart to be passé and insist on using more sophisticated display methods. In certain instances, this can be a mistake. As we will see, quite often nothing beats the blackboard or flipchart as a way of conveying persuasive information.

Blackboards and Flipcharts Help You Teach

Blackboards and flipcharts have at least three advantages over other methods of displaying graphics. To understand the first advantage, consider the following: You see a person with something to say up at a blackboard with chalk in his hand. Who do most people immediately think of? A teacher. Not an advocate. A teacher.

The association of "blackboard + chalk = teacher" is a strong one. This association often has a transforming effect on both the jurors and the lawyer. The effect on the jurors is fairly predictable. When jurors see you as a teacher your credibility will often rise in their eyes. The transformation on the lawyer is equally profound and often surprises counsel. Stand a person who has something to say in front of a blackboard, put chalk in his hands, and turn him loose. Watch what happens; he will often easily, naturally, and spontaneously slip into the role of—you guessed it—a teacher.

The effect often does not stop there; it continues to circulate and feed itself. The advocate slips into the role of a teacher; the jury perceives the advocate as teaching; the jury's perception helps the lawyer comfortably stay in his role as a teacher; this encourages the jury to perceive the lawyer as a teacher; and on it goes.

Blackboards and Flipcharts Allow Spontaneity

Blackboards and flipcharts provide a second advantage: spontaneity, both actual and planned.

Actual Spontaneity. Actual spontaneity is what you do when you are "dancing." Anyone who has tried more than a couple of cases knows what I mean by "dancing." It is what you do when things don't go as planned. I am not just talking about bad things. Sometimes unexpectedly *good* testimony can send your feet dancing.

When something unexpected happens (good or bad) and you need a trial graphic, the blackboard or the flipchart may be the only tool you have. Fortunately, it is also usually the best tool for this particular job.

Let's look at two examples.

▼▼▼

First example: Your witness should be on the stand for five minutes, six minutes max. All you need is to introduce her to the jury, establish that she knows the plaintiff, and testify that on a certain day she saw the plaintiff walking west on Third Street and then turn north onto Clay. With this, you should be done; you can thank the witness and she can head home.

Three minutes into your examination, you discover, much to your shock and horror, that your witness has "geographic dyslexia." You know the disease: The victims say "north" when they mean "south" and "east" when they mean "west." By the way, this condition is far more common than you might think and, for reasons I have never been able to ascertain, it is always your witness—never your opponent's witness—who has this malady.

Any way, by your seventh question, east has indeed become west and north has become south in the witness's mind, and the jurors are equally confused. Suddenly in your inner ear you hear the dance band starting to warm up.

There are several things that you can do. One is to spontaneously create a graphic on a flipchart or blackboard.

> **Q.** Excuse me, Ms. Van Ort, I am a bit confused. What street were you standing on when you saw the plaintiff?
>
> **A.** I was standing on Clay Street.

You draw:

Q. On Clay Street, between what two streets?

A. Between Third and Fourth Streets. Right at the southeast corner of Third and Clay.

You add in the cross streets and the witness's position:

Q. Let's put in which way is north.

You add the orientation to the map:

Whenever possible, north should always be pointing upward. After years of viewing maps, we are all more comfortable with this orientation. Actually, you have already established which direction is north by placing Ms. Van Ort in the prior sketch, but always draw north to help people viewing the map.

Q. Third Street would be up here and Fourth Street is down here. Right?

A. Yes.

I know this is a leading question (and some readers may say that I have been leading the witness for some time now). But, given the situation you find yourself in, it is probably worth taking the risk of asking the question in this manner. Judges usually recognize problems like the one you are in and are often sympathetic. Also, if the court does not allow you to ask this question, you can just ask the question again in a nonleading form.

> **Q.** So, where did you see plaintiff walking?
>
> **A.** Well, I saw him walking. . . . Oh, I misspoke earlier. I saw him walking west on Third Street—not east—and then plaintiff turned north onto Clay—not south.
>
> **Q.** So, plaintiff walked west on Third Street and north on Clay?
>
> **A.** Yes.

Just as plaintiff answers, you write:

At this point, I would mark the drawing as an exhibit. This guarantees that the clerk will keep track of it as part of the official trial record. You may never take the next step and have the drawing admitted (in fact, you probably will not), but if you need the graphic again at least the clerk will have it and it will not accidentally get thrown out as just a scrap of paper.

Second example: There are instances when you want to use a blackboard or flipchart after you find yourself dancing over unexpectedly *good* testimony. In this instance, you are cross-examining Mr. Ward, one of your adversary's key employees. In response to one of your questions, Mr. Ward uses a phrase that you have never heard him use before. He says that he told his boss that conditions at the plant were "a disaster waiting to happen." This phrase that came spontaneously from Mr. Ward at trial for the first time fits beautifully in with your theme. Now the music is playing in your head and your feet are starting to tap because you know you have the makings of a great spontaneous trial graphic.

Q. You said that it was a "disaster waiting to happen."

A. Yes.

You write:

Q. You thought it was a disaster waiting to happen because the fire escape doors were poorly marked. Right?

A. Yes.

You write:

Q. In fact, some of the escape doors were nailed shut?

A. Yes.

Q. That was another reason you thought this situation was a disaster waiting to happen?

A. Yes.

You write:

Q. Other doors were blocked by heavy boxes, weren't they?
A. Yes.

Q. That must have been another reason for thinking that this was a disaster waiting?
A. Yes.

You write:

By the time that you are done, you have created a memorable trial graphic, one that not only incorporates the unexpectedly good testimony from the witness but also lists the facts that you had previously planned to ask about without graphics.

Planned Spontaneity. "Her ad lib lines were well rehearsed . . . ."—Rod Stewart
Winston Churchill once confessed that the reason so many of his apparently spontaneous quips were so memorable was that some of them weren't really spontaneous. In fact, he actually spent considerable time thinking about what to say

long before he needed to do so. Trial lawyers can learn an important lesson from Sir Winston: Spontaneity sometimes takes considerable planning; nevertheless, the effort is worth it because the results can be highly effective.

Let's look at three examples of planned spontaneity and how you might display the resulting graphics using a blackboard or flipchart.

▼▼▼

First example: You represent a plaintiff who alleges that defendant should have foreseen and could have prevented a disastrous gas pipeline explosion. The defendant disagrees, claiming that it was forced to make a judgment call under extremely difficult circumstances and is now being unfairly criticized for having done so.

On several occasions during the pre-trial settlement conference, defendant's counsel uses the word "hindsight" and the phrase "hindsight is twenty-twenty" to criticize your case. You suspect that you will hear this again at trial, probably in defendant's closing argument, and you start thinking about how to counter this theme.

Sure enough, during defendant's closing argument, opposing counsel repeatedly states that your case is nothing but an "unfair attempt to apply hindsight, which is always twenty-twenty" to an instance where "the defendant made the best possible judgment call given what little information was known at the time."

When it is your turn for rebuttal, you walk without hesitation straight to the blackboard and, apparently off the top of your head, write:

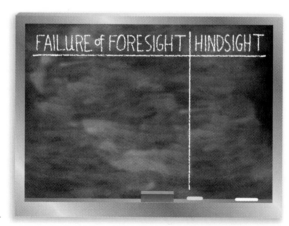

You then begin talking to the jurors about how defendant's argument is nothing more than an attempt to escape responsibility for its own failure of foresight. To reinforce this conclusion, you offer several examples. At the conclusion of each, you rhetorically ask the jury if the example demonstrates hindsight or defendant's consistent failure of foresight. Obviously, since the jury can't immediately respond, you (being the ever helpful advocate that you are) do so for them by summarizing each example using one or two key words and placing each resulting phrase in the "Failure of Foresight" column.

Two weeks before the gas leak, Peninsula Gas's engineering department concluded, in fact it was this report right here [you hold up the report], that its monitoring systems were accurate only 75 percent of the time. The authors of the report strongly suggested that management do something to drastically improve this failure rate. Peninsula ignored this report, figuring that 75 percent was good enough for the time being. I ask you, was the resulting explosion because of "hindsight" or a consistent "failure of foresight" for which you should now hold Peninsula responsible?

You write:

On the night of the gas leak and explosion, the sensor at Hilton Station recorded dangerously high pressure in the pipeline. The sensor acted like a circuit breaker and automatically stopped the flow of additional gas. The sensor did exactly what it was supposed to do; Peninsula did not! Peninsula should have sent someone out to inspect Hilton Station. Instead, it figured that since it was 3:00 a.m., it probably wasn't worth the hassle of getting someone out of bed to go do the job. I ask you again, was the resulting explosion "hindsight" or a consistent "failure of foresight" for which you should now hold Peninsula responsible?

You write:

Peninsula's night-shift supervisor had no data other than what the sensor was telling him. Nevertheless, he decided to manually override it, concluding "not much damage will happen if we override the automatic shutdown for just a few minutes and re-route high pressure gas through those pipes." Was the resulting explosion "hindsight" or a consistent "failure of foresight" for which you should now hold Peninsula responsible?

You write:

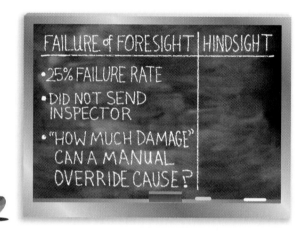

Unfortunately, the sensor was right. Within thirty seconds of Peninsula's overriding it, the entire pipeline exploded. Was this a result of "hindsight" or a consistent "failure of foresight" for which you must now hold Peninsula Gas liable?

You write:

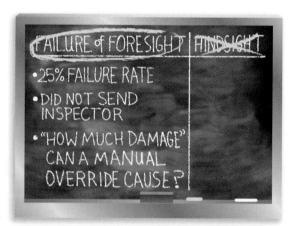

You conclude this portion of your rebuttal by emphasizing how hindsight had nothing to do with the explosion; instead, defendant's own consistent failure of foresight was the direct cause of the disaster and the reason that it must now pay for the extensive damage that it caused.

Second example: I have also seen a similar technique of planned spontaneity used quite successfully in opening statement as a simple way of introducing and imprinting your case theme in the jurors' minds. Here is a straightforward and simple illustration of how you might use this technique in opening statement.

Ladies and gentlemen, you are going to hear a lot of testimony but the evidence is going to show that this dispute is really only about two things: "Rights" and "Responsibilities."

As you speak, you write these words on the board:

Third example: There is a wonderful skill that certain lawyers have developed, which I call etch-a-sketching. This technique incorporates the slow and deliberate process of illustrating the lawyer's story as part of the storytelling itself. Trial lawyers who have perfected this technique are able to describe a series of events while at the same time drawing a map, flowchart, set of bullet points, or some other illustration that is tied directly into what is being said by the lawyer. Rather than completing the drawing all at once, these trial lawyers take their time to slowly draw the scene bit by bit as they verbally tell their story point by point. The verbal description supplements the drawing and, in turn, the drawing supplements the verbal description. When this technique is done well, it seems almost to hypnotize the jurors and capture their full attention.

I suspect that etch-a-sketching is effective for four reasons. First, it simultaneously appeals to two of the jurors' most important senses (vision and hearing) without overwhelming either with too much detail at any one time. Second, drawing involves physical action, which captures and focuses the jurors' attention. Third, there is a certain amount of anticipation or surprise as the jury waits to see what the lawyer will draw next. Finally, this spontaneous performance is somewhat equivalent to that of a tightrope walker performing without a net; people are morbidly curious to see if the performer, in this instance the trial lawyer, can actually pull it off or if he falls (metaphorically speaking) to a violent end.

Blackboards and Flipcharts Create Intimacy

Watching something being created can be spellbinding. I am reminded of this every time I walk past a building site and see captivated onlookers spending their lunch hours watching construction workers or when I see people watch artists creating a pot on a wheel or painting a portrait in public.

Why is spontaneity so powerful? I think for three reasons. First, there is something in human nature that perceives a spontaneous act or observation as being more heartfelt because it is unfiltered by long and potentially distorting conscious thought. Similarly, such acts are seen as directly connected to the core and therefore more deeply admired as somehow being more truthful.

Second, there is what I call the Odysseus factor, after the ancient Greek hero. To my mind, it is not a coincidence that Homer so often describes his most popular character as "clever Odysseus." Human beings are impressed by cleverness (so long as it is not used against them personally). They seem to admire cleverness even more when it is spontaneous.

Finally, in some Zen monasteries, the masters are known for periodically and unexpectedly hitting their students with specially designed wooden sticks that create a distinctive "whack" sound when used. The act is not intended to be a violent one. In fact, most people who have been hit this way will probably tell you that it did not really hurt so much as startle them, and immediately made them aware of what was going on around them. Unexpected spontaneous acts have a way of rousing the senses and naturally forcing people to pay attention. This, of course, is the Zen master's point in administering the whack. It should also be one of your reasons for using spontaneously created graphics and their associated display methods.

Rehearsed spontaneity is no less powerful than the real thing. The technique of walking up to the board and writing down key words or sketching a picture (even a rough one) captures the jurors' attention and holds it for a few added seconds, regardless of whether you planned in advance to do so. By their very nature, spontaneously created trial graphics create a certain level of attention and intimacy that may not exist in other forms of display. A spontaneously created graphic is created right then and there with the jury witnessing its creation. It did not exist prior to the lawyer walking up to the blackboard or flipchart. This creates a connection between the lawyer, the jurors, and the trial graphic that may not exist with prepared graphics.

I first realized this when a juror in one of my trials spontaneously whispered to me that I had just misspelled a word on a piece of newsprint paper. The juror's comment, which was just loud enough to be heard by almost everyone in the courtroom, came completely out of the blue. I had not planned the mistake; the juror had not planned to say anything—it just happened. There was some good-natured laughter by everyone. As a result of the incident, I not only corrected the mistake during closing, but also had the opportunity to go back and talk a bit more to the jury about what was substantively being raised by the spontaneously created trial graphic. In the end, it was one of those instances where I knew at least one person in the courtroom was awake and listening to me.

Blackboards and Flipcharts Follow the Rules of Information Architecture

The process of conceiving and developing spontaneous graphics is for the most part no different from the process you use for their pre-planned cousins. The rules of information architecture are identical. As evidence of this, let's look at three examples and examine what principles apply as you display them on blackboards or flipcharts.

First example: Your client manufactured a product that went through a rigorous quality control process prior to its leaving the plant. A few weeks later, when defendant used the product for the first time, it did not work. Plaintiff claims that the product was defective when it left your plant and will not pay anything. Your client believes that the product was fine leaving the plant and that it eventually failed to work because the defendant improperly stored the equipment prior to using it. You want to create a chart highlighting the tests that were performed in your client's plant and the fact that the product passed each quality control test.

Note that this example incorporates the following principles of information architecture discussed in Chapter 4: (1) use of a title to better explain the purpose of the graphic, (2) the Answer Board Principle, (3) Pacing Devices, (4) Selectavision, and (5) the Informational Honeymoon.

> ***Q.*** Ms. Zeiter, I want to talk with you about the tests that were done on your product before it was sent out. Does Zeiterco have a quality control process?
>
> ***A.*** Yes, it does.

You write:

Zeiterco Quality Control Process

You have created a title. This provides the advantages discussed above.

> ***Q.*** How many tests do you perform?
>
> ***A.*** We always do three tests.

You write:

You have started creating the internal parts of the trial graphic. You have also labeled the first column and indicated the number of elements that will eventually go there. This helps let the jury know what to expect. and if things get interrupted later will help you and the witness remember to list all the tests. And you have left space at the bottom of the graphic so that you can write in a conclusion when you are finished.

> **Q.** What is the first test?
> **A.** It is the high-frequency oscillation test.

You write:

> **Q.** What is the high-frequency oscillation test?
> **A.** [Witness gives a succinct description.]

> **Q.** Did you perform this test on the product that you sent to defendant?
> **A.** Yes.

As you speak, you write "Performed?" on the board, and add the witness's response:

Q. What was the result of that test?
A. It passed.

You write:

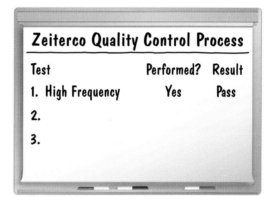

You have now created the entire perimeter of the graphic and through the use of testimony have explained what each column means. You continue questioning the witness, writing her answers on the board. Now you are not only bringing the jurors back to a trial graphic with which they are familiar, but also bringing them back to a format that they have seen before.

Q. What was the second test?
A. The medium-frequency oscillation test.

Q. What is the medium-frequency oscillation test?
A. [Witness gives a succinct description.]

Q. Did you do this test?
A. Yes.

Q. What was the result?
A. It passed.

You write:

Q. You mentioned three tests. What was the third test?
A. The low-frequency oscillation test.

Q. What is the low-frequency oscillation test?
A. [Witness gives a succinct description.]

Q. Did you do this test?
A. Yes.

Q. What was the result?
A. It passed.

You write:

Q. What did you determine as a result of doing these tests?
A. We determined that the product worked at the time it left our factory.

You write:

Q. In your mind, is there any doubt of this?
A. None.

Second example: Plaintiff alleges that he entered into a contract with your client. Your client claims that, while there were general discussions, the parties never agreed to anything. You want to educate the jurors about the requirements for a binding contract and show them that none ever existed in this case.

You know from pre-instructions and the charging conference that the judge will instruct the jury that a contract requires three things: (1) an offer, (2) an acceptance, and (3) consideration. In advance of the closing argument you write the following on the blackboard:

A Contract <u>Must</u> Have <u>All</u> These Things:

An Offer

An Acceptance

Some Consideration

You are going to do three things with this graphic. First, you are going to validate the graphic by linking its elements to the upcoming jury instruction. Next you will use it as a platform to talk about each element in turn and establish that there is no evidence for any of them. Finally, you will emphasize this by erasing that element from the graphic.

This example of a spontaneously created graphic relies on the following informational architecture principles: (1) the Answer Board Principle, (2) Pacing Devices, and (3) the Informational Honeymoon. It also relies on a technique that works particularly well with blackboards in closing argument—erasing material as a way to show that your opposing counsel could never prove an essential element of its prima facie case.

First step: Validate what you have written on the board. You tell the jury:

In a few minutes, Judge Golding is going to tell you about what the law requires in order for there to be a valid contract. There are three things, which I have written down here. There must be an offer, an acceptance, and consideration. Judge Golding is also going to tell you that you must have all three of these elements. If any one of them is missing, then the law says, "no contract." In other words, if any one of these elements disappears, all of plaintiff's case disappears as well.

You show the jury the blackboard.

Second step: Use the exhibit as a platform to talk about each element. You first get the jury to focus on the element of "an offer." You can discuss the law, you can use examples of how offers are made and, most important, you can argue why plaintiff has completely failed to establish that an offer was ever made. When you have finished and hopefully convinced the jury that there is no evidence on point, you erase that element from the board.

So now your graphic looks like this:

You go through the same step for acceptance. When you conclude there is no evidence of acceptance, you erase that element as well.

You go through the same step for consideration. Now your board is empty.

Just as each element has disappeared, so (you will argue) should plaintiff's entire case.

Third example: Defendant in this case willfully refused to produce all necessary documents. At the outset of discovery, defendant claimed no such documents existed. Slowly, through hard-fought discovery battles, a bit of information was found. After more intense discovery battles, more documents surfaced. Obviously, with cases of this type, there is no telling how much more information remains undiscovered. You have decided to "spontaneously" display this point to the jury and you have decided to do so using a visual analogy to make your point.

Three years ago, we asked defendant for all of its documents and were told that there were none.

You write the date of the original request on the board:

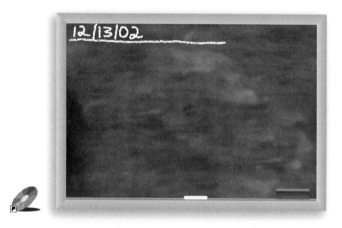

We did not believe them and began to dig and search. Sure enough, we found some of the supposedly nonexisting documents.

You draw:

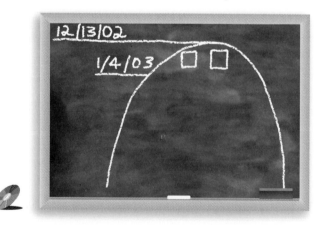

We asked defendant again, "Give us your documents." Defendants swore that was everything. We kept digging and sure enough there was more.

You draw:

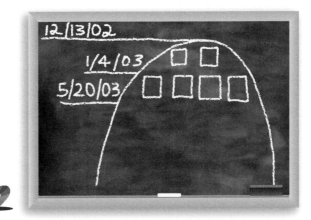

Each time we found the documents, defendants insisted that there were no more. Each time we found more.

You draw:

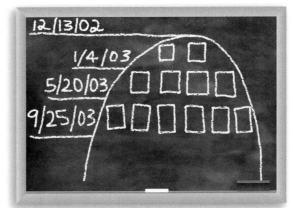

Don't you wonder what defendants still have buried out there and why they buried it?

You draw:

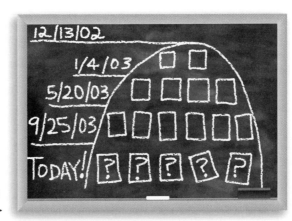

Limitations of Blackboards and Flipcharts

Now that I have praised spontaneously created trial graphics and the technologies used to present them (i.e., blackboards and flipcharts), we need to consider some inherent disadvantages with these display methods. There are generally three, all of them are fairly obvious.

First, such exhibits are for the most part intended to be temporary. Blackboards are easily erasable; newsprint paper is usually ripped off the flipchart and automatically discarded. To the extent that you are using these display methods merely for illustrative purposes, this is generally not a problem. But if you think you will need the material later, then you must be extra careful to make sure that your prized drawing does not end up in the recycling bin.

There is nothing improper about marking a drawing on newsprint paper as an exhibit. As noted earlier, what this usually means is that the court clerk will take possession of it when you are done drawing and include it in the trial record. This does not mean that the material is admitted into evidence, just that it has been deemed important enough to be marked as an exhibit. If you are going to introduce the material as evidence, you still need to go through the various steps prescribed in your jurisdiction. (See Chapter 5.)

If you are going to have the spontaneously created material become evidence, make sure you create a legible graphic that will make sense to the jury weeks later during deliberations. Additionally, it might not hurt for you to take a few moments to describe on the record what the document represents or shows. That way, if an appellate court is required to view the material years later, it can do so with the benefit of an official description of your drawing in the trial record.

Blackboards are even more problematic than flipcharts because you can't just tear off one of the sheets and save what you have just written. The blackboard is eventually going to have to be erased; there is no practical way around that fact. So, what do you do? First, try to avoid using the blackboard for anything except illustrative material that you have no problem erasing when you are done. But if you just can't avoid it, the next best thing (and it is not always that great) is to get the court's permission to take a photograph of the content of the board. I want to stress this is a very poor alternative, but if you really need to do it, then do it. Digital pictures or ones that develop instantly (like Polaroid) are the best ways to preserve the information on the blackboard. This way you will immediately know if the picture adequately preserves the image. The last thing you want is to take a picture, erase the board, take the film to be developed, and later discover that the picture did not turn out.

The second problem with this type of technology is that it takes time to write down your information on a blackboard or flipchart. Jurors are likely to lose interest if it takes you too long. This limits the amount of information that you can display. You can write a few words and keep the jury's interest, but since the jury can read much faster than you can legibly write, if you have a lot of information or data it is probably better to use an alternative display technology or to prepare your graphic before you come to court.

When I suggest that you prepare that graphic before you come to court, I do not mean that you must always pay to have a professional graphic artist prepare your exhibit for you. Just make sure that, whenever necessary, you write or draw whatever you plan on using on the newsprint paper during the break or evening before you need it. That way, you can flip to the material when you need it. There is very little cost in such a display process. The only investment is time. You must plan your use of these graphics in advance, which is another reason to begin and pursue mental mining early on.

Finally, you need to be very careful when you create these graphics. It is easy, in the heat of trial, to create a trial graphic that is a complete mess and looks like a drawing of a failed football play. Unless you have inherently neat handwriting, your words can appear messy. Unless you have carefully planned what you want to put into the graphic and where, you can forget where you want bits of information to go. So, save for a true emergency when you are "dancing" to create some unforeseen exhibit, practice creating your graphic several times before you go to court.

EXHIBIT BOARDS

The second phylum in the Nonelectrical Kingdom is reserved for exhibit boards, which are prepared graphics blown up and attached to a firm backing usually made of hard foam or cardboard.

I have already revealed my own personal prejudice—exhibit boards are undoubtedly my favorite method of displaying key graphics. Unlike their closest relatives, the spontaneously created graphics, exhibit boards come prepared with the information laid out the way you want it and with wording that you have carefully chosen in advance to convey just the right message to the jury. Unlike their slightly more distant cousins that display their messages electronically on a screen and then disappear, exhibit boards are solid and are always physically present. This constancy renders these boards the largest cue cards in the courtroom, enabling you to move confidently away from the podium without any apparent notes while still being able to rattle off facts and figures with confidence, merely by reading what you have had previously printed on the board.

Exhibit boards are talismans. You magically capture the jury's attention by slowly placing one up onto an easel. You stand next to a board hoping that the good juju in its message will magically transfer to you. You diffuse an overcharged courtroom or find time to regain your composure by slowly taking the exhibit board down from the easel. In my mind there is no more versatile way to display your trial graphics.

Now, having noted their versatility and after confessing that exhibit boards are my favorite way to display graphics, I need to offer some perspective. Most of the material I use myself and design for others is *not* displayed on exhibit boards; instead, I use other display media. Just because one medium is your favorite does not justify overusing it. As you will see, there are several legitimate reasons to limit the number of boards (or any other media type) you use. Unfortunately, just because a particular medium is your favorite does not exempt it from these rules.

Types of Exhibit Boards

Generally, there are four types of exhibit boards: static, fill-in-the-blank, dynamic, and specialty. Each has its specific advantages and disadvantages; each works in certain situations, but not in others.

Static Exhibit Boards. The comedian Flip Wilson used to occasionally dress in drag to portray a street-wise character he called Geraldine. As far as I can remember, Geraldine was known for two things. The first was her boy friend, "Killer," who never appeared onscreen but was supposed to be very big and very mean. The second was the line, "What you see is what you get!"—which she used in each of her comedy sketches.

With static boards, what you see is what you get. These are the simplest form of exhibit boards because their printed images never change. You generally design a static board to highlight a single point. Perhaps the clearest example of this is the classic textpull. (See Chapter 7.)

The fact that you can effectively display only a single point on a static board is both a limitation and a source of great persuasive power. The limitation is obvious—you can display only *one* point. The power comes from the fact that all of the board's emphasis is focused on this single point. For that reason, it is crucial that you choose just the right point for the board.

How do you determine whether a document warrants being displayed on a static board? I generally apply a three-step process. I first divide all of my documents into two groups: "crucial documents" and "everything else." The crucial documents should be by far the smaller stack and are the only ones that continue on in this process; the rest go back to the files. I next take the crucial documents and highlight those portions of the documents that really matter. Finally, I look at these highlighted sections in isolation and ask myself, "Which of these can stand on its own and make its point with little or no additional explanation by the lawyer?" The ones that can are potential candidates for this type of graphic display.

Because static boards are both simple and powerful, trial lawyers sometimes make two mistakes. First, they try to use the board to make more than one key point. Don't. This is usually confusing and dilutes the overall power of the board.

Second, a lawyer will occasionally appear in court with scores of static boards on which he has printed textpulls from every possible exhibit. Ironically, this is a very expensive way to cheapen the persuasive value of your static boards. You want to reserve static boards for a handful of your most crucial documents or points. If you put everything on a board, the boards are no longer special and what you display on them is less memorable to the jury.

You want the fact that you created a board in and of itself to mean something. You want to condition the jurors so that when you reach for a static board, they sit up and know that something important is about to happen. You want them to think, "This must be important, if the lawyer went to the time and expense of creating this board." Mass producing such exhibits desensitizes the jury so that eventually, printing something on a board has absolutely no independent significance whatsoever.

Fill-in-the-Blank Exhibit Boards. A half step above the purely static boards are those on which you have deliberately left blank spaces so that a lawyer or witness can generate additional jury interest by filling in the missing information at just the right moment.

Here are three examples. The first, Illustration 6-10, is a checklist of key questions. You can use a graphic like this at various points throughout trial. During opening statement, you can use it to preview the disputed issues to the jury. Then, as you work your way through your case-in-chief, you can check the appropriate box whenever a witnesses answers one of the questions.

Alternatively, you can wait until closing argument to first display the board. Then you can walk the jury through each question one at a time, remind them of the supporting evidence that they have seen on that point, and check the appropriate box thereby visually establishing that you have met (or your opponent has failed to meet) the burden of proof on an important issue or cause of action.

How the Lundys Were Treated

	YES	NO
Were the Lundys singled out?	☐	☐
Were the Lundys treated unfairly?	☐	☐
Were the Lundys treated that way because they were trying to open a home for Alzheimer's victims?	☐	☐
Were the Lundys damaged?	☐	☐

ILLUSTRATION 6-10. A Checklist of Key Questions

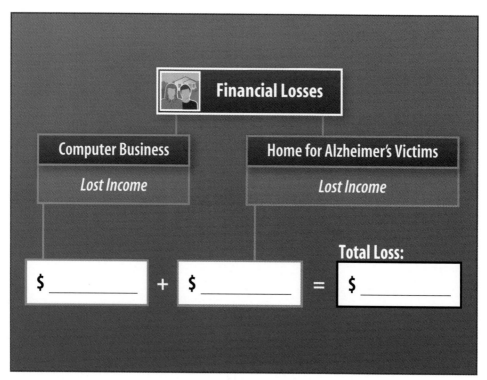

ILLUSTRATION 6-11. Leaving Strategic Blanks

The second example, Illustration 6-11, is a graphic designed to present key numerical figures to the jury. Rather than preprinting those figures on the exhibit, we have left the space blank. This particular example focuses the jury on your damages. Depending on the particulars of this case, either an expert witness (e.g., an accountant or economist) could write the appropriate number on the board during testimony or the lawyer could do the same in closing.

The final example is a blown-up version of the verdict form. It is important, particularly when the form itself is complex, to show your active jurors how you want them to complete it for you. This is a crucial step in helping these crucial participants get organized and off to a fast start in deliberations.

Perhaps one of the easiest ways to do this is to blow up the verdict form and make it into a fill-in-the-blanks exhibit board. A common mistake that lawyers make with this type of board is to rush through the form and complete it all at once. Generally, a better way to do this is to use the board as a way to introduce and review key bits of evidence. Serve the graphic course by course to the jurors. In other words, after you show and read the first question to the jury, take the time to review the key pieces of evidence that support your position. Write the important trial exhibit numbers down on the board and invite the jurors to do the same in their notepads so that they can review the actual exhibits during deliberations.

Earlier I mentioned that certain graphics naturally complement and supplement each other. In this particular instance, it often works well to display this fill-in-the-blank verdict board with other related graphics. So, for example, you can put this form on an exhibit board and place it up on an easel; at the same time, as you discuss a particular piece of evidence, you can either display your evidence on a second board or project it electronically onto a screen. (See Illustration 6-12.)

When you finish this review, check the appropriate box, urge the jurors to do the same in deliberations, and then repeat the process with each verdict question.

Dynamic Exhibit Boards. The third type of exhibit boards are what I call dynamic boards. These boards use a series of pacing devices to change the board's content in a predetermined and choreographed manner. Dynamic boards consist of two parts: the baseboard and the pacing devices you either add to or remove from the baseboard. The baseboard is the foundation that physically and visually supports the pacing devices. Depending on the type of board, the baseboard will sometimes be blank; other times it will contain the bulk of the exhibit's information.

Pacing devices are either made of the same material as the baseboard or, in the case of overlays, made of sheets of acrylic. The former are usually attached to the baseboard by magnets, Velcro, or some other adhesive. (See Illustration 6-13.) The latter are usually hinged at the top of the board and attached with highly durable tape. (See Illustration 6-16.)

There are specifically four types of dynamic boards, each of which is classified depending on the way you either add or remove the pacing devices from the baseboard itself. I call these four types: "buildable," "revealable," "combination," and "overlays."

The trial lawyer can put material on a board and place it on an easel, and at the same time discuss a particular piece of evidence on a second board or project illustrations onto a screen.

ILLUSTRATION 6-12. Using Complementary Graphics

The most common form of dynamic exhibit boards consists of two parts: (1) a Baseboard and (2) Cover Pieces.

1. Baseboard

2. Cover Pieces

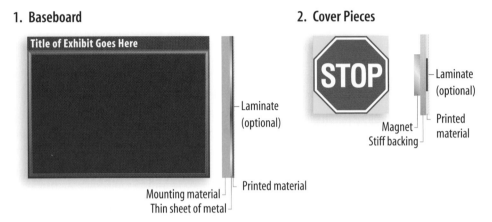

ILLUSTRATION 6-13

Buildable Boards. "Buildable boards" are boards to which you *add* pacing devices, which I call cover pieces, in order to increase the information presented by these graphics or to make the way that you present the information more dramatic or easy to understand. Generally, these boards use a baseboard with very little data (other than a title) printed on it. The space below the title bar is the area where you add the cover pieces. A typical baseboard for a buildable board might look like the one shown in Illustration 6-14.

The lawyer on his own (during opening statement or closing argument) or in conjunction with a witness (during testimony), will coordinate what cover piece to add to the baseboard and when. These add-ons usually have separate bits of information printed on them. When the time comes, the lawyer adds a piece. Later, as appropriate, he adds another and later another, until the graphic is complete.

The speed with which the lawyer builds this board can vary. At one extreme, the lawyer can build the board rapidly by quickly summarizing its contents in opening statement or closing argument. At the other extreme, the lawyer may take considerable time building the board using expert testimony where there may be a considerable time lag between the addition of each add-on.

Revealable Boards. The easiest way to describe revealable boards is that they are the opposite of buildable ones. In revealable boards, the baseboard has all of the desired information of the graphic already printed on it.

With revealable boards, the cover pieces are blank, often printed in a color to match the color of the baseboard. You place these cover pieces on the baseboard before you show the graphic to the jurors. As the lawyer and witness progress, they

① Baseboard and Cover Pieces

② Cover Pieces added to board

③ Completed exhibit

ILLUSTRATION 6-14. A Buildable Board

remove the cover pieces revealing the material printed beneath on the baseboard. A revealable board would transform like the one in Illustration 6-15.

Combination Boards. Combination boards use elements of both buildable and revealable boards. Where buildable boards have blank baseboards and magnetic cover pieces with data printed on them, and revealable boards have baseboards with data printed on them and blank cover pieces, a combination board has data printed on both the baseboard and on at least some of the cover pieces. This increases the amount of information that you can present at different times using the same

① Cover Pieces in position on Baseboard

② Cover Pieces removed

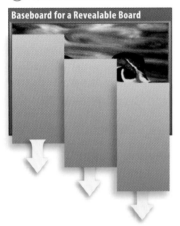

③ Completed exhibit

ILLUSTRATION 6-15. A Revealable Board

exhibit board. This technique works particularly well when you have a lot of material to cover, when you want to do it quickly, and when you do not want to lose momentum or distract the jurors by changing boards during your presentation.

Overlays. Overlays are generally acetate sheets on which information is printed or drawn. Tape attaches the top of the acetate to the top of the baseboard. You can flip the acetate sheet over the top to either cover the baseboard or put the acetate sheet behind it when you do not want it to be seen. It is possible to have more than one acetate sheet per graphic, but, for reasons discussed below, try to avoid this.

Overlay graphics can be displayed in two versions. The first is just the information on the baseboard. The second is the baseboard with acetate pulled down over it. Such a graphic might look like the one shown in Illustration 6-16.

There are three basic problems with overlays that make them less effective than other dynamic boards. The primary problem is that overlays are cumbersome and difficult to use. Second, acetate can get messy very quickly. This messiness can distort the ability of the jurors to see what is on or under the acetate. The final

The overlay is printed on a sheet of clear acrylic and attached to the top of the baseboard.	When it is needed, the overlay is folded over so that it lies directly on top of the baseboard.

Here, the baseboard is shown without the overlay, which has been temporarily flipped behind the board.	Here, the baseboard is shown with the overlay flipped over to cover the board.

ILLUSTRATION 6-16. A Board With Overlay

problem is that, despite what many lawyers imagine, you cannot effectively build a board by repeatedly adding multiple layers of acetate sheets on top of one another. After about two layers, the jurors cannot see through the acetate very well. If you want to create a multilayered trial graphic, you should consider using another display medium.

Which Type of Dynamic Board Should You Use? Once you have decided to use a dynamic board, how do you decide which type should it be? Ultimately, that is a purely personal decision for the lawyer using the board to make; having said that, I offer five observations that might help you make this decision.

First observation: Revealable boards are particularly effective and should be used when the exact location of the information on the dynamic board is important. Assuring this exact lining up would be difficult with a buildable board because of the likelihood that the lawyer might not place the necessary information in exactly the right spot. This is not a concern with a revealable board, in which the baseboard is printed with the information already in the right place. As long as you pull the cover pieces off at the right time and in the right order, there is nothing to worry about; the information will be perfectly placed.

Second observation: Buildable boards are safer to use if there is any reasonable question as to whether you can or want to use certain evidence. For example, I earlier showed you a buildable graphic that was used to define what a millirem of radiation was. In that example we showed that smoking one cigarette in a lifetime exposed a person to a millirem of radiation. To emphasize this point we created this magnetic pacing device to add to the baseboard.

Let's now assume that for some reason that you are either precluded from using this evidence (e.g., a judge rules in a motion in limine that this testimony is too inflammatory—I know that this is unlikely, but just assume it happens) or you decide you should not use the evidence (e.g., you discover that the likely foreperson of your jury is an adamant supporter of smoker's rights and smokes like a chimney during each break and you don't want to offend him). Using a buildable board as shown in Illustration 6-17 rather than a revealable one solves this problem for you. How? Simple; you just don't put up the magnetic pacing device and the jury is never the wiser.

Third observation: If your choice is between using a revealable board or a very large cover pieces with considerable data printed on it, generally go for the revealable board. Large magnetic pieces are unwieldy. You want to take the pieces off the baseboard and forget about them. Unfortunately, you can't just do this if you are using a buildable board with a pacing device containing substantial text. In such

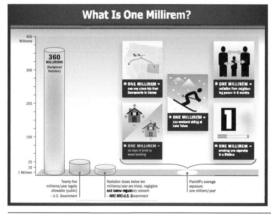

One of the advantages of a buildable graphic is that if you decide not to use a piece of data . . .

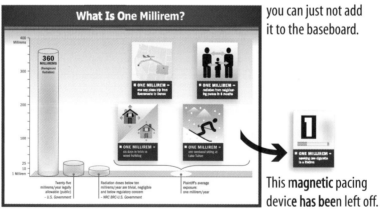

you can just not add it to the baseboard.

This **magnetic** pacing device **has been** left off.

ILLUSTRATION 6-17. When Buildable Is Better

a case, you need to make sure that the piece is in the right place, that it is not crooked, etc. Because of this, in such an instance it is far better to use a revealable board.

Fourth observation: When you want to be dramatic in a short period of time, a revealable board usually works best. As a practical matter, it is easier and faster to pull off blank cover-ups than to add pacing devices to a board. For example, we recently had a criminal case where the prosecutor made highly effective use of a revealable board. The baseboard of this graphic listed ten reasons why a particular defendant was guilty of a serious white-collar crime. The prosecutor was particularly effective in driving this point home by peeling off the cover-ups one at a time and letting the cover-ups dramatically drop to the floor. By the time he was done, the space around the podium was littered with the cover-ups and the board revealed a multitude of reasons why the jury should convict the defendant. The pile of cover-ups made the revealed information seem all the more ominous and had a profound impact on the jurors.

Final observation: Overlays work best in the rare situation when you want to add widespread data to an unchanging baseboard. The classic example of this is a graph (printed on the baseboard) that you want to cover with contrasting data over the entire graphic. If you are adding data to a very limited section of the graphic, overlays are not usually the best medium.

Specialty Exhibit Boards. Certain cases require that you come up with creative ways to display the information using nonstandard or specialty exhibit boards. Let me give you an example. In one of our cases, we were charged with finding a way to illustrate that plaintiff's expert's prediction of sales was completely unrealistic. We wanted to show that the predictions were inflated. The expert predicted that property sales in this desert town, which had been historically minimal, would jump twentyfold virtually overnight and remain that way for approximately forty years. Honest, I am not making this up, that was the prediction.

We came up with a specialty board that was a hybrid of a standard board and a sixteen-foot-long scroll. The board section contained the historical data, which showed minimal sales. To this board, shown on the left in Illustration 6-18, we added a scroll of information that could be unrolled to show the expert's unrealistic prediction that sales would explode for the next forty years. When fully extended, the specialty board dramatically made our point. (See Illustration 6-18.)

This trial graphic caused considerable laughter among those who viewed it. Laughter confirmed the fact that the absurdity of the expert's numbers was readily apparent to the jurors.

Advantages of Exhibit Boards

Exhibit Boards Are Immediately Accessible. There is something dramatic about reaching over, picking up a board, carrying it to the easel, and presenting it to the judge, jury, and witness. There is something comforting in knowing that the evidence goes

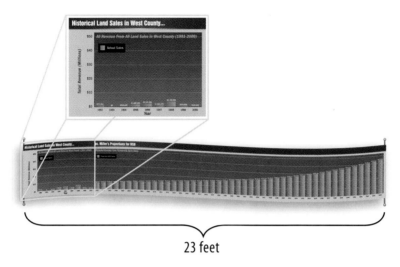

23 feet

ILLUSTRATION 6-18. A Specialty Exhibit Board

from you and the exhibit board (which is right next to you) directly to the jury, rather than through a considerably less personal projected image on a screen thirty feet away.

Exhibit Boards Come Ready to Use. Unlike graphics spontaneously created on flipcharts or blackboards, exhibit boards are already prepared and ready to show. You benefit in four ways from this. First, there is less of a chance that the graphic will contain errors since you will have reviewed it prior to coming to court. Second, there is no delay in getting the information onto the board and, thus, less chance for the juror's mind to wander as you spontaneously write out text or make a drawing. Third, you are able to focus all of your attention on using the graphic, rather than dividing your focus between creating it and using it. Finally, unless you are a quick sketch artist or one heck of a calligrapher, prepared graphics look a lot better and can be considerably more visually engaging. With visual engagement often comes understanding and retention by the jurors.

Exhibit Boards Can Be More or Less Permanent Fixtures in the Courtroom. At the beginning of your presentation, you can put an exhibit board up on a tripod and leave it there during your entire presentation. When you need the information on this board, you know where it will be. Just by sitting there, the exhibit board is available to be your lifeline when things get confusing or when you forget certain information. There is a comfort in knowing that, when you really need it, you always know where to find the board with its information.

Let me give an example.

When I tried cases or argued in court, I was always terrible with names and dates. As a result of a certain amount of low-level dyslexia, unless I had help, dates would get transposed, plaintiff would be come defendant, etc. One of the coping tools I used was a timeline that I would put up just as I started my presentation.

This timeline served a variety of purposes. It helped the jurors learn when key events took place and see when such events took place in relationship to one another. Equally important, the timeline was a place that I knew I could always turn to if I needed help. If I got into the heat of argument and could not remember whether something happened on 4/3/99 or 3/4/99, I knew with confidence that no matter where I was in the courtroom I could quickly turn for the information.

Graphics on Boards Are Less Ethereal Than Those Displayed Electronically. A colleague of mine once commented that electronically displayed graphics were "nothing more than shadow and lights." Fortunately in this day of increased reliance on television, videos, and computer screens, most jurors are not troubled by a bit of shadow and lights. At the same time, the comment does point out another advantage that exhibit boards have over other methods of displaying trial graphics—exhibit boards are solid and are more or less always accessible to and viewable by the jurors. When jurors enter and leave the courtroom, they see the boards that are scattered around there. Exhibit boards have a certain "hovering" quality that encourages jurors to keep looking at them. During boring examination (by your opponent, of course, not you), distracted jurors will read and reread some of the more interesting boards that you have propped for storage against counsel table. The point is, the boards are always there. Electronically displayed trial graphics are on the screen and then they are gone with no physical trace and, unless you are very careful, graphics sketched on newsprint paper accidentally end up in the trash can after you are done with them.

Exhibit Boards Seem More Personal to the Jurors. Recently, we worked on a case involving the alleged theft of trade secrets. Our client displayed many of her trial graphics electronically. But the most important graphics—the ones she wanted to go up and hug—those graphics went up on exhibit boards. The opposing counsel designed all of his trial graphics so that the only way he could display them was to project them onto a screen.

The differences in the presentations were profound. When our client used her exhibit boards (and remember that these were limited to the most important issues, documents, etc.), she would walk up close to the jury box and put one up on a tripod. She spoke directly to the jurors and used her hands to point at the important parts of each board. For exhibits that particularly favored her position, she would almost seem to embrace the board.

The opposing counsel used absolutely no boards. Whenever he showed the jury something, it was always projected onto a large screen across the entire courtroom from the jury box. He even displayed his most crucial documents electronically on a screen. In order to get the jury to see what he thought was important, he would take a laser pointer and direct a little red light onto the screen.

One of the things that happened was that the jury never saw the opposing counsel and his trial graphics at the same time. As soon as the jurors looked at him, he would direct them to look thirty feet away to a screen hanging from the back of the courtroom. There was no connection between the jury, the lawyer, and his trial graphics.

When the case was finished, all of the jurors who we were able to interview said that they felt much more positive about the lawyer who had used the boards. One juror commented that "it was very much like having a conversation in her living room." Another said, "You could really tell that those boards were important to her and that those were *her* exhibits." The point is, by judiciously using exhibits our client created a very important symbiotic relationship between herself and her most crucial graphics—a relationship that translated into positive feelings by the jurors toward the lawyer and (even more importantly) her client.

Exhibit Board Mechanics

Size of the Boards. When asked, "How long should a man's legs be?," Abraham Lincoln responded, "Long enough to reach the ground." Consistent with the tenor of this answer, when the client asks me how large we should make his boards, I always want to reply, "Large enough for the jury to see."

While most printers can create boards of any size, certain sizes are more or less standard. These range from 12 inches by 18 inches on the small size to 45 inches by 60 inches on the large. Within this range, your choice of size is affected by six variables. The first is perhaps the most important—the distance between you and the jury. Each judge has a different rule as to where you can or must stand when addressing the jury. You want to get as close as possible without intimidating the jury. The distance between you and the jury box will affect the size of the board. The greater the distance, the larger you have to make the board.

The second variable often gets overlooked—the size of the courtroom. Courtrooms vary greatly in size. I once tried a case in a rural California county where the courtroom was in a doublewide trailer. I kid you not. Fortunately, it was a bench trial. Exhibit boards 24 inches by 36 inches were about as big as would fit. Other courtrooms, usually federal courts, are huge. In most United States District Courts there is at least one "ceremonial courtroom" that is usually so large that the bench and jury box are in different zip codes. In such courtrooms, you can use—and you very well may need—boards as large as 45 inches by 60 inches.

Whenever possible, always send someone to the assigned courtroom as early as possible to observe how the courtroom is laid out and to ask the judge's clerk how and where the judge likes to display trial graphics and how much discretion the lawyer has to wander from the podium. Obviously, this information is crucial in determining what size your boards should be and should resolve any issues raised by the first two variables.

The third variable is the purpose for which you are using the board. Trial graphics are being increasingly used in situations other than trials (e.g., settlement conferences, arbitrations, and mediations). In these situations, the size of the board needs to be reduced. You may even want to consider using $8\frac{1}{2} \times 11$ inch copies printed on ordinary paper that can be handed out to the participants.

The height of the lawyer is the fourth variable. This is one thing that people who design boards often forget—and I speak from experience. I am only—let's just say I am less than 6 foot 2. The first time that I used professionally prepared trial graphics, I had one designed to be displayed vertically instead of horizontally. When I put this graphic up on a tripod, the top of the board was a good eight and a half feet up in the air. It was very sad whenever I had to refer to anything anywhere in the top third of the graphic. My hopping up and down to point to that portion of the board did little to increase my commanding image before the jury. Keep this in mind when you design your own boards and, if you are about my height, always carry a pointer.

The number of exhibit boards is the fifth factor that can affect the size of your board. Exhibit boards are not easy to transport to or store in court or to use once you get there. The problems associated with using the boards multiplies exponentially when you have more than a handful of boards. I have repeatedly advised that you limit the number of boards that you use; nevertheless, if you do need more than a handful, you might consider making them on the smaller size. Your back will thank you.

Finally, the size of the board may itself be part of the point that you are trying to make. We have seen several examples where the size of the board itself was part of the argument. (See, e.g., Illustrations 4-7 and 6-18.)

Special Lamination. Many commercial printers offer various laminates that can be added to the front of the exhibit board. These laminates provide a clear covering that goes over the picture, text, or whatever you are displaying to the jurors. As a general matter, the laminates protect the picture from stray scratches and dirt. The laminate also adds a more finished look to the graphics.

One of the laminates that is generally available allows you write on the board with a dry erase marker. When you are done, you can erase the markings by merely wiping the board. As you can imagine, this form of laminate can make certain graphics considerably more versatile. For example:

- If you have a map, you can have the witness mark where he was and then erase these marks when you are through.
- If you have a document, you can highlight different sections for different witnesses and then erase these highlights when the witness steps down from the stand.
- If you have a checklist, you can check off boxes with a certain witness and start over again with the next witness.

If you choose to have your graphics treated with this laminate, be aware of three things. First, the ability to erase the marking works only when you use dry erase markers. If you use a permanent marker, that is what you will get—permanent marks.

Second, as soon as you no longer need them, erase the marks you put on any specially laminated exhibit board. There have been occasions when I have waited several days and it is sometimes not easy to remove the marks after the ink is fully dry.

Finally, by definition, erasable marks will come off. If you need to preserve the marks for some reason, use permanent markers. I know, this sounds so obvious. But trust me, in the heat of trial, this is something that you can easily forget. The last thing you want to discover at that point is that the "permanent" exhibit that you specially prepared for trial is like the witch in *The Wizard of Oz* and is steadily melting away.

MODELS

Models are the final phylum in the Nonelectrical Kingdom. I divide models into two categories: replicas and representational models. Replicas are usually copies of things such as buildings, machinery, human hearts, or DNA strands. Representational models are more like three-dimensional "analogies" or "arguments" for your case.

Replicas

Replicas are usually miniature versions of things that you cannot otherwise see in the courtroom. For example, your client may need to show what a building looked like before it was destroyed or needs to show what a nuclear accelerator, which cannot be brought to court, looks like. Building a replica may allow the jury the opportunity to visualize things that they might not otherwise be able to do.

Replicas do not have to be reduced versions of an object. For example, in a biotechnology case, we built a replica of a mitochondrion—what our client kept referring to as "the powerhouse of the cell." We constructed a two-foot version of this microscopic part of a cell. Our replica (which by the way looked vaguely like a large kosher pickle) could be taken apart by our expert, who used it to show the jury the internal parts of this microscopic cellular organ.

Replicas do not always have to be 100 percent physically accurate. Let's assume that you want to show how various nucleic acids will bind only with certain specific other nucleic acids. I am not sure that anyone knows exactly what this physically looks like. Nevertheless, this should not stop you from using a replica to illustrate this concept.

Representational Models

There is a second kind of model that I do not believe lawyers have fully used in the past. These are what I call "representational" models. These models can be thought of as props for your argument. They are three-dimensional analogies or arguments. Whatever you call them, they are highly effective.

Recently, we had an intellectual property case where we were trying to show that as long as two elements were included in a product, the product infringed our client's patent. You could add a whole lot of other things, but if the two items were included, the patent was violated. To illustrate this point, we came up with a very realistic looking shopping bag. The only thing that was different about this bag was that it was made out of one-quarter-inch-thick acrylic sheets and, as such, you were able to see what was inside it. We also constructed various three-dimensional items that could be put into the bag. Two of these items represented the items protected by our patent. The other items were representations of other items not covered by the patent. We then created shopping lists that represented the makeup of the defendants' products. We went through each list and placed the representational items into the see-through bag. Afterward, we showed how each such shopping list did or did not include the two protected items. For those bags with the two items, we showed how such a combination was patent infringement.

Model versus Animation

A logical question that certain lawyers may ask is, "Why use models when you can give a virtual tour of the same thing using animation?" That is a great question. In some instances, it is probably better not to bother with a model. Realtors in my neighborhood now provide virtual tours of houses they are selling. The potential buyer is able to log on to a site and sweep through the house on what the realtors call a virtual tour. Similar systems can be and are used in lieu of physical models in court.

At the same time, there are certain instances when you want to have the permanence that only a model can provide. There are mainly two such instances. First, as I noted earlier, items projected on a screen are ethereal; they are shadow and lights. While they may have considerable impact when shown, that impact fades with time. Models, like exhibit boards, can and do stay in the courtroom. They create a "hovering" effect where jurors can linger over them.

Second, models allow for fiddling. For many years, I have had a small wooden top (the kind you can spin) on my desk. It was interesting to see what people did with it. During meetings in my office, many people would spontaneously (and without invitation) pick it up and start spinning it. I had no problem with people doing this, especially because it confirmed my belief that if it is there and attracts attention, a certain number of people will always fiddle. Jurors can and will play with models, especially if they are admitted into evidence and go into deliberations.

Let me give you an example of how fiddling with models can work to your advantage. We once had a case where the plaintiff claimed that if it had been allowed to use all of the construction equipment it wanted, it could have completed a job on time. Our client, the defendant, wanted to find a powerful way of pointing out that there was no way all of the equipment that plaintiff claimed it needed would have fit onto the construction site. To illustrate this, we created a representational model that was in the form of a puzzle. (See Illustration 6-19.) The outer bounds of the puzzle were cut to scale to represent the outer boundaries of the construction site. We then had an expert calculate the minimum amount of space each piece of equipment required. So, for example, plaintiff claimed it was ready to put two full-size cranes on the job. These cranes were

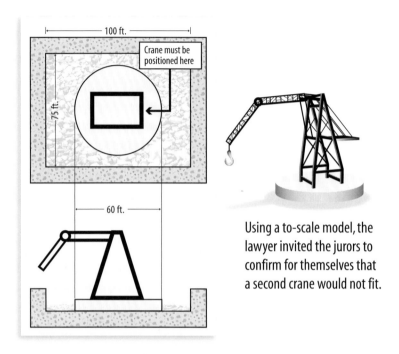

Using a to-scale model, the lawyer invited the jurors to confirm for themselves that a second crane would not fit.

ILLUSTRATION 6-19. A Model Exhibit

designed to swing around more or less 360 degrees and, as such, required circular workspace a certain number of feet in diameter. We created two circles that represented this workspace to scale and invited the opposing party to find a way to fit these two circles within the boundaries of the puzzle (i.e., within the boundaries of the construction site). As you have probably guessed, there was no way to do so. People who were exposed to this model could not help but fiddle with it. And, believe me, they fiddled with it and, when they did so, they *confirmed for themselves* that there was no possible way of arranging two cranes within the confines of the construction project. This is an example where you would never get the same result with animation.

Display Technologies From the Electrical Kingdom

"PROJECTION ONLY" SYSTEMS

The first phylum in the Electrical Kingdom is also the simplest. These are systems that use electricity to project a blown-up still image of a hard copy of a document or small three-dimensional item onto a screen. All that these tools do is project; they do not store images of the projected objects in any kind of an internal memory, such as in a computer hard drive; they do not allow the user to manipulate the content of the image once it is projected. These tools include overhead projectors and Elmos.

I doubt if there are many people who are still unfamiliar with overhead projectors. If you are like me, you first encountered an overheard projector in elementary school. The technology is that old and has not changed or improved much over the decades. These machines project light through acetate copies of a document or photograph and display the resulting image on a screen.

The three biggest advantages of using an overhead projector are fairly obvious. First, many courtrooms already have such machines and screens. The judges and clerks are familiar with the technology and will generally not think twice about letting you use them. Second, this is a very inexpensive way to display your documents. Most photocopying machines now allow you to copy directly onto acetate. This means that creating the projected material is something lawyers can do themselves or have done for a relatively low cost. Finally, this equipment is very easy to set up and use. In fact, I suspect that almost everyone reading this book has used such equipment at some point.

An Elmo is similar to an overhead projector, except that the person who uses it is not required to first transfer the material to clear acetate. Rather, an Elmo uses a small television-like camera to film whatever is placed before it and project these images onto a screen. The camera points downward and focuses on a flat base that is well lit by nearby lights. If you put a document on the base, the Elmo projects the document through the camera on to the screen. If you were to open a book and place it onto the base, it too would be projected by the Elmo. Even relatively small three-dimensional objects can be shown using this technology.

I am not a fan of this phylum. There are numerous problems with using an overhead projector or Elmo. The resolution is not great and the colors often appear washed out. Many of the older machines require that you turn out the lights in the courtroom in order to effectively see what is on the screen. Zinging someone on cross-examination in the dark with the only light in the courtroom coming from an overheard projector just doesn't quite seem to have the same effect as letting the jury watch the witness squirm in broad daylight during your scathing impeachment.

A word of caution—the fact that this technology is relatively easy to use does not relieve you from having to practice. Let me tell you a true story. We once worked on a case where the opposing counsel decided to use an overhead projector with very little forethought and even less practice. He enlisted the aid of a colleague to run the equipment while he delivered his closing argument.

Unfortunately, there was no coordination between the lawyer and his assistant; throughout the closing argument, the lawyer would talk about one topic while the assistant displayed something completely different. The low point in the presentation occurred when the lawyer forgot that the overhead projector could display only acetate versions of the documents. He handed his assistant a paper copy and insisted that she immediately display it to the jury. The assistant knew that this would not work, but was so flustered she put the paper onto the overhead projector anyway. Of course the result was a completely blank screen.

This did not stop the lawyer. Even though there was nothing on the screen, he kept pointing at the screen and describing the document as if there were something for the jury to look at. Finally, the assistant decided she had to do something, so she bravely picked up the 8½ × 11 inch document, held it in front of her, and charged up to the jury box holding paper within inches of some of the jurors' noses. Feeling that their personal space was being violated, the jurors pulled back away from the assistant. As they did, the assistant became even more determined to make sure that they could see the document and she kept pushing the document further and further into the jury box. This caused the judge, who by this point was quite alarmed, to interrupt the closing and firmly order the assistant to get away from the jurors. Needless to say, the net result was a complete and total disaster.

INTEGRATED PRESENTATION SYSTEMS

The second phylum in the Electrical Kingdom includes tools that not only project enlarged still images but also stores these images digitally on a computer hard drive. These tools are part of an integrated system that usually requires a computer, a high-definition projector or monitor, and presentation software, such as inData's Trial Director and Verdict Systems' Sanction.

These tools allow the lawyer to do two very important things that the overhead projector and Elmo cannot. The first is to create a digital database of documents and graphics by having this material scanned and exported into the system's hard drive. As part of creating this database, the system assigns a unique bar code to each page of each document. The program further allows the lawyer to use a bar code reader to *instantaneously* call up and project any particular document or graphic that has been stored on the hard drive.

The second thing that this technology can do is to manipulate the original image "on the fly" during trial. The exact extent to which the images can be manipulated depends on the capabilities of the software program. Typically, these programs allow the lawyer to spontaneously blow up sections and highlight portions of the digitally stored data. Additionally, these tools allow you to add or subtract layers, thereby creating an electronic version of a dynamic exhibit board. (See Illustration 6-20.)

The more sophisticated versions of this software also allow you to move nonlinearly through your material. That is, you are not required to go through the material sequentially. You can use the bar codes to jump around to any particular document in any particular order.

Just as you can have buildable boards, you can have buildable electronic presentations using this form of display. This requires that you create a series of different illustrations that you show sequentially. The advantage of doing this electronically is that you have greater flexibility than you would using an exhibit board and magnets. For examples, see the accompanying Visual Resource CD-ROM.

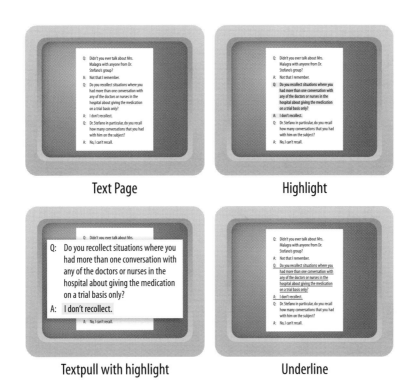

ILLUSTRATION 6-20. **Using Software to Display Text**

FILMED EVIDENCE

Lawyers are increasingly using filmed material in court. One of the most common uses is to show jurors filmed depositions. Other examples of how lawyers use this technology include filmed site inspections, filmed scientific experiments, and filmed tutorials showing how a particular process takes place.

Videotaped Depositions

Under all of the rules of evidence with which I am familiar, transcripts of party deponents may be used for any purpose, and depositions of nonparty witnesses may be used for impeachment. Most, if not all, courts reason that since written deposition transcripts can be read into the record, there is nothing that prevents showing films of that same deposition testimony to the jurors.

If you talk to jurors about what part of the case they found the most boring, they are likely to say, "Listening to lawyers read deposition transcripts into the record." Playing filmed deposition testimony is not as engaging as having the witness testify live. However, when a warm body is unable or unwilling to take the stand, jurors respond much more favorably to filmed deposition testimony than they do to lawyers reading the material into the record.

The fact that you can use these filmed depositions should be good news to most trial lawyers. I don't know about you, but I rarely feel so ineffective as when I read long passages of someone else's testimony into the record. It is not easy to do. I find myself wanting to talk like I normally talk; instead, I have to read words that were spoken with a different cadence and word choices than I am used to. If this is not bad enough, I know that, after a minute or two, no one is really listening to me. It is at this moment that I find myself wanting to re-enact the famous courtroom seen in Woody Allen's movie *Take The Money And Run*. For those who have not seen this comic masterpiece, Mr. Allen cross-examines himself. He does so by asking himself a question from counsel podium, then he runs to the witness stand to answer, then races back to the podium for a follow-up question, next runs back to the witness stand to answer, etc. This continues until Mr. Allen, as the exhausted witness, confesses on the stand.

For a reason I do not fully understand, many lawyers seem surprised when we suggest that they may want to use filmed depositions as part of their opening statement. Fortunately, an increasing number are following this advice and, as a result, many of these same lawyers are making stronger initial impressions during their opening statements. As with anything else, you should avoid excessive use of filmed deposition material in opening statement. Showing too much film in opening may lessen this evidence's impact later during trial.

Many lawyers are also surprised when we suggest that they consider editing various filmed depositions for use in closing argument. "Edit?" they ask. "How can you get away with editing filmed depositions?" The first thing that we assure them is that we are not changing the content of the testimony; we are not editing "yes" to "no" or "red light" to "green." Instead, what we do is to string together different parts of deposition testimony from one or more deponents in such a way as to maximize the impact of this testimony.

Let me give you two examples.

First example of film editing: We recently had a case where a middle-level manager, Mr. Phillips, ignored orders from each of his supervisors. Every one of his three superiors told him not to do something, but he went ahead and did it anyway. This happened not just once, but several times.

Our client filmed the depositions of Mr. Phillips and each of his three supervisors. In several instances, Mr. Phillips testified that he had authorization to take certain steps. In each of these same instances, each of Mr. Phillips's supervisors strongly denied that Mr. Phillips had such authority.

We wanted to find a way to immediately juxtapose Mr. Phillips's testimony with the contrary testimony of each of his supervisors. Edited videotape is one of the best ways to do this, and closing argument is probably the best place to play such a film.

For evidentiary reasons, each of the filmed snippets was introduced during our client's case-in-chief. By the time that we had finished doing so, most of the jurors knew that there was conflict between what was said by Mr. Phillips and each of his supervisors. At the same time, prior to closing argument, most jurors did not appreciate the degree of disagreement because the evidence was admitted in a somewhat disjointed manner (i.e., Mr. Phillips's filmed testimony came in on one day, the filmed testimony of each of his supervisors was admitted on other days).

For closing argument, we wanted to show how isolated Mr. Phillips was in his testimony. We wanted the jury to fully appreciate that every time Mr. Phillips said something was true, not just one but all three of his supervisors contradicted him.

To do so, we edited filmed testimony from four different depositions (Mr. Phillips and his three supervisors) so that our client could play it during closing argument in the following manner. The left side of a split screen showed Mr. Phillips saying, "I was authorized to do A." Immediately after his statement, the right side of the screen showed each of his supervisors, one at a time, contradicting his testimony.

Second example of film editing: Sometimes a lawyer will want to show how many different stories one deponent can tell about the same subject. One of the most effective ways to show this is to use what I call "Brady Bunch" editing. Those who used to watch the old *Brady Bunch* television show probably remember that the opening credits showed a screen that had been divided into three rows with three pictures in each one, like the one in Illustration 6-21.

ILLUSTRATION 6-21. "Brady Bunch" Editing

I will sometimes use this same type of screen to display filmed deposition testimony in closing. For instance, if a deponent has answered one question in a variety of different ways, I will start with a "Brady Bunch" screen showing four to eight images of the deponent at the same time. During closing, the lawyer can point out all of this contradictory testimony by playing one image at a time. The jury can see and hear the deponent make a statement, immediately followed by a different answer, followed by a third different response, a fourth different answer, etc.

Technology for Collecting and Showing Filmed Material

When you talk about using filmed material, you are really talking about three different technologies: (1) one for collecting and filming the material, (2) one for editing what you have collected, and (3) a third to display what you have collected and then edited.

While it is important to know that we are dealing with three different technologies, for our purposes we are not overly interested in the first two. These days, most filmed material is collected through some form of videotape. I always follow a three-step process in making technical determinations with respect to recording this material during the deposition. First, I hire a reputable videographer. Second, I tell the videographer how I hope eventually to use the material that will be filmed (e.g., I would like to be able to link the filmed material to a transcript that I can search electronically). Finally, I let my videographer decide what technology is appropriate. In other words, you should let those who know what they are doing decide which technology is appropriate for filming and recording your evidence.

The same is true with editing technology. This too is far beyond the expertise of most lawyers. Deal with experts and let them deal with these technology questions.

This leaves only the technology related to how you display your filmed material to the jury. This is probably the only place where your preferences as the trial lawyer will affect the choice of technology. There are two primary ways to display the filmed material: (1) on a videocassette recorder, if the material is stored on analog videotape, and (2) using a computer, if the material is stored digitally.

Each of these methods has its advantage. Videotape is relatively inexpensive and easy to display. It can be as simple as putting a videotape in the VCR, which is often already located in the courtroom. Jurors are familiar with and comfortable when watching events recorded on videotapes. Lawyers, even those who are not particularly technologically savvy, are not intimidated by VCR machines and generally are comfortable in their use.

Digitally stored film material is more expensive to prepare and to display. It does have a major advantage over videotape, however. Digital material can be viewed in any order you choose. With a videotape, you must proceed linearly. You must work your way through the tape from beginning to end. If you want to skip around, you can do so only by fast-forwarding or rewinding the tape itself. There is only one way to view the film: a-b-c-d-e-f.

You can view digitally stored filmed material in any order you choose. You are able to skip forward or backward with complete ease. In doing so, you do not need to take time to rewind or fast forward. You do not need to spend time trying to find the exact place where the film you want begins. If you want b-c-a-b-d-f-e, that is what you will get.

In addition, you can program the system so that it will immediately jump to whatever parts of the film you want. It can jump forward or backward. You can freeze on a particular shot. The combinations are virtually limitless.

The advantage of this system is fairly obvious. For example, during her deposition the defendant admitted that the light was red. This admission lies buried among all kinds of other testimony. At trial, you ask the defendant about the color of the light. She now says it was green. With digital technology, you can immediately jump to that portion of the testimony where she says the light was red. No hunting; with just a swipe of a bar code reader, you can go immediately to contradictory filmed deposition material.

This ability to *immediately* impeach a witness with contrary prior testimony has a powerful impression on the jury and the witness. The first time that we used this technology was in a case where the witness contradicted his deposition testimony a score or more times on the witness stand. Every time he did so, our client would pick up a bar code reader and on a large television screen would come the contradicting filmed deposition testimony. After a few rounds of this, the witness got conditioned. As soon as the lawyer picked up the bar code reader, but before he could use it, the witness on his own would correct himself.

ANIMATIONS

Broadly, there are two types of animations: simulations and illustrations. Simulations are, at least in theory, detailed and accurate recreations of what actually happened. They are created in two steps. First, an expert makes all necessarily calculations and measurements based on the actual conditions that lead to the lawsuit. For example, in a collision between two automobiles, the expert would carefully measure the dimensions of the intersection, the speed of the automobiles, the weight of each vehicle, etc. The number of measurements could run into the hundreds. Second, the expert would input all of this data into a computer program especially designed to simulate what would have occurred given the inputted data. The result would be an animation largely generated by the computer itself showing what it determined happened based on the data, the rules of physics, etc.

Simulations often become evidence; that is, they are admitted and become part of the official record. Generally this material requires the testimony of one or more experts to explain the data that was created and the reliability of the computer program that created the animation.

The effect of such graphics can be powerful. When you show a simulation to the jury you are effectively making them witnesses to what happened.

Simulations are often very expensive to produce and require considerable time. They are also routinely attacked (often successfully) by opposing counsel on a variety of grounds. These attacks often go to the accuracy and appropriateness of the data upon which the simulation is based. Consequently, simulations usually work best when as many of the underlying facts are fixed and the activity being simulated is subject to well-established scientific principles or formulas.

Illustrative animations are visual teaching aids used to explain the testimony of a witness. These illustrative tools are not usually admitted into evidence. As we discussed earlier, this material is not treated as the "truth" so much as a "study aid for the truth."

Animations such as these require considerable time and forethought to produce. The first step is to draw a storyboard, a series of sketches of the various scenes you wish to show. Let's use a simple example where the party wants to show how a junk pile built up and eventually polluted a nearby river. We might create a storyboard that looks like Illustration 6-22.

Once a storyboard is created, it is important to immediately get input from everyone who is likely to have any say in the final product. The storyboard needs

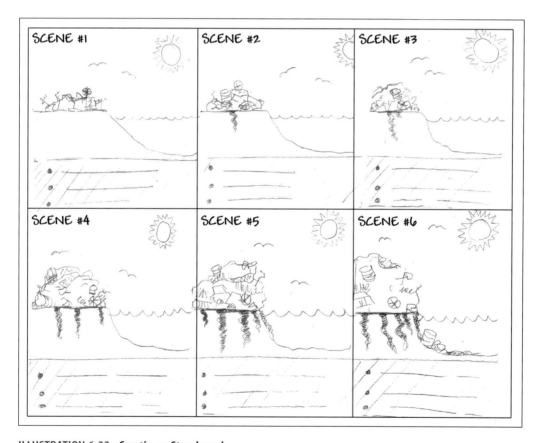

ILLUSTRATION 6-22. Creating a Storyboard

to be reviewed by the lawyers who will be using the animation. The experts and other witnesses who will rely on the animation must give their input as well. The reason for this is that once the creation of the animation starts, it is neither easy nor cheap to make changes. Perhaps the easiest way to understand the problems that changes create is to remember that when you make a change to an exhibit board, you change a single image. An animation is a series of thousands of images that are shown one right after the other. When you make a change to an animation, you must make this change to each of these thousands of images.

The actual technology of how to make animations is well beyond the scope of this book. What we can examine in this chapter is when it makes sense to use animation.

Andy Warhol once made a film of the Empire State Building. The film of a stationary object was shot with a stationary camera. All that the viewer saw for the whole movie was the same shot of the building minute after minute after minute. Very little, if anything, changed from one part of the movie to the next. While it may be art, it is not a great example of what might make a good animation.

Animation works best when it displays a dynamic process. Animations show how things change over time or during a particular process. Animations are also helpful at showing events that cannot otherwise be easily seen or photographed. The possible uses of illustrative animations are limitless. For example, the technology could easily be used to

- Illustrate how moving parts in a machine work together.
- Illustrate the process of building a product.
- Illustrate how years of exposure to the elements will cause metal parts to fail.

I have included examples of animations in the accompanying Visual Resource CD-ROM.

MacroMedia Flash

By now, virtually everyone is familiar with the Internet and the Web sites that are available through it. In my mind, these Web sites have become increasingly popular for three reasons: the depth of information on them, the increasing ease with which you can find this information, and the fact that the people who design the sites have found numerous ways to keep the viewer interested in what is being displayed. You should not be surprised that this same technology is increasingly available to trial lawyers as a way to organize information, display material, and educate jurors.

Before we discuss this judicial application, let's very briefly and in as nontechnical a way as possible review the overall structure of Web pages. At its core, each Web site has at least two important features. The first is a logical and carefully constructed hierarchy of information. The second is a set of navigational tools to help the user move effectively from section to section without getting lost.

The home or index page serves as the base upon which the informational hierarchy rests. Dispersed throughout this index page are various buttons, each associated with a major topic. These buttons serve both as portals that direct the user along the particular informational path he has chosen and navigational tools so that he can jump from topic to topic. Each path leads to a set of related sub-topics and sub-sub-topics, allowing the user to get deeper and deeper into the topic. The user can continue down this informational trail for as long as he is interested or until such a path comes to an end. Throughout this process, information is available in a variety of different formats; the user may see text, pictures, film, and animations all related to the same topic. In addition to this informational hierarchy, the user is able to jump in a variety of directions: forward to material not already viewed, backward to material the viewer has already seen, or sideways to different informational portals and data lines.

MacroMedia's Flash program is one of the tools used to organize and navigate on Web pages. This same technology is increasingly being used in the courtroom. In short, this program allows you to have all of the benefits of a Web site that I have described above without having to go onto the Web. So, for example, you can create an index page that features the key points of your argument or organizes your evidence into related categories. From this page, you can pursue any of these arguments or types of evidence and display text material, photographs, films, animations, or virtually any other form of data.

Clearly, the best way to appreciate this is to look at the example on the accompanying Visual Resource CD-ROM.

Mental Mining and Technology

At the beginning of this chapter I noted that, while you did not need technical expertise, you did need to know how to factor general information about technology into your overall mental mining process and thereby improve your entire case presentation. Let me explain what I mean by this.

I have repeatedly stressed that you should follow the same three-step process of first determining content, then choosing the best design/layout, and then (and only then) determining what the best way is to display what you have created. Without in any way contradicting this, I want to suggest a sub-step when you are determining what technology to use.

Make a mental checklist of the various types of technologies that are available to you. At some point in the mental mining process, run through this list in your mind and ask yourself if you have forgotten anything that you might effectively be able to use at trial. Let me stress that I am not suggesting that you do this so that you can find an excuse to brush off some old piece of equipment and use it again. I am suggesting that you go through this process as a cross-check and as a way to avoid missing content that might be important and effective.

Merely knowing what options exist broadens the lawyer's ability to think critically and ultimately results in better trial graphics. For example, several years ago, many of the lawyers with whom we worked never considered using edited videotaped depositions in their opening statements. Most did not have an explanation why they could not or should not use this type of technology; they just hadn't done so before and they were reluctant to start.

Many of these same clients now routinely use videotaped depositions in their openings; others do not. The important thing is not whether we "convinced" our clients to use videotaped depositions. Instead, what is important is that these clients now at least think about doing so and then make a conscious and informed decision as to whether their case will benefit from using this or some other technology.

Chapter **7**

Standard Forms

Types of Trial Graphics

In order to be considered a great jazz musician, tradition requires that a performer memorize, master, and be able to play in any key all of what are known as the jazz standards. These standards are jazz's most popular and influential compositions—those songs that collectively form the core of this musical idiom. Depending on whom you talk to, the list of standards ranges anywhere from a hundred to several hundred songs.

Knowing all the jazz standards assures performers of three things. First, they can play with other musicians that they have never met before, because all serious performers share the common knowledge of musical history and theory that mastering the standards provides. Second, the standards offer a framework within which they can improvise. Finally, musicians who know all of the standards can generally handle any situation that might unexpectedly arise during a performance.

The same principles apply to the process of creating trial graphics. We too have our own standards list, that is, a collection of trial graphic types that every lawyer needs to master. Fortunately for us, we are not required to memorize hundreds of standards—by my count, there are eleven such forms.

What are the standard forms? How do you determine which one to use? Eventually, you will answer these questions instinctively. Until then, I think the best way for you to make this choice is to imagine yourself in front of the jury with your graphic. At this point, never mind what that graphic actually looks like. Imagine you are able to speak directly to the jurors and hear yourself saying: "Ladies and gentlemen of the jury, here is a graphic that shows you _____."

The standard form that you should choose will depend on how you complete that sentence. For example, if you finish it by saying "here is a graphic that shows you important parts of key documents," then you will probably want to use a textpull. If you finish the sentence by saying, "here is a graphic that shows you where we're going over the next few hours of testimony," then you should consider using an outline.

Illustration 7-1 offers a summary of the most common answers to this crucial question and the corresponding standard form that you are likely to use as a result.

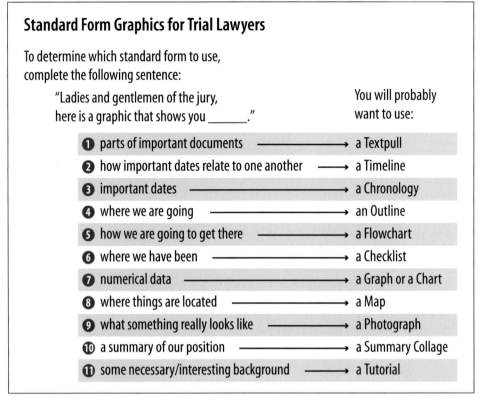

ILLUSTRATION 7-1

The purpose of this chapter is to classify trial graphics by standard form and to provide annotated examples for each classification. There is of course a major problem with this objective. Because there are an infinite number of ways to convey information to jurors, exactly classifying all graphics into strict categories is difficult and providing a complete set of examples is impossible. Nevertheless, this chapter is important. By studying these classifications and understanding what each standard form can and cannot do, the trial lawyer—like the jazz musician—can better improvise and handle any situation that might occur.

The balance of this chapter is divided into eleven sections—one for each of the major standard forms. The sections are in turn subdivided to include basic observations about each category—what works, what doesn't, when you might want to use each type of graphic, etc.

When you look at the following examples, you should not consider any of them as the definitive way to do a timeline, a textpull, or any other type of graphic. Instead, the examples in this chapter are just that—*examples.* Hopefully, when you look at them they will trigger ideas for your next trial. As is always the case with any mental mining technique, most of these ideas will ultimately not be useful; many will be; and with a bit of luck and perseverance, some of those will undoubtedly be great.

Textpulls:
Ladies and Gentlemen of the Jury, Here Is a Graphic That Shows You Parts of *Important Documents*

OVERVIEW OF TEXTPULLS

After oral testimony, documents are the most common way to present information at trial. When jurors see a document and read what is spelled out on paper in black and white, the events associated with the document seem all that more real and the ambiguities created by a witness's potentially faulty memory are often eliminated.

Textpulls are generally the most effective way to graphically highlight the crucial sections of your key documents. There are three reasons for this. First, human nature is such that when something is important, we generally write it down. Second, jurors recognize this element of human nature and give documents considerable weight, reasoning that if something was written down there is a better than average chance that it was important and true. Finally, most jurors generally do not want to have to read the entire document. They want you to pull the important text from the original document for them so that they can concentrate on it, read only what is absolutely necessary, and then move on to the next part of your case. Given these facts, it is no wonder that jurors give considerable weight to carefully prepared textpulls.

ANATOMY OF A TEXTPULL

There are generally four parts to most textpulls, as shown in Illustration 7-2.

❶ The scan ❷ The pull

❸ The citation ❹ The highlighting

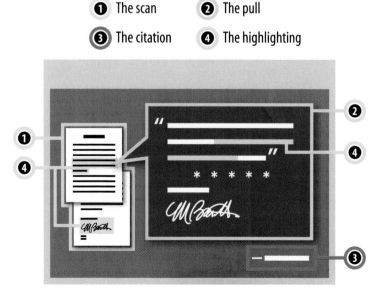

ILLUSTRATION 7-2. **The Components of a Textpull**

The Scan

The first part of a textpull is a small scan or copy of the original document from which you are pulling the key quotation. This scan is large enough so that the jury can visually identify the document, but not so big that it dominates or overpowers the rest of the graphic.

The scan helps authenticate the textpull. I am *not* using the word "authenticate" in the legal sense. That is, I am *not* using the word to mean "the document is what it purports to be." Instead, I use "authenticate" to refer to the increased respect that people usually have for items that they know are "real."

Let me give you an example.

Several years ago, my wife and I took our three children, who were quite young at the time, to my favorite museum—the Art Institute of Chicago. We showed them dozens of Monet's paintings, Grant Wood's *American Gothic,* Seurat's *A Sunday on La Grande Jatte*—nothing seemed to impress them.

In frustration, I commented that I was surprised that none of them was particularly interested in the art. My daughter, Kelsey, confided one of the reasons that she was not impressed: "I have seen all of these pictures before in books. These are just bigger copies hanging on the wall."

"Wait a minute!" my wife said. "These are not copies, these are the real things. These are the actual paintings."

For a moment, our children were quiet and looked confused. Slowly, it dawned on them. "You mean these are real?" asked Kelsey.

"Yes!" I replied.

"Oh," Kelsey said, "We need to go back and take a better look."

For the next several hours, our children carefully and enjoyably inspected the artwork, some of which they had previously passed by with little or no enthusiasm. Knowing that what they were seeing was the "real thing" made all of the difference in the world to them.

Jurors are comforted when they know that the information that they are relying on is the "real thing." That is one of the reasons I often suggest that trial lawyers include a scan of the original source document in their textpulls. The scan helps reassure the jury that the material is authentic and not just something made up by lawyers.

When possible, the scan should include the first page or cover and any page from which you are pulling text. Sometimes this is not possible. For example, sometimes including even small versions of all of these pages may take up too much room in your textpull or unduly distract the jurors from the pull itself. In such an instance, you have a choice: You can show a scan of either the first page of the document or the page from which you actually pulled the quotation. Which is better?

Usually you are better off scanning and displaying the first page. This not only authenticates the document but also makes it easier for the jurors to find the exhibit later on. Remember, while the original document from which you pull the text is usually admitted into evidence, the textpull itself (i.e., the graphic that you prepare to highlight the key passage) generally is not. When you hold up an actual exhibit in court for the jury to see (which many trial lawyers need to do more often), all the jurors usually see is the front page or cover of the document. That is the view they are likely to remember. During deliberations, the jurors are more likely to find the document you want them to use from among a stack of exhibits if they can remember what the first page of the document you showed them looked like. Scanning the cover of the document and including that scan as part of your textpull helps them do that.

The Pulled Quotation

The second part of a textpull is the pull itself. Since the point of a textpull is to single out an important sound bite from a key document, the pulled quotation is the guts of this standard form. To be effective, the pull needs to focus on a single point and be as succinct as reasonably possible. But be careful not to eliminate too much merely for the sake of brevity. Taking something unfairly out of context helps no one, least of all you. Do not pull any more than you reasonably need from the original document and do not eliminate material from your pull that takes or appears to take your quotation out of context.

There are three possible ways for you to display the pull. The first is to retype the text. Most of the time, this is the preferred method. Some exhibits are copies of copies of copies and, as such, do not scan well because the text is extremely grainy. Light portions of a letter disappear after multiple generations of photocopying. Retyping the text often makes this key portion of the graphic easier for jurors to read. (See, e.g., Illustration 7-7.)

The second way for you to present the pull is to blow up an unedited portion of the actual exhibit itself. There are certain parts of a document that you should blow up in their original form. For example, if it is important, you should blow up the actual signature. (See, e.g., bottom of pull in Illustration 7-7.)

The same is true of other portions of a document, such as diagrams or handwritten notes. In Illustration 7-3, the vast majority of the graphic's space is devoted to the scan; that is, there is no separate pulled text. As a practical matter, there is no other way to effectively display this complex drawing except to blow up the figure itself. Re-rendering the figure would be far more time consuming than merely blowing up the original. Additionally, the original sketch has a certain official feel to it that would be lost if you had an artist redraw it. Notice that there are four different colors of highlighting in this graphic. These four colors are used to help isolate and identify key sections in the original sketch.

The final way for you to display the pull is a combination of the first two methods—that is, to display some of the original material and then retype some or all of it to make it easier for the jury to read. This technique often works best if you want to show handwritten notes that are difficult to read or when the document is in a foreign language and you want to provide an English translation. (See Illustration 7-4.)

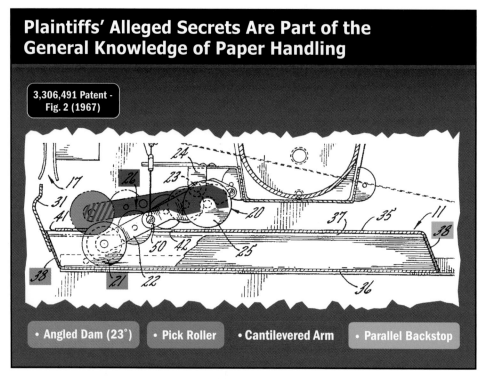

ILLUSTRATION 7-3. Textpulls Are Not Just for Text

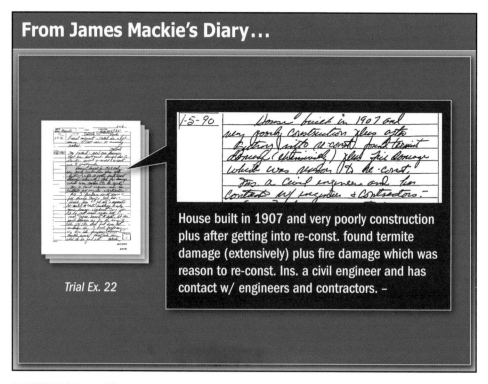

ILLUSTRATION 7-4. If Necessary, Retype the Pull

In addition to the key text, consider pulling some of the following items from your document:

❶ The company logo or letterhead

❷ The date

❸ The name of the person who received the document

❹ The name of the person who sent the document

❺ The signature of the sender

❻ The name of anyone who received a copy of the document

❼ Evidence that the document was received and read

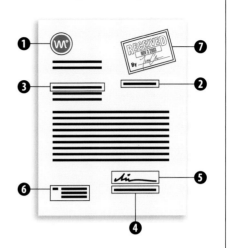

ILLUSTRATION 7-5

Once you have found a key document and decided you want to use it to create a textpull, what do you actually pull besides the key quotations? There is no absolute answer to this question. If the information is important, you should consider pulling it. As shown in Illustration 7-5, such material typically (but not always) includes a scan of the letterhead or company logo, the document date, the name of the people who sent and received the document, any evidence showing that the document was received and read, the document, and the author's signature. Remember, you are always involved in a balancing act—on the one hand you need to make sure that you have enough information to make your point and authenticate your material, on the other you must make sure that you do not overcrowd the graphic with unnecessary details.

The Citation

The third component of a textpull is the citation, which should identify exactly where the pull can be found in the original document.

Whenever appropriate, use two citations. The first is a straightforward, objective description of what the jurors are reviewing; for example, "Letter of 12/13/03 from Scott Wells to Bryan Wells." The second citation is the document's trial exhibit number, which, after all, is how most people will refer to the document throughout the trial.

At some point during the trial, politely (very politely) encourage the judge to take a few moments to explain the exhibit numbering system to the jury. Have the judge explain that the court clerk gives each exhibit a unique number (or letter) so that jurors can more easily locate a particular document from among the stack of evidence sent into the jury room during deliberations.

You should suggest that jurors write down key trial exhibit numbers and invite them to review these specific documents for themselves during deliberation. Some jurors will do so; others will not. But either way, jurors are likely to award you a few extra credibility points for letting them know that you have no problem with their checking on the facts for themselves.

Occasionally, you will create textpulls from statutes and case law for use at a hearing or bench trial. When you do, be sure to provide accurate citations. Check the citations in your graphics as carefully as those in any brief you file with the court.

Highlighting

The final component of a textpull is the highlighting, which principally serves two purposes. (See Illustration 7-6.) The first is to show, to the extent possible, where in the original document the pulled text is located. This helps to authenticate the pull itself and assists jurors in finding the material on their own during deliberations.

The second use of highlighting is to emphasize extremely important material in the pull itself. Remember, many jurors want to quickly know what is important so that they can absorb this information and then move on to the next fact. Ideally, the pull will be sufficiently pithy and its intended message so obvious that you will not need any highlighting. If this is not the case, first try to make it so. If this

In textpulls, highlighting is generally used in two different places for two different purposes:

❶ Highlight the scan to show where in the original document the pulled text is located.

❷ When necessary, highlight extremely important material in the pull itself. Don't overuse this technique or it will become meaningless!

ILLUSTRATION 7-6

proves impossible, use highlighting, but use it sparingly. Save highlighting in the pull for those occasions that really warrant it, or this technique will eventually become meaningless.

TYPES OF TEXTPULLS

Basic Textpulls

A basic textpull is, well . . . pretty basic. It is a static graphic that features a pull from a single document. Just because it is basic does not mean that this type of graphic displays unimportant information. On the contrary, documents displayed in this basic manner are often some of the most powerful and important in the case. These are the ones where the message is so clear that it requires no further graphic assistance in order to convey its significance to the jurors. Illustration 7-7 is an example.

Juxtaposed Textpulls

A juxtaposed textpull compares the text or testimony from two or more sources. Trial lawyers usually use juxtaposed textpulls for one of two purposes. The first is to emphasize that the material is convergent, that is, consistent. The simple convergent

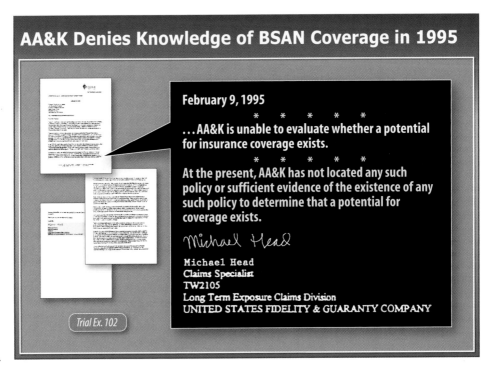

ILLUSTRATION 7-7. A Basic Textpull

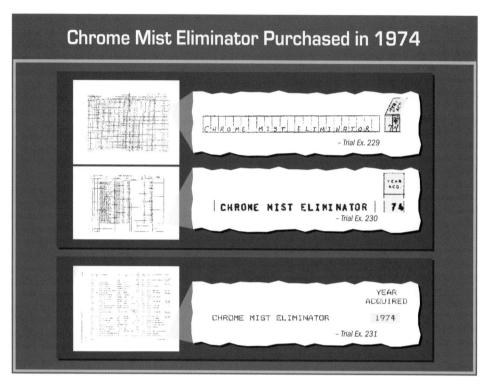

ILLUSTRATION 7-8. A Convergent Textpull

textpull in Illustration 7-8 juxtaposes text from three locations, all confirming that a crucial piece of equipment was purchased in a particular year.

The second common use of juxtaposed textpulls is to show that the material is divergent, that is, inconsistent. The divergent textpull in Illustration 7-9 juxtaposes two documents related to an insurance claim. The first shows the contractor's bid for repair: $45,000. The second shows what the insured submitted to the insurance company for payment: more than $133,000, about three times the amount paid.

Juxtaposed textpulls are often best displayed dynamically, i.e., as either buildable or revealable boards or electronic displays (discussed in Chapter 6). Generally, on a purely mechanical level, if you use an exhibit board to show more than two juxtaposed pulls, you are far better off making the graphic revealable. These boards are easier to use because everything that matters is already positioned on the baseboard exactly where you need it. This means that you do not need to concentrate on where to place the parts. Instead, all you have to do is pull away the appropriate cover pieces and voilà!—there is your message.

Thematic Textpulls

Thematic textpulls are an effective way to gather and display a variety of material all related to a specific topic or issue. The most common form of this graphic is to display a variety of quotations all dealing with the same issue. (See Illustration 7-10.)

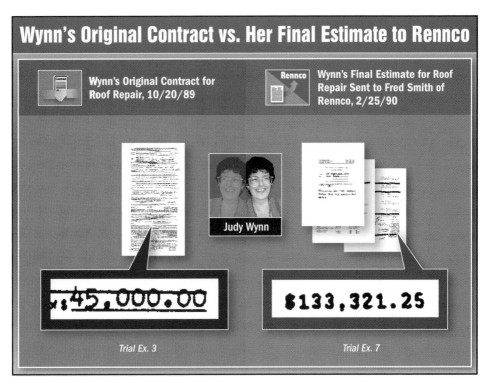

ILLUSTRATION 7-9. A Divergent Textpull

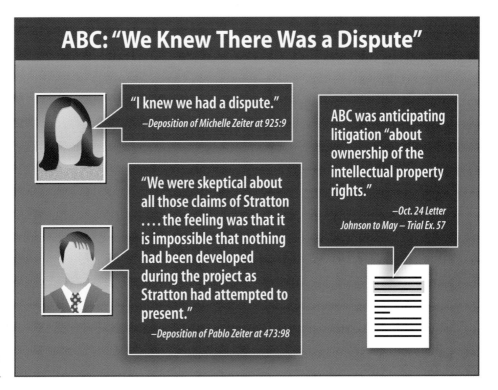

ILLUSTRATION 7-10. A Thematic Textpull of Quotations

An alternative way to create a thematic textpull is to use a single quotation, but then feature a series of references to different sources that relate to that particular quotation. The textpull in Illustration 7-11 begins with a single quotation from a patent at the top of the graphic. Distinct sections of the pull are highlighted in different colors, which correspond to the background colors of a list of related trial exhibits. This allows the jurors to know where to look to find evidence supporting this lawyer's argument concerning this key patent language.

Thematic textpulls work particularly well in closing argument or in other instances where you are summing up testimony on a particular subject. Like juxtaposed textpulls, thematic textpulls make excellent dynamic exhibits. You can reveal or add your first pacing devices, talk about that issue for a while, reveal or add a second pacing device and talk about that topic for a while, and so on. This dynamic format allows you to use Selectavision, the Informational Honeymoon, and the Answer Board Principle (discussed in Chapter 4) to convey information to the jury without overwhelming them.

Supporting Textpulls

Textpulls are an extremely effective way to annotate, beef up, or clarify other graphics. The most common example of this is using textpulls to supplement timelines.

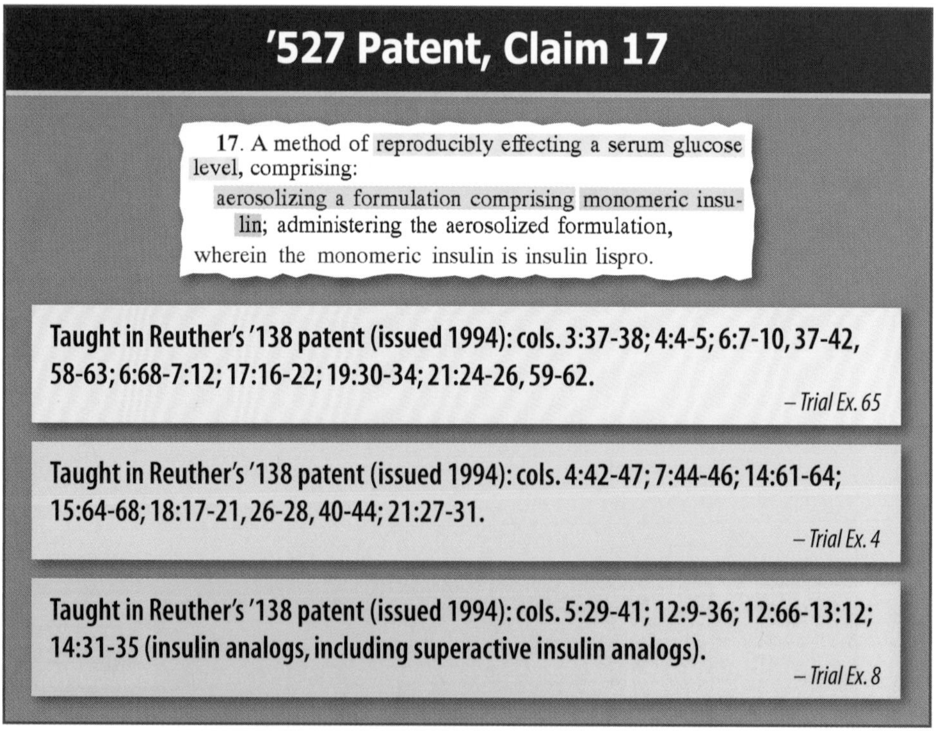

ILLUSTRATION 7-11. A Thematic Textpull of References

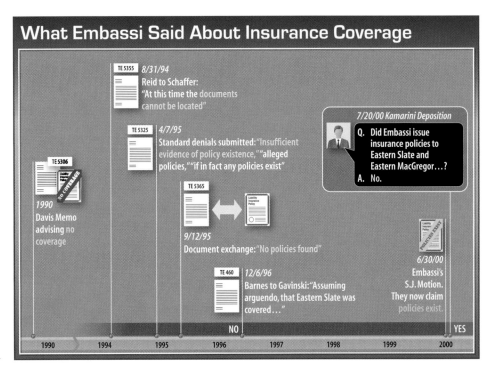

ILLUSTRATION 7-12. **Textpulls Supporting a Timeline**

As we will see in the next section, timelines help jurors understand what happened, in what order, and when. Annotating a timeline with "mini-textpulls" can help put key documents into their temporal context. (See Illustration 7-12.)

Timelines:
Ladies and Gentlemen of the Jury, Here Is a Graphic
That Shows You *How Important Dates Relate to One Another*

OVERVIEW OF TIMELINES

Timelines are important and powerful tools. For most people, organizing events chronologically is the first step in learning and understanding. It is as if the mind needs to walk through the calendar as a way of making overall sense of what happened. Take advantage of this fact, both to learn about your case and as a way to present what you have learned to the jury.

Placing things in chronological order provides you the greatest degree of flexibility in determining what to do next. As we have seen in Chapter 3, chronological order is not the only narrative style through which you can tell your story; it may be the most common way, but it is not the only way. Once you understand the events, you may decide to present them in a different order or through a different narrative style. Regardless of how you eventually present the case, remember that virtually every narrative style requires that you *start* with a temporal analysis and a chronological understanding of the facts.

You should prepare at least one timeline for each of your cases, regardless of whether you ultimately use the graphic at trial. Even if your timeline is never more sophisticated than a sketch on a single sheet of paper that you never show the jury—do it!

ANATOMY OF A TIMELINE

Most timelines consist of two parts: the timebar and the written entries tied to the timebar. Occasionally, trial lawyers will supplement the timeline by adding an illustration or scan to it. These illustrations and scans help to make the timeline more visually interesting and help communicate what happened at a key event or what is in an important document. (See Illustration 7-13.)

The Timebar

Perhaps the single most distinguishing characteristic of a timeline is the timebar that runs through the graphic. There are generally two issues related to timebars: (1) how to divide them into appropriate units and (2) where to place them in the graphic.

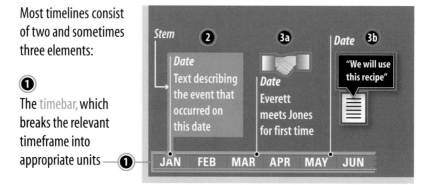

Most timelines consist of two and sometimes three elements:

① The timebar, which breaks the relevant timeframe into appropriate units

② Written entries, which usually include
- A specific date
- A description of the events
- A "stem" connecting this material to the timebar

③ Sometimes timelines include (a) an illustration or icon to visually communicate a key event or (b) a small textpull from a key document.

ILLUSTRATION 7-13

Dividing the Timebar into Appropriate Units of Time. The timebar breaks down the relevant timeframe into appropriate units, for example, years, months, or days. Within a case, there may be multiple timelines, and you may divide the timebars in each differently. For example, you may have an overall or "macrotimeline" that covers several years and consequently decide to divide the timebar in this graphic into annual or monthly segments. In that same case, during that same multiyear period there may also be a crucial month where considerable activity took place and needs to be shown to the jury. To illustrate this, you may want to create a "microtimeline" with the bar divided into daily segments.

I once worked on a case involving damages resulting from a major computer crash. Here the appropriate unit for the timebar in the macrotimeline was minutes—both before and after the crash. The microtimeline, which examined the events in much closer detail, used a timebar broken down into seconds. The way you divide your timebar will vary and will depend entirely on the facts of your particular case.

Placing the Timebar. When you design a timeline, you will typically place your timebar in one of two places: either at the bottom of the graphic (thereby leaving considerable blank space above the bar) or somewhere in the middle (thereby dividing the graphic into two parts—one above the bar and one below). (See Illustration 7-14.)

You will generally place your timebar either:

❶ At the bottom of the graphic →

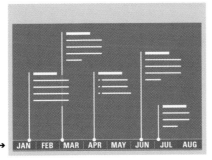

Advantages of placing the timebar at the bottom:

- Simplest form to create and read
- Permits most variation in stem length *(See Illustration 7-15)*

OR

❷ Somewhere in the middle →

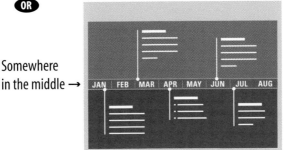

Advantage of placing the timebar in the middle:

Divides timeline into two layers so that one category of entries is displayed in the layer above the timebar and a second category is displayed in the layer below.

ILLUSTRATION 7-14

Placing the timebar at the bottom has three general advantages. First, this is the easiest way to create a timeline and the resulting graphic is extremely easy for the viewer to read. To determine what happened, she merely moves from left to right across the timebar.

Second, because placing the bar at the bottom leaves considerable space, you have the maximum flexibility to vary the length of each entry's stem. Varying stem lengths is one way to maximize the number of entries you place in the graphic. You are able to create "low-rise," "mid-rise," and "high-rise" entries all within a relatively narrow segment of the timebar itself. (See Illustration 7-15.) Having said this, let me caution you—cramming the maximum number of entries into a timeline is something you do only as a last resort, after you have made considerable effort to distill the entries down as much as possible.

Finally, if you want to, you can use the excess space above the timebar to display additional information related to the data in the timeline. (See Illustration 7-16.)

Alternatively, the timebar can be placed in the middle of the graphic. (See Illustration 7-17.) This placement creates two layers within the timeline itself—one above the timebar and one below it. Placing the bar in the middle provides two advantages. First, by alternating the entries (one above the bar, the next below, etc.) the trial lawyer can insert more entries in the graphic and still have them be relatively easy for the jurors to read. Again, this is a technique of last resort. Simplifying the content of the graphic is always better than trying to cram excess information into it.

Second, and more importantly, the trial lawyer can use the timebar as a way to usefully segregate information by type or party. For example, all activities related to one party can be placed above the line and all of the activities by the other party below. Dividing a timeline this way, i.e., segmenting the informational space into layers, creates what is called a layer cake timeline. We will discuss this form later in this chapter.

The Written Entry

The second part of a timeline is the written entry, which usually includes a date, a short description of what happened, and a stem that connects this information to the timebar itself.

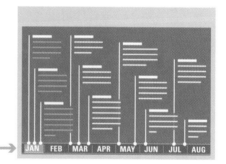

Placing the timebar at the bottom gives you the greatest flexibility in varying each entry's stem length. This maximizes the amount of information you can place in a relatively narrow segment of the timebar. ⟶

ILLUSTRATION 7-15

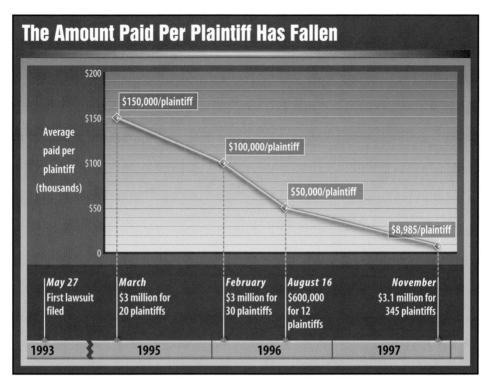

ILLUSTRATION 7-16. Using Space Above a Timebar to Make a Related Point

By placing the timebar in the middle, the lawyer can make the graphic easier to read by alternating entries one above and one below the bar.

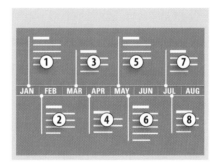

ILLUSTRATION 7-17

Determining what you should include in each of your entries is a process of constantly narrowing down and winnowing information. I almost always begin the process with way too many possible entries, each of which is far too wordy. This is obviously a problem since the ideal timeline has a limited number of entries, each of which has a relatively brief description associated with it.

You want there to be enough entries so the overall timeline makes sense. You also want each entry to have enough information in it to make sense to the jurors (even weeks later if they look at the timeline on their own). You do *not* want your timeline to be so full of clutter or other information that your viewers are distracted from your key points. In order to accomplish this, I make myself go through a four-step filtering process whenever I create a timeline. First, without spending too much time reviewing detailed language, I prioritize the various entries and eliminate those that neither are important nor further the basic theme of the case. This helps me focus on what is important and limits the remainder of the process to those entries that really matter.

Second, I cut back—way back—on each description. In doing so, it helps for me to remember that the lawyer can (and should) always supplement the entry *verbally* when presenting the timeline to the jury. For example:

April 3, 2000 Mr. Smith commences lawsuit against ABC Co. by filing a complaint for six causes of action, including breach of contract and fraud (121 characters)

can be edited to:

4/3/00 Smith sues ABC Co. (21 characters)

To which the lawyer can *verbally* add when he gets to this entry, "This is the lawsuit you, as jurors, are here to resolve. It is the lawsuit that involves the claims of breach of contract and fraud."

It is important for the lawyer to verbally describe the entries when using the graphic. It is a way to add relevant color without visually cluttering the timeline itself.

The third step is to determine whether certain recurring actions can be described using icons or symbols rather than more bulky groups of words. For example, if one of the parties makes a series of payments, it may be more effective to use an icon of a check to record each of these transactions rather than repeatedly writing out, "Payment made." (See Illustration 7-18.)

The final step is to repeat the three steps with what is left and, to the extent possible, keep cutting excess material until you are satisfied with the number of separate entries and length of each associated description.

How to Create Timelines

How do you create timelines? The short answer is, "Use your master chronology!"

I noted in Chapter 2 that while it takes considerable time and effort to create a master chronology, such efforts are worth it because of the variety of benefits that a trial lawyer can derive from such a document. The most immediate benefit is that the trial lawyer can use the information to start the process of learning the most important facts of the case. The second benefit is that different graphics naturally flow directly from the master chronology itself. As we will see, many of these graphics are timelines that help focus the trial lawyer and jury on what is important.

To better illustrate the process of how to use the master chronology, let me start by doing two things. First, Illustration 7-19 shows the master chronology

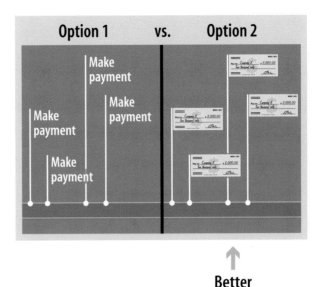

ILLUSTRATION 7-18. Saving Space With Symbols

from Chapter 2. As you may remember, it deals with a hypothetical case involving an automobile accident and the insured's unsuccessful attempt to get assistance from the insurance company to resolve the matter prior to a lawsuit. We will use this material to create examples of the four most common types of timelines: the macrotimeline, the microtimeline, the topical timeline, and the action/reaction timeline.

Second, let me tell you a story. Many years ago, a client visited my office in San Francisco. Since he was early, he went to get coffee at a nearby café in North Beach. This was several years before gourmet coffee was popular, so when he got to the counter and saw that the chalkboard menu listed all the drinks by their Italian names, he was not quite sure what to order. Figuring that the locals knew what was good, he asked for the same thing that the woman in front of him ordered—a triple espresso.

Later that morning my extremely hyper client told me how he had been initially shocked by how much the coffee cost and how little actual liquid there was in his small cup. At first he thought he was being ripped off, but later decided that the cost wasn't all that bad because, as he boasted, "I got at least two or three good cups out of that thing."

Evidently, it never dawned on my client to drink that small cup of espresso "as is." Instead, he sat happily in the café pouring a bit of the espresso into the bottom of a larger cup and then diluting it with hot water. My client repeated this process until what he called "the concentrated stuff" was all used up and he had consumed two or three good cups of "normal strength" coffee.

You should use your master chronology the same way as my client used his espresso—you should get at least two or three good graphics out of it.

A *Master Chronology* Is a Basic Learning Tool for Trial Lawyers

Master Chronology

1/4 Automobile accident – 3rd and Clay
"Vehicle 1 (Young) ran red light hit Vehicle 2 (Jernigan). Minor damage to Vehicle 2;
driver has neck injury." *[Doc. 5– Police Report]*

1/6 Initial contact with Big Insurance Company, Inc.
Young calls insurance agent. Claims Rep. Haskins faxes "Initial Report Form" to Young.

1/7 Young returns faxes "Initial Claims Report Form" to Big Insurance Company, Inc.
[Doc. 1– Completed form and fax transmittal]

2/10 Jernigan faxes first letter to Young
"I hope you are well. My neck really hurts, but all I want is to get my car fixed. Please have your
    insurance company call me. It's been 5 weeks. I have estimate for $500, which is all I want." *[Doc.
    2– Ltr 2/10 Jernigan to Young]*

    ∗Note: First letter seems very friendly compared with later ones after Young cannot get insurer to settle.

    Young forwards Jernigan 2/10 letter to Big Insurance Company, Inc. "Please take care of this
    while she [Jernigan] is still reasonable." *[Doc 3– Ltr 2/10 Young to Haskins]*

3/15 Jernigan calls Young to see if "can't we just resolve this"
"I said - 'I haven't heard from you. I just want my car fixed. I am starting to get upset.'
He said, 'I would love to help, but my insurance company won't call me back.'"
[Jernigan Depo. 19:1-7]

    Young calls Haskins and reports Jernigan's phone call. Leaves message: "I told him [Haskins]
    what she said and for the 20th time I asked him to please call me."
[Young Depo. 3:4-5]

4/20 Young pays his monthly insurance premium to Big Insurance Company, Inc.
    * Note: Get copies of canceled checks to show Young kept his side of bargain with insurance company.

5/21 Big Insurance Co. replies with form letter to Young
"We'll get to you as soon as possible. Have a nice day."
[Doc 6– Ltr 5/21 Haskins to Young]

5/25 Jernigan faxes Young
"I am really upset. If your insurer doesn't get a hold me by 5:00 today I am going to be
    forced to sue you for lot more than $500. Please let's settle this and get this mess
    behind us." *[Doc 8– Ltr 5/25 Jernigan to Young]*

    Young faxes letter to Haskins
"Please! Help me resolve this. I still haven't heard from you."
[Doc 4– Ltr 5/25 Young to Haskins]

5/30 Big Insurance Co. sends second form letter to Young
"Thank you for your recent inquiry. We will be in touch. Have a nice day."
[Doc 7– Ltr 5/30 Haskins to Young]

6/3 Jernigan calls Young
"I am tired of waiting for your insurance company. Resolve this by June 4 or this is going
    to my attorney." *[Tape from Mr. Young's answering machine]*

    * Note: What do we have to do to get audio tape admitted?

    Young calls Haskins
Leaves message updating Haskins on what is happening.

6/12 Attorney Shana Van Ort files/serves complaint
Alleges Jernigan suffered property and bodily injury 5 times greater than Mr. Young's
    policy limits.

6/20 Haskins sends third form letter to Young
"Can't find your Initial Claims Report. We need to start this process all over again. Please
    send/re-send notice of claim. We look forward to serving you."
[Doc 10– Ltr 6/20 Haskins to Young]

✱ possible exhibit ⟶

ILLUSTRATION 7-19

How is it possible to get multiple graphics from a single master chronology? Remember what you did to assemble your master chronology. You cast the broadest possible net and gathered as many facts as possible without prejudging or filtering them in any way. As a result, a master chronology will usually have all of the information that you will ever want and considerably more information than you will ever need.

As with all excesses, once you have assembled the master chronology, you need to cut back, to begin to discriminate, to insist on being selective. By narrowing the information in the master chronology, you create not only a more focused or specialized chronology (with which you yourself can better *learn* your case) but also, in turn, you can easily convert this material into a series of key trial graphics (with which you can *teach* the important facts of your case to the jury).

For our immediate purposes, let's define a case's theme as its core, its essence. (Case themes are discussed further in Chapter 3.) The theme is often (but not always) the *short* description that fills in the blank at the end of this sentence: "Cutting through all the crap, this case is really about _____." Your theme serves as a touchstone. Everything that you present to the jury, all of your facts, arguments, graphics, and other bits of evidence must be consistent with and/or supplement your case theme.

You will *not* use every detail in your master chronology to prove your case. Even if you could (i.e., if the court agreed to give you unlimited time to put on your case), you would not want to. Not every fact in your master chronology is consistent with your theme. In order to help yourself learn which facts are important, you must (metaphorically speaking) run your master chronology through a "What Really Matters" filter. When you do, you end up with what I call a thematically relevant chronology. This chronology separates what matters from what does not and isolates what you need from what you don't. (See Illustration 7-20.)

Occasionally, someone will ask me, "Why the extra step? Why *start* with a master chronology? Why not eliminate a step and just start right off selectively gathering information directly for a thematically relevant chronology?" The best answer I can give is to refer the questioner to Hercule Poirot, the retired Belgian police officer. Throughout Agatha Christie's novels, Monsieur Poirot faithfully gathered "curious little facts." Some were helpful; most were not. Until the end of his investigation, no one, including Poirot, really knew which facts were which.

Poirot always solved the murder mystery, but the point is he might *not* have been able to do so if he only looked for and gathered what he initially guessed to be "helpful" facts. To define a fact as "helpful" or "unhelpful" is to prematurely judge the fact and predetermine how you *think* the story should end. By doing so, you run the considerable risk of rushing to a conclusion that may not be the right one.

First, gather all of the facts in the form of your master chronology. Then and only then, based on the totality of what you have found, determine what the appropriate theme is for your case. Do not pick a theme and then try to find or shape facts to match your choice.

The Master Chronology Is the Source for Numerous Other Graphics

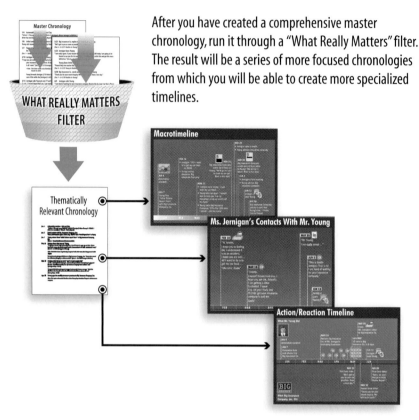

After you have created a comprehensive master chronology, run it through a "What Really Matters" filter. The result will be a series of more focused chronologies from which you will be able to create more specialized timelines.

ILLUSTRATION 7-20

THE MOST COMMON TYPES OF TIMELINES

Once you have assembled the thematically relevant chronology, you can easily use this data to create several different, commonly used trial graphics. For example, you can convert the information in the chronology into one or more of the four most common types of timelines: (1) macrotimelines, (2) microtimelines, (3) topical timelines, and (4) action/reaction timelines.

Macrotimelines

Macrotimelines provide jurors with an overview of the case, the "ten-thousand-foot view"; enough detail to help orient the jurors, but not so much as to overwhelm them. (See Illustration 7-21.) Trial lawyers generally use macrotimelines for introductory purposes. Macrotimelines are often one of the earliest organizational tools shown to the jury during opening statement. These types of timelines also work well as a way to summarize the facts in closing argument.

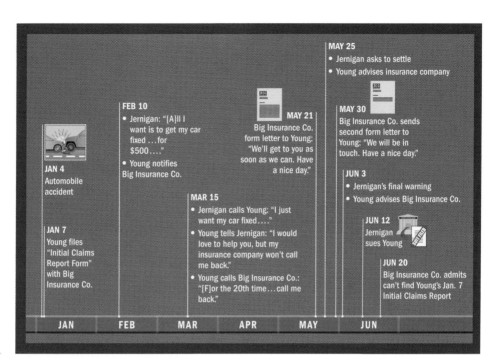

ILLUSTRATION 7-21. An Example of a Macrotimeline

Macrotimelines can benefit the lawyers trying the case. Specifically, you should design these trial graphics as safe harbors in which you can seek quick shelter whenever you need to check on a key date or the order of the most basic/important events. In this way, the macrotimelines act as cue cards allowing the lawyers to deliver much of their presentation without notes and from places other than behind the confines of a podium.

Microtimelines

Occasionally, information or activities will cluster together in a relatively short period of time. Assume that each of these activity periods is sufficiently important that it needs to be listed and discussed. How do you display the information without overwhelming the viewer?

You have a couple of options. One is to try to squeeze the data into a small area. For a variety of reasons, this is usually *not* the preferred way to convey both general and detailed information. You will often end up with a version that is too difficult to read and has entries that are so closely compressed together that the jurors will not be able to tell what happened when, or what proceeded/followed what. Illustration 7-22 is a horrible graphic, the result of trying to cram too much information into a single timeline. Better to have two different timelines—a macrotimeline (See Illustration 7-21) and a microtimeline (See Illustration 7-23).

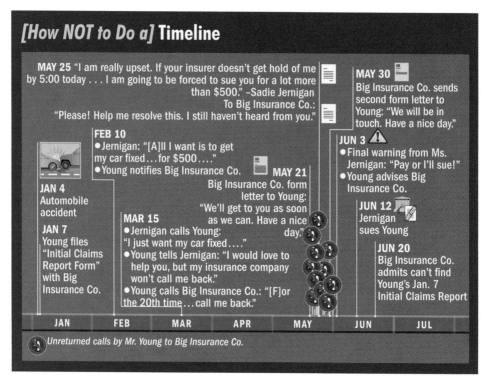

ILLUSTRATION 7-22. **This Example Tries to Force Too Much Data in Too Small of a Space**

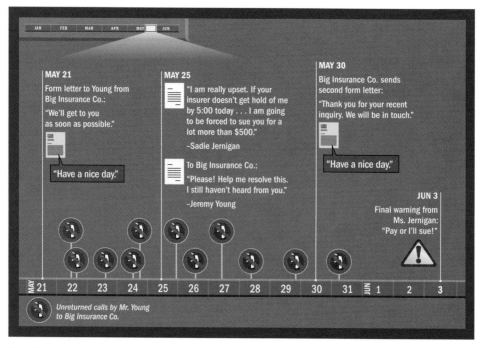

ILLUSTRATION 7-23. **An Example of a Microtimeline**

The better way to display clustered material is usually to create a microtimeline that devotes the entire exhibit to a relatively short period of time. Where the macrotimeline in Illustration 7-21 covers a period of six months, the microtimeline in Illustration 7-23 uses the same amount of space to cover just ten days. The larger scale makes the exhibit easier to read and easier for the jurors to appreciate the sequence of events leading up to trial. Note that the microtimeline does not entirely ignore a more global view of the case. For perspective, a miniature version of the macrotimeline is shown in the left-hand corner of the exhibit. A portion of that macrotimeline is highlighted in order to help the jurors see where this segment fits into the entire scheme of events. Thus, overview and detail are connected.

Topical Timelines

Information architects design topical timelines so that a presenter can gently, but clearly, force the viewer to concentrate on a single issue. (See Illustration 7-24.)

Events do not happen in isolation; they cluster together in a variety of different ways. Often, it is important to break a particular topic away from the rest of the story and examine that topic in isolation. By breaking down the overall picture into distinct topics, you force yourself to look for, and hopefully find, connections between what at first may have appeared to be a series of unrelated facts or events.

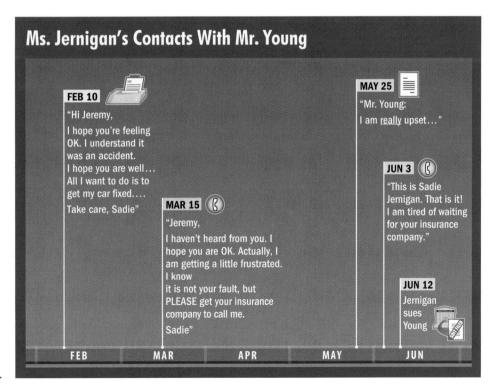

ILLUSTRATION 7-24. A Topical Timeline

Finding ways to divide the facts topically helps you see threads that connect some facts, but not others. It helps you see a trend or a lack of one.

The topical timeline in Illustration 7-24 isolates and focuses on a single subject—the telephone conversations between Ms. Jernigan and Mr. Young. One of the facts that becomes clear by isolating these events is the increasing frustration and anger expressed by Ms. Jernigan. At first she is willing to settle the whole thing for the cost of getting her car fixed. As time passes, her words become more angry and her demands increase. Mr. Young might be able to use this graphic to emphasize how much more easily the dispute could have been resolved if Big Insurance Company had merely returned his calls and contacted Ms. Jernigan early in the process.

Action/Reaction Timelines

The facts underlying lawsuits sometimes resemble Newton's third law of motion—for each action there is an equal and opposite reaction. Unlike Newton's law, the reactions between parties, while opposite, are rarely equal. Sometimes the reaction is disproportionately small. In such an instance, one party makes a considerable effort (action) only to be virtually ignored (reaction) by the other. In other instances, the response is disproportionately large and aggressive, like a penny-ante poker game: "Oh yeah, Mr. Tough Guy—I'll see your nickel and raise you a quarter."

One way of making sense of all this give and take is to create an action/reaction timeline. Such a timeline will allow you to visualize how one party's "tick" influences or is influenced by another party's "tock." For example, the action/reaction timeline in Illustration 7-25 shows Mr. Young's actions above the timebar and Big Insurance Company's actions (or rather, lack of actions) below. Using this format, the trial lawyer can effectively show the jurors how hard Mr. Young worked to get help from his insurance company and, in contrast, how the company did nothing in response. In fact, eight days after Ms. Jernigan filed her lawsuit, the insurer admitted it had lost Mr. Young's initial claims report.

OTHER TYPES OF TIMELINES

At the outset of this chapter I conceded that it is impossible to provide you with examples of every single type of graphic. Thus far we have examined four of the most common forms of timelines. While I cannot display all possible themes and variations, I want briefly to examine some of the other ways of conveying information using a timeline.

Segmented Timelines

The movie *The Sting* is about a hustle organized by one set of conmen against another set of conmen. Throughout the movie, you are never entirely sure who is conning whom. You are not sure how much is true and how much is hype. This is how many jurors cynically view a trial.

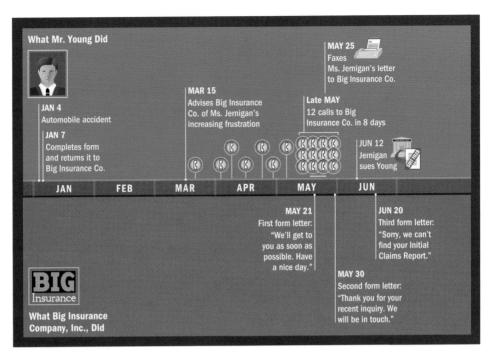

ILLUSTRATION 7-25. An Action/Reaction Timeline

One of the things that the director of *The Sting* did to help viewers keep better track of what was going on was to break the movie up into segments, each one of which corresponded to a discrete phase of the con. The director introduced each segment using a title slide with a cryptic description of what is about to occur.

For me, segmenting the movie had three effects. First, it helped me focus on what was going on. Second, segmenting the story and letting me know that we were moving from one segment to the next helped alert me to the fact that things were subtly changing. I might not know exactly what or how things changed until the end of the movie, but I understood that, because we were in a different segment, things were not quite exactly as they were earlier in the story. Remember, in the middle of a story knowing that there has been a shift is often as important to the viewer/juror as knowing exactly what that shift has been.

Finally, at the end of the movie (which, of course, had a nice little twist), the segmentation of the story helped me better appreciate what I had just witnessed. I could say to myself, "Now that makes sense. In the beginning I could not figure out why a character did that. Now it makes sense in light of what happened in the middle segment."

Often, when reviewing the events leading up to your trial, you will observe that these events naturally fall into distinct phases or segments. In such instances, you may find it easier to tell your story to the jury in segments, or chapters. When this happens, also consider using macro and micro versions of a segmented timeline to organize your presentation. Illustration 7-26 is an example of a segmented timeline with a macroview. The underlying events in this case fall into four segments, and each segment has been given a title. I would probably use this graphic in opening statement as an introduction to the case.

To the extent that you need to provide more detailed information, you can create a series of microtimelines, one for each segment. (See Illustration 7-27.)

Layer Cake Timelines

In any exhibit, space is a limited and scarce resource that needs to be carefully allocated. We are always trying to find ways to maximize our use of space and to do so in such a way as to convey more information effectively. Layer cake timelines let you do this. To create such a timeline, the trial lawyer divides the graphic into two or more layers and then assigns a particular type of information to each layer. (See Illustration 7-28.)

For example, assume that defendant was saying one thing in public and something different in private. As shown in Illustration 7-29, the trial lawyer might divide the timeline into two layers—one illustrating the public comments and the other illustrating the private ones. This simple technique provides jurors with a powerful way to compare the defendant's public and private actions.

There are three major advantages to using layer cake timelines. First, you are able to use space effectively and to combine information that might be on several different timelines into a single trial graphic. For example, if you find yourself

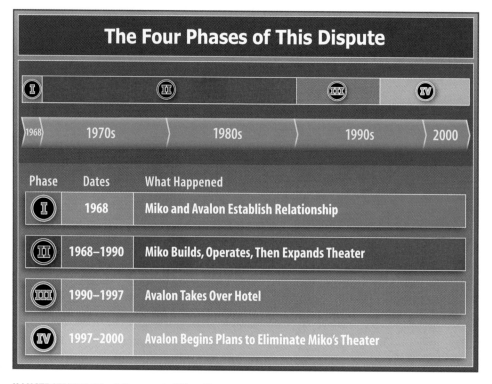

Phase	Dates	What Happened
I	1968	Miko and Avalon Establish Relationship
II	1968–1990	Miko Builds, Operates, Then Expands Theater
III	1990–1997	Avalon Takes Over Hotel
IV	1997–2000	Avalon Begins Plans to Eliminate Miko's Theater

ILLUSTRATION 7-26. A Segmented Timeline

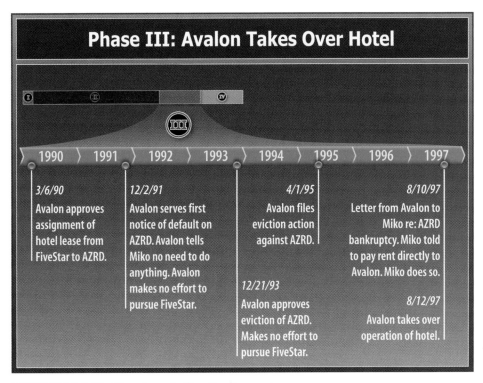

ILLUSTRATION 7-27. Microview of a Timeline Segment

Recipe for Creating a Layer Cake Timeline

Step 1:
Notice certain repeating
categories of activities

Step 2:
Divide the facts by category

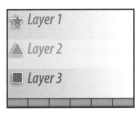

Step 3:
Create a multiple layer or "Layer Cake
Timeline" where each category of data
is assigned its own layer

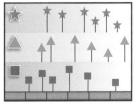

Step 4:
Place each entry in chronological
order within its assigned layer

ILLUSTRATION 7-28

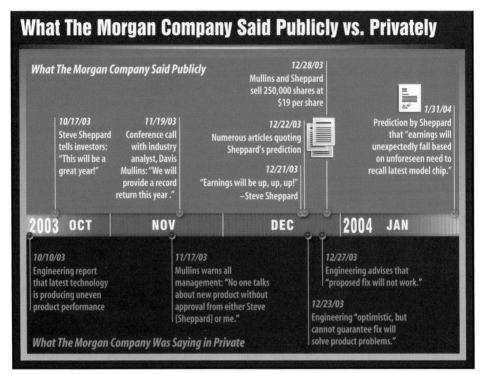

ILLUSTRATION 7-29. A Layer Cake Timeline

constantly referring to or comparing two different timelines when describing related events, consider whether you could effectively combine the two into a single layer cake timeline. However, this technique will not work in every case. Do not be penny wise and pound foolish by inappropriately cramming excessive information together and justify doing so by claiming that you are creating a layer cake timeline.

Second, layer cake timelines let you and your jurors know exactly where to go whenever you or they need particular information about an important subject. For example, in Illustration 7-29, if you need to know what was being said publicly, look at the layer above the timebar; if you need to know what the defendant was saying behind closed doors, look below.

Finally, layer cake timelines are the functional equivalents of an MRI scan. If you have ever seen the film developed from such machines, it's amazing. The machine is able to produce an image that is a slice right through the body at any specific location. We can do the same with a layer cake timeline. If you need to know what was happening on given fronts prior to a particular time, you can take a transverse slice out of the timeline. By doing so, you can see what was happening on all different layers during a discrete period of time. (See Illustration 7-30.)

Sequential or Relative-Order Timeline

Occasionally, the dates when certain events occurred are considerably less important than that the events took place in a certain sequence or relative order. You can display this in a "sequential" or "relative order" timeline. The graphic in Illustra-

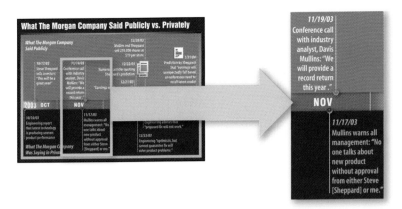

ILLUSTRATION 7-30. A Slice From a Layer Cake Timeline

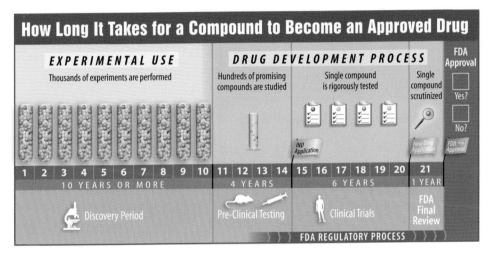

ILLUSTRATION 7-31. A Sequential or Relative Order Timeline

tion 7-31 is a sequential or relative order timeline. It outlines a compound's course from discovery to FDA approval as a drug. Though this particular case involved a specific drug, this graphic was designed to be generic in order to teach what generally happens in this process. The specific year that something took place is less important than the relative amount of time each phase of development takes and the length of the overall process, approximately twenty-one years.

Juxtaposed Timelines

Juxtaposed timelines operate the same way and serve much the same purpose as juxtaposed textpulls: They allow jurors to more easily compare and contrast information. As with juxtaposed textpulls, juxtaposed timelines can be either convergent (i.e., compare similar or confirming testimony) or divergent (i.e., compare contrasting material).

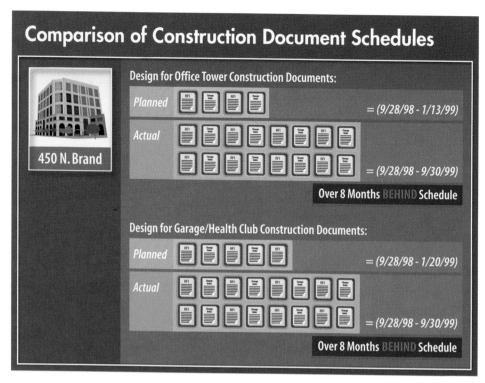

ILLUSTRATION 7-32. A Juxtaposed Timeline

One of the most common uses of juxtaposed timelines is to compare scheduled activities to actual performance. The timeline in Illustration 7-32 compares how long certain aspects of constructing a building were scheduled to take and how long those steps actually took to complete. It is easy to see the considerable delays in the construction of this building.

Chronological List: Ladies and Gentlemen of the Jury, Here Is a Graphic That Shows You *Important Dates*

You do not always need a timeline to show how events relate temporally. An alternative method is to use a chronological list of key events. Chronological lists are relatively simple trial graphics and generally have only two parts. The first is a column listing dates in chronological order. The second is a wider column, usually to the right of the first, describing in detail the events that occurred on each of the listed dates. (See Illustration 7-33.)

A typical chronological list is shown in Illustration 7-34. There are two things that you should notice about this graphic. First, this standard form tends to be very text-intensive. Unlike a timeline, chronological lists rely more on words than on space and symbols. Second, this type of graphic is a rare example of one which works better being printed vertically (in what is called a "portrait" setting) than hori-

Most chronological lists
consist of two parts:

1 ——————————

A column listing dates
in chronological order

2 ——————————

A wider column describing
events that occurred on
each of the listed dates

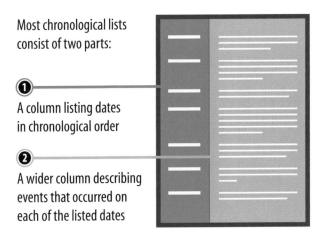

ILLUSTRATION 7-33

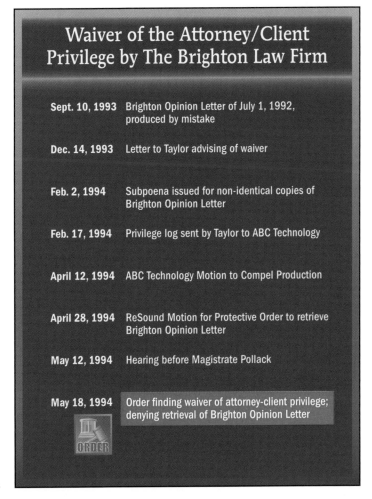

ILLUSTRATION 7-34. **A Chronological List**

This is vertical or "portrait"

More listed items but will not display well on screen

- Text wastes less space
- Many listed items
- Bullet point 1
- Bullet point 2
- Bullet point 3
- Bullet point 4

This is horizontal or "landscape"

Fewer listed items works well on a screen

- Text wastes more space
- Fewer listed items
- Bullet point 1
- Bullet point 2

ILLUSTRATION 7-35. Portrait and Landscape Formats

zontally (in what is called a "landscape" setting).[1] The reason for this is entirely practical. Since such exhibits tend to be fairly text heavy, a vertical frame wastes less space per line (See Illustration 7-35).

Chronological lists have a major disadvantage compared to timelines. It is virtually impossible to get jurors to intuitively *feel* how much time passed between events if the dates are all merely set out on a chronological list. Said differently, it is generally easier for a juror to visualize intuitively how much or how little time passed between two different events by looking at a timeline than looking at a chronological list. This is because in timelines large gaps are clearly visible and show when a long time passes between events. Likewise, jurors can easily see clusters of entries when events occur in rapid succession. In chronological lists, the

---

1. Graphics displayed in portrait format do not work well when projected electronically. Most screens are designed for the graphic to be displayed horizontally, not vertically. When shown vertically, there is often considerable wasted space around the graphic. (See Chapter 6.)

various events are listed at equal intervals. There would be as much space between events two hundred years apart as there would be between events one year apart. (See Illustration 7-36.)

How do you decide whether to use a timeline or a chronological list? While there is no definitive answer to that question, there are four factors that you should consider. First, if seeing temporal relationships is crucial, a timeline generally works better because it allows jurors to see how dates cluster or spread out. Conversely, if you want to *minimize* the jurors' ability to see how much or how little time passed (in other words, if time is the enemy of your case), a chronological list makes temporal relationships far less visible.

A second factor is preparation time. Chronological lists generally require less time and outside assistance to create than timelines do. Virtually any lawyer who knows a basic word processing program can create a decent $8\frac{1}{2} \times 11$ inch version of a chronological list, which can then be blown up into a board or shown electronically on an overhead projector or similar device. Not so with timelines, which generally require more effort and time to create.

Third, if you have a series of repeated activities, a timeline is often better than a chronological list. In a timeline you can use an icon or symbol to represent the

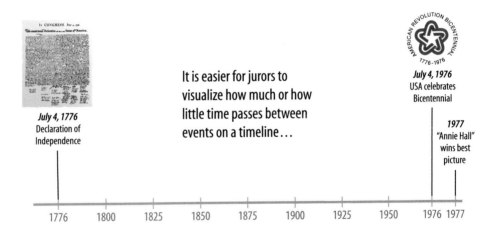

It is easier for jurors to visualize how much or how little time passes between events on a timeline…

July 4, 1776
Declaration of Independence

July 4, 1976
USA celebrates Bicentennial

1977
"Annie Hall" wins best picture

1776 1800 1825 1850 1875 1900 1925 1950 1976 1977

…than on a chronological list.

July 4, 1776   Declaration of Independence
July 4, 1976   USA celebrates Bicentennial
1977   "Annie Hall" wins best picture

In chronological lists, entries are evenly spaced no matter how much time passed between them

ILLUSTRATION 7-36

activity each time that it occurs. (See Illustration 7-18.) This technique generally does not work as well in a chronological list.

Finally, as a general rule, I believe that jurors appreciate a well-constructed timeline more than a chronological list. Everything being equal, you are generally better off using a timeline whenever possible.

Outlines:
Ladies and Gentlemen of the Jury, Here Is a Graphic That Shows You *Where We Are Going*

I used to prepare very detailed outlines for my cases. I would make sure that the outlines had everything in them that I needed. These outlines carefully listed the topics I felt I had to cover and important points that I wanted to stress along the way. I labored on these outlines. I would cut out large sections that were unnecessary and reorganize and reorder what was left until the internal logic was established. I would make sure that the font size was large enough so that I could easily find the information I wanted. When all this was done, I would carefully three-hole-punch the outline and stash it in a black three-ring notebook, which I would use at trial. (An added benefit: By this time, I really knew the case and how I wanted to present it.)

Then one day, it occurred to me, "If the outlines help me to keep things straight and to keep myself from getting lost, why am I the only one who gets to see them? If the outlines were helpful for me, after living with a case for months, wouldn't the outlines also be helpful to jurors who were hearing the story for the first time?"

So, at selected points in a trial or hearing, I tried putting up large versions of the notes on boards in the courtroom. I immediately noticed that the outlines did two things. First, they appeared to help jurors focus on what I was trying to say and where I was going. Second, I noticed, as I was speaking, certain people would write down what was on the outline. This made sense since the two most common things that students learn in a class are:

(1) When a teacher writes something on the board, you do the same thing in your notes, and
(2) When you study for a test, always review what the teacher wrote down and you then copied.

Finally, the outlines served as large cue cards that helped keep me on track and focused on the argument or examination.

I like to think of an outline as a way to show the jurors where you are going to take them at various points during the trial and what you think the jurors may find interesting and important along the way. Jurors, particularly active ones, will often write down the information from an outline and rely on these notes during deliberation. Merely writing down the information does not mean that they automatically accept it as being true. But at least some of the jurors will take at least some of your presentation into the jury room with them; I would rather them take something of *mine* than nothing.

For examples of outlines see the Expert Witness section of Chapter 8.

Flowcharts:
Ladies and Gentlemen of the Jury, Here Is a Graphic
That Shows You *How We Are Going to Get There*

I sometimes ask my clients to put together a flowchart of how they would like the jury to analyze their case. I do this because I have observed a high correlation between the ability to create an effective flowchart and the ability to put together a successful and well-organized closing argument.

A good flowchart—I mean a really good one—does not just happen. It requires the trial lawyer who creates it to do two things well. First, you need to determine what questions really matter. Next, you need to determine in what order you want to ask your questions in order to maximize your chances that the jury will reach the desired conclusion in an efficient and logical manner.

In a nutshell, that is what flowcharts do. They make you focus on both the substance and the order of your presentation. Because of this, just as I advised with timelines, you should create a flowchart for each of your cases. Even if it is a hand-sketched version on yellow legal paper—do it!

If, as I noted earlier, outlines show jurors where we are going, flowcharts are graphics that tell the jurors how we are going to get from here to there. Usually, no more than three or four Active Jurors set the direction of the discussions during jury deliberations. These jurors appreciate getting whatever order you may provide to this process. They particularly appreciate it when the order and flow that you offer takes them to the place that they believe they should end up. In other words, if you use a flowchart that goes in the direction a strong juror wants to go, it is not unusual to see that juror copy the flowchart into her notes and use the process outlined therein to try to influence how a particular issue is analyzed in the jury room after closing argument.

Flowcharts are helpful in a multitude of situations. Let's briefly look at five points in a trial where they might prove effective. First, flowcharts can help jurors analyze the verdict form. If you think about it, a well-drafted verdict form is often itself a flowchart. Consequently, these forms easily lend themselves to becoming such exhibits. Since the verdict form is the last piece of paper your jury is likely to consider in your case, a flowchart actually showing them how you want them to complete it can be very effective. Second, a flowchart can be helpful in showing jurors how to analyze jury instructions. Third, flowcharts are helpful in understanding contracts or other documents. This is particularly the case with insurance policies. Fourth, flowcharts can help provide instructions for understanding the case as a whole, a particular cause of action, or a particular affirmative defense. Finally, flowcharts can be used to help the jury understand the steps involved in a process.

Let's look at an example of a flowchart that you might use to help the jury understand how claims agents determine whether damage to a house is covered by an insurance policy. This process is set forth in a series of four graphics. (See Illustrations 7-37 and 7-38a–c.)

The first graphic in the series (Illustration 7-37) provides background or an overview of what exactly the steps in the process (as reflected in the flowchart) are. As you probably suspect, the lawyer and witness would likely start here as a way of explaining that the process involves a three-step analysis. The other graphics take the jurors through the steps.

More specifically, the lawyer and witness would establish that the purpose of the first step is to determine whether the plaintiffs have proven the damage was "accidental." If the answer to this is "yes," the analysis goes on to Step 2. If not, then the analysis stops at this point with a determination that the claim is "Not Covered." (See Illustration 7-38a.)

This process would continue on through the second and third steps. (See Illustrations 7-38b and 7-38c.)

I envision this series of graphics being used in at least two different places in the trial—first as part of a general discussion and then later to examine claims specific to the lawsuit and see how particular claims would move or not move through the flowchart.

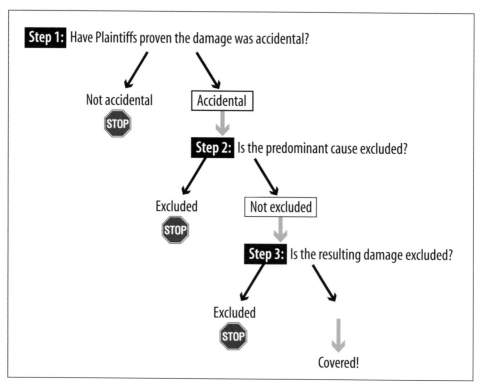

ILLUSTRATION 7-37. A Basic Flowchart

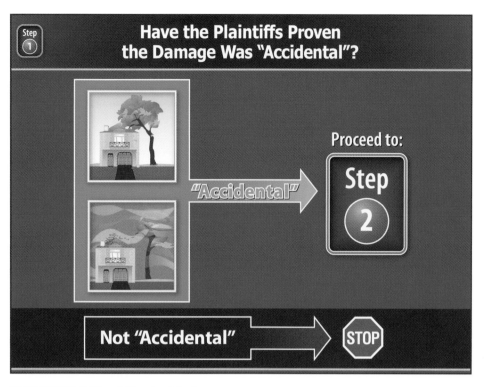

ILLUSTRATION 7-38a. A Flowchart Series

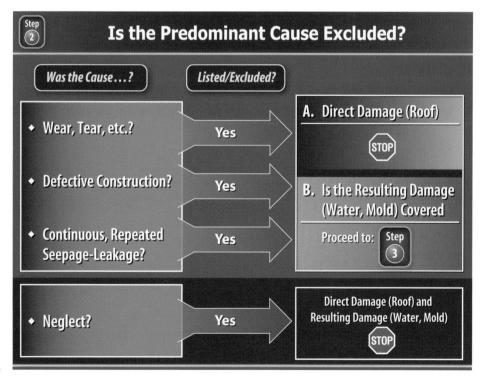

ILLUSTRATION 7-38b

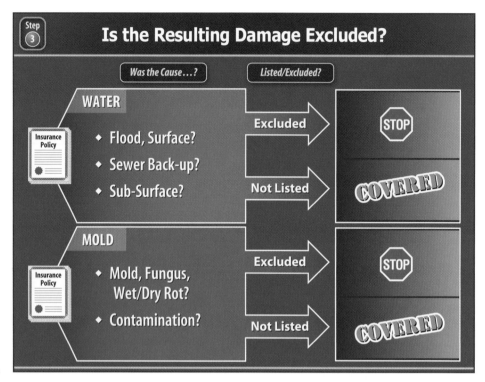

ILLUSTRATION 7-38c

Checklists:
Ladies and Gentlemen of the Jury, Here Is a Graphic That
Shows You *Where We Have Been and What We Saw on the Way*

If outlines illustrate where the jury is going to go during trial and flowcharts illustrate how the jury is going to get there, then you can think of checklists as being summaries of where the jurors have been and what they hopefully discovered along the way.

The typical checklist consists of two parts: (1) a series of statements (often presented as somewhat rhetorical questions) and (2) boxes that can be checked "yes" or "no." (See Illustration 7-39.)

The checklist can be as simple or as elaborate as you want. For example, checklists work very well as spontaneous graphics on either a flipchart or blackboard. They also work well as dynamic boards or electronic displays.

Let's briefly examine why something as simple as a checklist is so potentially effective in a jury trial. To do so, we need to revisit certain of the general information architecture principles discussed in Chapter 4. A trial lawyer who uses the same graphic baseboard over and over to make a point is taking advantage of the Answer Board Phenomenon. That is, all of the answers are concentrated in a sin-

A typical checklist consists of two parts:

 ① A series of
statements
or rhetorical
questions

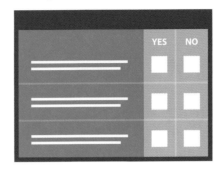

② Boxes that
can be checked
"Yes" or "No"

ILLUSTRATION 7-39

gle place. The jurors are encouraged to come back to that place to get an answer to the various questions posed by the lawyer. Since the jurors are already familiar with the baseboard, they are required to spend less and less mental energy to understand the point that is being made. Further, consistent with the Billboard Principle, the trial lawyer does not reveal all of the answers at once. She will talk about one issue, examine evidence for a while, come back to the second issue, and so on. This technique relies on a form of pacing devices. Additionally, each time she comes back and puts something new on the board (for example, checking a box), the trial lawyer will receive an Informational Honeymoon, that is, a few extra seconds in which the jurors will pay close attention to the graphic and the new data being communicated by the lawyer.

Graphs and Charts:
Ladies and Gentlemen of the Jury, Here Is a Graphic
That Shows You *Numerical Data*

GRAPHS

By now you know that I make no effort to hide my belief that successful trial lawyers must present themselves as if they are teachers. When I say this, most of my colleagues accept my statement without much argument. Occasionally, however, a client will grimace a bit and say something like, "Not like Mr. Burch," or some other name. The client does not even need to explain. These are not the teachers that former students remember with any fondness. These are the teachers that grown people still occasionally have nightmares about. You know the dream—you are about to take the final in Mr. Burch's class and you don't remember anything that was taught during the semester.

When I question people further about this, guess what the majority of these teachers taught. Guess what subject still gives people nightmares years after they took their last test. More often than not, these teachers taught some form of mathematics.

I mention this because for some reason, graphs often have the same effect on a small, but still significant, number of jurors. They see the graph; they think Mr. Burch; they freeze up.

Because of this, you need to be careful in presenting material in graph form. Am I saying do not use graphs? No. What I am suggesting is that you need to be careful and take extra effort when using a graph. You need to understand that it often takes a bit more information from you for the jury to understand a graph. A textpull, people usually get right away. The same is true with many timelines. For many people, though, graphs are not automatically intuitive.

It never hurts to take the time to explain what the x-axis and the y-axis represent. To the extent that you can illustrate what each means, do so. Take a second or two to explain, "As you go to the right, time is increasing; as you go up, the cost is going up." Take another second to explain, "As you can see, the cost went up from here in 1993 to here in 1995 and then it went down again; and in 1997, the cost was all the way down to $13.29."

Another way to avoid "graph anxiety" is to consider offering graph information in a format that does not look so much like a graph. The data in Illustration 7-40—how the price of an airline ticket is divided up—could be displayed in a bar graph or a pie chart. But the user-friendly graphic relays this information in a manner that most of the jurors could relate to as members of the traveling public.

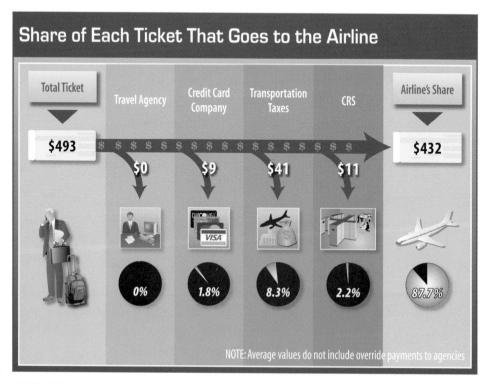

ILLUSTRATION 7-40. A User-Friendly Graph

CHARTS

Some people lump charts and graphs together. But they are not the same. I define a chart as a collection of data offered in a tabular form.

Most basically, a chart is an effective alternative to a graph. In fact, when you have limited data, that data can be better shown in a chart rather than a graph. To my eye, the chart works better than a graph for three reasons. First, limited data seems less limited in a chart than in a graph. Second, a chart looks more accurate. It can have numbers measured down to the thousandths. The graph may be equally as accurate in that the points were plotted to the thousandths as well, but it does not convey this as well as three actual numbers to the right of the decimal point in a chart. Finally, charts tend not to invoke the "Mr. Burch phenomenon." That is, charts do not inspire the same sense of anxiety that graphs do.

Charts also are extremely effective in conveying data collected from *more* than two variables. Let's look at a real example.

Here is a case where one of this country's most prestigious medical facilities was alleged to have consistently underpaid women and minority physicians. We were asked to show that this was untrue by ranking the staff physicians along three variables: race, gender, and income. Conveying this same information verbally is difficult. The chart in Illustration 7-41 shows this easily.

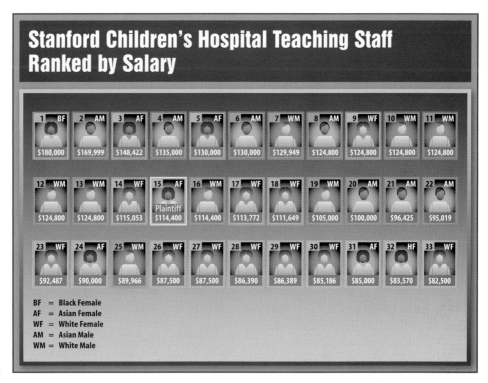

ILLUSTRATION 7-41. A Chart With Three Variables (Race, Gender, and Pay)

Maps:
Ladies and Gentlemen of the Jury, Here Is a Graphic
That Shows You *Where Things Are Located*

In my mind, timelines and maps are related graphics. This is not because they look alike (they don't) nor because you create them in the same way (you don't). Instead, I link these two forms because each addresses one of the two most common questions posed by a jury—*when* and *where*. As we have seen, the purpose of a timeline is to answer the former question, that is, to place events in their temporal context. The purpose of a map is to answer the latter question by helping jurors visualize the placement and movement of people, places, and objects in physical proximity to one another. (See Illustration 7-42.)

The most common way to use a map is to provide one of three geographic perspectives: (1) an overview, (2) a midlevel perspective, and (3) a detailed perspective. This is easiest imagined as a satellite taking three pictures, zooming its lens in closer each time.

The overview map provides the broadest perspective. A trial lawyer generally uses it in one of two situations. First, when the lawyer is dealing with some massive object and wants to help the jury appreciate how large the object truly is. The second common use is when the trial lawyer is presenting evidence about one geographic area to fact finders who are not entirely familiar with the area, usually

This map has
two parts:

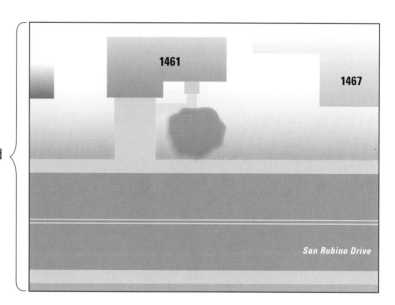

❶ The Baseboard
showing the
location

❷ These magnetic "cars" that the lawyer
and witnesses can move to various
places on the baseboard map.

ILLUSTRATION 7-42

because they are physically located far from the area depicted in the map. Such maps are generally not drawn to scale and are usually used purely for illustrative purposes, i.e., as a way of helping the jurors visualize the oral testimony of a witness.

Illustration 7-43 is an overview map designed for both of these purposes. It is of the Central Arizona Project (CAP). This massive public works project annually brings more than 1.5 million acre feet of water from the Colorado River to Phoenix and its surrounding communities. The project has over 330 miles of pipes, tunnels, and aqueducts. This map was used to convey both the enormity of the project and to help orient fact finders who lived in Washington, D.C., several thousand miles from the area depicted in the map.

Maps designed to convey a midlevel perspective are typically used in situations where the jurors are already generally familiar with a location. These maps tend to focus on a fairly confined area, but also include references to nearby well-known locations, such as freeways or buildings with which the jurors are likely to be familiar. (See Illustration 7-44.) Such maps may or may not be drawn to scale, depending on how the trial lawyer wants to use the graphic. My general observation is that most are not scaled and, like overview maps, most are used merely for illustrative purposes.

Maps providing a detailed perspective are generally drawn to scale and are sometimes (but not always) admitted into evidence after being appropriately authenticated

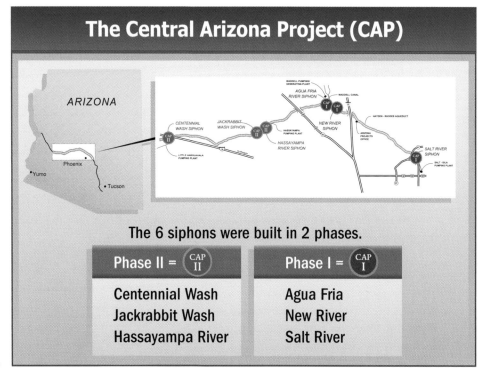

ILLUSTRATION 7-43. **An Overview Map**

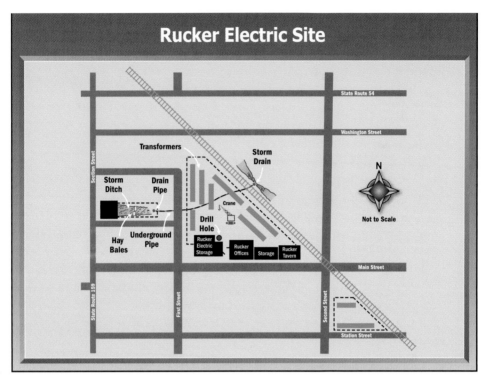

ILLUSTRATION 7-44. A Midlevel Perspective

and used by a witness. These maps usually feature a relatively small area that is directly related to the contested issues of that specific case. Such a map might show, for example, the intersection where the automobile accident occurred or the corner where the victim was shot. For example, in Illustration 7-45, the primary focus of the graphic is the detailed map to the right. Note the several small but important additions designed to make this graphic more user friendly for the jurors. To the left of the main map is a smaller city map that helps place where the events on the detailed map took place. The broader city map includes the location of a freeway and other prominent streets with which jurors from this area are likely to be familiar. The detailed map portion of the graphic includes two reference points that help place key witnesses and further confirm in the jurors' minds that this drawing is in fact accurate and can be relied on.

Trial lawyers will sometimes create a second version of the detailed map to be used for illustrative purposes. This version is used by witnesses to help describe what they observed to the jurors. Usually, the map will be part of a magnetic board. The baseboard will be a fixed version of the map on which witnesses can write information, draw what they observed, or move around magnetic pacing devices in the shape of cars or other objects.

Creative trial lawyers can also use maps not as the primary focus of the graphic but as a way to bolster another point or argument. Let me show you two

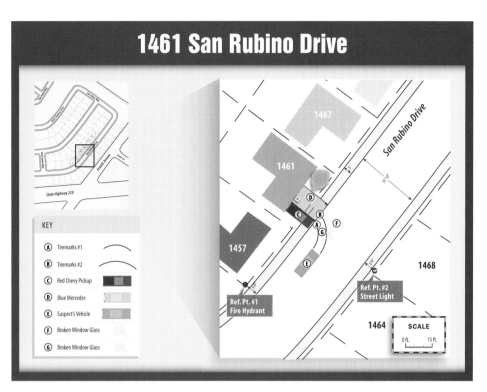

ILLUSTRATION 7-45. A Detailed Perspective

examples. Illustration 7-46 is a who's who of key players in a securities fraud case. The trial was held in the small Ohio town where the underlying events took place. In an attempt to avoid liability, higher-ups in the defendant company eventually became involved. Those higher-ups were located several hundred miles away in the New York City area. This graphic not only lists who is who but also where each such person was located and subtly (or perhaps not so subtly) suggests to the Ohio jurors that the cover-up against the small town was directed by the "big boys in the big city."

The second example is at the extreme end of a detailed map. Illustration 7-47 maps the relative office locations of four key executives on one floor of a high-rise building. In this case, the chief financial officer sold a substantial block of stock in the company two days after the president became aware of potentially very bad news and two days before that news was announced to the general public. The CFO claimed that he did not know about the bad news and that the timing of the sale was entirely coincidental. One of the things done to counter this argument was to include a map of the executive offices. As you can see, all of the key players are clustered together, all within literally a few feet of one another. How likely was it that, given this physical proximity and the fact that each of them spent sixteen hours a day in this location, the information was not shared between the president and the chief financial officer?

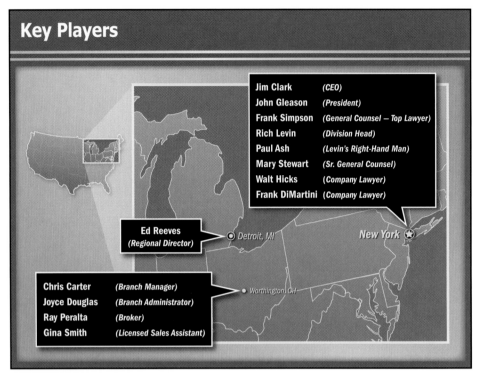

ILLUSTRATION 7-46. Linking People to Locations

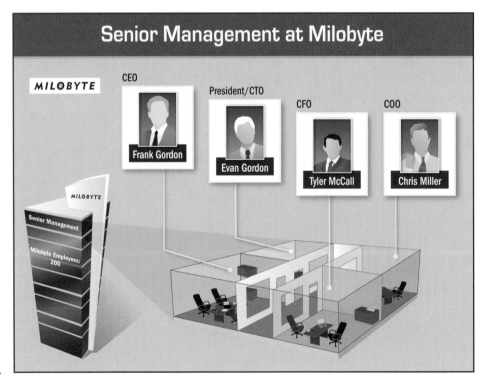

ILLUSTRATION 7-47. Showing Proximity

Photographs:
Ladies and Gentlemen of the Jury, Here Is a Graphic
That Shows You *What Something Really Looks Like*

Photographs can provide a powerful visual punch. As testament to their power, I suspect that if you were to examine all the evidence that courts have excluded as being relevant but unduly prejudicial, a large percentage of this material would be photographs.

A person seeing a drawing subconsciously understands that it is in some form a stylized version of reality. The drawing may display a horrific scene, but it is still understood to be at least on some levels not entirely real. In this sense, the drawing filters out a tiny bit of reality. Not so with a photograph. In such an instance jurors are more likely to see what is in the photograph as a specific object at a discrete location; in other words, it is reality. It is reality without filters. Because of this, photographs can make us stare, squirm, or cringe more than any sketch, model, or other form of graphic.

A trial lawyer generally uses photographs in three different ways. The first is to use the photograph on it own, as a stand-alone exhibit. These are probably some of the oldest forms of trial graphics and I suspect are used more often than almost any other form. These are straightforward graphics requiring no real additional discussion, except to remind you to check the rules of evidence in your local jurisdiction to determine what you must show if you intend to get the photographs admitted into evidence.

The second common way to use photographs is to juxtapose two as a way of comparing what something looked like before and after a crucial event, as in Illustration 7-48.

The third way to use photographs is as a reality check to confirm and authenticate other graphic forms. As we previously noted, jurors want to know that they are relying on the "real thing." For textpulls, you can assure jurors of this by including a small scan of the original document along with the textpull.

You can use a similar authenticating technique for other forms of graphics using photographs. Illustration 7-49 is a two-part graphic for a case involving building defects in hundreds of buildings. Since it is impossible to show every one of the buildings, Illustration 7-49a relies on a drawing designed to represent a typical such building. The second layer of the graphic (Illustration 7-49b) includes "real life" photographs showing examples of some of the actual construction problems. These photographs not only help educate the jurors, but also help assure them that they can rely on the graphics as authentic.

Trial lawyers will also often authenticate animations by interspersing photographs in the exhibit. For example, the animation may begin with an actual photograph of the site to confirm in the juror's mind that such a place actually exists. The lawyer may then have this photograph morph into an illustrated version of the location for the balance of the animation.

ILLUSTRATION 7-48. A Photographic Comparison

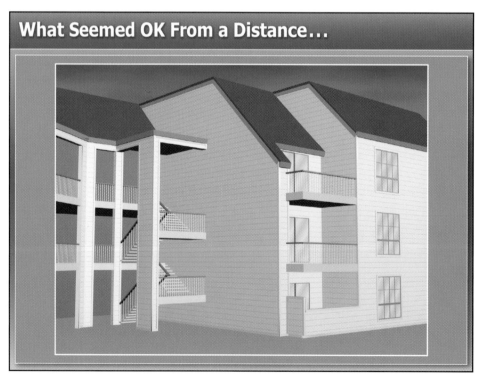

ILLUSTRATION 7-49a

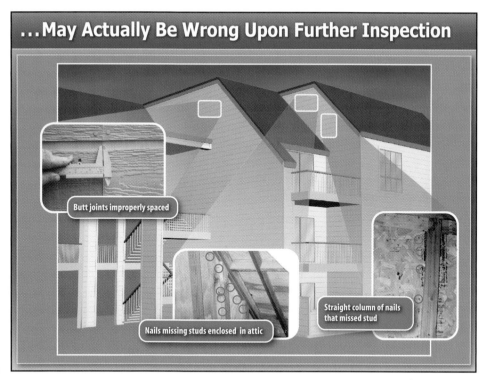

ILLUSTRATION 7-49b. **Using Photographs to Authenticate**

Summary Collages:
Ladies and Gentlemen of the Jury, Here Is a Graphic
That Shows You *a Summary of Our Position*

In Walt Disney's movie version of *Alice in Wonderland*—which I admit to liking more than the book—there is a wonderfully chaotic courtroom scene. Alice is being tried and the Doormouse is testifying against her. The more than slightly inebriated witness begins to recite, "Twinkle, twinkle, little bat, how I wonder what you're at! Up above the world you fly, like a tea tray in the sky!" Before he can finish, the Queen (who in the movie serves as the judge) yells to the otherwise unobservant jurors: "That's the most important evidence we've heard yet . . . WRITE THAT DOWN."

Summary collages are a wonderful way for you to graphically tell the jury, "This is important evidence . . *write it down!*" As their name implies, summary collages provide the jurors with a convenient one-stop place to get a collection of facts crucial to the case. Obviously, this is not a neutral analysis; it is your best shot as an advocate to highlight what you think matters and works best for your client.

Summary collages, like the ones shown in Illustration 7-50 and 7-51, bring together the key testimony from one or more live witnesses and textpulls from

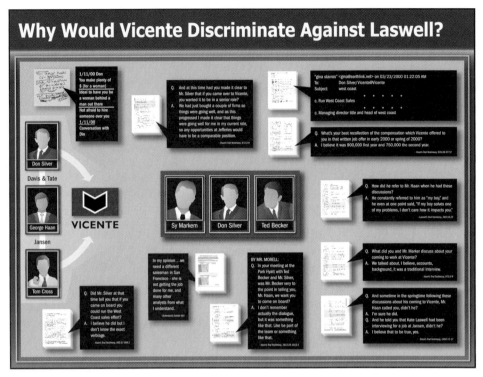

ILLUSTRATION 7-50. A Summary Collage

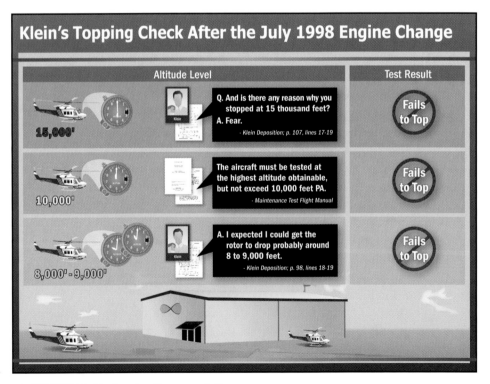

ILLUSTRATION 7-51. Another Summary Collage

crucial documents. You can create a summary collage using a blackboard or flip-chart. In such an instance, you carefully write the exhibit numbers down on the blackboard or flipchart and use this as your base. You would use this version by pointing to the exhibit number and then either describe the document, hold up a copy, or project a version on a screen. This simple method can be highly effective because many jurors will quickly write down all of the exhibit numbers you give them and then take their time in deliberations to review this material as part of evaluating your argument.

Tutorials:
Ladies and Gentlemen of the Jury, Here Is a Graphic
That Shows You *Necessary Background Information*

Generally when we talk about a standard form, we focus on a format for displaying information. For example, timelines come in a variety of different styles, but they all convey data in a similar way. The same is true of textpulls, outlines, checklists, etc. Tutorials are different. Tutorials are not so much about following a particular format as they are about making the commitment to find ways to educate jurors and adhering to the philosophy that you can persuade jurors by, among other things, educating them.

One of the things that I enjoy most about being a trial lawyer is that each case is different. I loved learning about how the stock market works in one case, how buildings are constructed in a second, and how police officers decide whether to search a stopped automobile in a third. As trial lawyers, we are paid good money to learn about these things. Why? We do so in order to ultimately teach what we have learned to jurors as part of convincing them that our client's position is "the truth."

In every case, there are concepts that require teaching. You need to teach the jury about these issues. Your role in court is that of a teacher. You are an advocate who, after educating your audience, derives the real benefits that jurors bestow on people who take the time to explain things to them in an organized, nonpatronizing manner. Such efforts are consistently appreciated by jurors and perceived as a sign that the lawyer who teaches has nothing to be afraid of or to hide.

Tutorials require only that you do two things. First, you must take the time to identify what issues the jury needs to have clarified. Identifying these matters is one of the objectives of the mental mining process described in Chapter 2. Second, tutorials require that you find simple and memorable ways to explain these concepts to the jury.

There are a wide range of tutorials. Some of your tutorials may be as simple as taking a little extra time to explain an important concept or term of art. Others may involve nothing more than a glossary to explain key terms. Some of your

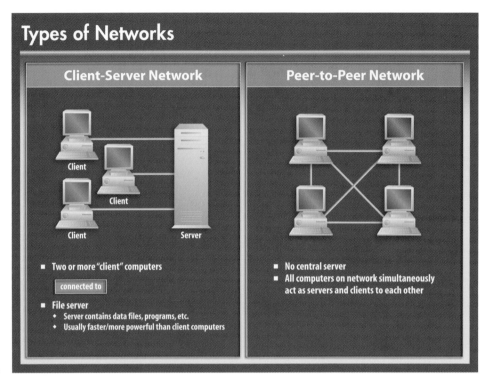

ILLUSTRATION 7-52. A Simple Tutorial

tutorials will require a level of greater preparation. Such tutorial exhibits will include one or more boards, such as the ones shown in Illustrations 7-52 and 7-53, to describe concepts that are easier to show than tell. Because tutorials often deal with complex unfamiliar issues, they often rely on analogies to make their points.

Whatever the format, make the philosophical commitment to teach your jurors.

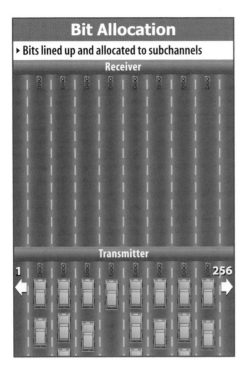

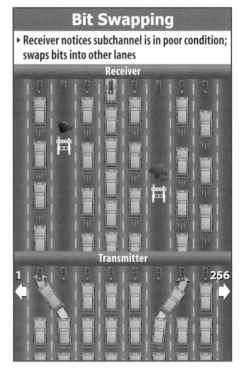

ILLUSTRATION 7-53. A Two-Board Tutorial

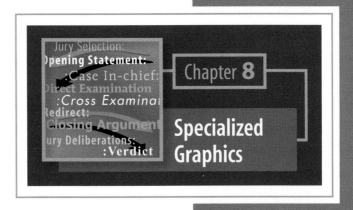

Chapter **8**

Specialized Graphics

Important Times to Use Graphics

By now, I hope I have convinced you that trial graphics are important and that by taking the time to properly create them you can greatly improve your case. This is true no matter where in your trial you choose to present this material. From opening statement through closing argument, you will benefit each time you use a well-prepared graphic.

Without detracting from the overall positive effect of using graphics *throughout* your case, this chapter focuses on three instances that are particularly well suited for their use—opening statement, expert witness testimony, and closing argument—and examines which types of graphics work well in each of these phases of trial.

In Chapter 7 we reviewed the standard forms of graphics. These are the most common and versatile graphics—the kind you repeatedly use throughout your trial. For example, you can put a timeline up on an easel at the beginning of your opening statement, repeatedly use that same graphic during each of your witness examinations, and then rely on it for a last time during closing argument.

The graphics in this chapter are more specialized; that is, you design them for a single purpose or for a discrete part of your case. Sometimes this is because the rules of evidence restrict when you can use certain tools (e.g., you can use argumentative graphics only in closing). Other times the graphics supplement a particular type of testimony (e.g., an expert accounting witness may need specialized graphics in order to help him explain the complex financial documents upon which he bases his opinions). Whatever the reason, these particular instances recur often enough that understanding what graphics you might want to use will increase your ability to persuade the jury.

Using Graphics in Your Opening Statement

I once had the opportunity to attend a master class conducted by one of the world's greatest cellists, Janos Starker. Master classes play an important role in training classical musicians. Various students play for the master, who is always a highly re-garded musician. Often audiences of interested spectators gather to watch and learn. The master listens to each student, stopping him abruptly at various points to compliment, criticize, make him play a portion of the piece over and over again—the process is nerve-racking.

In the class I attended, one of the students, who was extremely gifted, was flustered and started off by playing his piece badly. Everyone, including the student, realized this. Unfortunately, the bad start sent the student spiraling downward. After a minute or so, Maestro Starker mercifully stopped the student and began a firm (but avuncular) lecture on why you must always start off strong.

Starker admitted that even after playing professionally for decades he would still occasionally get very nervous before a concert. As a result, what he had learned over the years was to always start off his solos with great care. It was crucial for Starker to know, really know, exactly how he wanted the first few measures to sound and to be able to play them exactly that way. He would practice the beginning of the piece over and over—far more often than he would practice any other part. Eventually, he became so confident in his ability to play the beginning that he knew he could do so no matter what. The lights could go out in the concert hall, there could be an earthquake, it did not matter, Starker could always nail the beginning of any piece he played.

Starker went on to explain why this was so important: The quality of the beginning shapes all of what follows. When the performer starts off strong, something magical often happens. The musician somehow slips into a certain emotional state where instinct takes over and he can automatically continue playing at an extremely high level, no matter how nervous he might have been only minutes before.

I have since been told the same thing by many others, including trial lawyers and other performers. In fact, the Taoists describe this phenomenon as *wei wu wei,* "doing the non-doing." They use this phrase to describe the instances where the person and his actions merge. For example, when the dancer is so absorbed in what he is doing that he becomes his dance, a runner becomes his run, the writer becomes what he is writing, and so on.

In my experience, a similar thing can happen in a trial. Your performance in the opening statement (particularly the early part of your opening statement) will likely set the tone and quality of what follows.

When you sit down after your opening statement, you should have accomplished some or all of the following: (1) outlined what your case is about, (2) provided a chronological overview of what happened, (3) displayed your key documents and briefly explained why each is important without being too argumentative, (4) introduced the key players in the underlying dispute, (5) defined key terms or concepts, and (6) displayed a certain basic level of expertise and mastery of your case. Trial graphics can substantially aid you in accomplishing each of these six objectives.

TELL THE JURY WHAT THIS CASE IS ABOUT

Throughout the life of your case, but most particularly as you prepare for trial, you should force yourself to find a succinct and convincing way to fill in the end of the following statement: "When it really comes down to it, this case is all about _____!"

As you will soon discover, it is not always easy to fill in this blank in a way that makes the average person want to listen to your answer. Yet that is exactly what many jurors will be looking for you to do throughout your trial, but most importantly in your opening statement.

If you want to test yourself to see whether you have sufficiently distilled your case so that you can capture its essence, I suggest that you try what I call the PTA test. Go to a PTA meeting at your child's school or some other event where people spend at least a portion of the evening standing around politely talking. When someone comes up to you and asks, "So, what are you working on?" answer the question and observe your questioner's response.

If the questioner listens to your brief explanation and actually wants to know more, then you have successfully captured the essence of your case. If he lets you finish your answer, seems to understand but is not overly interested, then you are getting there. If, *before* you finish your answer, his eyes glaze over, he mutters something about having to get home, and he keeps inching toward the door, then you have a long way to go before *you* understand your case and even longer before someone else will as well.

When you can distill the complexities of your lawsuit down to the point where you can tell the jurors what it is about in a way they find interesting, you will have uncovered a major theme. You need to make this theme a central part of your presentation. One of the most effective ways to start doing so is to feature your theme at the beginning of your opening statement. There are four reasons why this is a particularly effective place to do so. First, the beginning of the opening statement is the point when most jurors really need the overview that the theme often provides. Second, this is when jurors are most likely to be actually listening to what you have to say. Third, this is the place where you are least likely to draw an objection if your description is a bit (and don't ever let it be more than a bit) argumentative. Finally, and most importantly, putting this information at the beginning of your opening statement will help you get off to a strong start, thereby setting the tone that will hopefully help carry you through the entire trial.

There needs to be a connection between your opening statement and your closing argument. Obviously, each serves a different purpose, but the most successful closing arguments can usually trace their rhetorical antecedents directly back to the opening statement. Consequently, whenever possible, you need to rhetorically and graphically link the two.

I mention this connection because, while this section deals with opening statement, I have included several closing argument graphics. I have included several closing argument graphics in this section of the book which is supposed to be devoted to opening statements. This should allow you to see how what you say or show at the beginning of the trial can directly connect with what you argue at the end.

Let me give you two examples.

The first deals with a case about numbers—widely diverging and contrasting numbers. On the one hand, there were the large numbers—over 3,000 unauthorized stock transactions by a broker affecting hundreds of retirees and their families.

On the other there was the smallest number—zero, which reflected what the broker's employer did to prevent the illegal transactions and what it did to reimburse its injured investors.

The trial lawyer wanted to find a way to plant these numbers in the jurors' brains during opening statement and then argue their significance during closing argument. He accomplished this by creating two related "fill in the blank" graphics on boards—one for opening and one for closing. At the beginning of his opening statement, the lawyer placed the first board up on an easel. Consistent with the answer board phenomenon (discussed in Chapter 4), he did not fill in the blanks all at once. Instead, as he mentioned each of the figures in his opening statement, he went up to the board and handwrote that number in the appropriate spot. (See Illustration 8-1.)

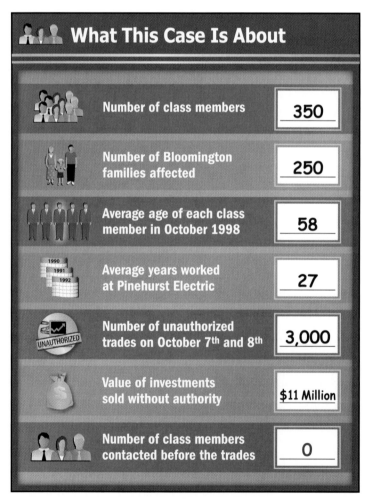

ILLUSTRATION 8-1. Connecting the Opening Statement . . .

The lawyer used his second related board (Illustration 8-2) in closing. In his closing argument, the lawyer used the same process of filling in the blanks as a way to *argue* to the jury what the case was about. As you can see, while the questions and answers are different, the lawyer deliberately created this graphic to have the same general look and feel as the one in his opening statement.

Here is generally what the lawyer said while completing the graphic shown in Illustration 8-2:

This case is about Adam Sorensen, a stock broker: who made 3,000 unauthorized trades in three days; who liquidated over 350 retirees' accounts worth over $11 million dollars; and who violated 17 rules of the New York Stock Exchange. This case is also about how Sierra Brokers, the company responsible for Mr. Sorensen, did nothing to stop him from illegally liquidating 350 accounts and how Sierra Brokers did nothing to reimburse 350 of its clients whose retirement funds were financially devastated by Mr. Sorenson.

ILLUSTRATION 8-2. . . . With the Closing Argument

The second example of tying your opening statement to your closing argument involves a situation where the lawyer did not use any graphics during his opening statement. Instead, he used the opening statement to plant his theme in the jurors' minds verbally. The trial lawyer in this bad faith insurance case stressed that every time the insurer tried to resolve the underlying claim, the plaintiff would "set up a roadblock to prevent a fair resolution." This "roadblock" theme resurfaced several times during the insurance company's case-in-chief as various witnesses described how they tried to resolve the claim "only to be blocked by plaintiff." At the end of the case, the trial lawyer tied this familiar theme of being blocked into his closing argument using the graphic shown in Illustration 8-3.

PROVIDE A CHRONOLOGICAL OVERVIEW

Part of what you are doing in opening statement is telling a story to the jury. The jurors need the framework of a story in order to make sense of all of the information you are providing to them. Without such a framework, the material will seem to the jury to be nothing more than a series of random facts.

We have already discussed the characteristics of a good story and how designing graphics will help you develop one for your trial. We have also discussed the fact that, while it is not the only way to tell a story, presenting what happened in chronological order is the most common way to do so, and the most common way to tell a story chronologically is to use timelines, as described in Chapter 7.

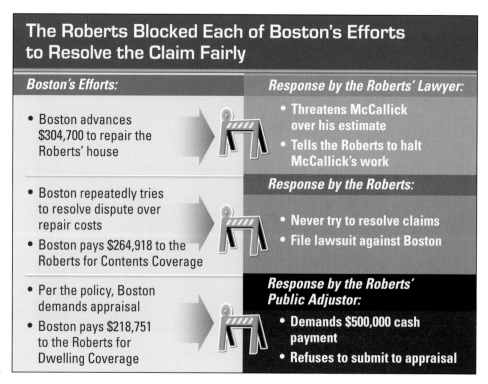

ILLUSTRATION 8-3. Reprising a Theme

For our immediate purposes, I am not going to repeat my earlier discussion concerning timelines. (See Chapter 7.) Instead, I want to continue to focus on the connection between graphics first used in an opening statement and then again in a closing argument.

In this next example, one of the plaintiff's themes was that the defendant repeatedly saw the warning signs "but consistently ignored these red flags" and kept charging forward, much to the detriment of plaintiff. In opening statement, plaintiff used a very simple timeline to highlight certain key events for the jury. (See Illustration 8-4a.)

Plaintiff's counsel continued to use this timeline throughout his case-in-chief as various of his witnesses pointed to certain key dates and described what happened at each point. The net result was that the jurors were not only extremely familiar with the timeline but also had come to rely on it as a way of keeping the facts straight.

At the beginning of his closing argument, plaintiff's counsel put the familiar timeline up on an easel next to his podium. At the appropriate time, he repeated his comment from opening statement that this was a case where the defendant had plenty of warning, but "intentionally and consistently disregarded the red flags." He walked up to the familiar board and began discussing each of the entries, reminding the jurors what had happened at each instance and what supporting evidence there was in favor of the plaintiff. But this time he did something different. When he finished with each entry, he put a magnetic pacing device in the form of

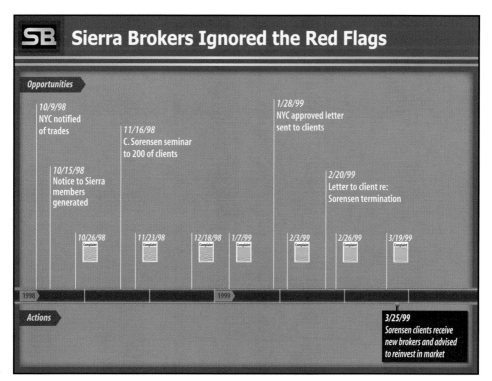

ILLUSTRATION 8-4a. Opening Statement: A Simple Timeline

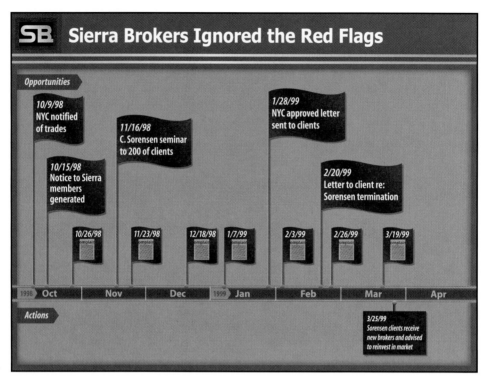

ILLUSTRATION 8-4b. **Closing Argument: A Dramatic Finale**

a red warning flag up on the timeline. He proceeded to do this throughout his closing. When he was finished, the graphic he first showed the jury in opening statement was plastered with red flags. (See Illustration 8-4b.) The lawyer had effectively connected an image from his opening statement to his closing argument through the use of a theme and a trial graphic already familiar to the jurors.

SHOW THE JURY YOUR KEY DOCUMENTS AND EXPLAIN THEIR IMPORTANCE

Opening statement is a good time to introduce your key documents to the jury and briefly describe what the evidence will show with respect to each. Textpulls (discussed in Chapter 7) are the best way to do this.

I have three suggestions about using textpulls in opening statement. First, remember that in opening statement you can rely only on admissible evidence. Many judges apply this rule loosely and will allow you to show and refer to documents in opening if you make a good faith representation that you will later have the material admitted into evidence; others will not. Always check with your judge or his clerk.

Alternatively, consider stipulating with your opposing counsel that certain key documents (these are the ones you are most likely to want to show to the jury during opening) are admissible and get the court to adopt/approve that stipulation prior to trial.

Second, the more basic the textpull, the better for purposes of opening statement. Some judges perceive anything beyond basic textpulls to be argumentative and will not let you use, for example, a juxtaposed textpull comparing or contrasting evidence. Again, if you want to use anything other than a basic textpull, check what rules apply in your judge's courtroom.

Finally, you need to be careful that you do not overdo it by using too many textpulls or showing the same one to the jurors over and over again. Even the most dramatic textpull can lose much of its punch if the jury sees or hears about it too many times. I am not suggesting that you hold back and not show such graphics to the jurors in your opening statement. Instead, I am merely suggesting that you need to carefully choose when it makes sense to do so.

INTRODUCE THE KEY PLAYERS TO THE JURORS

I can be notoriously bad with names. In fact, when we were first dating, I once forgot my wife's name—fortunately, Jill saw the humor in this and forgave me.

I am particularly bad when someone rattles off names and I have no way to categorize who is who or how one person/entity relates to another. This is an affliction that troubles many people. Opening statement is a perfect time to help people to learn this crucial information.

There are several easy ways to do this graphically. The simplest way is to provide a who's who list of the names and positions of key people, most of whom will eventually testify in the case. Illustration 8-5 shows a basic format for a very straightforward who's who graphic. The purpose is to help identify the key characters and help the jury remember who they are and how they relate to one another.

ILLUSTRATION 8-5

Photographs for this type of exhibit can be obtained directly from the people pictured, from the Internet, and from videotaped depositions, among other avenues.

Explaining who the parties are is particularly important in a class action. The jurors want to have a feel for who all of these hundreds or thousands of people are. At the same time, there is often a need to humanize the class by describing certain individuals in particular. Illustrations 8-6, 8-7, and 8-8 are examples of this

ILLUSTRATION 8-6

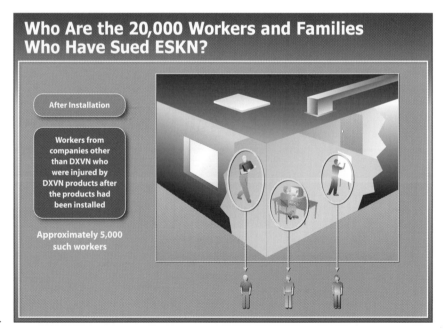

ILLUSTRATION 8-7

ILLUSTRATION 8-8

type of graphics. Notice that Illustration 8-8 incorporates a portion of Illustration 8-7 to tie the individual into the overall class.

Trial graphics that introduce key players are an excellent way to add context to your opening statement. For example, you could use a graphic to help explain what your client does. The graphic in Illustration 8-9 presents the plaintiff, a brake distributor. It also helps explain what the distributor does, what other companies it works with, and its role in the industry.

You should consider introducing the opposing party to the jurors in opening statement, particularly if there is some significance about that party, such as its size or resources. Do so in a fair manner, but in a fair manner that is consistent with the way you want the jurors to perceive the other side. For example, in order to avoid any claim of misstating the facts, the graphic in Illustration 8-10 contains a quotation directly from the opposing party's petition indicating how large it is and what its revenues were.

Another variation is to use an introduction graphic in your opening and then use a modified version of the graphic to make an argument in your closing. For example, Illustration 8-11a shows a straightforward organizational chart. It shows who the key officers of the corporation are and who reports to whom. This graphic would work well in opening and possibly during witnesses examination as well.

Notice that in designing the graphic, the trial lawyer left blank space at the bottom of Illustration 8-11a. That is so the already familiar graphic can be used in closing by, for example, displaying testimony or other material related to the key players on this organizational chart, as shown in Illustration 8-11b.

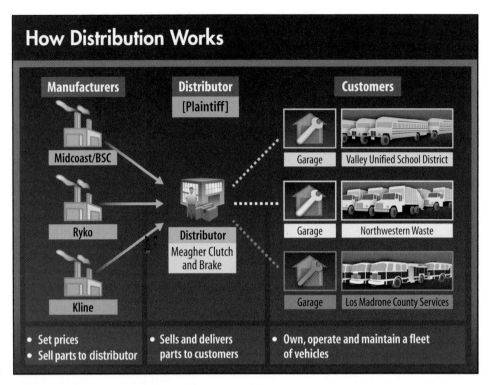

ILLUSTRATION 8-9. Introducing the Client

ILLUSTRATION 8-10. Introducing the Opposition

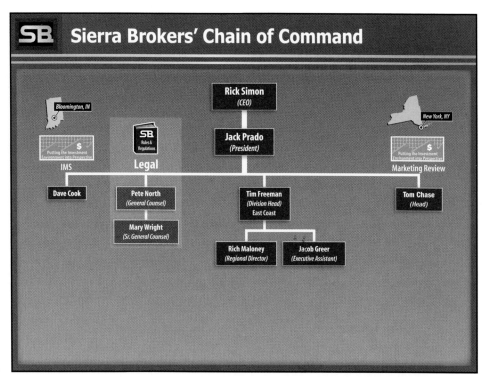

ILLUSTRATION 8-11a. Leaving Space in an Introduction Chart . . .

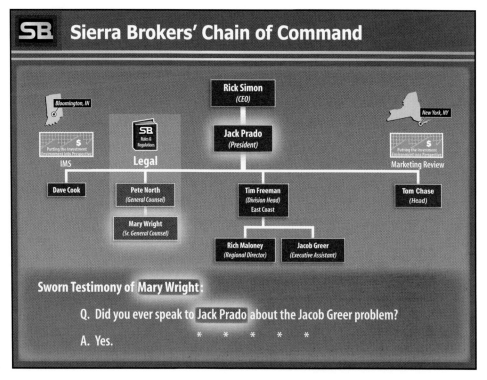

ILLUSTRATION 8-11b. . . . to Use in Closing

INTRODUCE KEY CONCEPTS TO YOUR JURORS

My colleague Joel ben Izzy is a professional storyteller. Joel tells this wonderful tale:

> Clarence Darrow told a story of a trial early in his career. It was a civil case, being tried in a rural courthouse, and he was worried that the jury might not catch the subtleties of the law. He soon decided though that there was at least one very educated member of the jury, and, from that point on, he directed his remarks to him.
>
> Sure enough when the jury came back from deliberations, Darrow was gratified to see that this man had been chosen as foreman.
>
> "Have you reached a verdict?"
>
> "No, Your Honor," said the man, "we have not. We need more information. You see there are two words that have been used constantly throughout this trial that we do not understand."
>
> "Which words?" asked the judge.
>
> To which the man replied, "One is 'plaintiff,' the other is 'defendant.'"

After living with a case for months, if not years, dealing with technical terms and concepts often becomes second nature to trial lawyers. Most jurors do not have that advantage. They need someone to define these terms for them and they often benefit from having these definitions presented to them in the opening statement so that they can better understand key testimony right from the beginning.

The lawyer who takes the time and makes the effort to define key terms or concepts benefits in a variety of ways. For example, jurors are often impressed by and positively predisposed to vote for those lawyers who take the time to teach. Additionally, if you offer a definition or explanation and your opposing counsel does not, the jurors will naturally understand the concept only one way—yours.

Not all definitions require graphics. You can often effectively convey the information verbally by merely taking the time to define a particular term. For example, I was once involved in a case where I need to explain how shifting soil had created a reverse gradient in a community's sewer system. Over the years, the pipes had gone from being downward sloping, to flat, to slightly upward sloping—which, by the way, is not good for a system that usually relies on gravity to move waste *away* from, not *toward,* homes. I displayed this concept merely using my arm and altering the different angle of slope showing how the pipe had shifted from going downward to going slightly upward instead.

If you decide that you want to use a graphic to define your key terms, one of the easiest ways to do so is to create a series of annotated definitions. (See Illustration 8-12.) The ideal way to do this is to first display this material on a board during opening statement. Explain to the jurors that these are some of the key definitions that witnesses will testify about at trial and that you are showing them this graphic to help them keep track of those definitions. Take the time to discuss the handful of terms that need to be explained. Continue to use the definition board during witness testimony so that the jurors will learn and use *your* definitions.

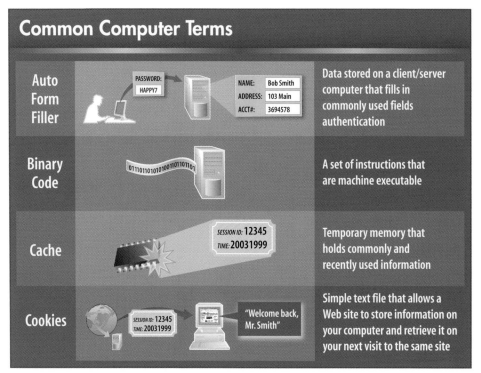

ILLUSTRATION 8-12. **Defining Key Terms**

Another way to define key terms is to illustrate them for the jurors using an analogy. Illustration 8-13 is an example of this. This graphic uses a lock and key analogy to explain certain biological terms. The analogy and the drawings within it substitute for a complex written definition.

In certain cases, jurors will need assistance in understanding how a particular transaction occurs. An effective way to do so is to illustrate the basic steps of that transaction and have your expert witness walk the jury through it. Unfortunately, sometimes jurors cannot wait until your witness takes the stand before being introduced to the process. If you feel that your jurors might benefit from early exposure to such graphics, you should consider showing the jury these graphics in your opening statement.

For example, Illustrations 8-14a through 8-14e demonstrate how a commercial loan works. In this case, it was important for the jurors to understand this process in order to better appreciate how the developer had failed to adhere to the terms of his contract with the bank. Using such a series of graphics allowed the trial lawyer to show how the bank provides money to the developer who must use it to build the project, in this instance a hotel. (See Illustrations 8-14a and 8-14b.) The hotel generates profits, which are first paid back to the bank in monthly installments. (See Illustrations 8-14c and 8-14d.) If any money is left over after paying the bank, it goes to the developer. (See Illustration 8-14e.)

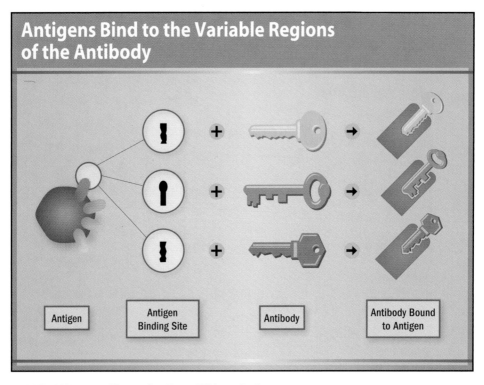

ILLUSTRATION 8-13. Illustrating Terms With an Analogy

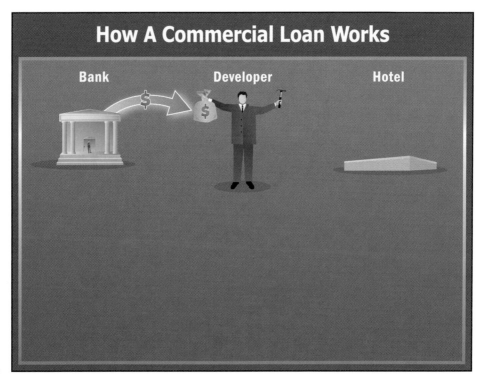

ILLUSTRATION 8-14a. Explaining a Key Concept

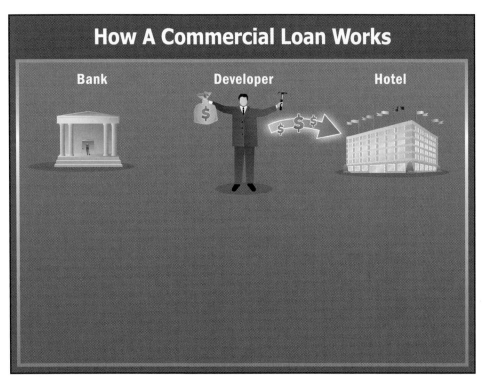

ILLUSTRATION 8-14b

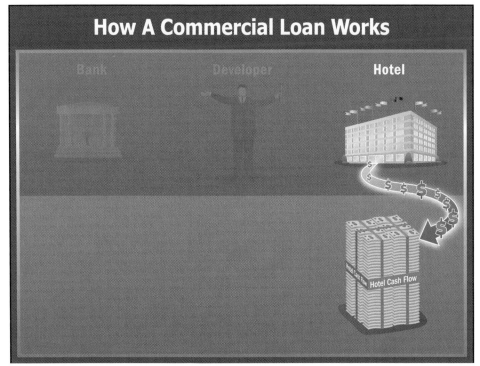

ILLUSTRATION 8-14c

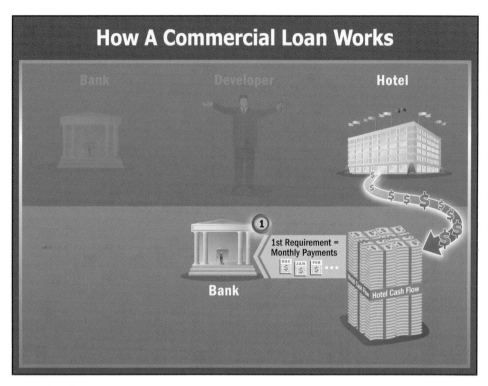

ILLUSTRATION 8-14d

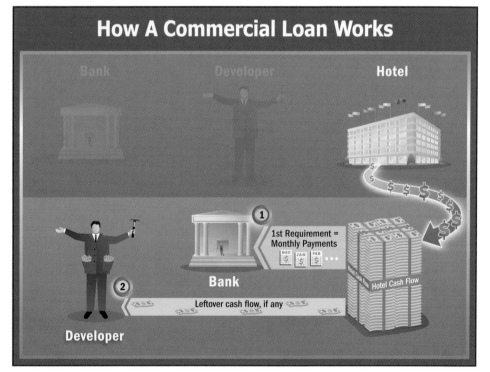

ILLUSTRATION 8-14e

Jurors also benefit when trial lawyers take the time to define the steps in what might initially be perceived as being a complex process. Illustrations 8-15a through 8-15c show how huge pieces of reinforced pipe (over twenty feet in diameter) are assembled, transported, and installed.

DISPLAY MASTERY OF YOUR CASE

It is important to make a good first impression—we all know that. After all, isn't that why our parents cleaned us up for the first day of school and why we do the same with our children?

Trial graphics can help you make such an impression in your opening statement. The process of creating trial graphics forces you to think, really think, about your case and to find better ways to organize the way you present your story to the jury. Jurors respond positively to well-prepared graphics. This material makes the adversarial process more interesting and easier for them to understand. Finally, using graphics helps lawyers who might otherwise feel the need to stand behind a podium with notes to move away from the podium and more directly engage the jury.

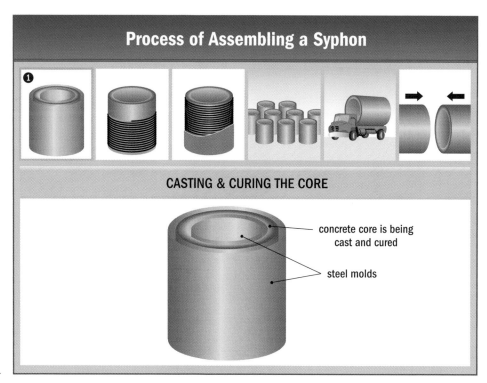

ILLUSTRATION 8-15a. **Explaining a Complex Process**

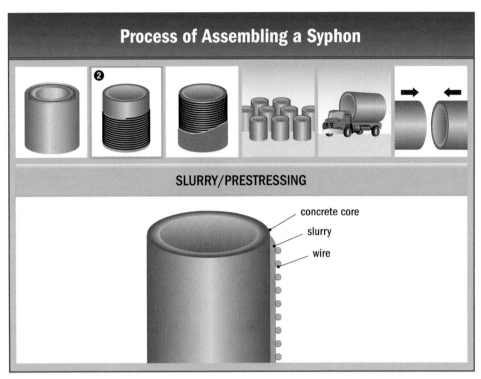

ILLUSTRATION 8-15b

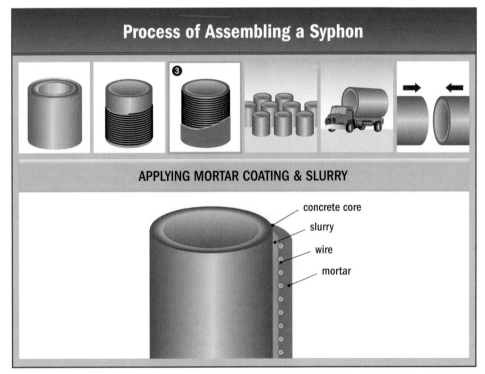

ILLUSTRATION 8-15c

Using Graphics During Expert Witness Testimony

EXPERT WITNESSES PRESENT NUMEROUS CHALLENGES

When judging how much time to spend preparing an expert to testify at trial, the lawyer would do well to remember an old nursery rhyme.

> *There was a little girl who had a little curl*
> *Right in the middle of her forehead.*
> *When she was good, she was very very good.*
> *But when she was bad, she was horrid.*

It is often the same with expert witnesses. I have seen some amazingly good experts; I have also seen some who have severely hurt their clients. I have even seen a couple of experts who I firmly believe cost their clients the case. Trial graphics can have a substantial impact on how effective the expert witness is in conveying his information to the jury.

Expert witnesses start out with three distinct disadvantages—all of which you need to appreciate and spend time designing around. First, many jurors are not entirely sure why the expert is there in the first place. Jurors intuitively understand why other witnesses are in court. The other witnesses are . . . well, witnesses—they experienced the events surrounding the dispute. They saw the cars crash or heard the defendant threaten the victim. But the experts, most of them were not even around when any of these events occurred. Why, many jurors wonder, are these people testifying and why are they doing it in such a boring manner?

The second problem is that experts often know too much for their own good, or rather, experts often know too much for the jury's good. Good expert witnesses harness this knowledge and use it to educate the jurors. Usually this requires that experts take more time at the beginning of their presentation to introduce key concepts to the jurors. Good experts talk directly to the jurors using as few technical terms as possible and, when they do use one, they explain what it means. In short, good experts respect the jurors. Those experts who are not as good do not share this sense of respect or at least do not display it when they testify.

The final problem is that expert witnesses are viewed with considerable distrust. They are being paid to be there and, wouldn't you know it, they always seem to travel in pairs—one saying something that favors the plaintiff and the other saying the opposite in favor of the defendant. Such factors cannot help but cause jurors to become skeptical about this kind of testimony.

The way you structure your expert examination and the graphics that you use during expert witness testimony can go a long way toward reducing (I am not sure you can ever eliminate) these problems.

"Gingers" and "Blah Blah Blahs"

I divide what experts tell jurors into two broad categories: "Gingers" and "Blah Blah Blahs." These terms come from an old "Far Side" cartoon by Gary Larson, who to my mind is one of the most gifted cartoonists ever.

One of my favorite of Larson's cartoons shows a man talking to his dog. The first frame, which is labeled "What We Say to Dogs," shows the owner yelling at his dog: "Okay, Ginger! I've had it! You stay out of the garbage! Understand, Ginger? Stay out of the garbage or else!" The second frame, which is labeled "What They Hear," shows the conversation from the dog's perspective. All that the dog hears is "Blah blah GINGER blah blah blah blah blah blah blah blah GINGER blah blah blah blah blah." You get the point.

The same can be said about expert witness testimony. The jurors usually only care about and understand a small percentage of what the expert tells them. I call these bits of testimony the Gingers.

Jurors are not looking for long dialectics on esoteric issues. The law of your particular case may require that you provide such information for the record, but do not expect most jurors to understand or appreciate it. This information is what I call the Blah Blah Blahs—material from which most jurors derive very little information, let alone persuasive information.

I am confident that I have insulted a number of experts by describing the bulk of what they have to say as being blah blah blah. I may even have insulted prospective jurors. That is not my intent. Instead, I have three objectives in using this Gary Larson analogy. First, I want to dramatically emphasize that, like it or not, this is reality. Second, I want to make sure that lawyers and experts understand what Gingers are and work to convey as much information as possible during this portion of testimony. Finally, I want lawyers and experts to concentrate on finding ways to increase (even slightly) the amount of information that jurors take away from the Blah Blah Blahs. Trial graphics and the process of creating these graphics are crucial in accomplishing the second and third of these objectives.

Maximize Your Gingers

Now that I have categorized expert testimony as being either Gingers or Blah Blah Blahs, let me give my theory of how many jurors decide whether to believe an expert's testimony. Most jurors will not be able to "peer review" what an expert says on the stand. It is the very rare juror who will understand regression theory or other technical ways of analyzing data.

Instead, most jurors are looking for other tools to evaluate your expert—tools that they can use as a substitute for in-depth technical knowledge. I suspect that most jurors look for these clues early in the expert's testimony, make a decision based on what they find, and then feel that it is safe to stop listening to the technical data that tends to take up the bulk of the expert's time on the stand.

Whatever information the jurors take away from an expert witness will likely come to them through the Gingers. You need to maximize both the amount of information you convey in this portion of the expert's testimony and the likeli-hood that jurors will actually pay attention to this information. As such, you gener-ally want to offer the Gingers relatively early in your expert's testimony; you want the information to be easy for the jurors to follow; and, when possible, you want to convey the information both verbally and visually.

The most common Gingers—that is, issues that jurors understand and care most about—are answers to the following five questions: (1) What did the expert do? (2) What did the expert find? (3) Why is this important? (4) Does what the expert did to come to his conclusions seem fair? and (5) Why should the jurors believe one expert as opposed to the other?

Help Jurors Understand What the Expert Did, What He Found, and Why It Is Important

Simple outlines are an extremely effective way of helping your jurors understand your answers to the first three Gingers, that is, What did the expert do? What did the expert find? and Why is what the expert found important?

Illustrations 8-16a through 8-16c are examples of a set of simple outlines that you might consider using with an expert witness. In this instance, we can break down testimony into three such layers, all of which nest in or connect to one another. You can start with the broadest outline in order to provide an introduc-tion. (See Illustration 8-16a.) Next, you can refer to the middle version that outlines

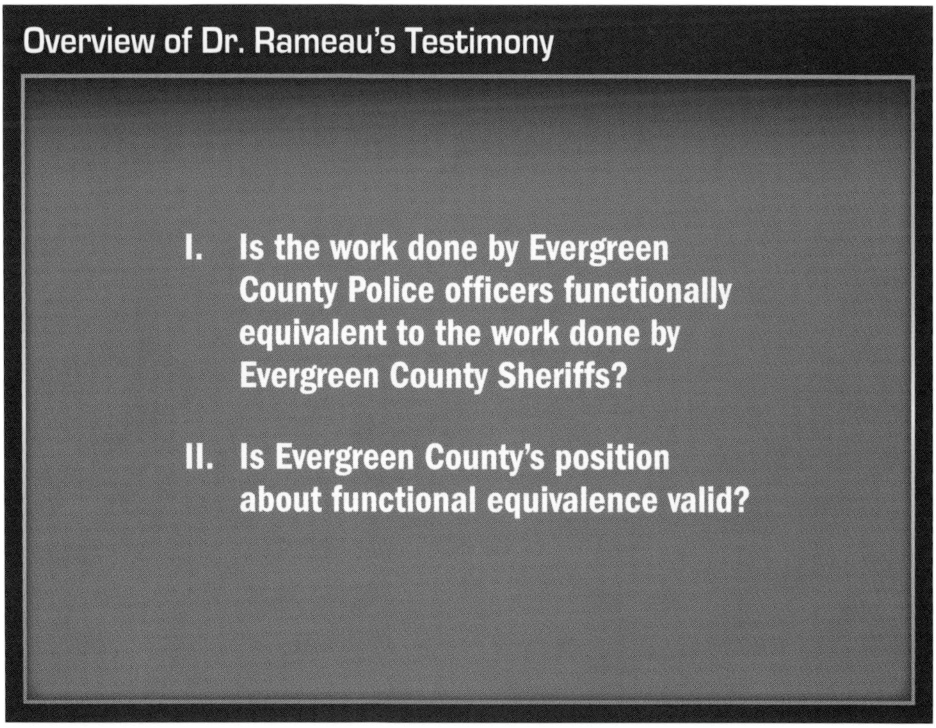

Overview of Dr. Rameau's Testimony

I. Is the work done by Evergreen County Police officers functionally equivalent to the work done by Evergreen County Sheriffs?

II. Is Evergreen County's position about functional equivalence valid?

ILLUSTRATION 8-16a. Outlining Expert Testimony

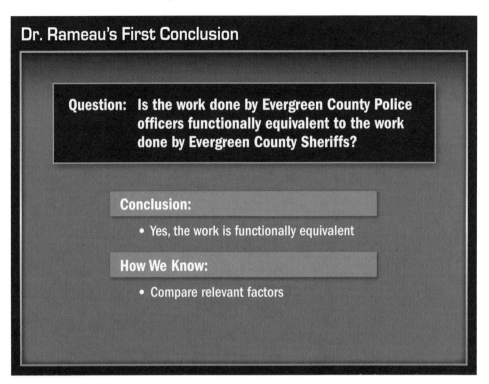

ILLUSTRATION 8-16b

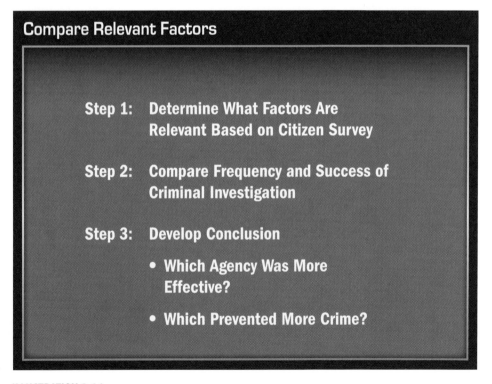

ILLUSTRATION 8-16c

a subsection listed in the first outline. (See Illustration 8-16b.) Finally, you can use a fine version that analyzes a point in more specific detail. (See Illustration 8-16c.)

This series of graphics is what I call a nesting-doll outline. I base the term on the Russian wooden matryoshka dolls, where there is a doll inside a doll inside of a doll, and so on. In this instance, each of the outlines is connected to and builds off of the one shown immediately before it. (See Illustration 8-17.)

Outlines such as these have an additional advantage. In order to create effective outlines, the lawyer and his expert need to spend considerable time together sketching out and refining the scope of the witness's testimony. Here again, the process makes for better testimony regardless of whether you actually create a graphic to show during trial or not.

Help Jurors Understand That the Expert's Methodology Was Fair

Jurors are rarely going to be able to understand and critique the expert's methodology from a technical perspective. Instead, what a typical juror will want to know is whether the methods and procedures used by the expert generally make sense and seem fair. There is a better chance that jurors will accept your expert's testimony if they can answer both questions with "Yes."

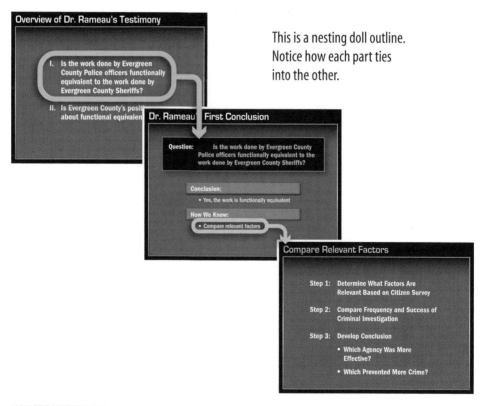

ILLUSTRATION 8-17

Let's look at an example in a class-action lawsuit in which racial discrimination was alleged. In this case the defendant was a county that operated two different law enforcement agencies—the county police department, which hired mostly minorities, and the county sheriff's department, which hired mostly white officers. The County paid its police officers only 60% of what it paid the sheriffs.

The plaintiffs' economic expert determined that the county disproportionately paid higher salaries to white officers and lower salaries to minority officers. The process by which he came to this conclusion involved highly complicated tests and procedures. Instead of trying to explain all of the steps to the jurors, the lawyer decided to use a three-step analogy to generally illustrate what was done. But, before he turned to the steps, he made sure that the jurors understood that the data that was used came directly from the defendant. This preliminary step helped authenticate the result and added a sense of fairness and accuracy to what the expert did. (See Illustration 8-18.)

Once the expert established where the data came from, he then proceeded to use an analogy to describe what he did to come to his conclusion. Here are the graphics the expert used and approximately what he said.

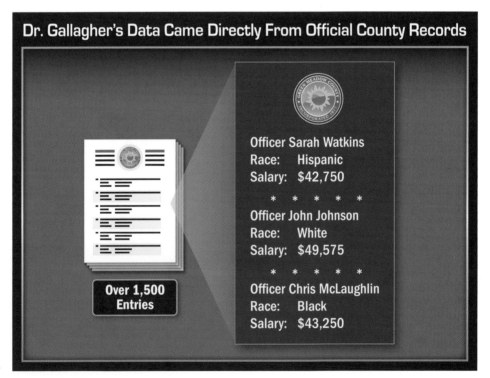

ILLUSTRATION 8-18. Authenticating Expert Data

▼▼▼

The first thing that I did was to gather information about every single police officer and sheriff's deputy. All of this data came directly from the county's official records. What I was looking for was the race and salary of each person. I took this information for each person and put it together.

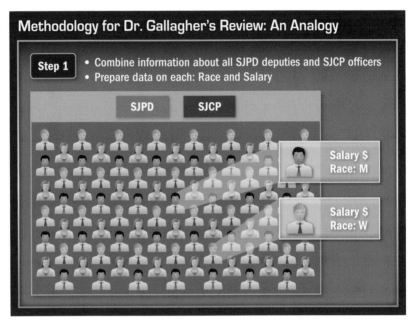

The best way to imagine what I did was to create an index card for each person on which I listed that person's race and salary. I pulled all of the index cards together without looking to see who was who and put all this data together as if it was in a big barrel.

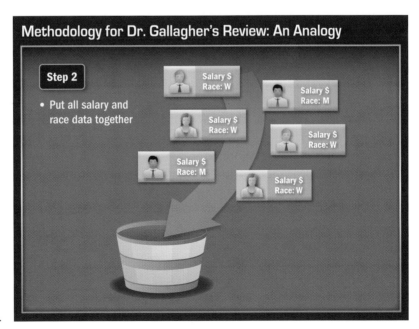

I then pulled the slips out one at a time and ranked them in order starting from the highest salary to the lowest salary. Once I had done this I went back and looked to see if there was any pattern based on race. What I found was that the county disproportionately paid higher salaries to whites and lower salaries to minorities.

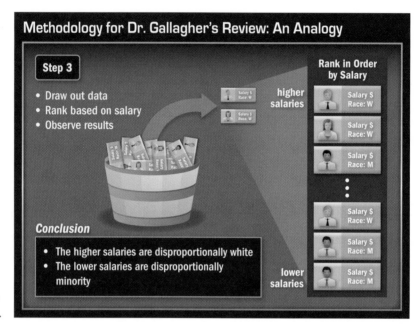

This series of graphics worked very well, with all of the jurors later reporting that they understood and believed this witness's conclusions. I think this approach and these graphics were very effective for two reasons. First, the process seemed fair. The underlying data, for example, was not something that the expert made up; instead, it was official governmental data that came directly from the defendant. Second, the process made sense.

Obviously the expert did a lot more than this and his methods involved a process considerably more elaborate. But the point is, this simple analogy helped the jurors understand and accept what was done and the analogy was probably much more effective than describing in detail the computer models and fancy theory that might have been used.

Remember, jurors may not understand much of what the expert says but they will be scrutinizing that portion that they do understand to see whether it seems fair and makes sense based on their ordinary knowledge of how things work. I have heard numerous jurors say that they accepted what one particular expert said because, while they did not understand all of it, what they did understand seemed to be fair and make sense.

Help Jurors Understand Why They Should Believe One Expert Over the Other

As I previously noted, experts tend to travel in pairs with one offering evidence in favor of the plaintiff and the other offering opposite information in favor of the defendant.

In most, if not all jurisdictions, the jurors are not required to choose one expert over another. Instead, jurors can, if they so choose, disregard both. There is an increased likelihood of this happening if the lawyers fail to offer evidence as to why one expert's conclusions are more reliable than the other's.

There are numerous ways to illustrate why one expert is more believable than the other. One way is to simply compare each expert's qualifications and potential biases.

A second way is to compare what assumptions were made by each. This is often used when comparing calculations made by accountants or economists where one side made its assumptions using conservative numbers compared to the other side's more speculative assumptions using inflated numbers. (See Illustration 8-19.)

A third way to compare the conclusions of two competing experts is to offer an example of how one expert's assumptions are more likely to produce a realistic answer than the other. Consider, for example, the series of graphics in Illustrations 8-20a through 8-20d, which shows how two experts calculated the total amount due to a large class of plaintiffs.

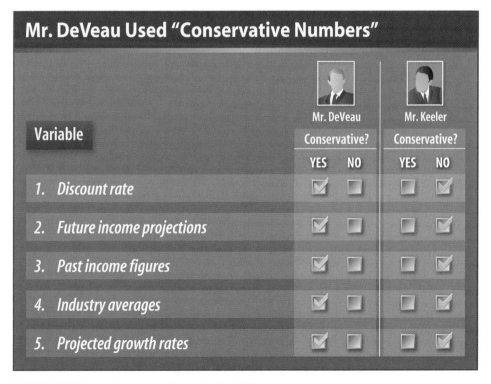

	Mr. DeVeau Conservative?		Mr. Keeler Conservative?	
Variable	YES	NO	YES	NO
1. *Discount rate*	☑	☐	☐	☑
2. *Future income projections*	☑	☐	☐	☑
3. *Past income figures*	☑	☐	☐	☑
4. *Industry averages*	☑	☐	☐	☑
5. *Projected growth rates*	☑	☐	☐	☑

Mr. DeVeau Used "Conservative Numbers"

ILLUSTRATION 8-19. Comparing Expert Believability

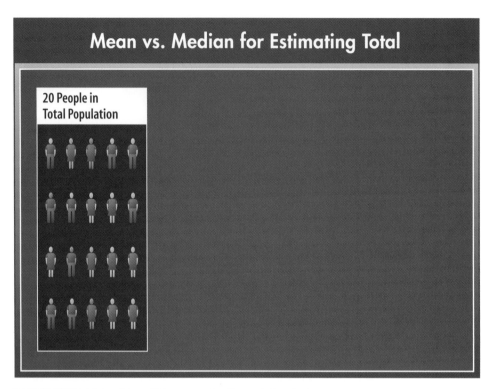

ILLUSTRATION 8-20a. Discrediting Opposing Expert's Conclusion

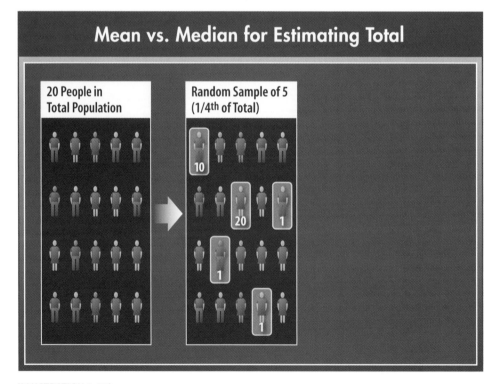

ILLUSTRATION 8-20b

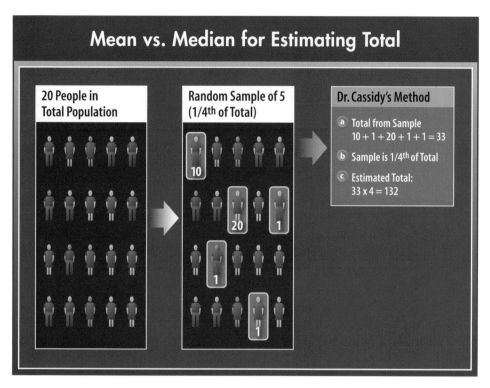

ILLUSTRATION 8-20c

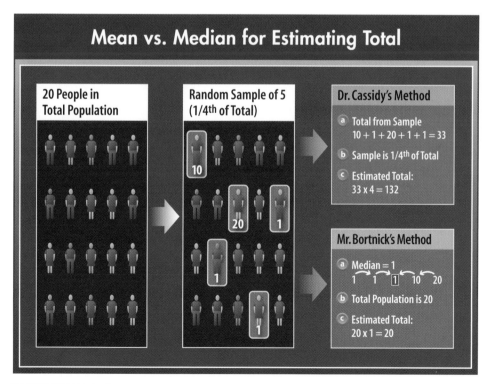

ILLUSTRATION 8-20d

The actual class included 2,000 plaintiffs. Experts from both sides agreed that gathering information from all 2,000 would be unduly expensive and time consuming. So the experts agreed to take one sampling and each use that data to calculate total damages.

The experts differed in that one calculated from the mean, or average, of the sample, so that the final number was representative of the total number of people in the class. The other expert, in a clear attempt to minimize damages, took the data from the sampling and calculated the median number (i.e., the number in the middle of the sample) and multiplied that median by the total number of class members. In this case, calculating from the median grossly minimized the amount of supposed damages.

Trying to explain this verbally was difficult. So the first expert developed a graphic that showed how the process worked for each expert using hypothetical numbers. The jury immediately understood the problem and dismissed the second expert's conclusions.

MAKE THE MOST OF YOUR BLAH BLAH BLAHS

The bulk of most expert testimony will fall into the Blah Blah Blahs, that is, it is likely to be information that most jurors will have considerable difficulty understanding. Often when I tell this to experts, they seem to believe that I am suggesting that there is nothing that they can or should do to help improve communication with jurors during this portion of the testimony.

Such a conclusion is wrong. There are numerous things that the expert can and should do to try to maximize the chances that some of this information is understood and used by the jurors.

Give the Expert Some Toys

I have had a number of expert witnesses affectionately characterize the material that they use during the bulk of their testimony as their "toys." These are items that they can use to help capture and hold jurors' interest.

Illustration 8-21 is an example of such a toy. It is an illustration showing the various parts of automobile brakes. The lawyer designed this graphic to help make the expert's testimony more interactive with the jurors. To help keep attention, the expert can get up, walk to the graphic, and point out various features of the brakes for the jurors.

There is no real limitation to the types of tools that you might use in such an instance. The point is to find ways to help the expert visually supplement his verbal testimony and to do so in a way that captures jury attention.

Help the Expert Explain Technical Terms

Often experts cannot stop themselves from using (and sometimes are required to use) technical terms during their testimony. There is nothing inherently wrong

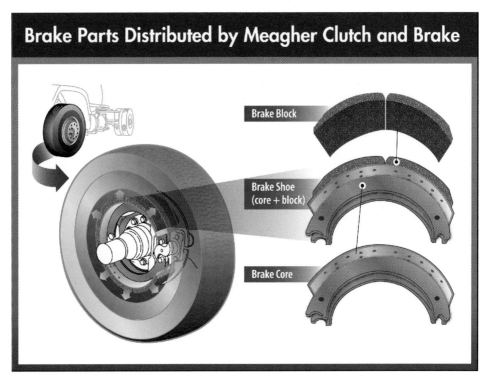

ILLUSTRATION 8-21. An Expert's "Toy"

with this so long as the expert takes time to explain such terms when they are introduced. Illustration 8-22 shows how an expert witness might annotate a definition of "prior art," an important concept in intellectual property cases.

Illustration 8-23 shows how an expert might use an analogy to explain a technical term. In this instance, the expert was required to explain a "1 to 1,000 *reverse stock split.*" Specifically, the lawyer wanted to demonstrate that in such a transaction, while the stockholders would have fewer shares, the total value of those shares would not decrease. As the analogy points out, this is the same as a person taking one thousand single dollar bills to the bank and converting them into a single thousand-dollar bill. While the number of bills has decreased (from one thousand to one), the value has not changed.

Keep the Expert Focused

Is it just me or has anyone else noticed that some experts seem to have a difficult time focusing on what it is they are supposed to talk about? As a friend of mine in the "communications business" says, experts have a hard time "staying on message." I would like to think that they have this problem because they know so much and are just trying to be helpful. Unfortunately, whatever the cause, the result can be disastrous. Experts who fail to stay on message can miss a crucial point or bury that point among unnecessary information someplace in their excessive wanderings.

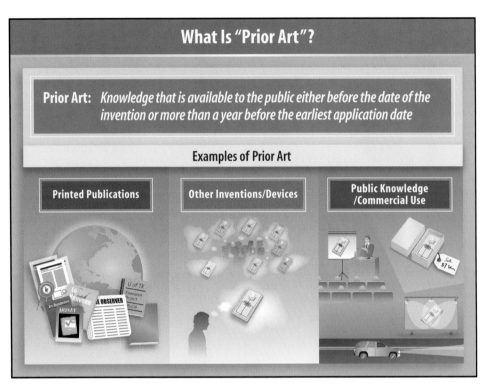

ILLUSTRATION 8-22. **Explaining a Technical Concept**

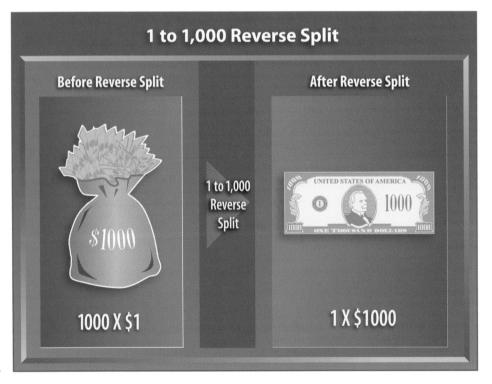

ILLUSTRATION 8-23. **Using an Analogy to Explain a Technical Term**

If you have such a witness, you might want to consider the following kind of graphic. I am going to show it to you in four versions. All you are seeing in the first version is the baseboard, which is how the exhibit would look before you started adding to it. (See Illustration 8-24a.) The second and third version show the baseboard after it has been covered by a portion of the magnetic add-ons. (See Illustrations 8-24b and 8-24c.) The final version is the board after all of the magnetic add-ons have been placed on the baseboard. (See Illustration 8-24d.)

Specifically, with respect to this exhibit, the expert would have testified that an airplane typically went through fourteen steps before receiving an "air worthiness certificate." You would put up an icon describing the first step and all of the activities that are involved in this step. You would continue on through each step until you are done.

This board fulfills the dual purpose of providing the jury with a tutorial and, at the same time, keeps the expert focused on exactly what you are looking for by way of an answer. For example, if at the fourth step the witness begins to wander onto a collateral issue, you can gently pull him back to focus on the fifth step.

Yes, Capt. Jones, this is very interesting about the type of the carburetor used by the Red Baron during the First World War. Maybe we will come back to that later. *[You are thinking, like hell we will.]* But, for *now [strong emphasis on now]*, what about step five *[you point to the fifth box]*, what is the fifth step *[now you are tapping on the empty fifth box]* right here, the fifth step in certifying an airplane as being airworthy?

ILLUSTRATION 8-24a. **Keeping Your Expert Focused**

ILLUSTRATION 8-24b

ILLUSTRATION 8-24c

ILLUSTRATION 8-24d

Help the Expert Explain Conclusions

As we have previously discussed, one of the most important questions that trial lawyers should be asking themselves is "Compared to what?" In other words, how do you get jurors to compare new and often technical information to material with which they are already familiar? We have already examined numerous examples of graphics that could be used during expert testimony in just this way.

One final example is one which helps an expert explain what it means to say that a person has a "one in a million chance in a lifetime of developing cancer." Without in anyway trivializing this figure, I once tried to find a way to put it into perspective. (See Illustration 8-25.)

Help the Expert Explain Key Working Documents

In my mind the worst part of watching expert witnesses give testimony is listening to them explain the content of highly technical documents or how they calculated some complex figure. The worst example of this is testimony by accountants who run through spreadsheets and other incomprehensible documents. Some run through the material very quickly and provide no real benefit from this testimony. Other accountants go through the material in painful detail, completely losing all of the jurors in the process.

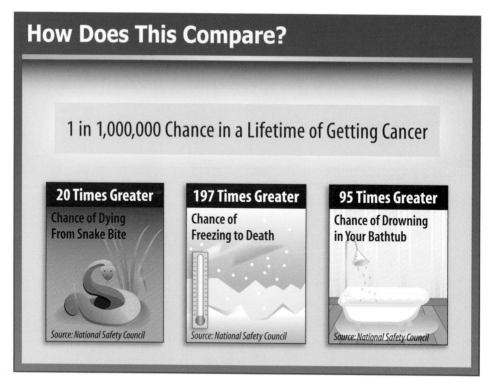

ILLUSTRATION 8-25

Let me show you a better way for such experts to testify. This process, which can be used by all experts—not just accountants—consists of four parts.

The first is to provide a very high-level overview of what the expert needed to calculate. (See Illustration 8-26.) In this example, the expert, an accountant, needed to calculate "total losses," which consisted of "past losses" and "future losses." At the beginning of his testimony, the expert writes this information on a flipchart and

ILLUSTRATION 8-26. Begin With an Overview

briefly describes each type of loss. Note that he will come back to this graphic at the end of his hypothetical testimony.

The second part of the expert's testimony describes the various steps that went into calculating each figure. (See Illustration 8-27a.) The witness does so by using a board on which the various steps were listed. The point of this step is not to make the jurors expert accountants, but to briefly explain the steps and to leave at least some of the jurors feeling that the steps seem logical and fair.

The third part of the expert's testimony consists of tying the six steps to his key summary document. Illustration 8-27b is the first in the series of these documents. It shows the six steps, each color coded, on the left of the graphic and the key document, already admitted into evidence, on the right.

The expert then proceeds through the steps and highlights on the key document where the data related to each step is located. The first two of these six graphics are displayed in Illustrations 8-27c and 8-27d.

Calculating Total Losses Requires Six Steps:

Past Losses

Step 1: Start with Linda Lundy's actual past earnings

Step 2: Project what she would have earned

Step 3: Reduce her projected earnings for new business costs

Step 4: Subtract what she earned or could have earned

Future Losses

Repeat steps 1-4

Step 5: Reduce future earnings to present value

Step 6: Add past losses and future losses together

ILLUSTRATION 8-27a. **Show the Expert's Steps**

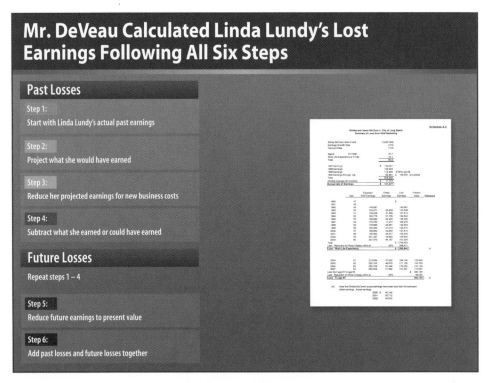

ILLUSTRATION 8-27b. Compare the Steps to the Expert's Report

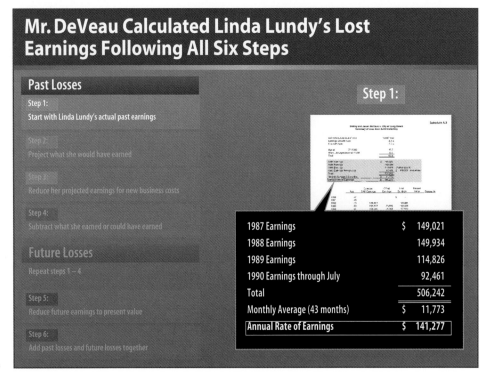

ILLUSTRATION 8-27c. Show Where the Data for Each Step Is Located

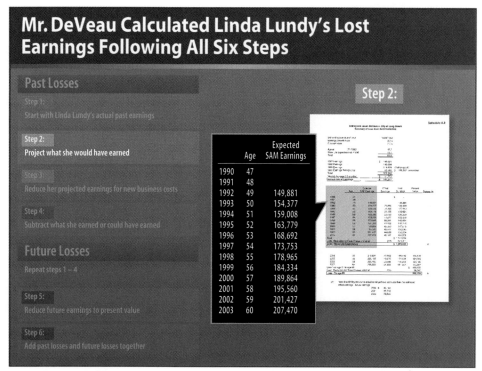

ILLUSTRATION 8-27d

Again, the purpose of this third step is not to make jurors experts. Instead, this step helps to authenticate the expert's conclusion and helps those jurors who are interested and might actually understand some of the numbers know where to go and look during deliberations.

The final step is to go back to the flip chart and fill in the actual numbers for the jurors. (See Illustration 8-28.)

Past Losses	4,600,000
+ Future Losses	+ 3,700,000
Total Losses	8,300,000

ILLUSTRATION 8-28. End With the Expert's Conclusion

Using Graphics During Your Closing Argument

A jury consultant once told me that he felt that closing arguments were unnecessary. He insisted that most jurors had already made up their minds by this point in the trial and, as such, the closing argument was merely for the lawyer's ego. I disagreed and asked him whether he actually ever advised his clients to waive their closing argument. "Of course not!" he replied with a look that suggested that I was a fool for even suggesting such a thing.

I believe that closing arguments do make a difference, although perhaps not in the ways we trial lawyers generally think. I will concede that many of the jurors have formed opinions (sometimes very strong opinions) before closing arguments start. While they have formed these opinions and may even have decided who they think should win, what some jurors lack is the ability to articulate exactly why.

This fact, that is, the need that many jurors have to be able to articulate why they are voting a particular way, should guide the entire structure of your closing argument. Jurors do not need for you to repeat your opening statement—I don't care how good it was. Jurors are long past needing an introduction of the case or a witness-by-witness summary of what was said. They need more than that; they need for you to remind them of what really matters and for you to explain exactly why it does.

Here is where I believe closing argument plays two important roles. First, closing argument helps many jurors articulate for themselves why they feel the way they do, thereby decreasing the likelihood that someone on the other side will change that juror's mind. Second, closing argument is the last place where Active Jurors often get the ammunition they need to argue why the side they favor should win.

Closing argument is the last opportunity trial lawyers have to tell our story to the jurors. It is our final chance to convince them that our client's version is the truth. Ironically, it is also the first and only time that we get to use all of the tools, including graphics, at our disposal.

During closing argument, trial graphics are particularly helpful in four ways: (1) isolating selected pieces of evidence from your case and arguing why each is important, (2) turning your opponents' own graphics against them, (3) addressing the law and arguing how and why it should be applied in your favor, and (4) arguing—just plain arguing.

ATTACKING WITH GRAPHICS

Certain types of exhibits that you have already created for earlier parts of your case readily lend themselves to summarizing the evidence and/or explaining why it is important. Many of these we have already discussed in other sections of this book and do not require much additional examination here. For example, you can use timelines and textpulls to help remind jurors of key events. But remember that just mentioning these dates or documents is insufficient for closing argument. Instead, you need to provide three additional bits of information about each key date and document: (1) why each is important, (2) what other evidence (besides your word) exists that confirms the information is important, and (3) how this particular event or document fits into the overall context of the case.

In addition to these already existing graphics, you might consider preparing two other types of graphics that you can use in closing argument to bolster your version of the facts. The first are special graphics that you have prepared based on themes and other key points you have made in opening statement, as we discussed at the beginning of this chapter. The second are "argumentative" versions of other standard graphic types, such as argumentative textpulls.

The graphics that we examined in Chapter 7 were for the most part not particularly argumentative. When closing argument rolls along, you should consider changing that and making them so. Let's look at a few examples.

We have previously discussed juxtaposed textpulls. To some extent, merely juxtaposing two texts for the purpose of comparing and contrasting what each says is technically a form of argument. What I am suggesting here goes beyond that. What I am talking about is comparing two documents and overtly showing why you believe one to be superior or more truthful than the other.

For example, let's assume that both sides prepared estimates concerning how much certain extensive repair work would cost. One of the estimates was professionally prepared by a licensed contractor who spent hours carefully detailing his work. The other was not. In closing, you might very well use a graphic such as Illustration 8-29 to emphasize the differences in the two documents and then use this difference as a basis to argue why the jury should rely on the more accurate version.

Comparing the Estimates

	Paxton Builders' Estimate		Brown's Scope Increase	
Pages of detail?	42	✓	3	✗
Detail for each room?	YES	✓	NO	✗
Quantity & unit detail?	YES	✓	NO	✗
Detailed price estimates?	YES	✓	NO	✗
Prepared by a licensed contractor?	YES	✓	NO	✗

ILLUSTRATION 8-29

You can also prepare argumentative graphics attacking the testimony of your opposing party's witnesses or comments made by opposing counsel in opening statement. At the outset, let me tell you that while these graphics can be very effective, you need to be careful that you do not appear too strident when you use them.

Illustration 8-30 juxtaposes testimony from four of the defendant's witnesses. Notice how this graphic has been organized. At the top are three boxes, each one of which is labeled to reflect a particular failing by defendant. Each of these topics is an area that the lawyer who created this graphic intends to argue as evidence of defendant's malfeasance. In each box, the lawyer has included crucial testimony from one of defendant's own witnesses. Additionally, notice the box at the bottom of the graphic. This box also contains a key quotation, which is labeled "Conclusion." Obviously such a designation is argumentative, and that is exactly why it is there.

Illustrations 8-31a and 8-31b combine to form another version of a trial graphic that attacks testimony by opposing party's own witnesses. Since this graphic is a more direct attack on those witnesses, some jurors might be offended by such a graphic.

We have previously noted how opening statement and closing argument need to be connected. When you are making your opening statement, do not overcommit yourself.

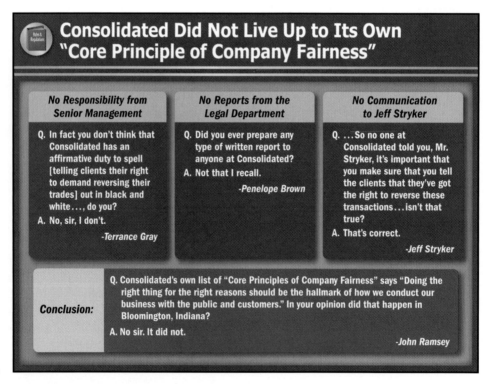

ILLUSTRATION 8-30. Juxtaposing Testimony

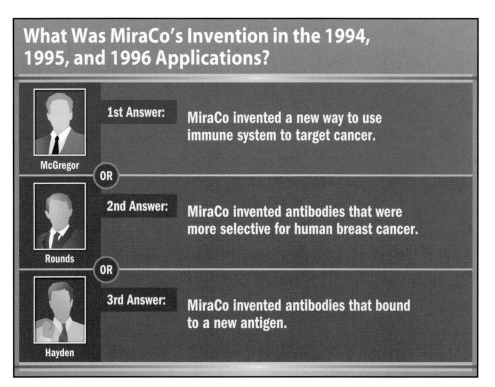

ILLUSTRATION 8-31a. Confronting Opponent's Witnesses

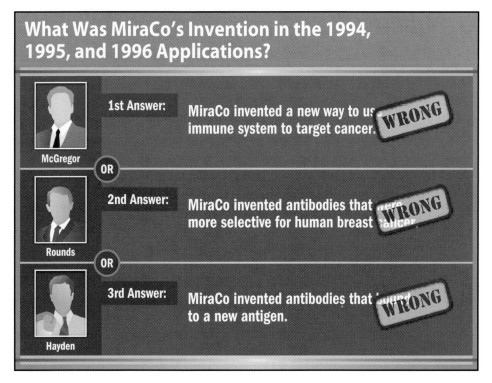

ILLUSTRATION 8-31b

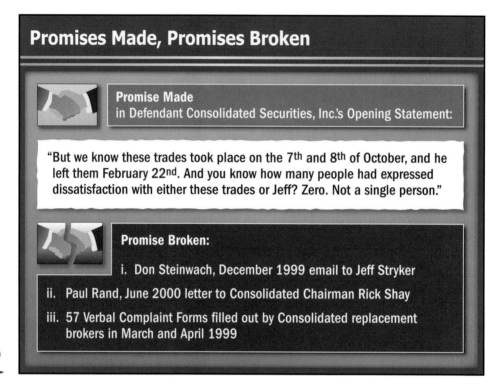

ILLUSTRATION 8-32. Attacking Opposing Counsel's Statements

Should your opposing counsel choose to disregard this advice, you may find it appropriate to use a graphic such as the one shown in Illustration 8-32. This direct attack on the opposing party's counsel focuses on certain unfulfilled promises made in opening statement by that lawyer.

TURNING YOUR OPPONENTS' OWN GRAPHICS AGAINST THEM

One of the most satisfying things you can do is to turn your opposing counsel's own graphics against him. One of the most frustrating things that can happen to you is when your opposing counsel turns one of your own graphics against you. You must be on the lookout for both possibilities.

There are a variety of ways to turn your opponent's graphic. The simplest is to put your opposing party's graphic up during your closing argument and verbally point out all of its faults.

Alternatively, you might consider creating various pacing devices that you can use to put on your opposing counsel's graphic as a way of highlighting problems. I found that the simplest way to do this was to use "stickies"—those colored pieces of paper with a reusable adhesive on the back. Consider getting a pad of these that are large enough that you can write a key word or phrase on each and then plaster your opposing counsel's graphic with them to point out weaknesses or problems with the graphic.

Another way to attack your opposing counsel's graphic is to make a copy of it yourself and have a graphic designer annotate it for you. Illustration 8-33 shows an example of this. The bottom of this graphic is a copy of a timeline that plaintiff used throughout its case. The jury was familiar with it and did not need to be reminded what it was. One of the problems with plaintiff's graphic (in addition to it being very badly designed in general) is that it failed to list some very key events. Defendants' attack on the graphic, in the top portion, points out the events that plaintiff "forgot" to show.

INSTRUCTING THE JURORS

Never forget how important the law is in almost every single case. There is a group of jurors, often highly articulate professionals, who rely almost exclusively on the law to make their decision. These are jurors who carefully parse through the jury instructions to see whether each element has been met. These are jurors who, in criminal cases, understand and can articulate the differences between alternative criminal counts. These are jurors who can do all this and, at the same time, are often intellectually capable of making forceful, well-reasoned arguments to support their position during deliberations. These are the jurors you want on *your* side.

Consider offering these jurors five types of graphics.

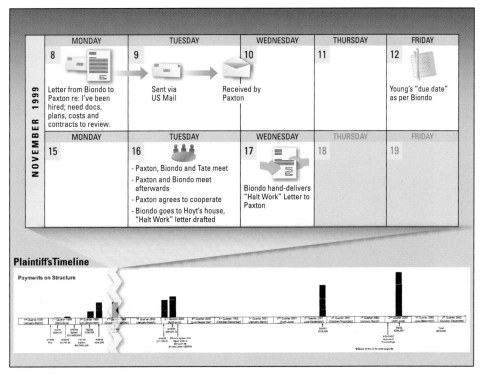

ILLUSTRATION 8-33. Spotlighting Flaws in Opponent's Graphic

The first is a simple textpull of the applicable law or jury instruction with the most important language, that is, language you are most likely to use in closing, highlighted for the jury. (See Illustration 8-34.)

The second type of this graphic is a tutorial that helps explain what the law means. Such graphics often work best in displaying how one or more parties is required to act or treat another party. (See Illustration 8-35.)

We have previously discussed the third type of graphic—organizing tools. For an example of this, see the series of graphics in Chapter 3 explaining the concept of implied malice in the case of the vicious dogs.

The fourth type is what I call a factually annotated jury instruction. These straightforward graphics generally have language from a jury instruction printed out verbatim at the top of the graphic. Below this is a sampling of evidence showing how a party has either met or failed to meet this legal requirement. The final portion is a summary at the bottom of the graphic. (See Illustration 8-36.)

The final example is an analogy that helps illustrate the jury instruction. These graphics are particularly helpful and important for those jurors who tend to be visual learners. Some jurors can understand the gist of an instruction merely by hearing it read by the judge. Others, equally intelligent and articulate, can better understand it if the material is visually laid out for them.

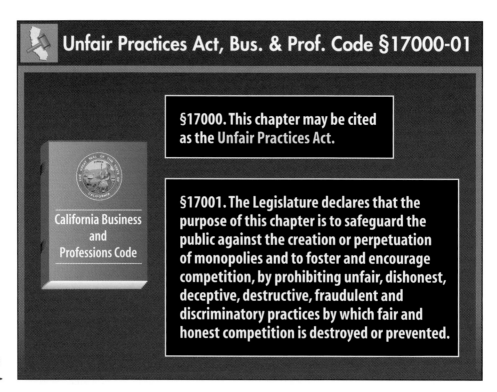

ILLUSTRATION 8-34. A Closing Textpull

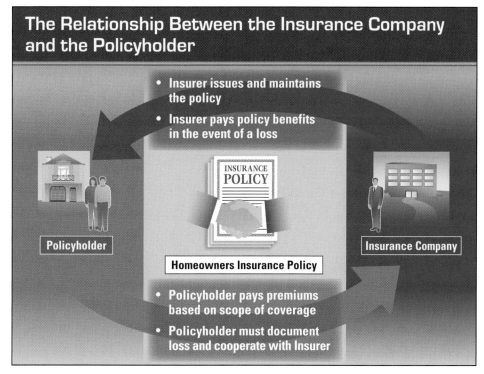

ILLUSTRATION 8-35. A Closing Tutorial

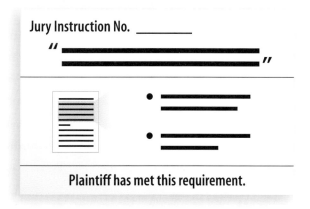

ILLUSTRATION 8-36. Annotated Jury Instructions

Illustration 8-37 is an example of this type of graphic. The graphic deals with an instruction in an intellectual property case defining the "doctrine of equivalents" test, which, when two patents are being compared, requires a party to show that the function, way, and result are identical. Some jurors have difficulty understanding what it means for the function, way, and result to be identical. Others forget that in order to meet the test, all three of these requirements must be established.

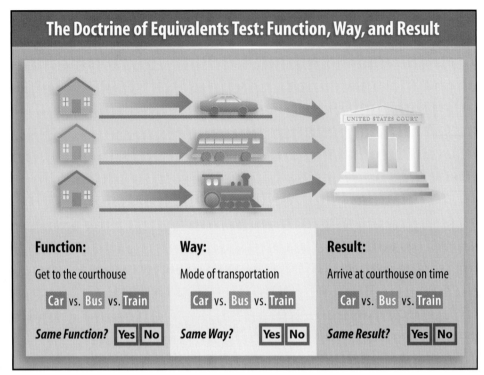

ILLUSTRATION 8-37. Using Analogy in Jury Instructions

The graphic offers an analogy of three different jurors getting to the courthouse from their homes each morning. One takes a car; the second a bus; the third a train. As the analogy shows, the "function" of these three modes of transportation is the same—each gets the juror to the courthouse. Likewise, the "result" is the same—each arrives at court on time. But the "way" is obviously different. Using this analogy, the lawyer is able to focus on an important issue of law, explain what it means, and help jurors understand how it might apply to a real-world situation with which all of them are familiar. Clearly, it is much easier for jurors to follow this argument than trying to understand what might otherwise be very technical portions of the actual patent itself.

ARGUING ABOUT DAMAGES

Information about damages is often presented in a very disjointed way during trial. Jurors often hear a total figure during opening statement, with very little explanation of what went into calculating this figure. Throughout the parties' cases-in-chief, various damages witnesses often go into details about the various pieces, but offer no comprehensive picture of what the total should be. Because of this, it is very important in closing argument for you to explain to the jurors exactly what the damages should or should not be.

The simplest way to do this is to provide a graphic that merely lists and totals the amount of damages. You do not need anything overly fancy for this. You can display this information on a blackboard or on a flipchart. (See Chapter 6 for examples of blackboards and flipcharts.)

Don't forget, when appropriate, to argue about your damages. Many less experienced lawyers forget that they are entitled to do so in closing argument, and, as such, they are not merely limited to reciting numerical figures. (See Illustration 8-38.)

USING GRAPHICS FOR NO OTHER PURPOSE THAN ARGUING

Sometimes I wonder whatever happened to a good old-fashioned argument. I am not talking about a heated exchange of words that occurs spontaneously in anger. No, I am talking about the kind of closing argument that motivated many of us to go to law school and become trial lawyers. The kind that we imagine Clarence Darrow giving at the end of one of his cases or Atticus Finch making to rouse the jury to do justice.

Many trial lawyers tell me that such arguments are no longer in vogue because jurors no longer favor such inspired displays of advocacy. These are the same lawyers who often tell me how jurors are getting younger and seem fascinated by fast-moving and dramatic movies, music, and television.

As you probably can tell from the last sentence, I strongly disagree that arguments, even forceful arguments, are passé.

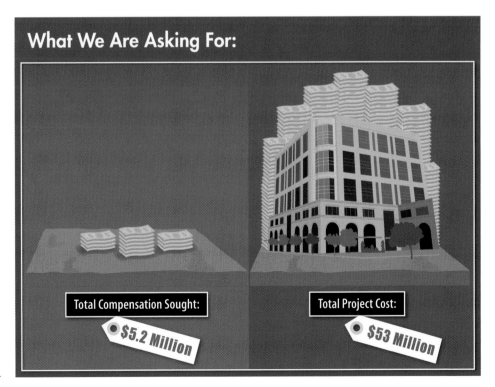

ILLUSTRATION 8-38. Summarizing Damages

I believe that good old-fashioned arguments are less common for three reasons. First, it is the rare (and in my mind, the fortunate) lawyer who regularly gets the opportunity to go to court for a jury trial. Arguing and persuading through arguments are skills that require considerable preparation time and experience. As lawyers spend less time in front of juries, many find it easier to merely pass off a slightly beefed-up version of their opening statement as an argument. It is not.

Second, I believe that many lawyers spend untold hours preparing the facts or law of their case without spending sufficient time contemplating how to argue those facts and law. This is because for most lawyers gathering facts in discovery and arguing the law in motions takes up the bulk of case preparation time.

Finally, I suspect that there are fewer arguments because many lawyers are not quite sure how to go about conceiving of, playing with, and refining these rhetorical tools.

I strongly believe that creating argumentative illustrations for closing argument will help you overcome all three of these hurdles.

Each of the following examples came from a mental mining session that the lawyer undertook long before the trial began. Beginning this process early is important both because it takes time and, as we have previously discussed, because some of the rhetorical antecedents to a good argument have to be laid out in opening statement. Waiting until the night before closing argument to start this process will not allow you to do so.

For two reasons, I encourage you to walk yourself through the process of designing argumentative graphics even if you never actually use such tools in trial. First, the process is highly personally satisfying for those who do so. After all, didn't you decide to become a trial lawyer because you enjoyed the intellectual stimulation of arguing (again, not fighting—just arguing)? Second, your case cannot help but improve by going through this process.

One of the reasons that arguments are so fascinating is that no two are ever alike, even when they deal with the same subject. What follows does not even scratch the surface of the kinds of graphics that you can develop. I offer them as examples to encourage you to spend time coming up with your own. I promise that this will be time extremely well spent.

MAKING THEMATIC ARGUMENTS

Thematic arguments are those that are not directed at a particular point. Instead, they attack your opponent's case or bolster your case as a functional unit rather than a series of discrete parts. These arguments go to the gestalt of either party's case. They address issues fully integrated throughout the formal and informal structure of that case. When people see illustrated versions of these arguments they tend to have two reactions—"That is very argumentative, but wow, it goes straight to the point."

Let's look at two examples. The first deals with a situation that arises quite often in litigation, a plaintiff taking inconsistent positions and trying to win using

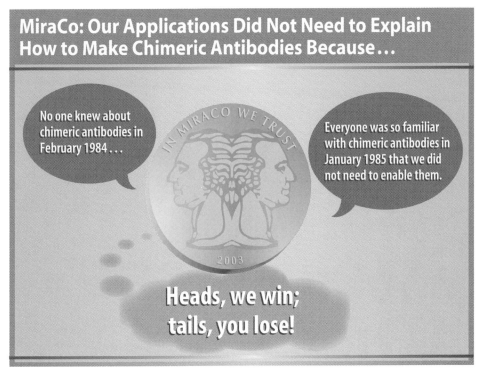

ILLUSTRATION 8-39. **Exposing Opponent's Inconsistencies**

both of them. (See Illustration 8-39.) Since this is often verbally described as a "heads I win, tails you lose" situation, why not visually show it as such?

The second example involves an insurance bad faith case where the insurance company came up with one excuse after another to deny payment. Throughout the course of several years, the insurance company lost alleged defense after alleged defense. At trial the company raised two final defenses.

The policyholder had various arguments that specifically addressed each defense, but it wanted more; it wanted the jurors to be able to judge the final defenses in the context of what had been years of unsuccessful delay by the insurance company. In effect, the policyholder wanted to emphasize the general theme that the trial was further indication of the insurance company's true intent—that is, rather than pay a legitimate claim, it would stall and make life so difficult and expensive for the insured that he would eventually give up and either take less than he is entitled to or just go away.

Illustrations 8-40a through 8-40e show five slides from a series of twelve. (The complete series can be viewed on the Visual Resource CD-ROM.) Each of the insurance company's attempts to avoid paying the claim is illustrated using a roadblock sign. In closing argument, the plaintiff's counsel went through each and described how the insurance company had raised each defense seriatim and ultimately lost on each such ground. After seeing and hearing about nearly a dozen such instances, the jurors concluded that the trial was merely the latest attempt at this strategy of delay and that the insurer had acted in bad faith.

ILLUSTRATION 8-40a. Revealing Opponent's Delay Tactics

ILLUSTRATION 8-40b

ILLUSTRATION 8-40c

ILLUSTRATION 8-40d

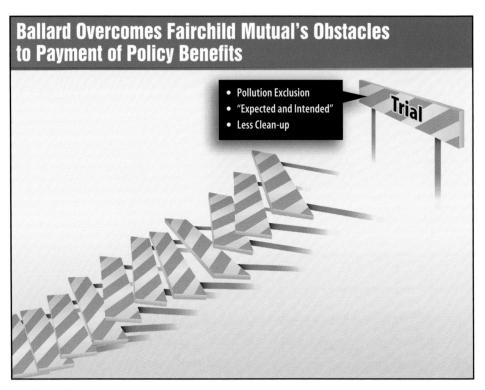

ILLUSTRATION 8-40e

Show Alternatives the Opposing Party Ignored

Around the dinner table at my house, one argument that eventually gets brought up in any political argument is what the offending politician should have done. Do not forget this technique for your closing arguments. Creating a graphic illustrating what one party should have done but failed to do can be an extremely effective way to make your point. I have found such arguments to be particularly helpful when state of mind is at issue. Jurors understand that a person's state of mind is important and that it is often difficult to prove. Jurors also strongly embrace the concept that actions speak louder than words and will naturally look to see whether actions, words, and professed state of mind all align.

The easiest way to show what a party should have done is by way of a "report card" graphic. This is usually a simple chart on which various actions (that were done or should have been done) are listed. To the right of such a list are boxes or other tallying mechanisms to see whether what was done was consistent with what should have been done. (See Illustration 8-41.)

A slightly more elaborate way to show this is to prepare a flowchart listing the steps that should have been followed if the party really wanted to accomplish what he now professes he wanted to accomplish. The lawyer can trace along the flowchart while reviewing the evidence, showing that the party was either consistent or inconsistent with what he has testified to in court.

What Jeff Stryker Should Have Done

		Did Stryker Do It?
1	Communicated immediately that transactions were done and that they were unauthorized	NO
2	Communicated that what he did was illegal	NO
3	Communicated available options to the clients	NO
4	Communicated his reasoning behind his actions	NO
5	Communicated what other brokers and specialists were telling and advising their clients at the time	NO

ILLUSTRATION 8-41. Giving Opponent a "Report Card"

Appeal to Common Sense

I recently met a young man who wore a band around his neck to which he had attached his car keys. The initials WWJD were woven throughout the band. I asked him what the initials stood for and he advised me that they were the initial letters to "What Would Jesus Do?" It seemed that whenever this young man was unsure what to do or how to behave, he would turn to these four letters for inspiration. Living near Berkeley, California, with its broad diversity, I have since seen numerous variations of this necklace advising followers of a variety of faiths to ask What Would Buddha/Mohammad/Other Wise Person Do?

People in my house are notorious for not reading directions or instructions that come with new products. Things are just too easy that way. Instead, we tend to rely on directions and instructions only as a last resort. Some trial lawyers are this way with common sense. They will construct long and elaborate arguments without even pausing for a moment to use the most basic reasoning technique—common sense.

For those lawyers, I strongly suggest that you repeatedly ask your self WWMD—"What Would Mom Do?" as a way of considering whether there is a common-sense argument that should be made in your case.

Obviously, when I say "Mom" I am merely suggesting an archetype for any wise person who somehow has the uncanny ability to cut through the most complex situations by pointing out a simple answer or straightforward solution.

Let me show you an example. In this case plaintiff had important information that he passed on to the defendant. According to plaintiff everyone knew when the information was transferred that it was very important, that time was of the essence, and that plaintiff expected the defendant to act immediately. Defendant did not act immediately and, as a result, plaintiff was substantially harmed. Defendant countered that, while the information eventually became important, no one including plaintiff understood that it was so crucial at the time it was transferred and that he (the defendant) cannot be faulted for not acting immediately.

By the time of trial, this case, like many others, was buried in thousands of documents. There were numerous percipient and expert witnesses who testified about the horrible result of delay. Each side had hired several experts to talk about standards in the industry and what was and was not considered important. Needless to say, both sides' experts disagreed on what should have been expected.

During the mental mining session, a secretary to one of the lawyers asked a simple question: "How did plaintiff deliver the documents to the defendant?" When the lawyer told her that the plaintiff mailed the information, she paused and stunned a handful of lawyers by saying, "Well, that does not make any sense. These guys [plaintiff and defendant] had offices only four blocks away from each other. If plaintiff really believed that the documents were so important, why didn't he just drive them over to the defendant's office? I mean, come on, common sense tells you that is what you should do if you are truly worried about getting important documents delivered quickly. On top of that everyone drives past defendant's office building to get to the freeway to get home. It was right on the way."

This approach immediately translated into a very simple, yet effective common-sense argument and graphic. (See Illustration 8-42.)

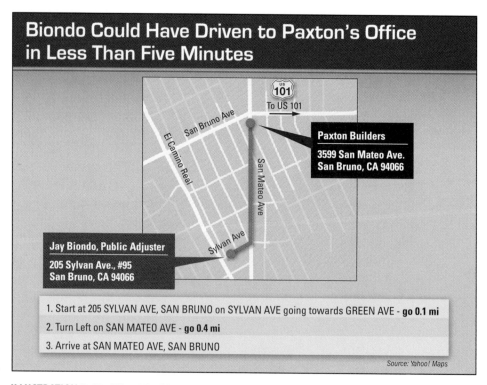

ILLUSTRATION 8-42. **What Would a Person With Common Sense Do?**

Chapter **9**

Hypothetical Cases

Introduction

What follows are four hypothetical fact patterns along with a select number of sample graphics for each. To fully appreciate the material in this chapter, you will need to review it in conjunction with the accompanying Visual Resource CD-ROM. Ideally, you will examine the material in the book, find some or all of the graphics interesting, and then review them in greater detail using your computer. This is important because some of the graphics as displayed in the book may appear "cluttered" or too full of information. The only way to view them as if they were actually being used in court is to do so from the Visual Resource CD-ROM. The CD-ROM will allow you to witness "Selectavision" in action and understand why the amount of information in each graphic is appropriate.

While some of what follows is based on actual cases, much is entirely fiction. In any event, we have made two types of changes to the "facts." First, if the material comes from a real case, we have changed names and other identifying information. Second, for teaching purposes, we have simplified the facts and much of the testimony (especially expert testimony) associated with the graphics.

Whenever you do this, you inevitably destroy much of the subtlety of a real dispute and for this I apologize in advance, particularly to those readers who have expertise in any of the factual or legal areas covered by these hypothetical examples. However, there is good reason for this simplification (some might argue oversimplification). The focus of this chapter is, as it should be, on concept and example—not strict factual accuracy.

At the beginning of my real cases, I will often prepare preliminary sketches of possible graphics for my clients. Ideally I am able to do so at a period very early in the case, when I am able to say (only half in jest) that my imagination "has not yet been overly hampered by the facts." [1]

---

1. In this I like to paraphrase the jazz performer Louis Prima—"I'll tell you hun, I read a little bit, but not enough to hurt me none."

When I give these preliminary sketches to my clients, I start off by admitting that the graphics contain errors, but then I quickly remind the lawyers that the purpose of the drawings is not factual accuracy. Instead, I want the lawyers to use the sketches as a way to think about possibilities and potentialities and to do so without their imaginations having been overly hampered by the facts. The time for absolute factual accuracy will come, but just not so early in the mental mining process of the case.

The same can undoubtedly be said about the following fact patterns and graphics. Do not review this material for the purpose of learning about some area of substantive law or fact. Additionally, do not assume the types of graphics in each hypothetical are somehow restricted to that unique fact pattern. Instead, examine these examples for their intended purpose—as possibilities of the types of graphics that you might consider using in one of your future cases regardless of its particular subject matter.

Hypothetical Case Number One:
SOAR Technologies vs. Cylindrical Systems

FACTS

SOAR Technologies Inc. was a relatively small software developer based in San Francisco. The company was founded by two former college classmates, Rebecca Stein and Patrick Sullivan. While attending Stanford, Stein and Sullivan developed a revolutionary translation software, which they call Smart Quotes. Smart Quotes not only allows different computer operating systems to communicate flawlessly with each other, it also translates text in foreign languages into English and vice versa.

In June 2002, SOAR Technologies demonstrated Smart Quotes at Comdex in Las Vegas. Comdex is the industry's largest convention. Products that do well at Comdex usually get considerable industry publicity and tend to go on to be the star performers in the market. Smart Quotes was considered to be one of the most impressive products that year at Comdex. SOAR Technologies, Sullivan, and Stein received considerable publicity and sales of Smart Quotes began to rise rapidly.

Lou Castro is president of Cylindrical Systems, one of the largest computer software companies in the world. Cylindrical Systems created and marketed a translation program known as Clear Content. Clear Content does a good (but not perfect) job of allowing different operating systems to communicate. Clear Content does not translate any foreign languages into English. In fact, all of Cylindrical's attempts to develop such foreign language translation programs have failed miserably.

After seeing how well Smart Quotes worked, Mr. Castro sent an e-mail to Cylindrical's senior management telling them, "We are in trouble. Unless we stop these guys [SOAR] we are dead meat." Two days later, Castro sent another e-mail to Edward O'Donnell, Cylindrical's senior vice president and chief technology officer, "[W]e are in trouble with SOAR and its Smart Quotes software. . . . You better figure out how we are going to prevent this or it's your job!"

SOAR Technologies was scheduled to make an initial public offering (IPO) of its stock on July 25, 2002. On July 21, *World Computer Press,* the industry's leading daily publication, received an anonymous e-mail from "someone close to SOAR." The e-mail claimed that Stein had discovered several programming errors with Sullivan's work on Smart Quotes that would undoubtedly present considerable problems for future end-users. The e-mail also alleged that SOAR's management was in complete disarray because Sullivan and Stein had been arguing for weeks and were no longer even talking to each other. None of this was true.

On July 22, *World Computer Press* published a short article in its "Word on the Street" section. This section is popularly known in the industry as the "Crash and Burn Pages" because companies that appear here usually are in trouble and often eventually fail. The article mentioned without attribution the rumors in the anonymous e-mail. The article caused considerable commotion in the investing public. SOAR's IPO, which should have been a success, was a complete failure. SOAR never recovered and eventually declared bankruptcy. Cylindrical's Clear Content software remains the dominant product in the industry.

Suspecting that Cylindrical was behind the sending of the anonymous e-mail, SOAR sued Cylindrical and others. As part of discovery in its case, SOAR uncovered Castro's two e-mails about Smart Quotes. In addition, one of SOAR's expert witnesses was able to use a variety of forensic techniques to trace the source of the anonymous e-mail back to Mr. O'Donnell and his work computer.

SAMPLE GRAPHICS

For this hypothetical, I created graphics for six aspects of SOAR's case: (1) basic textpulls to show the key portions of important documents to the jury; (2) introductory material concerning the parties, the key players, their products, and the relative strength of the competing products; (3) a basic timeline; (4) a simple tutorial on how IPOs typically work and why they are so important to the continuing growth of a new company; (5) tutorial material to be used by SOAR's expert to explain how she was able to conclude that Mr. O'Donnell sent the anonymous e-mail to *World Computer Press*; and (6) a limited amount of argumentative graphics for closing argument.

Basic Document Textpulls

There are several key documents in this case—documents with which the jurors must become familiar in order to fully understand what happened. I have designed a series of textpulls to assist the jurors with this task. These textpulls are in two different formats—a more typical or standard style for Illustrations 9-1 through 9-4 and an alternative version for Illustration 9-5.

Illustrations 9-1 through 9-4 are examples of basic textpulls. Notice certain key characteristics about each of them. For example, each has a title describing exactly what the key point is of the document displayed in that graphic. This helps the jurors understand the significance of the material every time they see it—whether it is the first time the lawyer shows the document to them or weeks later when they see the graphic lying around in the courtroom. Whenever possible, in order to avoid the claim that a title is too argumentative, we rely on a direct quotation from material in the actual document itself.

These sample graphics "authenticate" themselves in a variety of ways. For example, each includes a scan showing the source of the original material. Additionally, we have included two citations. The first is the trial exhibit number. This is the number that you should encourage the jurors to remember and write down in their notebooks so that they can more easily find the original version of this document from the stack that goes with them into jury deliberations. The second citation is a more detailed description of what the document is and where the information came from (e.g., "E-mail from Lou Castro to Edward O'Donnell, June 25, 2002").

Illustration 9-3 further authenticates its content by including photographs of Mr. Castro and Mr. O'Donnell so that the jury can better understand who sent and who received the document. I do not suggest using this authentication method for all documents. Instead, I would limit its use to the most important material, such

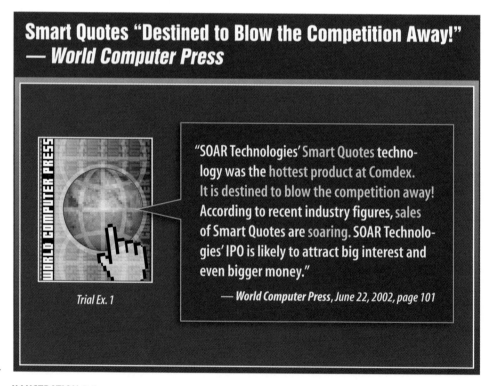

ILLUSTRATION 9-1

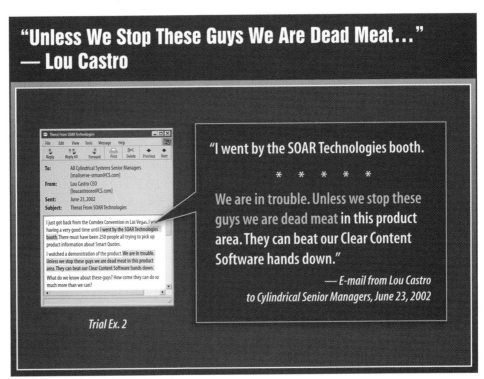

ILLUSTRATION 9-2

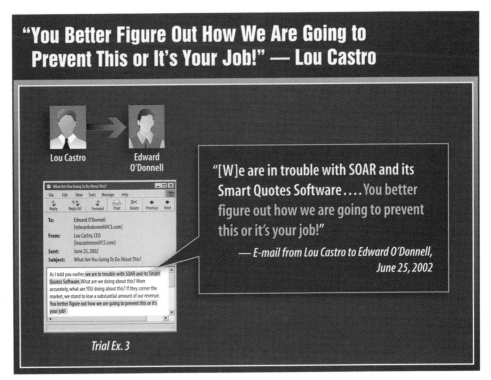

ILLUSTRATION 9-3

as this e-mail, which probably best explains Mr. O'Donnell's motivation to harm SOAR and Smart Quotes.

In order to make it easier for the judge and jurors to read the material (particularly at a distance), each of these graphics displays its key text in light type on a dark background. Additionally, I have highlighted key sections of the pulled material itself to help the lawyer and jurors focus on what really matters.

These graphics are likely to be used by the lawyer throughout the trial. They could, for example, be used in opening statement, during witness examination, and in closing argument. The lawyer could display this material either on exhibit boards or through some form of electronic media.

Illustration 9-5 is an alternative form of a textpull that you might consider using when you want to show the jurors more material than can be easily displayed in a typical pull box. This graphic displays the entire "Word on the Street" article in order to help the jurors put the false comments about SOAR into context, that is, to allow the jurors to see the material as a typical reader of the article would have seen it. To help the jurors focus on what is truly important within that article, we have put a border around information related to SOAR.

Since this graphic is in portrait format (i.e., vertical), the trial lawyer will not be able to easily use electronic media to show it to the jurors because most screens and monitors usually display material in a landscape (i.e., horizontal) format. The trial lawyer is likely to use a graphic such as this in opening statement, during wit-

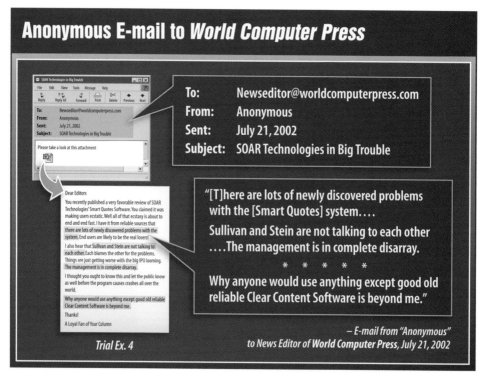

ILLUSTRATION 9-4

The "Facts" in *World Computer Press* Article Were All False

World Computer Press article

July 22, 2002

Lots of talk on the street this week about products not performing like they should. **Real McCoy** out of Santa Clara has had to recall a number of its products that just did not deliver as promised. Users were hoping to be able to start relying on the **Basho 2002** software last month. No such luck. *The Word on the Street...* Real McCoy – Isn't!

There is similar bad news coming out about the darling of this year's Comdex convention. As we previously reported, **SOAR Technologies** is going public this month. Until recently, no one had anything bad to say about **Rebecca Stein**, **Patrick Sullivan**, and their new software **Smart Quotes**. But, is there trouble brewing? Rumors are circulating about newly discovered problems with the software that will likely lead to major problems with any system using this product. Pressure is building at SOAR with its upcoming IPO. It has even been suggested that Stein and Sullivan are not even talking to each other, that is how bad things are at Soar. *The Word on the Street...* This IPO may be DOA!

Word on the street is that there are some real problems with hardware manufactured by **Bhatt Circuits, Inc.** Users of Bhatt products from all over the country claim they are having problems. Bhatt denies there is any such problem, but the complaints just keep on coming. *The Word on the Street...* Bhatt Times Ahead!

Trial Ex. 5

ILLUSTRATION 9-5

ness examination, and during closing argument, and will probably need to do so displaying the material on an exhibit board.

Introductory Material Concerning Parties, Players, and Products

I have prepared a series of sample graphics for the plaintiff's lawyer to use to introduce the parties, the key players, and the company's respective products.

Illustration 9-6 provides basic information about SOAR Technologies. The graphic also features background information about two of the most important witnesses who are likely to testify on behalf of that company—Mr. Sullivan and Ms. Stein. In contrast, Illustration 9-7 contains no such personalizing information about Mr. Castro or Mr. O'Donnell. Instead, this graphic emphasizes how large Cylindrical is in comparison to SOAR. These graphics provide factual background and corroborate a potential theme of "small vs. big" or "David vs. Goliath."

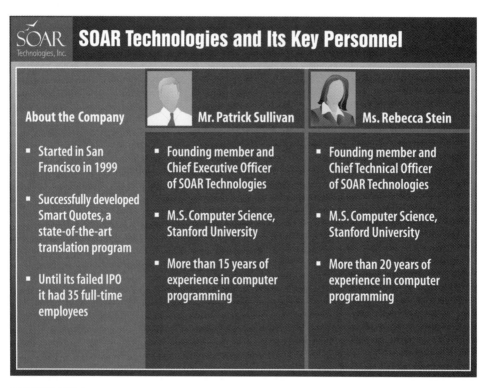

ILLUSTRATION 9-6

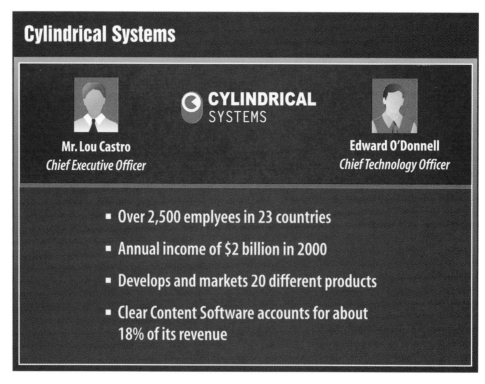

ILLUSTRATION 9-7

These examples could be presented as either static or dynamic graphics. The trial lawyer is most likely to use them in opening statement and/or in closing argument.

One of this case's important issues is the relative benefits and strengths of each company's product. More specifically, SOAR will want to educate the jurors about what each product can do and show how/why Smart Quotes was superior to Clear Content. This information is not only important background but also it helps explain what motivated Cylindrical to send the disparaging material to *World Computer Press*.

Illustrations 9-8 and 9-9 illustrate what each product can do. Notice that in Illustration 9-8 we have included an example of how the program might be used by an American user to translate foreign languages into English and vice versa. Since Clear Content could not perform such translations, this information is noticeably absent from Illustration 9-9. Illustration 9-10 compares the two products in a way that clearly favors Smart Quotes.

The trial lawyer is likely to use some or all of these graphics in opening statement, during witness testimony, and in closing argument. This material could be displayed either on boards or by way of an electronic media. The graphics could be either static or dynamic.

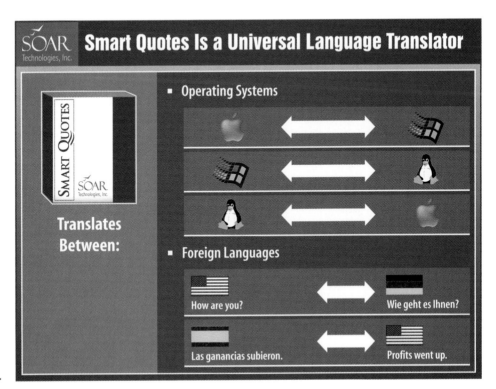

ILLUSTRATION 9-8

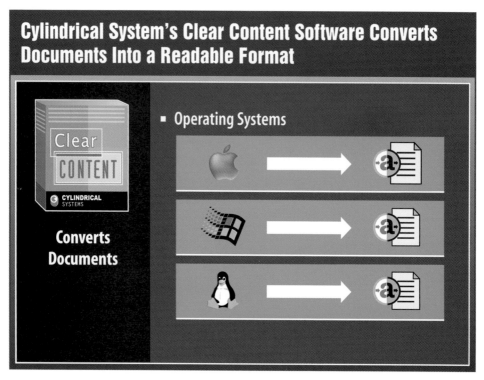

ILLUSTRATION 9-9

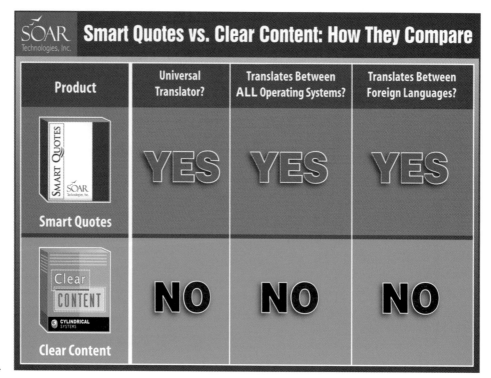

ILLUSTRATION 9-10

A Basic Timeline

Illustration 9-11 is a layer cake timeline that SOAR could use to show the jurors the relative order in which key events occurred. All entries concerning SOAR are above the timebar; below the timebar is material related to Cylindrical as well as the anonymous e-mail and resulting article (both of which the trial lawyer hopes to link to Cylindrical in the jurors' minds).

We have included a variety of scans and other illustrations in the timeline in order to make the graphic more visually engaging and to help jurors better understand where key documents (i.e., the scanned documents) fit in the story.

As discussed in Chapter 7, I generally believe that it is best to display timelines on exhibit boards, and I particularly recommend doing so with this example.

A Simple Tutorial on Initial Public Offerings (IPOs)

SOAR will want to establish the following sequence of events: the anonymous e-mail led to the unfavorable news article, which led to the failure of the IPO, which led to SOAR's bankruptcy.

I suspect that some of the jurors will not fully understand what an IPO is, how it works, and how its failure could directly lead to SOAR's being driven out of business. Illustration 9-12 is a very simple tutorial that SOAR can use to help jurors understand these important facts. The graphic displays the overall IPO process as

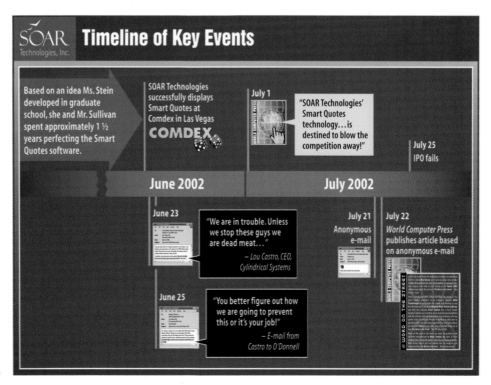

ILLUSTRATION 9-11

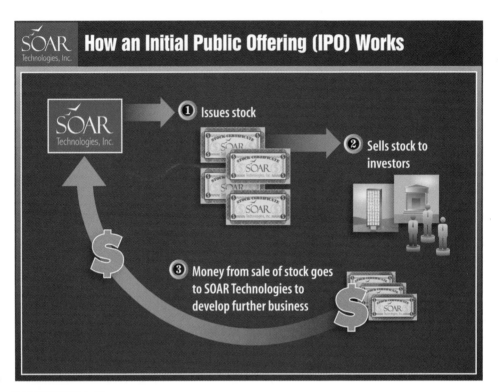

ILLUSTRATION 9-12

involving three steps: (1) SOAR issues stock, (2) SOAR sells that stock to investors, and (3) the money from the sale goes back to SOAR so that it can use the funds to develop further business. Some may find this explanation overly simplistic—but for these purposes, it is supposed to be.

This graphic could be displayed either in a static form or dynamic format. All other factors being equal, I would probably display this graphic electronically in a dynamic format. The lawyer would likely use this material in opening statement, during witness examination, and/or in closing argument.

Tutorial Material for Plaintiff's Expert

SOAR hired an expert to determine who sent the offending e-mail to *World Computer Press*. In order for SOAR to prevail, it will need to help the jurors understand the expert's conclusions and what the expert did to reach those conclusions. Additionally, the lawyer needs to convince the jurors that the expert's techniques and conclusions are fair and accurate, even if jurors do not understand exactly what the expert did.

Introduction to the Methodology Used by the Expert. Our hypothetical expert is going to testify that she was able to trace the offending e-mail back to Mr. O'Donnell's computer in three ways. These methods included (1) using information in the e-mail itself to trace its path backward from recipient to sender, (2) locating

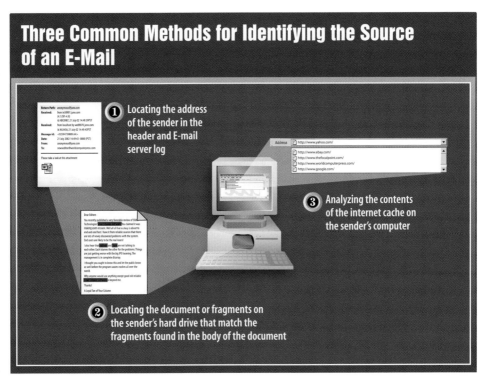

Three Common Methods for Identifying the Source of an E-Mail

1. Locating the address of the sender in the header and E-mail server log

2. Locating the document or fragments on the sender's hard drive that match the fragments found in the body of the document

3. Analyzing the contents of the internet cache on the sender's computer

ILLUSTRATION 9-13

document fragments on the hard drive of Mr. O'Donnell's computer, and (3) analyzing the content of the internet cache on Mr. O'Donnell's computer.[2]

Illustration 9-13 is an example of a graphic that the expert could use to help introduce the jurors to this overall process as well as to each of the three specific methods she used during this process. As you can see, this graphic lists the methods and describes each very generally.

This graphic would work well as an exhibit board that the lawyer could put up on an easel and display throughout the expert's entire testimony. In this way, I see the graphic being used in at least three different ways.

First, the lawyer would use it at the beginning of the expert's testimony as a way of preliminarily surveying what work the expert did. Here, the expert and lawyer would use the board to provide an overview of the process to the jury. This would not involve any detailed testimony, merely a general introduction of the more detailed testimony that would soon follow.

Second, the lawyer could use the board to help the expert make her transitions into more detailed discussions about each search method. For example, the lawyer might point to the graphic and say, "Ms. Expert, now that we have concluded your

---

2. Having worked with such computer experts before, I acknowledge that what follows does not do justice to what these talented people can really do.

testimony about the first method, let's talk about the second method you used. What was that method?" The expert would then use the board to launch into a more detailed discussion of that method.

Finally, at the end of the expert's testimony or in closing argument, the lawyer might use the graphic to summarize the expert's conclusions. Pointing to the graphic, the lawyer might say, "Ms. Expert, now that we have concluded your testimony, what again was your conclusion with respect to method three?"

Method One: Using Information in the E-mail to Trace It Back to the Sender. The expert's first forensic method to trace the e-mail was to use information in the e-mail itself to trace it backward from the recipient (i.e., *World Computer Press*) to the sender (i.e., Edward O'Donnell). This involved three steps. First, the expert obtained an "extended header" from the e-mail itself. Next, she used information unique to that extended header to trace what e-mail account sent the message. Finally, she subpoenaed information concerning that account and was able to determine who opened it. Illustrations 9-14 through 9-23 illustrate and walk the jurors through this process.

Illustration 9-14 identifies the two basic parts of any e-mail. Most of the jurors are already likely to be familiar with this information, which I have displayed by way of a simple textpull. Nevertheless, I suggest that you start at this basic level for two reasons. First, some of the jurors will not be familiar with this terminology and

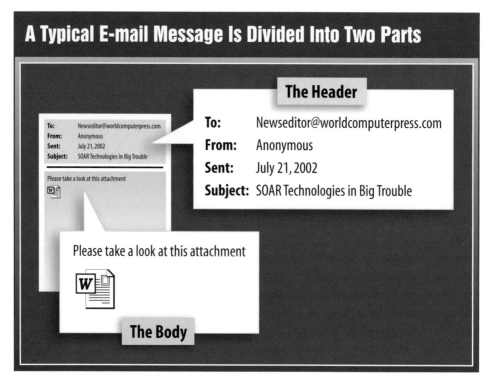

ILLUSTRATION 9-14

they will eventually need to be in order to understand the other steps in the process. Second, even more technically sophisticated jurors find it psychologically easier to begin learning new material (which is much of what the expert's testimony will be) if you start with something with which they are already familiar, such as the parts of a typical e-mail.

Illustrations 9-15 and 9-16 introduce the jurors to the concept of "extended e-mail header" and the unique information that it contains. As with Illustration 9-14, this information is conveyed using simple textpulls. Hopefully, these three introductory graphics (Illustrations 9-14 through 9-16) will help the jurors understand that: (1) this type of information is accurate and (2) that it is objective—i.e., that it is not merely something created by SOAR or its expert for the purposes of this case.

Illustration 9-17 shows what the expert was able to do with the information that she obtained from the extended e-mail header. Specifically, she traced the e-mail address to an account administered by Juno.com. This information lead directly to an AOL account which was opened by someone (presumably Mr. O'Donnell) using one of Edward O'Donnell's credit cards.

The information in Illustration 9-17 would work well in a revealable exhibit board. The graphic would originally appear with each of the steps covered up. As the expert talked about each step, either she or the attorney could remove a magnetic covering to reveal an illustration of what that step was and what that step found.

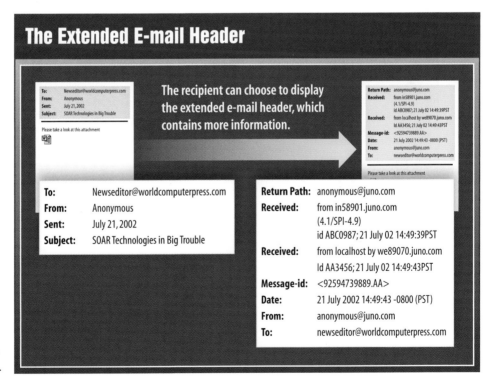

ILLUSTRATION 9-15

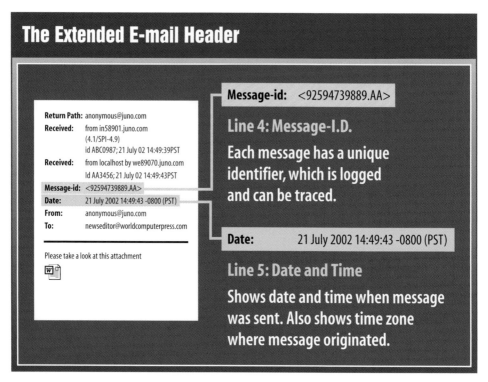

ILLUSTRATION 9-16

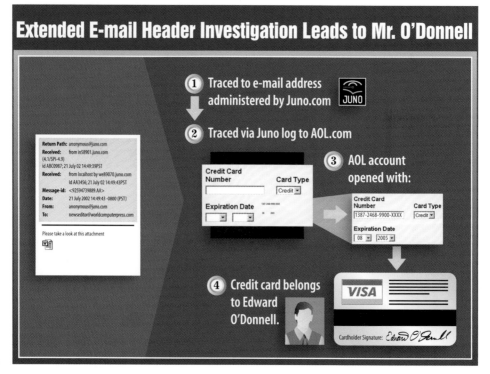

ILLUSTRATION 9-17

In order to further assist the jurors, the lawyer would ask the expert to explain any important new terms or concepts used in describing the process displayed in Illustration 9-17. For example, "Ms. Expert, you just used the phrase 'internet service provider'—what is that?"

By making Illustration 9-17 revealable, you will not trigger the jurors' Yikes! Alarm; you will get all of the other benefits of using pacing devices; and you will create some sense of suspense as to what information will be revealed in the final step (e.g., the account was opened using a credit card belonging to Mr. O'Donnell).

Method Two: Locating Document Fragments on the Hard Drive of Mr. O'Donnell's Computer. Many people believe that when they tell their computer to delete something from its hard drive that the information is completely and permanently deleted. This is not the case.

When you "delete" something, all you are really doing is letting the computer know that in the future it is free to reuse the space where the saved document was previously stored. Until such time as the computer actually stores new information directly onto that space, the original material is still electronically present in the computer, and the "deleted" material can, with certain techniques, still be retrieved by an expert. Additionally, even if the computer saves a new document on the hard drive where the old material was previously stored, often not all of the space previously used by the deleted document will be directly covered over by the new material. Consequently, there will occasionally be fragments from the original document remaining on the hard drive long after the user thought it had been deleted.

To help explain this point, you might want to offer the jurors an analogy in an area where they are likely to have greater experience. For example, let's assume that you have a cassette tape recorder and you record a message that is ten seconds long. When you are done, you decide to record another message over the first. If the second message lasts twelve seconds, all of the original recording will be recorded over and you will not hear any of the first message. If, however, the second message is only eight seconds long, the first eight seconds of the initial recording will be lost, but a fragment of the original message (the last two seconds) will remain and can be retrieved from the cassette tape. (See Illustration 9-18.)

Computer experts can subpoena a computer that they believe may have generated a particular document. They can then make exact copies of that machine's hard drive and search these copies to see whether they can find fragments of the original document.

Ideally, the experts will find words or phrases on the hard drive that match those in the deleted document. Merely finding matches does not guarantee that the suspect machine was used to generate the original document. For example, certain common words (e.g., "a," "the," "this," and "that") are going to be found on any computer, even one completely unrelated to the questionable document. Consequently, the expert looks for unusual words or combinations of words that are both on the suspected computer's hard drive and in the document. The more

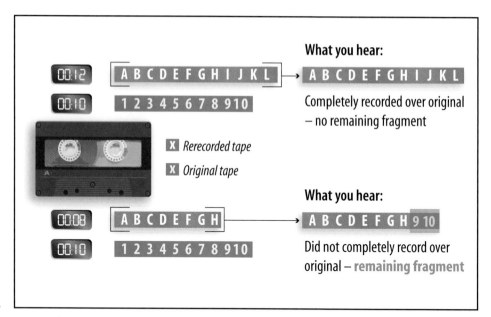

ILLUSTRATION 9-18. This Tutorial Relies on an Analogy

unique or unusual the matching words that the expert can find, the more likely it is that the document was generated on that particular machine.

Illustrations 9-19, 9-20, and 9-21 help illustrate this process. Illustration 9-19 provides a very basic platform from which the expert can do a variety of things. For example, she can use this graphic to define certain terms. She can also use it to correct the misperception that many jurors may have that once they push the delete button the material is completely wiped off the computer.

The figures in Illustration 9-19 are not intended to be exact representations of what happens. Instead, this graphic is more of a prop or a teaching aid that the expert and lawyer can use to illustrate the point.

Illustration 9-20 is a tutorial graphic designed to show the steps an expert follows in recovering information from the hard drive and comparing what she finds to the text of the original document. You will notice that this graphic is a general one and does not deal with the specific facts of the hypothetical case. This is intentional, because I very much want the jurors to understand the process and believe that it can be done before turning to the specifics of this case. Once they have such an understanding and belief, it will be easier for them to accept the final conclusion in Illustration 9-21; that is, Mr. O'Donnell created the text of the offending e-mail.

Method Three: Examining the Internet Cache on Mr. O'Donnell's Computer. The third method that the expert used to trace the e-mail was to inspect the internet cache on Mr. O'Donnell's computer. As the expert will explain, the computer's internet cache automatically keeps a list of Web sites recently visited by the user.

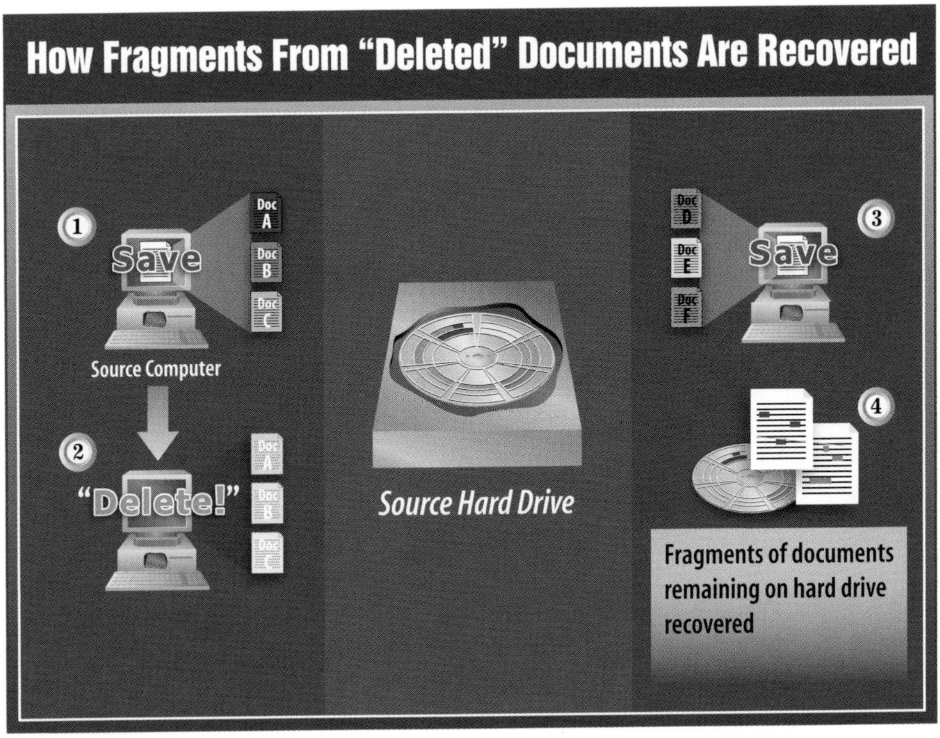

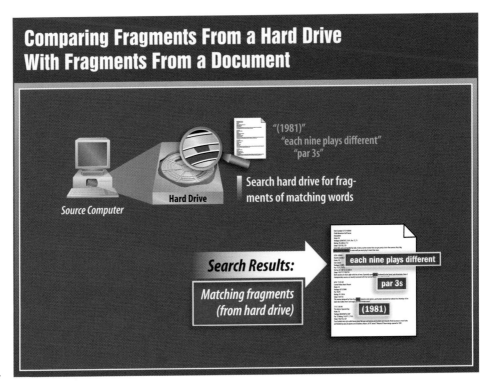

ILLUSTRATION 9-19

ILLUSTRATION 9-20

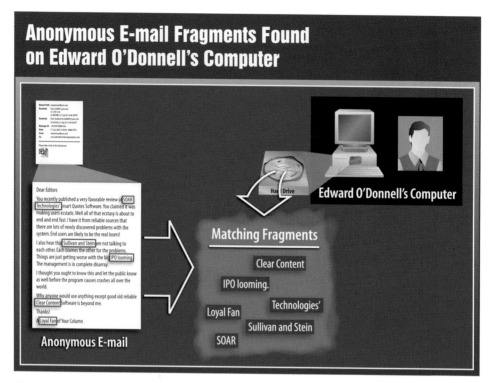

ILLUSTRATION 9-21

Obviously, by itself, this information is not particularly helpful because a popular Web site visited by millions of people will appear on millions of different computers. However, combining this information with the conclusions of the prior two tests will help further establish that Mr. O'Donnell created and sent the offending e-mail to *World Computer Press*.

The expert could use a graphic such as Illustration 9-22 as a prop to help establish what the internet cache is and what it does. As we did with the prior series of graphics, we believe that it is important to get the jury to understand and accept this information in the *abstract* before going on to a graphic that shows the particulars of what the expert found in this particular case. (See Illustration 9-23.)

Material for Closing Argument

The lawyer in this hypothetical could use several of the illustrations that we previously discussed in closing (e.g., Illustrations 9-17, 9-21, and 9-23). In addition, she might also use a graphic like Illustration 9-24 to help establish defendants' motive in sending the e-mail.

Finally, those trial lawyers who feel that they need to "slam the door shut" during closing could use a graphic such as Illustration 9-25. As you will see from the Visual Resource CD-ROM, Illustration 9-25 is a composite board that summarizes the evidence—all of which points directly to Mr. O'Donnell.

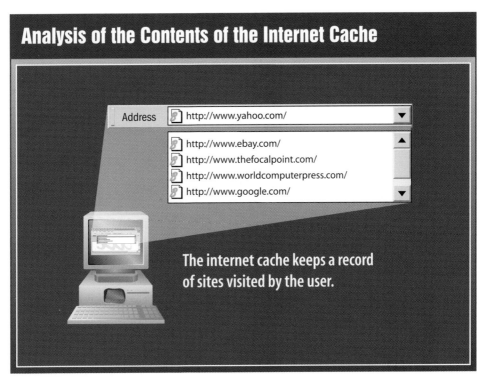

ILLUSTRATION 9-22

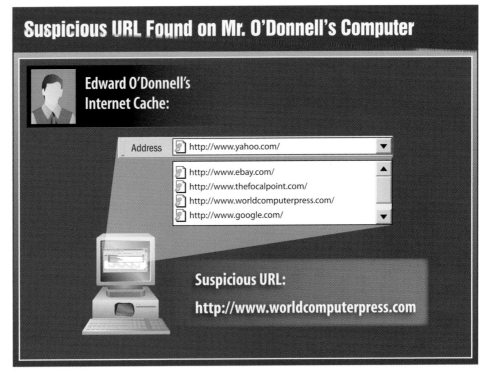

ILLUSTRATION 9-23

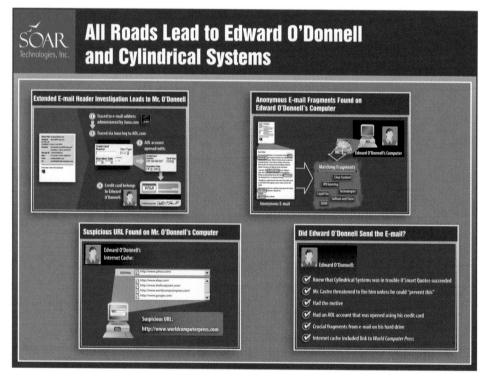

ILLUSTRATION 9-24

ILLUSTRATION 9-25

Hypothetical Case Number Two:
Midwestern University vs. Salem Guaranty Insurance Company

FACTS

Midwestern University (MWU) is a large public university with over 45,000 students. It has a large and active athletic program with over 9,400 students participating in over twenty-five athletic teams and clubs. MWU maintains a fleet of approximately six hundred buses, cars, and trucks. It uses these vehicles for a variety of purposes, including transporting student athletes to other campuses to compete in sporting events.

MWU has an extensive automobile insurance program in place to protect itself against any liability. The program includes coverage protecting the university should a student athlete get injured or injure a third party while using a university-owned vehicle. MWU administers its own self-insured retention (SIR) program that pays for $1 million in liability. TAG Insurance, a large automobile insurer, provides MWU with $15 million coverage in excess of the university's SIR.

Salem Guaranty Insurance Company also insures MWU. It alleges that it intended to provide MWU with $1 million of comprehensive general liability coverage. This Salem Guaranty policy generally excludes coverage for automobile injuries. As a concession to the university, Salem agreed to issue an endorsement that would provide MWU $1 million in automobile insurance that was supposed to trigger only after both MWU's SIR and TAG's $15 million excess policies were exhausted. Salem charged MWU only $103 for this endorsement.

A clerk at Salem issued the wrong form. Instead of attaching an endorsement indicating that Salem would pay only after MWU had exhausted $16 million in coverage, the clerk sent out a form that provided *primary* insurance coverage; that is, Salem would pay its $1 million first, before either MWU's SIR or TAG's excess policy.

Unfortunately, there was a bad automobile accident and MWU must pay over $1 million in damages.

Salem did not discover its policy mistake until after the accident when MWU tendered its claim to Salem. MWU has sued Salem for breach of contract and bad faith for failing to pay its $1 million. Salem has filed a counterclaim seeking reformation of its contract to reflect what it believes to have been the true intent of the parties, that is, that Salem would pay auto insurance claims only *after* MWU had exhausted both its SIR and its TAG coverage.

There is considerable evidence in Salem's favor. For example, several individuals from both Salem and MWU who were involved in the purchase of the policy have testified that no one ever discussed purchasing primary auto liability coverage from Salem. In addition, Michael Merrill, a former claims administrator at MWU, has testified that he would have expected to pay "between $250,000 and $300,000" for a primary–coverage policy. MWU paid only $103 for the coverage, which is consistent with a high-level excess policy. Further, immediately after the accident, in response to interrogatories filed by the injured driver, MWU did not list Salem as its primary insurer.

SAMPLE GRAPHICS

For this hypothetical, I created graphics for three aspects of the Salem Insurance Company's case: (1) a graphic that the insurer could use not only in opening to summarize the party's positions but also as part of closing argument, (2) a chart that Salem could use to summarize the legal requirements for reformation, and (3) a series of related graphics that summarize Salem's evidence with respect to each reformation requirement.

A Graphic Summarizing the Parties' Respective Positions

Occasionally, jurors find it helpful when the lawyer explains (usually in the opening statement) exactly (1) what is and is not in dispute as well as (2) what the parties' relative positions are on key contested issues. I designed Illustration 9-26 to provide this information to the jury first in a nonargumentative format and then, as we shall see later, used the same format to create an argumentative graphic to be used during Salem's closing.

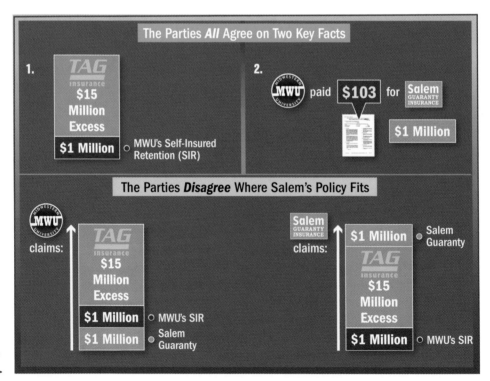

ILLUSTRATION 9-26. The Parties' Respective Positions

For purposes of opening statement, Illustration 9-26 consists of two sections. The top section shows the key undisputed facts to the jury: that separate and apart from the Salem policy, MWU has $16 million in automobile liability insurance coverage, and that MWU paid Salem $103 for an additional $1 million in insurance.

The bottom section of Illustration 9-26 summarizes where the parties disagree. The bottom left shows MWU's claim that the Salem insurance is the first layer of insurance coverage; that is, it is primary and Salem must pay first on any automobile liability claim. Salem's position is illustrated at the bottom right of the graphic. Salem contends that its policy is an excess policy that pays last, only after the $16 million in MWU's SIR and TAG's policy limits are exhausted. I suggest that this graphic be displayed electronically.

In closing, the trial lawyer can use a slightly different version of this graphic to argue that Salem's position is the correct one. In this variation, Salem has changed the subtitle in the lower half of the graphic to be "Where Does the Salem Policy Fit?" (See Illustration 9-27a.)

The lawyer would point out this change to the jury and then she would do three things to this second version of the graphic. First, she would add the quotation from Mr. Merrill stating that he would have expected to pay between $250,000 to $300,000 for such primary coverage. (See Illustration 9-27b.)

Second, she would highlight the undisputed fact that MWU paid only $103 for the $1 million dollars of additional coverage. (See highlight around $103 in Illustra-

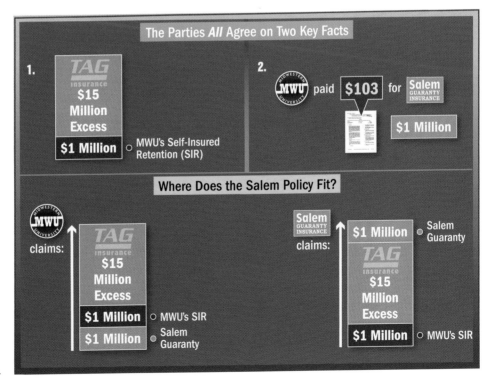

ILLUSTRATION 9-27a

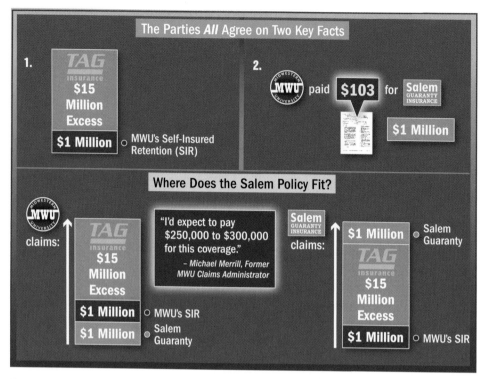

ILLUSTRATION 9-27b

tion 9-27b.) Finally, she would use this disparity (i.e., $250,000 versus $103) to argue that the parties must have intended for Salem to provide excess coverage, *not* primary insurance. (See Illustration 9-27c.)

A Chart Summarizing the Requirements for Contract Reformation

The law in this hypothetical jurisdiction requires that any party seeking to reform a contract must meet four requirements. It must first establish the true intention of the parties. Second, it must show that a mistake was made. Third, it must prove that the mistake was mutual. Finally, it must establish that the instrument (in this case the policy) does not reflect the true intentions of the parties.

Illustration 9-28a is a checklist setting forth each of these four requirements.

I designed the graphic so that the lawyer could use it for three purposes in closing argument. First, she could use it to provide an overview of the law. Second, she could use the graphic as a launching pad for a more detailed discussion of the facts in the case. Finally, at the appropriate time, she could check the box to show that she had met each individual requirement. (See Illustration 9-28b.) I suggest displaying this graphic on a board that the lawyer could leave up during the closing argument and, as suggested above, check the boxes at the appropriate time.

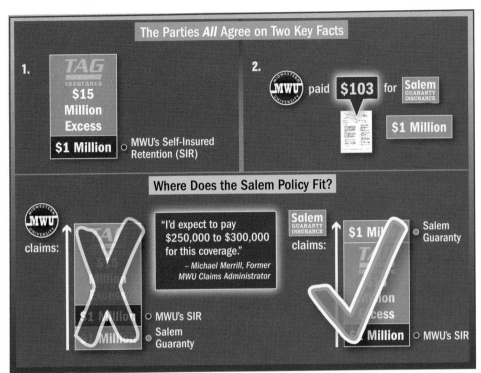

ILLUSTRATION 9-27c

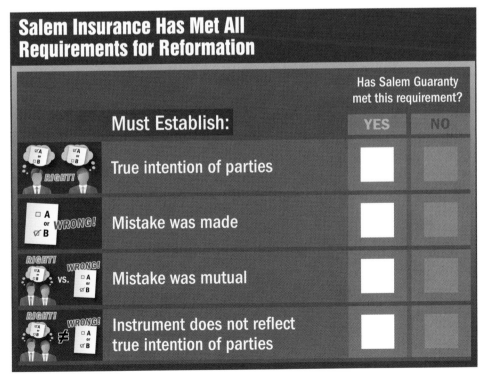

ILLUSTRATION 9-28a

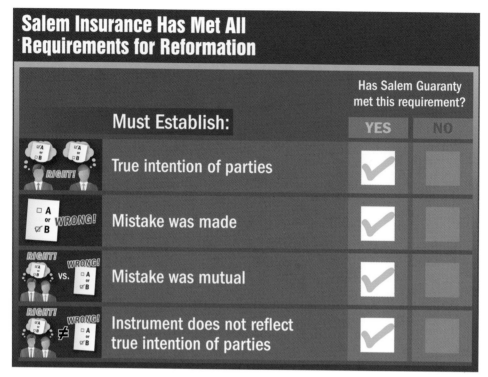

ILLUSTRATION 9-28b

A Series of Graphics Summarizing the Evidence for Each Requirement

Illustrations 9-29a through 9-29d are a series of interrelated graphics. Each summarizes the evidence that supports Salem's position with respect to one of the reformation requirements listed in Illustrations 9-28a and 9-28b.

As you can see, each of these graphics includes an icon from Illustration 9-28a representing one of the four reformation requirements. This icon is in the upper left corner of the title bar. The title includes a written description of that particular icon. Additionally, since the requirements generally mandate that the mistake be mutual, I have included icons from MWU and Salem on each exhibit to show that they were both part of the error.

After reviewing each of these evidence summaries, the lawyer can go back and check the appropriate box in Illustration 9-28b. She would do so until she had checked each box and was happily finished.

Depending on the trial lawyer's resources, she might consider also creating a series of textpulls, one for each of the documents referred to in Illustrations 9-29a through 9-29d. The lawyer could use these textpulls throughout the trial.

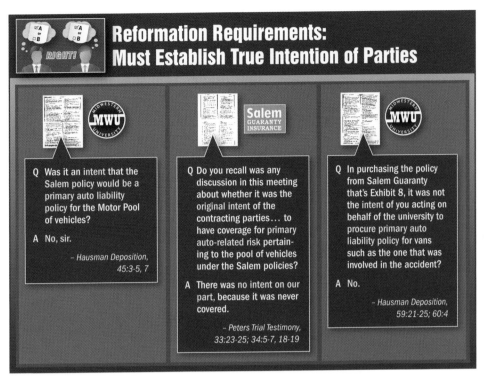

ILLUSTRATION 9-29a

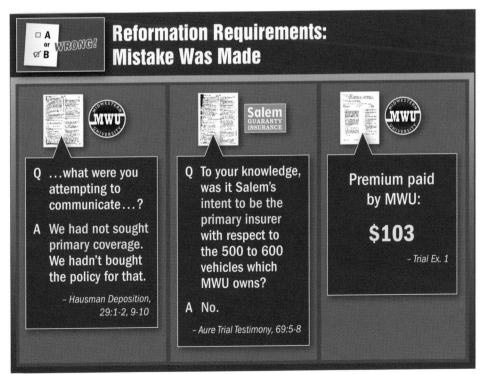

ILLUSTRATION 9-29b

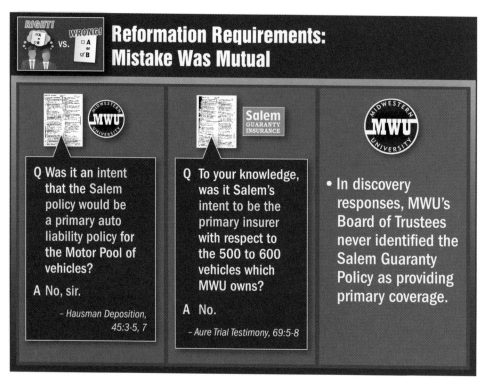

ILLUSTRATION 9-29c

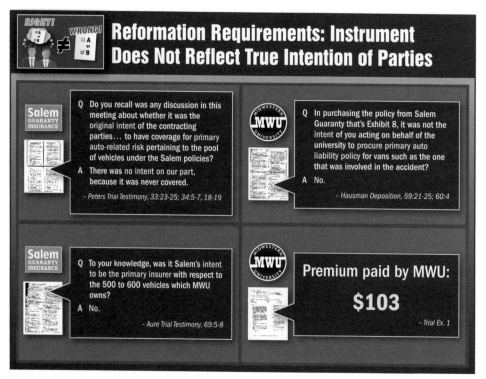

ILLUSTRATION 9-29d

Hypothetical Case Number Three:
Sean Cleveland et al. vs. The River Hotel

FACTS

The River Hotel is a large facility in Nevada. Its facilities include more than a thousand guest rooms, conference facilities, recreational facilities, and several restaurants, including one that recently received a four-star rating.

The River Hotel has approximately 2,500 employees, many in the food preparation and handling services. A large percentage of these workers are employed on an hourly basis and have no real long-term job security. In order to discourage its hourly staff from missing work, the River Hotel decided to adopt a new work policy whereby (1) workers would not get paid whenever they stayed home sick, and (2) anyone missing work for any reason, including illness, would receive a written warning threatening termination. A copy of the warning would be placed in the employee's personnel file.

Shortly after implementing this policy, Andrew Procter, the workers' union representative, advised Alex Chavez, the general manager of the River Hotel, that while such a policy would undoubtedly save the hotel money, it was also likely to result in large numbers of employees coming to work sick because they would fear losing their jobs if they took time off. Mr. Chavez ignored this warning and stringently enforced the "no pay/written warning" policy for what he later admitted were purely economic reasons.

In May, a single employee was sick with the Norwalk virus. This virus, which is extremely contagious, causes a severe illness with symptoms including fever, violent vomiting, severe nausea, abdominal cramps, and uncontrollable diarrhea. Fearing that he might lose his job if he stayed home, the employee continued to work throughout his illness. Guests and other employees began to fall ill to the virus. The spread was slow at first; however, after about thirty days, the number of infected people exponentially jumped from less than a handful to hundreds. All total, 1,320 people (935 hotel guests and 385 hotel employees) contracted the virus and became violently sick.

The River Hotel consistently denied that it had any responsibility for the spread of the virus. Several of the guests disagreed and filed a class action lawsuit against the hotel.

SAMPLE GRAPHICS

For this hypothetical, I created graphics for six aspects of the plaintiffs' case: (1) a basic tutorial related to the Norwalk virus, (2) summaries of the hotel's unsanitary practices, (3) the scope of infection among the River Hotel's employees, (4) timelines, (5) a summary of how the River Hotel violated Nevada health laws, and (6) a summary of a key element of plaintiffs' closing argument.

Basic Tutorial on the Norwalk Virus

The next four illustrations show basic tutorial material related to the Norwalk virus, the symptoms of those infected with it, and how the virus is typically transferred.

The first two of the graphics (Illustrations 9-30a and 9-30b) are intended to inspire a certain sense of "yuck" in the jurors' minds when they see them. This is necessary to help the jurors appreciate the very serious nature of the pathogen and to help ease them into what is likely to be some very explicit and unpleasant testimony by those who suffered from or have studied the effects of the virus.

The final graphics in this series show how the virus is transmitted. The first layer, Illustration 9-31a, displays how kitchen workers transmitted the virus among themselves. The second layer, Illustration 9-31b, shows how these employees transmitted the virus to the River Hotel's guests. As you will see, the icons developed in Illustration 9-31a are used again in Illustration 9-31b as well as in a number of other subsequent graphics.

I suggest displaying these graphics to the jurors electronically.

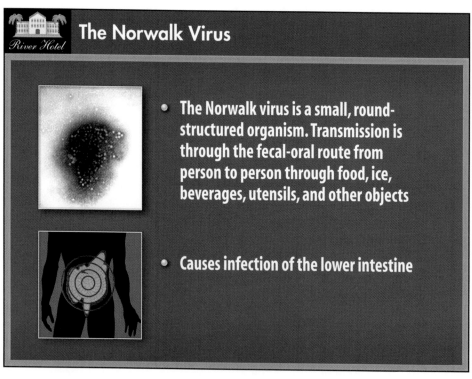

ILLUSTRATION 9-30a

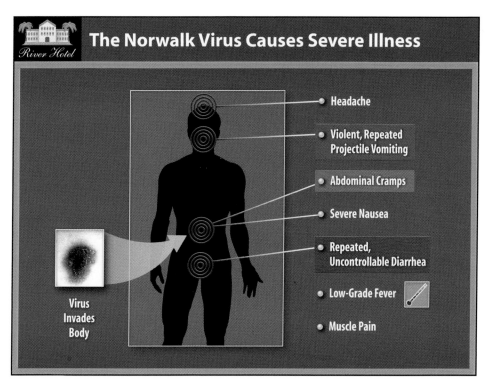

ILLUSTRATION 9-30b

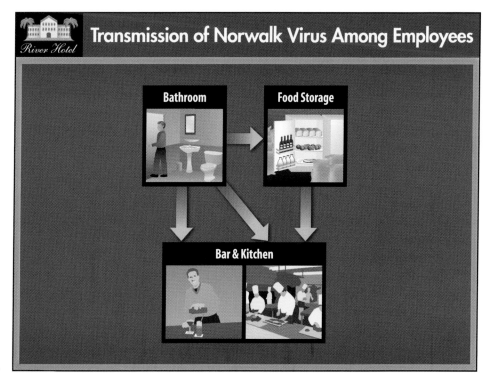

ILLUSTRATION 9-31a

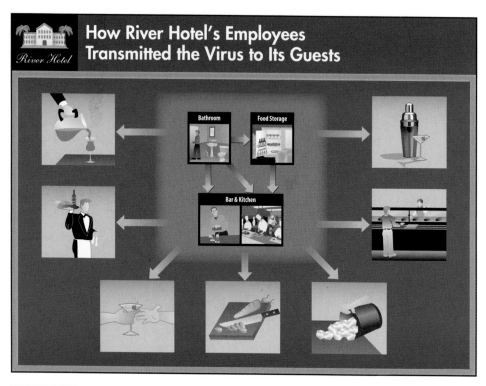

ILLUSTRATION 9-31b

Summaries of the River Hotel's Unsanitary Practices

Once the jurors have a general understanding of the virus and how it is transmitted, they need to learn about the River Hotel's unsanitary practices that were specifically responsible for spreading the virus among hotel guests and employees.

Illustration 9-32 lists such specific examples. As you can see, this graphic continues to rely on the general icons developed in Illustrations 9-31a and 9-31b.

Illustration 9-33 lists further violations related to unsafe water and ice handling practices at the River Hotel. This graphic includes a summary of findings in a handbook issued by two federal agencies—the United States Department of Health and Human Services and the United States Food and Drug Administration. I authenticated this material using each agency's very official-looking logo.

Illustrations 9-32 and 9-33 are designed so that the jurors are likely to think "yuck" when they read what the River Hotel did or did not do. I suggest displaying these graphics to the jurors electronically so as to make them easily buildable.

Some of the River Hotel's Unsanitary Practices

- Failed to instruct employees in proper washing of hands and arms
- Failed to provide proper handwashing facilities
- Failed to provide soap and towels
- Permitted improper handling of food utensils and serviceware
- Permitted handling of ice with hands or unclean utensils

- Unclean food prep areas
- Improper food handling
- Improper food storage
  - Raw meat on top of perishables (fruit, vegetables, etc.)
  - Cat running loose in food warehouse

ILLUSTRATION 9-32

Inspectors Found Unsanitary Water and Ice at the River Hotel

U.S. Department of Health and Human Services

U.S. Food and Drug Administration

"Norwalk gastroenteritis is transmitted by the fecal-oral route via contaminated water and foods. Secondary person-to-person transmission has been documented. Water is the most common source of outbreaks..."
— *Food Pathogenic Microorganisms and Natural Toxins Handbook*

- Discarded waste in main ice room
- Ice machines in employee cafeteria not cleaned regularly: heavy mineral buildup
- Ice buckets used for other purposes *e.g. food storage, sanitizing water for towels*
- At least 10 potential points of contamination of potable water by nonpotable water
- Several back-flow preventers in water system not functioning

ILLUSTRATION 9-33

The Scope of Infection Among River Hotel Employees

Illustrations 9-34a through 9-34d and 9-35 dramatically show the scope of infection among both the River Hotel's employees in general and, more specifically, among those employees working in the kitchens.

Illustration 9-34a establishes that River Hotel had approximately 2,500 employees. Of these, 1,757 employees voluntarily completed a questionnaire administered by the County Health Department. (See Illustration 9-34b.) Twenty percent of the employees (approximately 500 people) showed symptoms associated with the devastating virus. (See Illustrations 9-34c and 9-34d.) Of these, 55 percent (over 250 infected individuals) continued to work even though they were violently sick. (See Illustration 9-35.) As we will see, those who stayed at home came back to work prematurely and did not stay off work for the period required by law in order for them not to be contagious.

Each of these graphics makes extremely effective use of icons and the theory of small multiples. I suggest displaying this buildable material electronically.

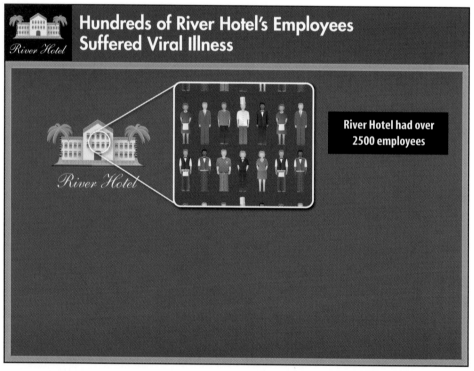

ILLUSTRATION 9-34a

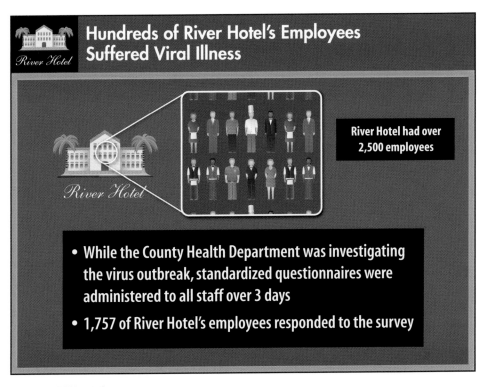

ILLUSTRATION 9-34b

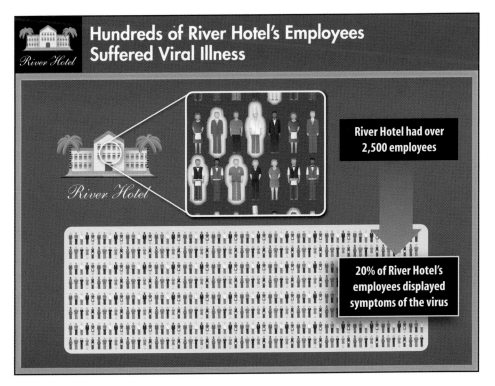

ILLUSTRATION 9-34c

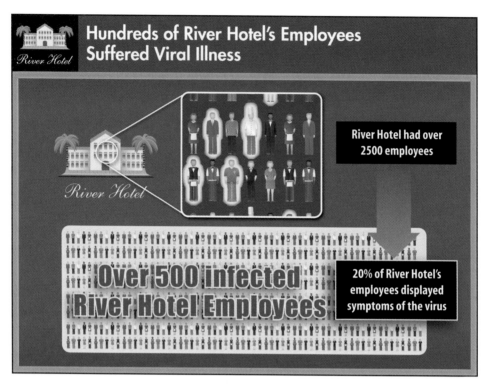

ILLUSTRATION 9-34d

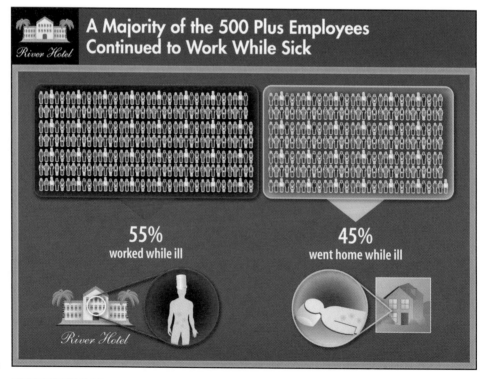

ILLUSTRATION 9-35

Over 21 percent of the employees working in the kitchens at the River Hotel got sick. (See Illustration 9-36.) This included the executive chef, who was in charge of the overall operations of the kitchens, two of his sous chefs, ten cooks, and numerous support staff. (See Illustration 9-37.) The vast majority of these sick employees continued to work rather than taking time off as legally required to protect guests and other workers.

Again, these two graphics (Illustrations 9-36 and 9-37) make highly effective use of both icons and the theory of small multiples. I would display this material either electronically or, since the image of the number of sick food handlers is a powerful one, on boards.

Timelines

Illustrations 9-38, 9-39a, and 9-39b are important related timelines. The first plots the number of people struck by the virus at the River Hotel. As you can see in Illustration 9-38, these numbers increased geometrically from less than a handful a day in May to well over one hundred a day in early June. This graphic breaks down the illnesses by employees and guests. This information is important, but it becomes even more so when you put it into context as shown in Illustrations 9-39a and 9-39b.

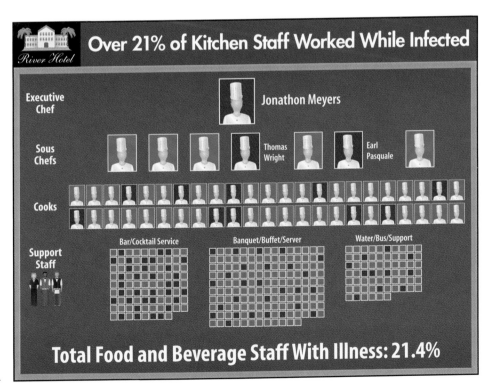

ILLUSTRATION 9-36

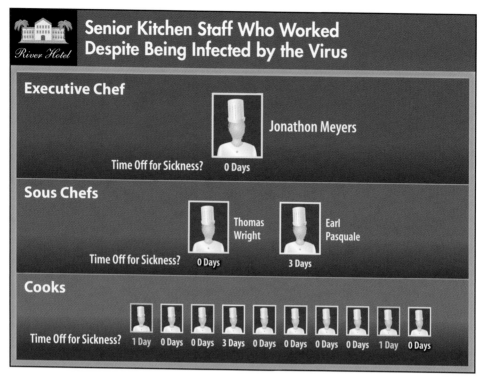

ILLUSTRATION 9-37

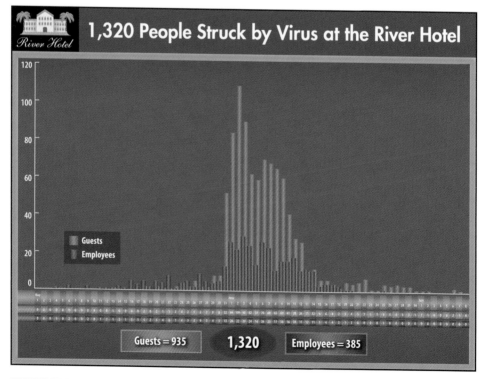

ILLUSTRATION 9-38

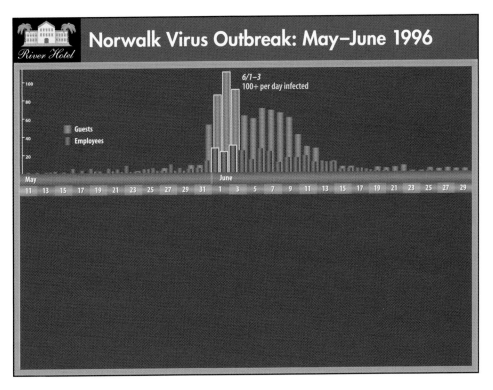

ILLUSTRATION 9-39a

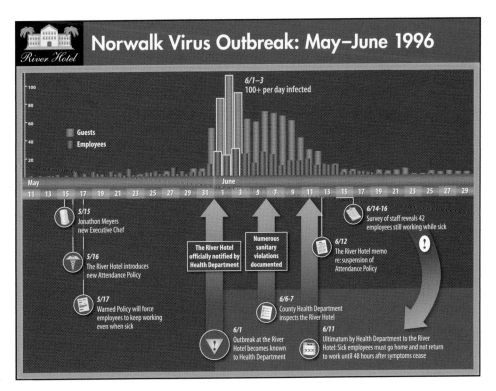

ILLUSTRATION 9-39b

Illustrations 9-39a and 9-39b are part of a multilayer, dynamic, layer cake timeline. The first layer (Illustration 9-39a) starts by showing the jurors a smaller version of Illustration 9-38, a graphic with which the jurors have already become familiar. These figures take on additional significance as the lawyer adds events occurring at the River Hotel below the timebar.

Illustration 9-39b is the final layer of this graphic. (For the complete buildable version, see the Visual Resource CD-ROM.) Of particular importance for the plaintiffs' case is the fact that forty-two of the River Hotel's employees were still working while sick in mid-June. This was despite the fact that on June 11, the county health department had already warned the River Hotel that it must not allow any more sick workers to continue to work. In other words, despite over 1,300 people getting sick and repeated warnings from health officials, the River Hotel continued to violate the law.

I suggest that the trial lawyer prepare two versions of Illustrations 9-38 and the 9-39 series. The first version could be displayed electronically. This would allow you to more easily "build" the graphics (especially the 9-39 series). This helps eliminate the Yuck! Factor. I still suggest that you display the graphics on boards. This allows you to leave them up throughout the trial.

Graphics Illustrating That the River Hotel Violated Nevada Law

As part of expert witness testimony or in closing argument, the plaintiffs will likely want to show the jury how the River Hotel violated Nevada law by allowing sick employees to continue to work *and* by not forcing those sick people who stayed home to remain there long enough so that they would not be contagious when they returned to work. The graphics in Illustrations 9-40 and 9-41 provide this information.

Illustration 9-40 is a straightforward juxtaposed textpull. The first layer (Illustration 9-40a) summarizes a key provision of the Nevada Administrative Code. The second (Illustration 9-40b) juxtaposes the provision of the Administrative Code with an already familiar graphic summarizing symptoms experienced by the River Hotel's employees who continued to work even while sick. As you can see, to make the point even more obvious, color coding is used to match the prohibitions in the Code with the symptoms experienced by those affected by the virus.

Illustration 9-41 is a slightly more complicated graphic illustrating how the River Hotel violated the law by having employees either not stay home or not stay home long enough so as to be no longer contagious. The first layer summarizes Nevada law. (See Illustration 9-41a.) The second layer shows that 55 percent of the employees continued to work even though they should have stayed at home for anywhere from 72 hours (three days) to 108 hours (four and a half days). (See Illustration 9-41b.) The third layer shows that those workers who went home stayed away from work an average of 1.3 days, still well below the 72–108 hour minimum. (See Illustration 9-41c.) The final two layers ask and answer the key question—"Did they stay home long enough?"—"No!," thereby further arguing that the River Hotel violated Nevada law. (See Illustrations 9-41d and 9-41e.)

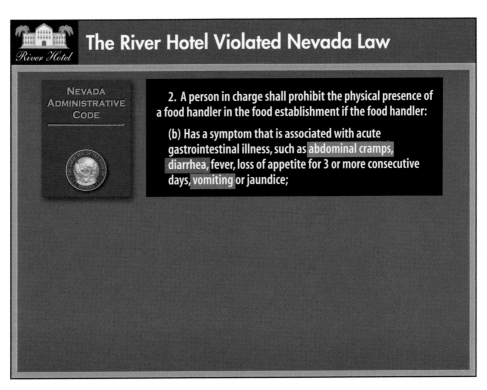

ILLUSTRATION 9-40a

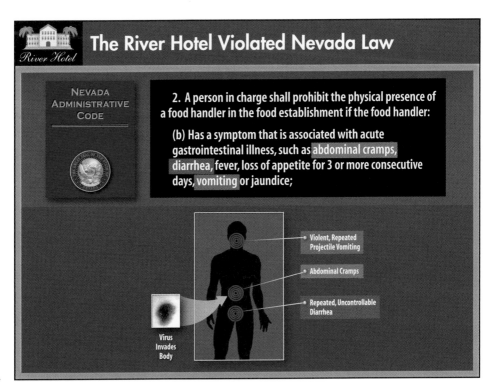

ILLUSTRATION 9-40b

ILLUSTRATION 9-41a

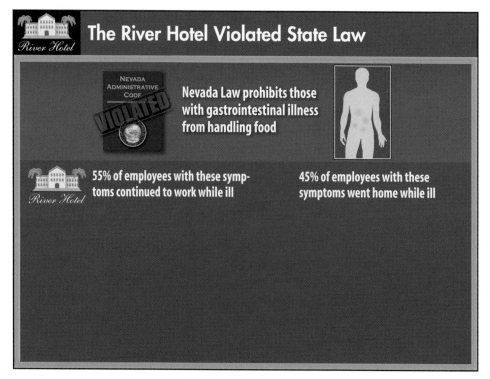

ILLUSTRATION 9-41b

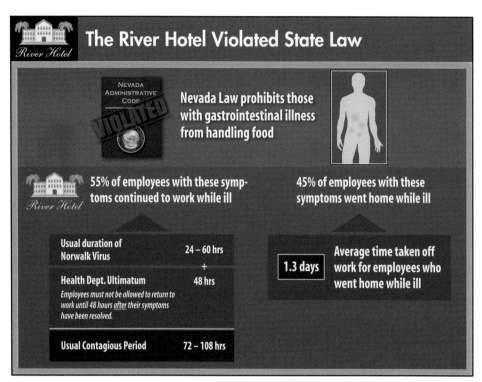

ILLUSTRATION 9-41c

ILLUSTRATION 9-41d

ILLUSTRATION 9-41e

Selected Closing Argument Material

As noted earlier, Active Jurors start out as "searchers for the truth" and eventually become "advocates of the truth." As advocates of the truth, these Active Jurors are one of your most important weapons during deliberations. Hopefully, your argument during closing becomes their argument during deliberations. You can increase the chances of this by providing jurors with tools that help them better understand and articulate your key points or arguments. Illustrations 9-42 and 9-43 are examples of what you might provide to jurors in this case.

Illustration 9-42 is a dynamic and multilayered graphic. The first layer juxtaposes a picture of sick workers with the Nevada Administrative Code that required sick food handlers to wait 48 hours after they were no longer sick before going back to work. (See Illustration 9-42a.)

The second layer includes the question that we want to encourage the Active Jurors to ask during deliberations: "What prevented so many sick employees from taking time off of work?" (See Illustration 9-42b.)

In the final layer we answer the question for the jurors in the way we hope our Active Jurors will if asked by others during deliberations. (See Illustration 9-42c.) This massive level of sickness was a direct result of the River Hotel's policy of not paying and threatening workers who stayed home while sick.

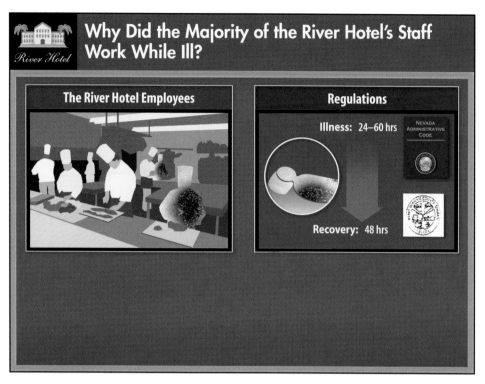

ILLUSTRATION 9-42a

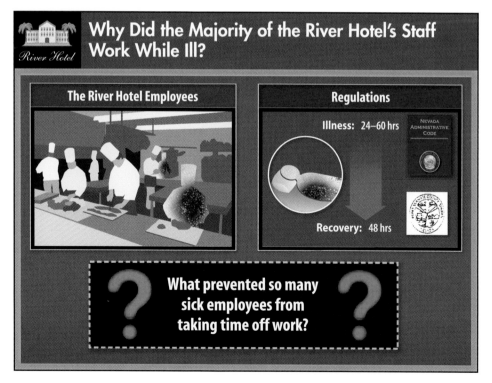

ILLUSTRATION 9-42b

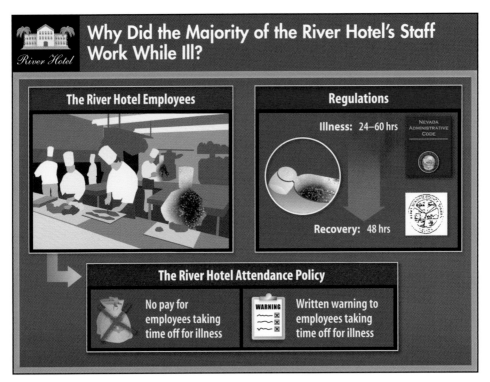

ILLUSTRATION 9-42c

The lawyer could then end this argument by asking one final question, "Why did the River Hotel have this drastic policy that forced sick workers to come to work? Why? Because the River Hotel wanted higher profits." The trial lawyer could then end by putting up a key textpull previously used in opening statement and during your examination of witnesses. This is the letter by the workers' union representative to the River Hotel's general manager predicting that, while the policy might save money for the hotel, the implementation of the attendance policy would undoubtedly lead to numerous employees coming to work even though they were seriously ill. In short, the lawyer would argue, the River Hotel had been warned of a potential disaster, which it completely disregarded for the sake of making more money. (See Illustration 9-43.)

Hypothetical Case Number Four:
Brown vs. Acme Insurance Co.

FACTS

On April 15, 1999, the Browns had a fire at their home. Fortunately, no one was injured. Unfortunately, the fire destroyed much the house and its contents. The Browns were insured by Acme Insurance Company.

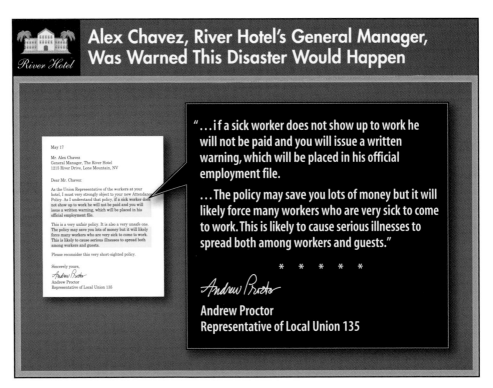

ILLUSTRATION 9-43

Initially, the relationship between the Browns and Acme was relatively amicable, given the tragic circumstances. Within twenty-four hours of the fire, Acme met with the Browns and started advancing money to them to cover damages and other expenses related to the fire.

Based on Acme's strong recommendation, the Browns hired Smith Construction Co. to do emergency repairs and to rebuild their house. Smith Construction gets about 50 percent of its income doing repair work on homes insured by Acme.

Within the first six months after the fire, Acme advanced approximately $335,000 to the Browns to cover repairs, lost personal property, temporary housing, etc. As part of its repair work, Smith Construction prepared a forty-two-page detailed report outlining what work needed to be done and the exact cost of this work. Ultimately, Acme paid $1,066,829 to the Browns for their home repairs and losses.

In November 1999, the Browns hired Gary Franklin, a public adjuster, to assist them with their claim. Public adjusters are advocates hired by the insured in order to recover to the fullest extent of the claim. They are generally paid a percentage of whatever they can persuade the insurance company to pay the insured.

Shortly after the Browns hired Mr. Franklin, their relationship with Acme became considerably more adversarial. Franklin persuaded the Browns to fire Smith Construction. Franklin then submitted a very general estimate prepared by Lucas Hurst, an architect (not a licensed contractor as required by the insurance policy), insisting that the Browns were entitled to much more money than had been estimated by Smith Construction and advanced by Acme.

Franklin also began to threaten Acme with a bad faith insurance claim, claiming that Smith and Acme were in collusion to lowball how much would be paid to repair the Browns' house. The Browns, through Franklin, eventually hired an attorney (Colby Nelson) and then another attorney (Allison Palandrani) to pursue a bad faith insurance claim against Acme.

Acme eventually demanded an appraisal (as provided in the insurance policy) to determine how much it owed to the Browns. The appraisal, which was issued by a neutral umpire selected by the parties, determined that Acme had already paid 97 percent of what the Browns were entitled to under the policy. Acme then immediately paid the difference between what it had already paid and what the umpire ordered. Despite this, the Browns continued to pursue their bad faith lawsuit against Acme.

SAMPLE GRAPHICS

For this hypothetical, we created graphics for six aspects of the defendant's case: (1) a series of timelines with which jurors can evaluate the overall facts of the case as well as how things changed once Mr. Franklin became involved, (2) a tutorial of what was covered by Acme's insurance policy, (3) a comparison of the Smith Construction Company's estimate to that prepared by Lucas Hurst, (4) a tutorial about how the appraisal process works, and (5) charts comparing how much Acme was required to pay with how much it actually did pay.

Timelines

The jurors in this case will undoubtedly benefit from having one or more timelines available to them in order to better understand what happened. Illustrations 9-44a through 9-45c are examples of types of timelines that the trial lawyer might consider using in this case.

Illustration 9-44a is a macrotimeline covering the *entire* disputed period. Let me start off by acknowledging that this graphic has a lot of information (but not too much) on it. There are at least two reasons for this.

First, the trial lawyer intends to display this graphic using an exhibit board and relying on it throughout the case. This will allow her to use the board as a large and reliable cue card so that she can move away from her notes at the podium at virtually any point during the trial and still be confident that, if necessary, she can quickly check on key dates, names, sequence of events, etc.

Second, she wants to be able to have one graphic that she can use to show all of what Acme did to resolve the claim and all of the Browns' efforts to defeat Acme's hard work.

This timeline includes a variety of design features intended to make it easier for the lawyer and jurors to use. (See Illustration 9-44b.) First, notice how the timeline is laid out. It is a layer cake timeline, with all of Acme's activities placed above

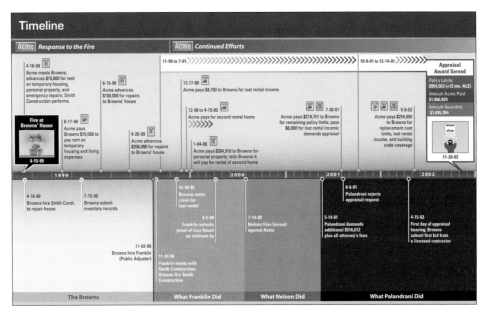

ILLUSTRATION 9-44a. A Layer Cake Macrotimeline

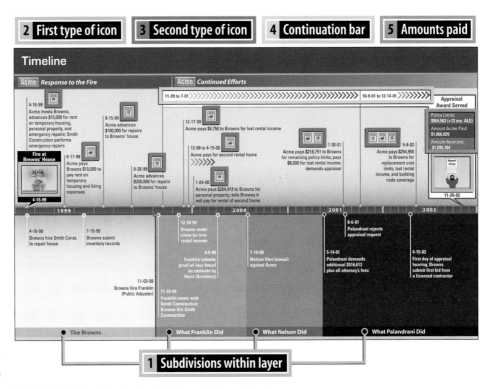

ILLUSTRATION 9-44b. Design Features of Macrotimeline

the timebar and all of the Browns' below. In addition, each horizontal layer is further subdivided vertically. You can most easily see this division by looking below the timebar. I divided this layer into four subparts, each corresponding to either the Browns or one of their legal advisers. To help distinguish these subdivisions, each is in a slightly different color. (Notice that the color deepens along the timeline, becoming increasingly red, to indicate that plaintiffs' demands are becoming more extreme.) So, for example, the first subdivision below the line shows the time between the fire and the Browns' hiring of Gary Franklin. The second subdivision shows "What Franklin Did"; the third shows "What Mr. Nelson Did"; and the final subdivision shows "What Ms. Palandrani Did." (See Illustration 9-44b, Point 1.)

Dividing this layer this way makes it easier for jurors to read and understand the graphic. Additionally, this way of dividing the graphic is consistent with defendant's theme that initially there was considerable cooperation between the parties and it was not until the Browns' legal professionals got involved that there was a problem.

A second design feature of note is the extensive use of icons. There are two such sets of icons. The first denotes the beginning ("Fire at Brown's House") and what should have been the ending of this dispute ("Appraisal Award Served"). Both of these are key events that warrant their own icons. The icon at the end is of the umpire that rendered the neutral decision concerning how Acme should pay; as you will see, this icon is repeated in a variety of different exhibits that are connected with this crucial event. (See Illustration 9-44b, Point 2.)

The second set of icons is used each time Acme pays money to the Browns. (See Illustration 9-44b, Point 3.) As you will see in subsequent graphics (Illustrations 9-46a through 9-46f), the insurance policy itself is divided into distinct sections, each of which is represented by a distinct icon. This allows the jurors to see what each payment covers, an issue that becomes important later on when Acme argues that it has not only paid more than the total of what was required, but also paid at or above the maximum amount for each separate type of coverage.

A third design feature is the use of continuation bars. You can see this in the upper layer starting in November 1999 and running through the end of the timeline. (See Illustration 9-44b, Point 4.) Using such bars not only indicates ongoing efforts by Acme but also eliminates the need to repeat separate entries detailing exactly what was done.

Finally, on the top layer at the far right you can see a series of numbers. (See Illustration 9-44b, Point 5.) These compare what for the defendant are the three most crucial figures in the case: (1) the face amount of the policy (i.e., what the policy requires be paid), (2) the actual amount paid by Acme, and (3) the amount awarded by way of the appraisal.

Although it is somewhat unusual to include such numbers in a timeline, it is justified in this instance for at least three reasons. First, these numbers are the basis of one of defendant's key arguments. Second, many people (including our hypothetical trial lawyer) have problems memorizing numbers. These people often transpose numbers or cannot remember the numbers at all. By having the information at a fixed and obvious spot on the timeline, the lawyer knows exactly where to look for a reminder of exactly what these numbers are. Finally, the lawyer wants to encourage the jurors to write down, remember, and learn the significance of these numbers. Since the trial lawyer is likely to have this graphic up on an easel throughout the case, it is a perfect place to display this information.

Illustrations 9-45a, 9-45b, and 9-45c are hybrid timelines. They are part micro-timelines because they focus in great detail on a relatively short period of time. They are also part topical timelines because they focus on one topic (i.e., the deteriorating relationship between the parties once the Browns hired a public adjuster and a lawyer specializing in insurance bad faith.)

Because this graphic will ultimately contain much information, I have designed it to be dynamic. The first layer helps orient the jurors about the overall timeframe covered by the graphic. (See Illustration 9-45a.) The second layer isolates and reviews in considerable detail the relatively amicable period between the time of the fire and when the Browns hired Gary Franklin. (See Illustration 9-45b.) The final layer examines how the relationship became considerably more adversarial once Mr. Franklin became involved in managing the Browns' claim. (See Illustration 9-45c.)

Acme's Insurance Policy and What It Covered

A common problem that an insurance company has is convincing jurors that the insurance policy limits what it is required to do. To help make this point, Acme

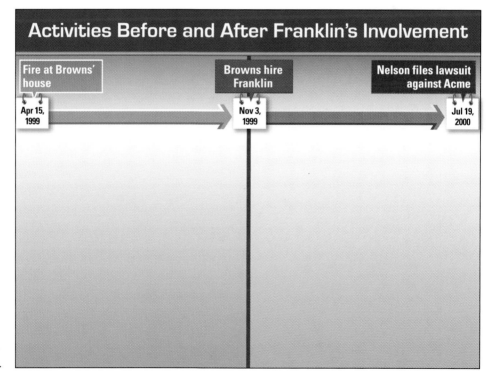

ILLUSTRATION 9-45a

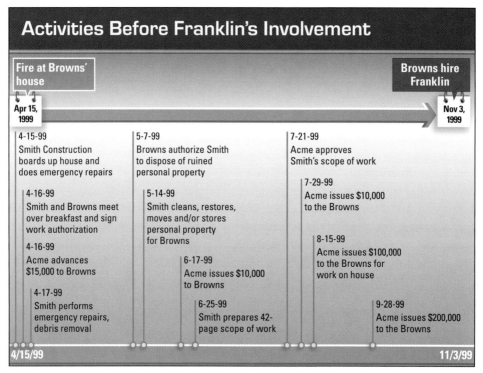

Activities Before Franklin's Involvement

Fire at Browns' house

Browns hire Franklin

Apr 15, 1999 ——————————————————————→ Nov 3, 1999

4-15-99
Smith Construction boards up house and does emergency repairs

4-16-99
Smith and Browns meet over breakfast and sign work authorization

4-16-99
Acme advances $15,000 to Browns

4-17-99
Smith performs emergency repairs, debris removal

5-7-99
Browns authorize Smith to dispose of ruined personal property

5-14-99
Smith cleans, restores, moves and/or stores personal property for Browns

6-17-99
Acme issues $10,000 to Browns

6-25-99
Smith prepares 42-page scope of work

7-21-99
Acme approves Smith's scope of work

7-29-99
Acme issues $10,000 to the Browns

8-15-99
Acme issues $100,000 to the Browns for work on house

9-28-99
Acme issues $200,000 to the Browns

4/15/99 11/3/99

ILLUSTRATION 9-45b

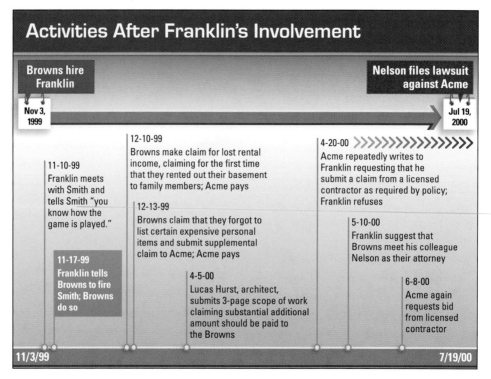

Activities After Franklin's Involvement

Browns hire Franklin

Nelson files lawsuit against Acme

Nov 3, 1999 ——————————————————————→ Jul 19, 2000

11-10-99
Franklin meets with Smith and tells Smith "you know how the game is played."

11-17-99
Franklin tells Browns to fire Smith; Browns do so

12-10-99
Browns make claim for lost rental income, claiming for the first time that they rented out their basement to family members; Acme pays

12-13-99
Browns claim that they forgot to list certain expensive personal items and submit supplemental claim to Acme; Acme pays

4-5-00
Lucas Hurst, architect, submits 3-page scope of work claiming substantial additional amount should be paid to the Browns

4-20-00 〉〉〉〉〉〉〉〉〉〉〉〉
Acme repeatedly writes to Franklin requesting that he submit a claim from a licensed contractor as required by policy; Franklin refuses

5-10-00
Franklin suggest that Browns meet his colleague Nelson as their attorney

6-8-00
Acme again requests bid from licensed contractor

11/3/99 7/19/00

ILLUSTRATION 9-45c

might consider creating a series of tutorial graphics such as Illustrations 9-46a through 9-46f.

Illustration 9-46a is an introductory graphic that the trial lawyer can use to start this tutoring process. It contains an actual scan from the first page of the Acme policy. The scan helps authenticate this graphic and the subsequent related textpulls in Illustrations 9-46b through 9-46f. As you can see, Illustration 9-46a uses the analogy of a jigsaw puzzle to make the point that the policy has different parts that fit together and complement each other.

There are a variety of reasons for using this analogy. For example, it helps Acme argue and the jurors hopefully understand that the policy is not merely some hodge-podge of terms, but a carefully considered and designed program providing a previously agreed-to type and amount of coverage for the insured. Additionally, as you will see in later exhibits, this division helps the lawyers argue not only that Acme paid more than required by the overall amount of the policy but also that it paid at or above the maximum sub-amount required by each individual section of the policy. (See Illustrations 9-52a and 9-52b.)

Illustrations 9-46b through 9-46f are a series of textpulls and annotated definitions of key parts of the Acme policy. The trial lawyer could display these graphics in court either electronically or on boards. Given the number of these graphics, all other issues being equal, I suggest that the material be displayed electronically, thereby saving the greater impact of boards for other more limited and crucial information.

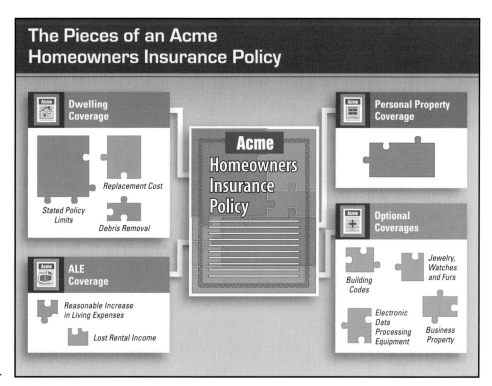

ILLUSTRATION 9-46a

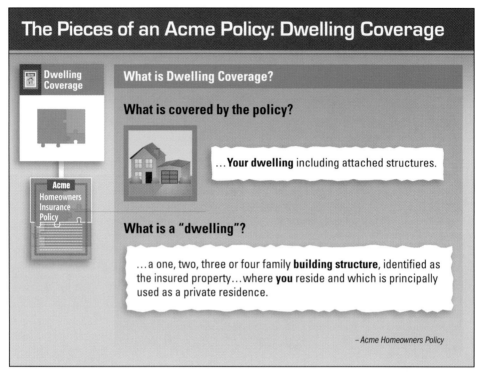

ILLUSTRATION 9-46b

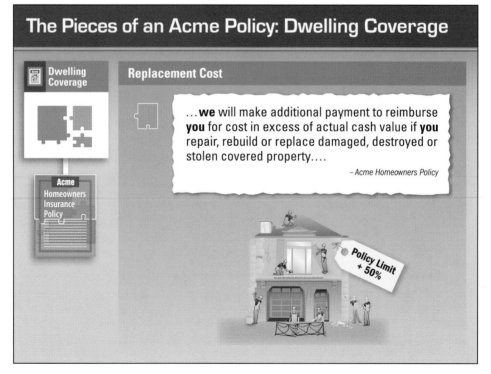

ILLUSTRATION 9-46c

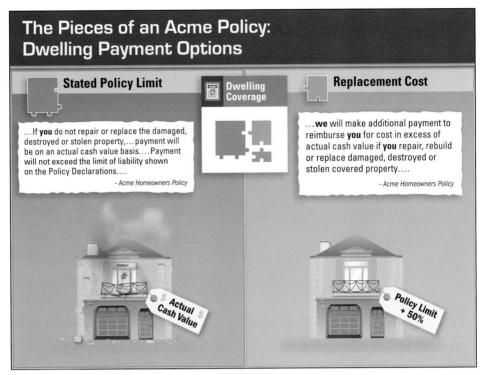

ILLUSTRATION 9-46d

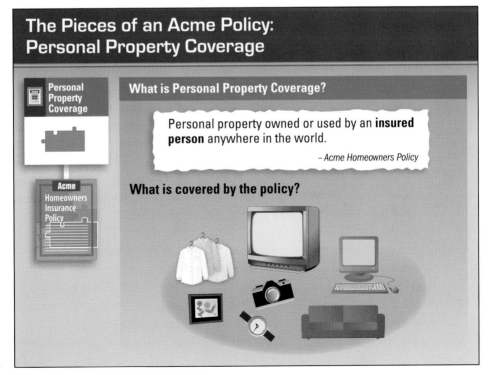

ILLUSTRATION 9-46e

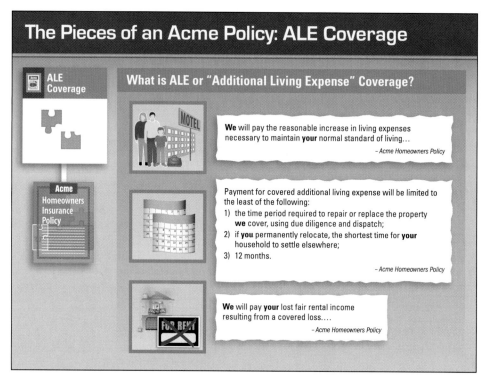

ILLUSTRATION 9-46f

Comparison of Each Party's Estimate

The Browns allege that there was collusion between Acme and Smith Construction. Specifically, the Browns claim that, as a favor to Acme, Smith Construction (which gets 50 percent of its income from Acme's referrals) underestimated how much it would cost to repair the Brown's home. As evidence of this, they offer a report done by their architect, Lucas Hurst, that claims the cost to repair the Brown's home is considerably more than estimated by Smith Construction.

I designed the graphics shown in Illustrations 9-47a through 9-47c to compare the two estimates and to call Mr. Hurst's objectivity and reliability into question. Illustration 9-47a provides an overview of Smith Construction's estimate; Illustration 9-47b lists the categories of repairs analyzed in it. Illustration 9-47c is a blow-up that provides a small sample of the level of detail in the estimate. Some of the readers and hypothetical jurors might see these exhibits as being a bit crowded and as containing a lot of material. I intentionally designed the graphics this way to subtly reinforce how much information is in the Smith Construction documents. At the same time, I made sure that the information in these graphics is not so crowded or too difficult for the jurors to read and understand.

Illustration 9-48 lists the characteristics and content Mr. Hurst's report. Notice that I use a different color scheme in this graphic from that used in Illustration 9-46. I did this to help emphasize that Illustration 9-48 is *not* one of Acme's documents or witnesses.

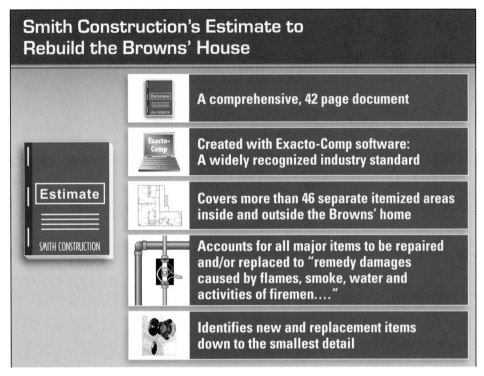

ILLUSTRATION 9-47a

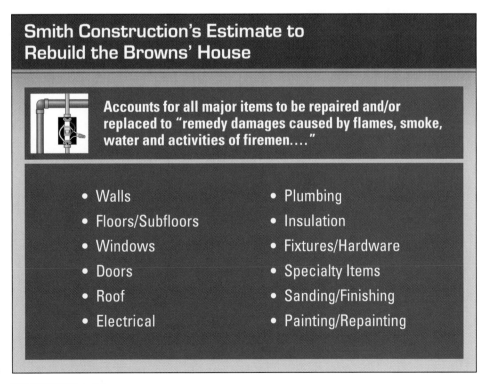

ILLUSTRATION 9-47b

Smith Construction's Estimate to Rebuild the Browns' House

 Identifies new and replacement items down to the smallest detail

ROOM	DESCRIPTION	UNIT		REMOVE	REPLACE	TOTAL
Basement	Carpet pad	31.12	SY @		4.51	140.35
Kitchen	R&R Dimmer switch	1.00	EA @	2.93+	22.32=	25.25
	Sink faucet - high grade	1.00	EA @		175.14	175.14
	Range hood	1.00	EA @		213.18	213.18
Foyer/	R&R Door buzzer remote opening unit	1.00	EA @	2.00+	38.50=	40.50
Entry	Door peep hole	1.00	EA @		21.61	21.61
	Paint door trim & jamb (per side)	3.00	EA @		19.86	59.58
Master	Toilet	1.00	EA @		267.27	267.27
Bath	Soap dish	1.00	EA @		12.75	12.75
	Toilet paper holder	1.00	EA @		17.15	17.15
	Towel bar	2.00	EA @		14.60	29.20
Rear	Paint balustrade	18.00	LF @		2.97	53.46
Stairway	R&R Light fixture	3.00	EA @	3.84+	76.04=	239.64
	Paint stair riser	32.00	EA @		4.95	158.40
	Paint stair tread	32.00	EA @		5.16	165.12
	Paint stair stringer - both sides	72.00	LF @		0.65	46.80

ILLUSTRATION 9-47c

Lucas Hurst's "Fire Damage Scope"

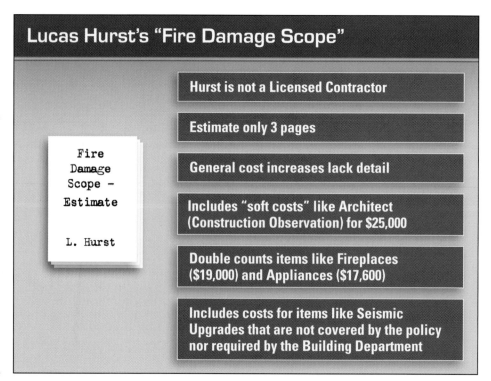

Fire
Damage
Scope –
Estimate

L. Hurst

- Hurst is not a Licensed Contractor
- Estimate only 3 pages
- General cost increases lack detail
- Includes "soft costs" like Architect (Construction Observation) for $25,000
- Double counts items like Fireplaces ($19,000) and Appliances ($17,600)
- Includes costs for items like Seismic Upgrades that are not covered by the policy nor required by the Building Department

ILLUSTRATION 9-48

These graphics could be displayed either electronically or on boards. The advantage to using boards is that the trial lawyer could put both up at the same time, on separate easels, so that the jury could more easily compare the two estimates and hopefully conclude that Mr. Hurst is not to be trusted.

Tutorial on Appraisal Process

As the fact pattern indicates, when the parties could not agree on the amount owed, Acme demanded an appraisal pursuant to the terms of the insurance policy. The appraisal, which was issued by a "competent and impartial umpire" selected by representatives of both parties, found that Acme had already paid the Browns over 97 percent of what was due under its policy. Acme wants to show that its having made this level of voluntary payments—in an amount so close to what the "competent and impartial umpire" found was actually required—is compelling evidence that it acted in good faith.

For the jury to fully appreciate this argument, Acme's lawyer will need to make sure that the jury understands (1) what the appraisal process is, (2) that the process is provided for under the insurance contract agreed to by both parties, and (3) that it is a fair process. The graphics designed to provide this information to the jury are shown in Illustrations 9-49 and 9-50.

Illustration 9-49 shows a combination of a textpull and an annotated definition. The top half (Illustration 9-49a) is a direct quotation from the Browns' policy.

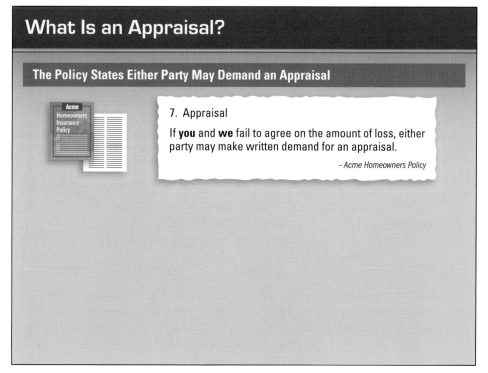

ILLUSTRATION 9-49a

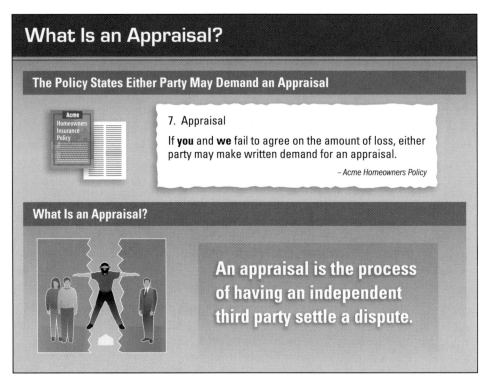

ILLUSTRATION 9-49b

Illustration 9-49b shows an analogy of the language. The fact that the lawyer is relying on terms agreed to by both parties increases the credibility of the graphic in general and the appraisal system in particular.

Notice the icon of an umpire at the bottom left of Illustration 9-49b. This icon will be used again in later graphics.

Illustration 9-50a is a hybrid of a textpull, an annotated definition, and a process information flowchart. The drawings in Illustration 9-50b annotate the process of how the umpire is picked by both parties and how she makes her decision based upon input from each party's representative. As you can see in the second panel in the bottom half of the graphic, the attorney has intentionally highlighted the terms "competent and impartial umpire" as a way of helping to validate the fairness of the process and its ultimate conclusion.

Illustration 9-51 is a simple chart comparing three figures: the policy limits, the amount paid by Acme before the umpire's decision, and the total amount the umpire determined Acme needed to pay. The graphic relies on the umpire icon to show the total of what she ordered to be paid; it relies on the Acme logo to show what had already been paid prior to the umpire's decision; it uses a pie graph to show that what had already been paid constituted the vast majority of what the umpire eventually ordered be paid to the Browns.

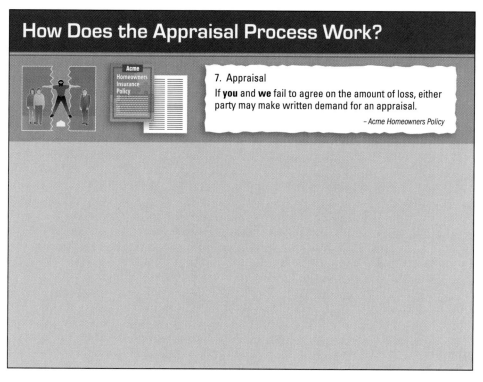

ILLUSTRATION 9-50a

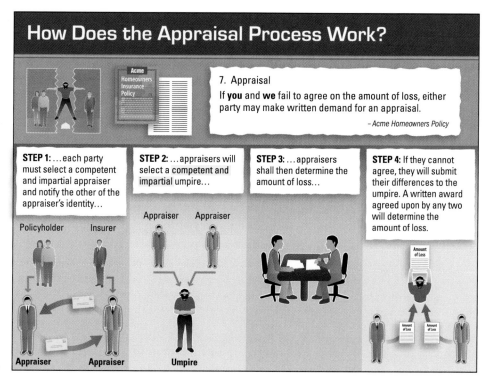

ILLUSTRATION 9-50b

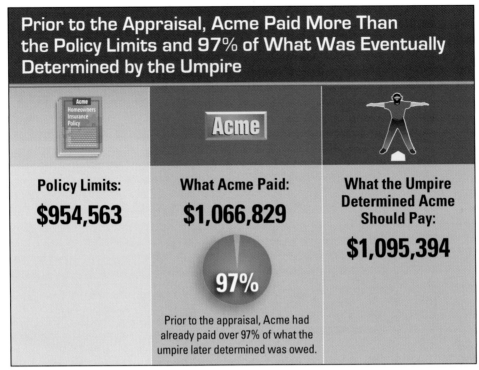

Prior to the Appraisal, Acme Paid More Than the Policy Limits and 97% of What Was Eventually Determined by the Umpire

Policy Limits: $954,563

What Acme Paid: $1,066,829

97%

Prior to the appraisal, Acme had already paid over 97% of what the umpire later determined was owed.

What the Umpire Determined Acme Should Pay: $1,095,394

ILLUSTRATION 9-51

Acme Paid the Browns More Than Required Under Its Policy

As further evidence that it acted in good faith, Acme will undoubtedly want to show that it paid the Browns more than was required under its policy. The simplest way for Acme to do this would be to list and contrast two different numbers—one being the *policy limits* and the other being the total *amount actually paid* by Acme. Acme can do this by merely writing the numbers on a blackboard or a flipchart.

If the trial lawyer's resources permit it, she could convey this information in another way that is likely to have a far greater impact on the jury. As you can see, Illustrations 9-52a and 9-52b break the insurance policy down by section and provide both numbers for each. Breaking down the payments this way is consistent with the earlier graphics which also analyzed the insurance policy section by section. (See Illustrations 9-46a through 9-46f.)

Additionally, displaying the information this way allows the lawyer to argue that not only did Acme pay more in the aggregate than it was required but also it paid the Browns at or above the policy limits for each and every individual section of the policy. In other words, Acme paid in whole and in part more than it was required to do.

Illustration 9-52b adds what I call editorial comments, pointing out that the amount of each payment is at or above the maximum amount required by the insurance contract.

Policy Limits vs. Amount Paid

		Stated Limits at the Time of the Fire	Amount Acme Actually Paid
Dwelling Coverage	Stated Policy Limit	$424,250	$424,250
	Replacement Cost	$212,125	$212,125
	Debris Removal	$21,213	$21,213
Personal Property Coverage		$296,975	$296,975
ALE Coverage		Up to 12 Months	12 Months ($69,841)
Building Codes Coverage		$0	$42,425
TOTAL:		$954,563 + 12 Months ALE	$1,066,829

ILLUSTRATION 9-52a

Policy Limits vs. Amount Paid

		Stated Limits at the Time of the Fire	Amount Acme Actually Paid
Dwelling Coverage	Stated Policy Limit	$424,250 MAXIMUM	$424,250
	Replacement Cost	$212,125 MAXIMUM	$212,125
	Debris Removal	$21,213 MAXIMUM	$21,213
Personal Property Coverage		$296,975 MAXIMUM	$296,975
ALE Coverage		Up to 12 Months MAXIMUM	12 Months ($69,841)
Building Codes Coverage		$0 ABOVE MAX	$42,425
TOTAL:		$954,563 + 12 Months ALE ABOVE MAX	$1,066,829

ILLUSTRATION 9-52b

The trial lawyer could use Illustration 9-52a in opening statement and/or in witness examination. Because of the editorial comments in Illustration 9-52b, it is probably more appropriate for the trial lawyer to use this second version during closing argument. Both of these graphics could be displayed either electronically or on a board.

Index

Note: Page numbers followed by the letter "i" indicate references to illustrations; page numbers followed by the letter "n" indicate references to footnotes.

A Note on the Typography

Text for this book was set in Dante, a contemporary typeface redrawn from the original font designed by Giovanni Mardersteig at the end of World War II. Mardersteig wanted to create a new book face with an italic version that worked harmoniously with the roman. It was adapted for digital composition by Monotype in 1993.

This book was designed and composed by Lachina Publishing Services in Cleveland, Ohio.

Printed and bound by Quebecor World, Inc., Kingsport, Tennessee.